Core Concepts of
CONSULTING
FOR
ACCOUNTANTS

Nancy A. Bagranoff, D.B.A., CPA

Professor
Department of Accountancy
Miami University

Stephanie M. Bryant, Ph.D., CPA

Assistant Professor
School of Accountancy
University of South Florida

James E. Hunton, Ph.D., CPA

Quinn Eminent Scholar in Accounting Information Systems
School of Accountancy
University of South Florida

JOHN WILEY & SONS, INC.

New York   Chichester   Weinheim   Brisbane   Toronto   Singapore

EXECUTIVE EDITOR	Brent Gordon
MARKETING MANAGER	Clancy Marshall
SENIOR PRODUCTION EDITOR	Norine M. Pigliucci
SENIOR DESIGNER	Dawn L. Stanley
PRODUCTION MANAGEMENT SERVICES	Hermitage Publishing Services

This book was set in Garamond Book by Hermitage Publishing Services and printed and bound by Hamilton Printing. The cover was printed by Lehigh Press.

This book is printed on acid-free paper. ∞

Library of Congress Cataloging in Publication Data:
Bagranoff, Nancy A.
    Core concepts of consulting for accountants/Nancy Bagranoff, Stephanie M. Bryant, James E. Hunton.
        p.   cm
    Includes bibliographical references.
    ISBN 0-471-39086-0 (pbk.: alk. paper)
    1. Business consultants. 2. Consultants. 3. Accountants. I. Bryant, Stephanie M. II. Hunton, James E. III. Title.

HD69.C6 B34 2001
657—dc21   2001026007

Printed in the United States of America

10 9 8 7 6 5 4 3 2 1

To my husband, Larry, for his patience and encouragement.
Nancy A. Bagranoff

To my husband, Gary, who has always been the wind
beneath my wings.
Stephanie M. Bryant

I am deeply appreciative of the understanding and compassion
shown by my wife (Betty) and daughter (Christy)
during the writing of this book, as I spent many hours away
from them in the process. Without their love and support,
I could not have focused as much time and energy on this "project."
James E. Hunton

PREFACE

We wrote this book to respond to a variety of pressures and opportunities facing the accounting profession. In writing it, we have come to believe even more in the importance of educating accountants as consultants. We also learned how intertwined the professions of accounting and consulting have been throughout their histories.

There are many reasons to teach consulting to accounting students. First, much accounting work is of a consultative nature. Accountants can apply many consulting skills and knowledge to traditional tax and audit work. For example, tax and audit engagements are projects in themselves, and project management skills would come in handy in planning and budgeting them. Making partner in an accounting firm usually requires developing client relationships and selling new business, just as in consulting organizations. The consulting process that entails writing proposals, solving problems, and providing deliverables to clients is much the same for a variety of accounting jobs.

Audit and tax services also frequently lead to "advice-giving" of one sort or another. It is no accident that the ten biggest consulting firms in the United States have included the Big Five accounting/professional service firms. True, some of these firms are now spinning off or selling their consulting practices. But they are certainly not getting rid of all consulting. At a minimum, the practices remaining with the CPA firms include many assurance and advisory services. Pairing accounting and consulting is natural for these organizations. A company's accountants are external parties who know about the business. They are the logical third parties to turn to when managers need advice.

A third reason to teach the "tricks of the trade" of consulting to accounting students is that today many accounting students accept consulting jobs upon graduation. Accounting is a great foundation for consulting. In our book we describe many of the consulting services that accountants are uniquely poised to offer. A fifth year of education allows us to help accounting students develop consulting and other competencies, such as information systems, that will make them sought after by consulting recruiters.

In a recent report, *Accounting Education: Charting the Course through a Perilous Future,*[1] W. Steve Albrecht and Robert J. Sack report a survey finding that shows large increases in business consulting and advising jobs for accounting graduates. The report also suggests that accounting educators might follow the AICPA and the Institute of Management Accountants in creating accounting curricula that develops students who are educated to be business consultants and advisors. This book will provide a faculty member interested in developing such curriculum with a resource to do so.

---

[1]W. Steve Albrecht and Robert J. Sack, *Accounting Education: Charting the Course through a Perilous Future,* Accounting Education Series, V. 16, American Accounting Association, 2000.

ACKNOWLEDGMENTS

Many people helped us with this book. Our students have been patient with us as we "tried out" some of our material on them. Two students in particular have been helpful. Marci Alba, Miami University, helped in editing and proofing. Wendy Jennings, University of South Florida, helped to edit the project management chapters and worked through the examples included in Appendix A.

Kevin McNeilly, Professor of Marketing at Miami University, deserves special thanks. She provided many of the materials that served as a foundation for the chapter on marketing professional services. We also thank Mark Hanna, Professor of Management at Miami University, who provided the audit engagement assignment we include in the appendix.

Several accounting professionals helped us as well. Harry Ballman and Kevin Martin shared information about their firms that we allude to throughout the book. David Woodworth at Arthur Andersen, LLP provided some training materials that helped in writing about process mapping. Kevin Cash of Ernst and Young LLP gave us some process maps that served as the foundation for some figures included in that chapter. Many other accounting consultants provided anecdotes about their practices that were helpful as well. We'd like to give a general thanks and acknowledgment to all the accountants in practice, who offer value-added consulting advice to their internal and external clients on a daily basis.

ABOUT THE AUTHORS

Nancy A. Bagranoff received her A.A. degree from Briarcliff College, B.S. degree from the Ohio State University, and M.S. degree in accounting from Syracuse University. Her DBA degree was conferred by The George Washington University in 1986 (accounting major and information systems minor). From 1973 to 1976 she was employed by General Electric in Syracuse, New York, where she completed the company's Financial Management Training Program. Dr. Bagranoff is a Certified Public Accountant, licensed in the District of Columbia, since 1982. She spent Fall 1995 as Faculty in Residence at Arthur Andersen where she worked for the Business Systems Consulting and Computer Risk Management groups. Professor Bagranoff has published many articles in such journals as *Journal of Information Systems, Journal of Accounting Literature, Computers and Accounting, The Journal of Accounting Education, Journal of Accountancy, Strategic Finance,* and the *Information Systems Audit and Control Journal.* She is coauthor, with S.A. Moscove and M.G. Simkin of *Core Concepts of Accounting Information Systems.* Currently Dr. Bagranoff is Professor of Accountancy and Director of the Master of Accountancy program at Miami University.

Stephanie M. Bryant, Ph.D., CPA, is an Assistant Professor of Accounting at the University of South Florida. She previously taught at James Madison University, in Harrisonburg, Virginia, where she served as the Director of the Accounting Information Systems Program. She earned her Ph.D. in accounting (concentration in information systems) at Louisiana State University. Dr. Bryant teaches graduate and undergraduate classes in consulting, accounting information systems, and information systems audit, and previously worked for KPMG Peat Marwick. Dr. Bryant has published numerous articles appearing in such journals as *Advances in Behavioral Research in Accounting, Journal of American Taxation Association, Journal of Accountancy, Issues in Accounting Education, International Journal of Accounting, Review of Accounting Information Systems, International Journal of Intelligent Systems in Accounting, Finance, and Management,* and *Accounting and Business.*

James E. Hunton earned his B.B.A. degree in accounting from West Texas State University. He received his M.B.A. degree in management from Rivier College in Nashua, New Hampshire, and earned his Ph.D. in business administration (majoring in accounting and information systems) from the University of Texas at Arlington. Professor Hunton is also a C.P.A. (Texas). Before beginning a Ph.D. program in 1991, he was a finance officer for the U.S. Army, information systems auditor for Arthur Young, financial analyst and controller for Mobil Oil Company, and controller and general manager for a publishing company located in southeast Texas. Since earning his Ph.D in 1994, Dr. Hunton has served as Assistant Professor at Virginia Commonwealth University and currently serves as an Associate Professor at the University of South Florida, where he also holds the prestigious position of Quinn Eminent Scholar in Accounting Information Systems. He has published numerous articles in accounting, information systems, and psychology journals. Some of the many accounting journals in which he has published are: *The Accounting Review, Accounting, Organizations & Society, Auditing: A Journal of Practice and Theory, Behavioral Research in Accounting, Journal of Information Systems, Advances in Accounting In-*

formation Systems, and *Journal of Accountancy.* Other journals include: *Journal of Applied Psychology, Organizational Behavior and Human Decision Processes, Journal of Behavioral Decision Making, Management Science, Decision Sciences,* and *MIS Quarterly.* Professor Hunton is an active member of the AICPA and American Accounting Association. Additionally, he is a Professor of Accounting Information Systems at the University of Amsterdam.

CONTENTS

PART ONE

INTRODUCTION TO CONSULTING SKILLS

Chapter 1

The Accountant as Consultant

> *Computers already can do most of the number-crunching and data-intensive work CPAs used to do, so to grow, or even to survive, small CPA firms will have to expand into consulting.... Fortunately, the prepared CPA is the best person for the job.*
>
> "Bill Gates' Win-Win Scenario for CPAs," R. J. Koreto, *Journal of Accountancy,* May 1997, p. 61.

INTRODUCTION

Accountants have always been consultants. Their knowledge of accounting and finance provides them with a valued business perspective. Accountants' understanding of business processes, capital markets, controls and security, tax law, and so on allows corporate or management accountants to make valuable contributions to the companies for which they work. Similar knowledge about a variety of organizations enables public accountants to provide similar value-added services to their clients.

For many years, despite the value added by accountants in their consultative role, the profession has possessed a narrow and somewhat unflattering image. But today's "bean counters" are moving beyond that image and reestablishing themselves as the business partners and consultants they have always been.

Today, consulting has become such a large part of the work performed by what we used to call public accounting or CPA firms that these firms now face independence conflicts and other issues. How this will be ultimately resolved, we don't know. We do know that businesses have long looked to accountants for advice on many matters and will likely continue to do so.

In this chapter we look at the evolution of the accounting consultant. We first consider the accounting profession's roots. Next the chapter examines the history of consulting services. Following that discussion, we describe the convergence of the accounting and consulting professions today through three case studies. The chapter also examines the future as seen by two professional accounting organizations: (1) the American Institute of Certified Public Accountants (AICPA), and (2) the Institute of Management Accountants (IMA). In that section of the chapter, we also discuss what we call the "accounting consultant paradox"—the imperative for accountants to act as consultants and the impediments to doing so.

Finally, this chapter describes two important aspects of consulting practice: (1) the consulting skill set and (2) the consulting process. These are the primary topics of this book. We introduce the topics here and will return to them throughout the remaining chapters.

TWO PROFESSIONS EVOLVE

Accounting and consulting share a common history. An examination of the early years in both professions highlights their similarities and differences.

Accounting's Roots

Depending on the definition, accounting's origins may be traced as far back as the Stone Age, when humanity first began counting, or to some time in the middle of the second millennium A.D. when a "money economy" emerged. Luca Pacioli, a fifteenth-century Franciscan monk, gets credited with creating accounting's system of double entry bookkeeping. As for the first known accounting course—it may have been one taught in Venice in 1581. The official acknowledgment of accounting as a scientific practice occurred in Italy in 1742.

In 1896, New York passed a law providing certification of public accountants. During that same year, Charles Haskins and Elijah Sells opened the first of the U.S. Big Five firms in New York. Figure 1-1 shows the origins of today's largest public accounting firms. For some time these firms have referred to themselves as professional service firms in an attempt to reflect the broad array of services they offer their clients. Interestingly, pressures from the SEC to scale back service offerings has relegated some of the CPA firms once again to simply "accounting" firms. Nonetheless, diversification and technology have changed the accountant and accounting firms. Well, to some extent anyway. Consider a quote from a 1964 publication on the history of accounting: "The statement frequently heard, 'Accounting is a tool of business,' is true, but not the whole truth. Accounting is also a vital partner of management in business today!"[1] That same 1964 publication also noted the interest areas of the accountant as including: economics, equity laws, finance, business analysis, and

Firm	Year Founded (City of Origin)
Andersen Consulting	1989
Arthur Andersen	1913 (Chicago)
Arthur Young	1894 (Chicago)
Cooper Brothers & Co.	1861 (London)
Coopers and Lybrand	1957
Deloitte	1854 (London)
Deloitte, Haskins, and Sells	1978
Deloitte and Touche	1989
Ernst and Ernst	1903 (Cleveland)
Ernst and Whinney	1979
Charles Waldo Haskins	1886 (New York)
Haskins and Sells	1895
KPMG Peat Marwick	1987
Lybrand, Ross Brothers, and Montgomery	1898 (Philadelphia)
Marwick, Mitchell & Co.	1897 (Glasgow)
Peat Marwick International	1911
Price Waterhouse	1849 (London)
Touche	1900 (London)
PricewaterhouseCoopers	1998
Whinney, Smith, and Whinney	1849 (London)
William Barclay Peat & Co.	1870 (London)

FIGURE 1-1 The origins of the largest public accounting organizations.

---

[1] History of Accounting (Dayton, OH: The National Cash Register Company, 1964), p. 15.

psychology. So, perhaps accountants have been doing many of the same things in the past that we believe are new today.

As the twenty-first century opens, accountants continue to engage in financial audit and tax work. The SEC mandate for an external audit is likely to continue. So long as it does, accountants will perform structured financial statement audits. A less complex tax structure, one that would alleviate the need for tax professionals, may be the vision of some politicians, but it is likely that the U.S. tax code will retain sufficient complexity to warrant tax planning. Nevertheless, it is clear that audits in particular are a mature product. Price competition in the audit industry is fierce as clients view the service as a standard commodity. There is little or no growth in most professional service firms from the practice of financial audit. While both audit and tax revenues evidence single-digit growth for many CPA firms, growth in the area of consulting services is exploding. The Big Five's worldwide revenues grew, more than 20 percent in 1998 and almost 16 percent in 1999. The source of this growth came largely from consulting services in key business areas, such as information system security, enterprise resource planning (ERP), e-business, internal auditing, "back office" support, business process reengineering, risk analysis, legal services, and mergers and acquisitions.

A Brief History of Consulting

For so long as men have had assets to protect, power to wield, and goals to achieve, there has been a need for impartial, objective advice on how to do so.[2]

There are many definitions of consulting. In this book we will use the formal definition given by the American Institute of Certified Accountants (AICPA)'s Consulting Services Team. The definition is as follows:

Consulting provides value by diagnosing, strategizing, designing, constructing, integrating, operating, or implementing solutions. Consulting utilizes relevant knowledge, based on integrity and objectivity, in both expert and advisory roles.[3]

What most definitions of consulting have in common is that the practice involves *transferring expertise*. We usually think of this expertise coming from a party *outside* an organization. This is not always true though, because internal consultants, like internal auditors and internal management accountants, may transfer their expertise *within* the organization.

If a consultant is simply anyone who gives advice, we can trace the origins of consulting back much farther than the beginnings of accounting. Modern management consulting, however, has more recent beginnings. Some historians credit Frederick Taylor, father of the scientific management concept, as most influential in developing the practice of management accounting. Frederick Taylor, an engineer, timed processes in his efforts to increase worker productivity. Some argue that this work was related more to industrial relations than management consulting.

---

[2] S. A. Washburn, "Challenge and Renewal: A Historical View of the Profession," *Journal of Management Consulting,* November 1996, p. 47.

[3] www.aicpa.org/members/div/mcs/index.htm.

"Management engineering," the forerunner of management consulting, began with engineers and accountants. Large accounting, engineering, and law firms emerged at the end of the nineteenth century. These firms employed professionals who could offer their skills and advice to America's growing industrial organizations. Professional firms still known today, such as Arthur D. Little, Arthur Andersen, Ernst and Ernst, and Seidman and Seidman, offered engineering, accounting, and legal expertise to corporate clients. (Figure 1-2 shows the 50 largest consulting firms in the world today.) Accountants started many of these firms. Case-in-Point 1.1 provides one example.

> **Case-in-Point 1.1**   Marvin Bower, who led McKinsey & Co. from 1937 until the mid-1970s, is credited with turning consulting practice into a legitimate profession. Bower himself was not an accountant, but an accountant founded his firm. James O. McKinsey, in fact, was an accounting professor at the University of Chicago. He took a broad view of accounting, believing in its ability to help management. He used his genius at interpreting the numbers to diagnose a company facing financial difficulties. The McKinsey "banker's survey" evolved into a general management audit plan of business that is still in use today.

Following the Great Depression, the SEC's mandated financial audits had an impact on management consulting. During these public audits, accounting professionals were able to collect large quantities of data about their clients' organizations that they could use to help organizations solve problems. World War II added other types of management consulting, such as operations research and strategic planning.

The emergence of computer technology in the mid-1950s created yet another specialization for management consultants: management information systems (MIS). Public accounting firms developed a business called Management Advisory Services (MAS) to help their clients integrate the new technology into their organizations. In 1958, MAS became a special interest section of the American Institute of Certified Public Accountants (AICPA). With new information technologies, these practices grew rapidly, particularly in recent years.

ACCOUNTING CONSULTANTS TODAY AND TOMORROW

Many accounting organizations today are changing or broadening their client services. Some CPA firms, believing that consulting can be more lucrative than traditional services, position themselves in specialized consulting niches. Others develop these services to fuel new revenue outlets and add more offerings that are valued by clients. In this section we look at three different CPA firms and their evolution. We then discuss the evolution of two professional accounting organizations, the Institute of Management Accountants (IMA) and the American Institute of Certified Public Accountants (AICPA). Finally, we look at the "accounting consultant paradox"—the consulting imperative and impediments to it.

Three Case Studies

The accounting and consulting professions are converging today in new ways. The role of the accountant has expanded throughout history to a consultative role. Man-

Firm	Main Office
1. Accenture	Chicago, IL
2. PricewaterhouseCoopers	New York, NY
3. Ernst & Young (now Cap Gemini Ernst and Young)	Cleveland, OH
4. Deloitte Consulting	New York, NY
5. CSC	El Segundo, CA
6. KPMG	New York, NY
7. McKinsey & Company	New York, NY
8. Cap Gemini	Paris, France
9. Mercer Consulting Group	New York, NY
10. Arthur Andersen	Chicago, IL
11. A. T. Kearney	Chicago, IL
12. Towers Perin	New York, NY
13. Booz-Allen & Hamilton	McLean, VA
14. IBM Consulting	Somers, NY
15. American Management Systems	Fairfax, VA
16. Keane	Boston, MA
17. Hewitt Associates	Lincolnshire, IL
18. Sema Group	Paris, France
19. Logica	London, United Kingdom
20. The Boston Consulting Group	Boston, MA
21. Watson Wyatt Worldwide	Bethesda, MD
22. DMR Consulting Group	Montreal, PQ, Canada
23. CMG	London, United Kingdom
24. Aon Consulting	Chicago, IL
25. Cambridge Technology Partners	Cambridge, MA
26. Arthur D. Little	Cambridge, MA
27. Bain & Company	Boston, MA
28. Debis Systemhaus	Fasanenweg, Germany
29. PA Consulting Group	London, United Kingdom
30. Woodrow Milliman	Seattle, WA
31. Origin	Eindhoven, The Netherlands
32. Telcordia Technologies	Morristown, NJ
33. Buck Consultants	Secaucus, NJ
34. Metzler Group	Chicago, IL
35. Roland Berger & Partner	Munich, Germany
36. Technology Solutions Company	Chicago, IL
37. Whittman-Hart	Chicago, IL
38. CTG	Buffalo, NY
39. CBSI	Farmington Hills, MI
40. Renaissance Worldwide	Newton, MA
41. Hay Group	Philadelphia, PA
42. Mitchell Madison Group	New York, NY
43. Perot Systesms	Dallas, TX
44. INS	Sunnyvale, CA
45. McGladrey & Pullen	Schaumburg, IL
46. CIBER	Englewood, CO
47. Monitor Company	Cambridge, MA
48. First Consulting Group	Long Beach, CA
49. Horwath International	New York, NY
50. Hagler Bailly	Arlington, VA

FIGURE 1-2 The 50 Largest Management Consulting Firms. (Reprinted with permission from *Consultants News,* 2000. All Rights Reserved. Kennedy Information LLC, 800-531-0007, www.kennedyinfo.com)

agerial accountants have become internal consultants and strategists for their organizations. Public accountants are business advisors to their clients. To illustrate this point, in this section we examine three accounting practices, their beginnings, and the services they offer today. We will refer to these case companies periodically throughout this book.

Harry Ballman, CPA   Harry Ballman retired from his partnership at Grant Thornton in 1978, at the age of 38, to open his own accounting practice on Capitol Hill in Washington, D.C. He had spent 16 years with Grant Thornton but wanted to return to practicing accounting and serving clients in a smaller office environment than was possible in a firm with more than 1,200 partners.

Harry has always taken a consulting or business advisory approach in meeting client's needs. He viewed financial statement and tax return preparation as a means to planning the future. His business is a sole proprietorship, but he subcontracts much of the work he cannot do to other professionals.

About four years ago, Harry became concerned about the converging of financial services by CPAs, lawyers, broker/dealers, and insurance companies, along with traditional accounting/tax packages becoming less expensive and available via CD ROM and on-line services. He decided he could "fight, flee, or flow" if his practice was to survive and thrive in this environment. Harry chose to "flow" in a way that met client expectations. He became certified in insurance and as a Registered Investment Advisor (Series 65). He began to deliver full personal financial planning and wealth-building services. Such services included advising about mutual funds and other investment products and forming alliances with mortgage bankers, realtors, insurance agents, and law firms to better serve the "whole" picture for his clients.

Today, Harry Ballman does not limit his accountant role to performing needs assessment, risk management, and asset allocations, but goes further and delivers the products needed to meet his client's business objectives. He can recommend the benefit of a retirement plan for personal and business clients and then deliver the 401-K, Keogh, or other investment and retirement plans needed to implement the plan. His estate planning service doesn't end with the conceptual framework for a client to have a living will, durable powers of attorney, health care proxies, revocable living trusts, and so on. Rather, his law firm alliances let him offer a full range of estate planning services. Clients see this as delivering true value to their organizations. As a result, Harry Ballman's business is growing at a faster rate than ever.

Martin and Associates   Kevin Martin is a CPA with an educational and professional background in accounting and information systems. He left the firm of Coopers and Lybrand in 1988 to develop an accounting practice with the primary objective of advising clients on accounting software. Today, Kevin is the managing partner of a firm of about 25 professionals.

Martin and Associates was never conceived as a traditional public accounting organization. The intention from the beginning was to derive almost 100 percent of firm revenues from consulting services. Kevin saw a need for mid-size businesses to get advice in choosing and implementing accounting information systems. He felt that accountants with information systems expertise could position themselves well in this market.

Martin and Associates is a value-added reseller of Sage and Microsoft Great Plains accounting software. Client targets are mid-range privately held or smaller public companies willing to pay moderate consulting fees (approximately $100 per hour for up to 100 hours) in acquiring an accounting software solution. Martin and Associates helps clients to conduct a needs analysis, select the best software, enhance the software to fit the client organization, and train and support client software users. For this work, Martin and Associates' ideal hire is a graduate with both accounting and information systems expertise. Business is growing and the consulting firm expects to hire up to eight new employees during the next year.

What is most interesting about Martin and Associates is that the firm did not begin as an accounting firm offering accounting services—and subsequently developing a consulting business. Rather, Martin and Associates *began* as a consulting company, offering traditional audit and tax services as a sideline. The firm's growth, from one individual to about 25 professionals in little over a decade, illustrates the growth potential of consulting services that build on accounting skills. It also shows the enormous opportunity when you identify a consulting niche that's a good fit between your skills and services needed in the marketplace.

The Andersens   Recently, some large public accounting firms have made decisions to sell or spin off parts of their consulting practice. Splitting off consulting practices from core accounting practices of tax and audit is not a new phenomenon. Arthur Andersen and Andersen Consulting (now Accenture) made this division several years ago—although the "divorce" is only recently final.

For most of the twentieth century, Arthur Andersen was known as an accounting firm, even though its first foray into the consulting arena was not with Andersen Consulting. Arthur Andersen has employed engineers and systems experts to evaluate client systems since 1919. The company entered the information technology consulting business in 1952, when it implemented a business computer system at General Electric. Arthur Andersen developed its consulting practice to meet the needs of its clients for expertise in finance, strategy, business processes, and information technology. The business of information systems consulting grew within the company until, in 1989, Andersen Consulting emerged as a separate business unit. In 1997, problems within Andersen Worldwide attracted public attention. One problem was that the consulting practice was growing more rapidly, in terms of both revenues and profits, than the accounting side, yet profits were shared. There were also cultural differences that are expected when a younger, more aggressive practice begins to outgrow its parent company. These cultural differences increased when the accounting and consulting sides separated.

Andersen Consulting first became known for technological consulting. However, as audit and tax services matured, Andersen Consulting developed into a full-service consulting practice. Arthur Andersen's Business Consulting group first started offering technology consulting to companies that were too small for Andersen Consulting to take on as clients—Andersen Consulting primarily serviced Fortune 500 companies. This left a niche for Arthur Andersen in the consulting business. Arthur Andersen was becoming increasingly involved in consulting, advising clients on information technology, human resources, legal issues, strategy, finance, and reengineering.

In 2000 the split was final, and Andersen Consulting announced its new name in late 2000: Accenture. The split-off of Andersen Consulting, though, is hardly the end of consulting practice at Arthur Andersen. The new Arthur Andersen is far removed from the traditional accounting practice it once was. What was "audit practice" is now "assurance services," and it includes risk management and computer security assessment, in addition to basic financial statement attestation. Figure 1-3 shows a web page for the newly separate Arthur Andersen. The company offers nine service

9 answers. 1 promise.

**Economy demands new mindsets and new solutions.
Start thinking.**

To be a force for change, you need to be the embodiment of change. Within each of our nine global market offerings, you will find the depth, dimension and experience you need to both create and innovate. In fact, our offerings have been specifically redesigned to enable ambitious organizations and dynamic people to unleash the potential of all their assets. It is time to reinvent, rediscover and revolutionize. Ready to be bold?

Our global offerings

> Assurance
> Business Consulting
> Corporate Finance
> eBusiness
> Human Capital
> Legal Services
> Outsourcing
> Risk Consulting
> Tax Services

FIGURE 1-3   An excerpt from Arthur Andersen's March 2000 web site, www.arthurandersen. com. (Used with permission.)

lines—most of which are value-added advisory services. (Notice that in Figure 1-2, Arthur Andersen is listed as the tenth largest consulting firm.)

Vision for the CPA

The American Association of Public Accountants was formed in 1887. Since its inception, the AICPA has witnessed many changes in the profession, including controversies about the scope of CPA services. Consulting isn't a new idea for accountants—they have been doing it for decades—but they called it management advisory services. Today, the AICPA faces its biggest challenges in the form of litigation, rapid development of information technology, a new 150-hour education requirement for CPAs, legal oversight, and an identity crisis in the profession.

At a 1993 meeting in Santa Fe, New Mexico, members of the CPA profession gathered at a conference called by the AICPA to address issues surrounding the market decline in demand for audit and attestation services. The meeting resulted in formation of the AICPA Committee on Assurance Services. The AICPA charged this new committee to develop assurance services that would broaden the service offerings of CPAs and build on their unique skill set. Both the initial meeting group and the assurance committee adopted a customer focus, examining the marketplace for service opportunities. At the time the Assurance Committee issued their recommendations, the audit business was generating about $7 billion for the accounting profession. The committee estimated that expansion into recommended service lines could double or triple this market. Two information technology-related assurance services, CPA WebTrust[SM] and CPA SysTrust[SM], are a direct result of the committee's work. Web-Trust[SM] is an AICPA certification on the security, privacy, and business policies of a client's consumer web site. SysTrust[SM] is assurance over the security of a client's information system.

Many assurance services are consulting-related services. The AICPA correctly recognized in the early 1990s that failure of the accounting profession to develop new services created the threat that other professional groups would take advantage of market opportunities where accountants could offer value-added services to clients. The accounting profession was faced with the choice of offering only those services considered commodities or they could be proactive in developing consulting services their clients would value.

Initiatives in the assurance service area were a forerunner to the AICPA's creation of a Vision Statement for the future of the public accounting profession. In 1998, the AICPA released a special report, *CPA Vision 2011 and Beyond: Focus on the Horizon.* The report is the result of the first phase of the CPA's Vision Project, a process meant to redefine and reposition the accounting profession. The CPA Vision Project elements include a vision statement, core purpose statement, and identified

---

Vision Statement: CPAs are the trusted professionals who enable people and organizations to shape their future. Combining insight with integrity, CPAs deliver value by: communicating the total picture with clarity and objectivity, translating complex information into critical knowledge, anticipating and creating opportunities, and designing pathways that transform vision into reality.

National Top Five Values
1. Continuing education and lifelong learning
2. Competence
3. Integrity
4. Attunement with broad business issues
5. Objectivity

National Top Five Competencies
1. Communication skills
2. Strategic and critical thinking skills
3. Focus on the client and market
4. Interpretation of converging information
5. Technological adeptness

National Top Five Issues
1. The future success of the profession relies on public perceptions of the CPA's abilities and roles.
2. CPAs must become market driven and not dependent on regulations to keep them in business.
3. The market demands less auditing and accounting and more value-adding consulting services.
4. Specialization is critical for the future survival of the CPA profession.
5. The marketplace demands that CPAs be conversant in global business practices and strategies.

National Top Five Services
1. Assurance
2. Technology
3. Management Consulting
4. Financial Planning
5. International

FIGURE 1-4 Elements of the CPA Vision Project.

core values, competencies, issues, and services of CPAs in the twenty-first century. The core purpose of CPAs is "making sense of a changing and complex world" (AICPA, CPA Vision Project). Figure 1-4 shows the other elements. The Vision Statement appears to position CPAs as consultants, who provide their customers with a variety of professional services that leverage their unique skills and competencies. Note that the issues and competencies refer directly to consulting.

According to advertisements run by the AICPA in 2000, CPAs offer: consulting services, financial planning, performance management, technology services, international services, information integrity, and assurance services—in that order. These services are quite different from the traditional audit and tax services that the public would typically associate with a CPA. All these service lines might be said to be advisory services. And only some of the assurance services, specifically those associated with financial statement attestation, actually require the CPA certification. Some of the slogans from recent AICPA advertisements appear in Figure 1-5.

In addition to the AICPA assurance services group, there is a division of the AICPA devoted specifically to consulting. The Consulting Services Team suggests consulting in assurance services, financial planning, technology, expert consulting (e.g., business valuation and litigation support), and advisory counseling (e.g., strategic planning and human resource consulting). The AICPA's *Statement on Standards for Consulting Services No. 1—Consulting Services: Definitions and Standards* is available at the AICPA web site, www.aicpa.org.

The AICPA is also adding to its CPA credential by creating new accreditations. In 1999, the professional group announced a new information technology accreditation for CPAs involved in strategic planning, implementation and management of information technology. The new accreditation, Certified Information Technology Professional (CITP), is an outgrowth of the vision process' identification of information technology as a core service and core competency. Another proposal is for a global credential that complements the CPA credential and would have global standardization and recognition.

The New Corporate Accountant

Many CPAs work as corporate or managerial accountants. These accounting and finance professionals have their own professional organization. The Institute of Management Accountants (IMA) was founded in 1919. In 1999, the IMA renamed their primary journal publication *Strategic Finance,* replacing the old name, *Management Accounting.* The name change reflects the repositioning of the manage-

---

> EVERY BUSINESS PLAN
>   HAS A FEW WRINKLES. OR SO THEY SAY.
>
> ON A CLEAR DAY, YOU CAN SEE
> THE FUTURE OF YOUR BUSINESS.
>
> **The CPA.** *Never underestimate the value.*[SM]

FIGURE 1-5 Advertising slogans from American Institute of Certified Public Accountants (AICPA) print ads.

ment accountant as a financial advisor. This mirrors many of the changes within the profession.

The personal computer and the information age prompted much of the change in the practice of management accounting. Computers both freed corporate accountants from mundane data-crunching tasks, and also provided them the opportunity to analyze the data and use it to help manage their companies. As information technology impacted the practice of managerial accounting, competitive forces affected the corporate finance function. Reengineering, the startover from scratch approach for changing organizational processes, confronted internal finance departments. From 1988 to 1996, the cost of operating a finance department in business organizations dropped 37 percent.[4] This shrinkage is likely to continue, and in some cases corporations are choosing to outsource their finance functions. Managerial accountants who do not change their traditional orientation are likely to find themselves either out of a job or employed in fairly low-level positions.

The IMA has been proactive in the last decade in researching and responding to changes in the profession of management accounting. In 1994, the organization commissioned a baseline study to determine the accounting knowledge and skills needed for the practice of management accounting today. The results of this research were published in the report, *What Corporate America Wants in Entry-Level Accountants.* The report identifies the following knowledge and skill areas as most important for management accountants: budgeting, working capital management, product costing, strategic cost management, asset management, control and performance evaluation, consolidated statements, and information system design. The research also identifies a *preparation gap,* the difference that exists in expected versus actual preparation in these knowledge and skill areas. In 1995, the IMA commissioned a scientific study of the profession. This study, *The Practice Analysis of Management Accounting* was updated again in 1999.

The 1999 update showed that today's management accounting and finance professionals provide increasing value to their organizations, use more interpersonal skills, work in business units rather than central headquarter locations, and work more on cross-functional teams. The new management or corporate accountant's workday is also pretty different from that of just a few years ago. Figure 1-6 shows the changes in how these accountants spend their time today as compared to five years ago and Figure 1-7 is a similar bar graph of changes anticipated in the next three years. It's pretty clear there's a dramatic shift *away from* collecting, compiling, and reporting data and *toward* information interpretation and involvement in decision-making.

"The rapid automation of traditional accounting functions has transformed the corporate accountant into a financial analyst and internal consultant—roles that require new knowledge, skills and abilities—resulting in calls for a profound shift in academic preparation and corporate recruiting."[5] Depending on perspective, the challenges facing today's corporate accountant are either a threat or an opportunity. For managerial accountants who want to evolve as business advisors and consultants, the future may offer more promise than the past.

---

[4] G. Hackett, "How Does Your Finance Department Measure Up?" *Journal of Accountancy,* January 1997, p. 50.

[5] Institute of Management Accountants, "Major Shift Away from Traditional Accounting Functions Revealed In Largest Continuing Analysis of Management Accounting." *IMA Focus,* September–November 1999, p. 1.

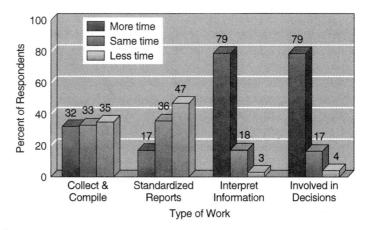

FIGURE 1-6 Change in the nature of management accounting work between 1994–1998. (*Counting More, Counting Less,* August 1999. Adapted with permission, Institute of Management Accountants, Montvale, New Jersey, www.imanet.org)

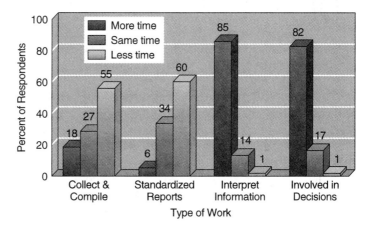

FIGURE 1-7 Change in the nature of management accounting work anticipated between 1999–2002. (*Counting More, Counting Less,* August 1999. Adapted with permission, Institute of Management Accountants, Montvale, New Jersey, www.imanet.org)

The Consulting Imperative

As we have said, the history of consulting is closely linked to accounting. Charles Waldo Haskins, who started his accounting practice in 1886, described the public accountant as "the consulting physician of finance and commerce." We believe the future of accounting *is* consulting—in the form of value-added business advising. This is the *consulting imperative* for the accounting profession. As C. W. Haskins knew, the value of accountants is not just the work they do that's mandated by audit and tax regulation, but the real value is in the advice they provide to both internal and external clients.

Financial audits and tax compliance work, the public accountant's core service offerings for much of the past century, are *mature products*. This is a marketing term that describes a stage in the product life cycle characterized by slow market growth, decreasing profitability, intense competition, and an undifferentiated product. In the past few decades, the users of audit and tax services have come to see these service products as commodities. Fortune 500 companies need attestation services. Their audit committees tend to believe that a Big Five audit opinion is important. But, beyond that, they are largely indifferent as to *which* large professional service firm they engage. This indifference, or perception of indistinguishable products, creates price competition that forces prices and profits down. Business managers know that when you have mature products, your days are numbered unless you begin to bring new products to market.

Where accountants are concerned, product maturity creates a consulting imperative—the need to develop new value-added specialty service products. Chapter 12 describes many of the consulting services that accountants are uniquely equipped to offer.

Impediments to Consultative Accounting

Although the opportunity for accountants to assume a consultative role with clients is an imperative, there are obstacles to changes in the profession. This is what we call the "accounting consultant paradox." The impediments to consulting include independence issues, resistance to change, threats from competition, and the public perception of accountants.

> *While for many years some critics of the profession have raised questions concerning the compatibility of performing consulting and auditing services simultaneously for a client, it is only in recent years that these concerns have been expressed by official bodies responsible for the oversight of the profession.*[6]

Was this written in the year 2000? No, this quote appeared in a 1980 article in the *Journal of Accountancy.* For some time, government regulators, particularly the Securities and Exchange Commission (SEC) have expressed concerns about auditor independence when public accountants offer consulting services to audit clients. The independence concern represents one of the biggest impediments to consulting.

Independence concerns may or may not have been the *primary* reason for the split between Arthur Andersen and Andersen Consulting. However, there is no doubt that this issue had a lot to do with recent decisions by several Big Five professional service firms to spin off or sell their consulting businesses. The heart of the issue is whether or not auditors can keep their independence and issue tough, negative opinions on a client's financial statements—while at the same time offer lucrative consulting services to that company. In some cases, those consulting services might be helping to design the system being audited.

Although the big professional service firms might be shedding some consulting services, it's unlikely that they will be getting out of the consulting business altogether. Look again at Arthur Andersen's web page (Figure 1-3). Traditional audit and tax are just a small piece of what they offer—and this is *Arthur Andersen*—AFTER the

---

[6] J. C. Burton, "A Critical Look at Professionalism and Scope of Services," *Journal of Accountancy,* April 1980, p. 48.

split. Many assurance services are also more consultative today, rather than just attestation. Finally, IT auditors cannot help offering security advice to audit clients. IT audit practices are growing in the double digits for this reason. Independence concerns are a problem, though. Chapter 11 discusses the legal and ethical issues surrounding the accounting consultant in some detail.

Apart from independence concerns, the resistance of accountants, like anyone, to change is a problem. For many years, audit and tax were growth industries. And maybe that made accountants become a little complacent. In the 1960s, accountants "owned" the information systems world. MIS departments reported to the head of accounting in most organizations. Unfortunately, accounting systems did not provide marketing, manufacturing, personnel, and other functional units in companies with the information they needed to manage and grow their businesses. As a result, MIS moved out of the accounting domain, and an opportunity for accountants to become the premier information specialists was lost. This is just one example of what happens when you don't change. As our discussion about the AICPA and the IMA indicates, the profession is now trying to make up for lost time. The competition has gotten stiffer. Companies like American Express are offering accounting services and many professionals are interested in offering various kinds of assurance services.

A final problem for accountants in being hired for consulting work is their image. The stereotypical "bean counter" is not someone you would look to for help in changing business processes, selecting an ERP, or developing risk management strategies. The middle-aged, thin, balding, "unlucky in love" male might be a great image for someone you want to evaluate your financial statements and prepare your tax return. But for consulting services, the image needs work. The AICPA's image enhancement campaign is a step in the right direction.

CONSULTING PRACTICE

Because consulting requires only that someone seek your advice (usually for a fee), there is a broad range of consulting practices and not much regulation. The Institute of Management Consultants (IMC), founded in 1968, does inject some standardization into the profession. The IMC maintains a code of ethics, provides a certification program (Certified Management Consultant), produces professional development activities, and publishes a journal. Consultants, however, may choose a certification in their own area of expertise, rather than opt for the more general consultant license. Figure 1-8 lists some of the professional certifications held by consultants specializing in accounting, finance, and information systems.

In this section, we talk about two important aspects of consulting practice: (1) the skill sets of a consultant, and (2) the consulting process.

The Consultant's Toolbox

Although any professional expertise may qualify an individual to be a consultant in some respects, there are certain skills that the profession requires for success. In this section of the chapter we briefly describe these skills. Chapter 2 discusses these skills in some depth and we reinforce them throughout the book.

Certification	Organization	Web Site Address
Certified Government Financial Manager (CGFM)	Association of Government Accountants (AGA)	www.agacgfm.org
Certified Financial Planner (CFP)	Financial Planning Association	www.fpanet.org
Certified in Financial Management (CFM)	Institute of Management Accountants	www.iimanet.org
Certified Information Systems Auditor (CISA)	Information Systems Audit and Control Association	www.isaca.org
Certified Internal Auditor (CIA)	Institute of Internal Auditors	www.theiia.org
Certified Management Consultant (CMC)	Institute of Management Consultants	www.imcusa.org
Certified Public Accountant (CPA)	American Institute of Certified Public Accountants	www.aicpa.org
Chartered Financial Analyst (CFA)	Association for Investment Management and Research	www.aimr.org
Certified Microsoft Professional (CMP)*	Microsoft, Inc.	www.microsoft.com

* This is one of many technical certifications available to information technology (IT) professionals. Certifications for IT professionals tend to be technology-specific.

FIGURE 1-8　Certifications for accounting, finance, information systems, and management consulting professionals.

In addition to specialized expertise, consultants need skills in a number of areas. These include communication and people skills, plus skills in change management, time/project management, negotiation and marketing, and critical thinking. Good interpersonal skills are especially important. Consulting is interactive and requires cooperation among consulting team members and with client employees.

Communication Skills　Writing skills are a *must* for consultants. Consultants prepare several documents in a client engagement. These include the engagement letter, proposal, progress reports, and a final report. Consultants must be able to write both clearly and concisely.

Oral communication skills are also necessary. Consultants usually present their proposals orally. A poor presentation can literally "blow" your chance of winning a project. Presentation skills include technical expertise with presentation software, plus the ability to speak to a group. The final report is generally delivered both in written and oral form to the client. Convincing the client of the value of the work done requires strong communication skills in packaging the deliverables. Chapters 2 and 4 cover communication skills.

"People" Skills　There are several different "people" skills required in consulting. Group skills include team-building and the ability to function as part of a team. (Chapter 2 discusses team-building in some detail.) In a consulting environment, work is rarely done by just one individual. The consulting *team* completes the project. Managers of the team have to be able to generate enthusiasm for the project and create a cohesive goal-directed working team. The team leader needs to be knowledgeable about, "forming, storming, and norming" the team.

Team members need to appreciate the value of working in a team. There are countless exercises and simulations available that teach us the superiority of teams over individuals in solving problems. For example, some teachers use a combination of group and individual tests in the classroom. In this exercise, students first complete an exam individually. They then retake the exam in their group. Group scores are almost always higher than individual grades. Exercises like this one "prove" to team members that the team will do better. They help to convince the team member who believes he or she will always know best that they should listen. Survivalist-type exercises also reinforce the superiority of teams over individual thinking. Many MBA and corporate training programs use these exercises.

Working in teams requires other people skills, including an understanding and appreciation of diversity and the ability to resolve conflict. Teams are likely to consist of diverse group of individuals. In fact, the most effective teams are diverse. Different thinking among group members leads to consideration of a wider range of possible solutions to a problem. Being able to manage this diversity is critical to successful problem-solving. It also requires an understanding of the perspectives of individuals of a different gender, age, skill set, personality, culture, or ethnicity. Again, simulations and other exercises can be helpful in developing an appreciation of diversity and understanding how to listen.

A good team leader can resolve conflicts and create consensus. Some conflict is necessary for teams to operate most effectively. There is a difference, though, between constructive and destructive conflict. The project leader needs to know which is which. Constructive conflicts can be lead toward consensus. Destructive conflicts may require intervention, sometimes even removal of a team member. Conflict resolution and consensus-building require interpersonal and communication skills.

Yet another people-related skill is effective interviewing. This is a skill that successful accountants are likely to have. Tax accountants and auditors must interview their clients. Failure to elicit full disclosure of pertinent information can sabotage tax planning or audit efforts. Similarly, failure to capture the complete picture will result in unsuccessful consulting engagements. Effective interview techniques include structuring questions appropriately and listening skills. Solutions to a problem require an understanding of the problem and a client's business processes. Consultants always run the risk of finding the *right* solutions for the *wrong* problems. Problem identification is an early step in client engagement. This identification can only take place if interviews are conducted properly and if the consultant *listens*. Listening skills are often emphasized as one of the most important in a consultant's tool kit. Chapter 8 covers interviewing.

Time and Project Management   Time and project management go hand-in-hand. Projects have to be managed to stay on target. The longer it takes to complete a consulting engagement, the more costly it is, both in terms of consulting fees and postponing the changes that will increase a client's profitability. Consultants have a number of tools to assist them in managing projects. These tools include Gantt charts, PERT analysis, and schedulers. Software packages, such as *Microsoft Project,* incorporate these techniques. This book includes *Microsoft Project* software with it. We discuss the software and how to use it in Appendix A at the end of the book. Chapters 5 and 6 discuss project management in detail.

Change Management Skills   Companies engage consultants because they are thinking about making changes. Yet change is not comfortable for many individuals. Change brings threats and risks to the status quo. Sometimes employees see change as a threat to their jobs. The need for change implies that employees are not doing their work correctly, or at least not as efficiently and effectively as possible. When employees learn that management has engaged consultants to, for example, reengineer business processes, they might associate that effort with downsizing. So it is likely that many employees will be less than enthusiastic about possible changes. Skill at managing change requires, once again, open communication. It also requires identifying attitudes toward change. In any given situation, it is likely that there will be one group of individuals who welcome change, another group somewhat neutral about change, and yet another that is resistant to any change. Those who are skilled at effective change management know to direct their efforts at the first and second groups. Although you do not want to abandon the third group, concentrating most efforts at making them go along may only lead to frustration and the loss of positive attitudes of the others. Because change management is essential to consulting success, we discuss it in detail in Chapter 10.

Negotiation and Marketing Skills   By nature, accountants are probably not the most comfortable people with marketing or selling. Traditionally, accountants considered audit and tax work as annuities. Once a client chose a firm as their auditor, for example, they were unlikely to make a switch so long as the work was performed satisfactorily. Today's competitive business environment changes that scenario. Auditors and tax accountants are finding themselves bidding for jobs and negotiating prices for their services. This requires them to be adept at marketing their audit and tax products.

Consulting engagements are even more likely to require marketing efforts. (Chapter 3 discusses marketing professional services in some depth.) These services are not mandated by legislation so a client has to be able to see the benefits that a consultant can offer. Accountants are frequently familiar with their clients' businesses and have an understanding of issues like no one else outside the client organization. This puts them in a favorable position to suggest consulting engagements. For example, an auditor might be concerned about the client organization's security over its information system. The auditor can offer consulting services to assist the client in managing this risk. In recent years the largest professional service firms have developed advertising campaigns to promote their image as seen in Case-in-Point 1.2.

> ***Case-in-Point 1.2***   Ernst and Young advertises the firm with the line, *FROM THOUGHT TO FINISH*™ and PricewaterhouseCoopers has patented a firm slogan, "Join us. Together we can change the world."[SM]

Critical Thinking Skills   Consultants are problem-solvers. Skill at critical thinking is vital to finding optimal solutions to problems. We hear a lot today about "thinking outside the box." Critical thinking includes the ability to do just that. Creative and innovative solutions are often the best ones. Accountants are traditionally quite skilled at analytical thinking but they are not typically associated with creativity. There are many ways to develop critical thinking skills and we discuss some of these in the next chapter.

An Overview of the Consulting Process

A consulting engagement typically follows a certain sequence of events, beginning with a proposal and ending with a deliverable to the client. The final section of this chapter provides an overview of this process. Chapters 4 through 9 cover the process in depth.

Project Proposals   The consulting process begins with an engagement proposal. It ends with a satisfied client. Throughout the process the consultant collects data and documents findings. Delivering the solution to the client does not necessarily mark the end of the engagement. Obtaining feedback on the solution and following up are important in ensuring success. Figure 1-9 is a flowchart of the consulting process. We will briefly discuss each phase here and examine them in detail in the remainder of the book.

Proposed projects have many different beginnings. Most, however, are the result of a marketing effort or problem identification. Some consulting projects are internal; others are external. This book focuses on external consultants, but the consulting process, apart from the original source of the project, is similar. An audit or tax client may express some concerns or an accountant might notice an issue that needs attention. An accountant, based on familiarity with a client through audit or tax work, might notice a problem area where professional services can be of help. As an example, a large professional services firm might offer e-commerce services to a client. Or, as happened often in the late 1990s, the outside auditor could offer firm services related to Y2K concerns. An accounting and consulting organization might attract new clients through advertising and other promotion efforts. Regardless of the initiating contact, the consulting project will begin with an engagement proposal.

A client may request a proposal from a consultant directly or the proposal can be a response to a general request for proposal (RFP). The first type is not likely to be subjected to a competitive bidding process. A proposal written as an RFP response is somewhat different because the RFP is likely to specify at least some of its content. It is also going to be compared with competitive proposals.

There is a fairly standard format to proposals, regardless of type. Each proposal should begin with a brief executive summary or introduction that "sells" the client. This section contains an introduction to the consultant or the consulting firm, a brief summary of relevant experience, and an overview of the proposal content. You should also include any particularly noteworthy features of the proposal to capture the reader's immediate attention. Remaining sections of the main body of the proposal are a statement of objectives or requirements, the project organization and approach the consulting firm will take, the project scope, deliverables, staffing, details about qualifications and experience, and a listing of timing and fees. Appendices to the proposal document will include resumes and any disclaimers or needed legal language. Chapter 4 describes the client proposal in depth.

If the project is not approved, you may or may not have the opportunity to revise it and resubmit. In any case, some follow up is called for. Obtain any information possible about why the client did not approve the project.

Data Collection and Analysis   Once a client accepts a consulting proposal, work begins. The primary work is data collection and analysis. Chapter 8 discusses a variety of techniques for collecting data. In that chapter we will also cover tools for analyzing data. Data collection and analysis can take anywhere from a few weeks to a few years, depending on the nature of the project. For example, implementing an enterprise resource planning (ERP) system took most Fortune 500 companies, such as Procter and Gamble, several years. The data collection and analysis phase may include some design activity, particularly if the consulting project involves information systems.

Parallel Activities   Certain activities take place during the main project work. These are project management, documentation, and progress reporting. Keeping the project on track with the proposal time and cost specifications is important. Consultants should report significant variances to the client. The contract may specify the timing of progress reports. If it does not, you should, at a minimum, report progress after reaching certain milestones. Documenting findings in graphical format may be

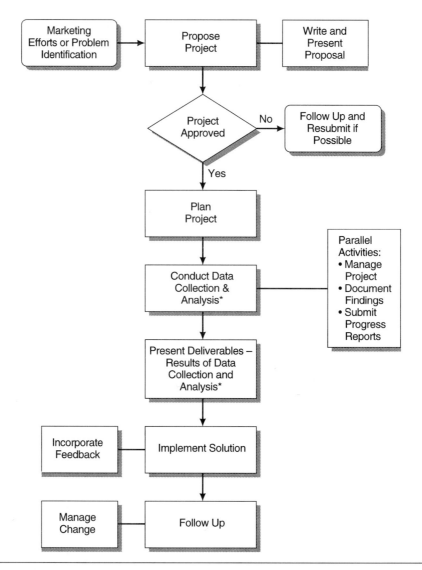

* In the case of an information systems project, these stages include systems design and implementation.

FIGURE 1-9 The consulting process.

a significant factor in developing deliverables or solving issues. You may want to provide the client with any flowcharts or process maps you develop that are of potential use. For example, in a reengineering project, a consultant will create a map of existing processes. This document may be enlightening to the client.

Project Deliverables Deliverables come in many forms. Perhaps the primary deliverable is a newly functioning information system. On completion of the main work, the consultant is likely to provide both a written and oral report of some kind. If the client is not satisfied, consultants may decide to do more work. Some follow-up, based on client feedback, is typical. Follow-up work may also be needed to ensure that the consulting solution works after the consultant leaves. For instance, consultants may need to train employees on a new system or about new processes. Chapter 9 discusses deliverables, feedback, and follow-up.

SUMMARY

The profession of accounting is an old one. Trade transactions require accountability. Many of today's largest professional service or CPA firms trace their beginning to the mid-nineteenth century. From early on, accountants thought of themselves as business consultants and, in fact, many of the early practitioners of "management engineering," the forerunner to management consulting, were accounting professionals.

Today's accountants must be consultants. The traditional service offerings of public accountants, audit and tax, are mature industries. An increasingly competitive business environment, combined with advances in information technology, call for third parties to provide value-added services, such as consulting. Audits and tax work are commodities, with price competition and flat growth rates. Information technology has also changed the work of management accountants. They no longer need to spend their time making complex cost calculations and analyzing the past. Computers do much of that work for them, allowing internal accountants to assume a more proactive role in business.

Both the American Institute of Certified Public Accountants (AICPA) and the Institute of Management Accountants (IMA) are working hard to redefine the profession of accounting. The AICPA, in its Vision Project, is defining accounting largely in consulting terms. The Vision Project identifies new service areas for accountants that leverage their unique skills. The IMA is repositioning the corporate or management accountant as a strategist, offering internal consulting to management.

As accountants assume more of a business advisory role, they are faced with both opportunities and challenges. Independence concerns are particularly problematic. While accountants are frequently in a position to understand a client's business from a unique perspective that positions them well in terms of consulting, that same relationship may compromise the very independence that enables them to express an unbiased opinion of the business.

The practice of consulting requires not only knowledge of business, but also a set of skills. While accountants have many of these skills, there are others that they need and don't always get. These skills include communication and people skills, plus skills in change management, time/project management, negotiation, marketing, and critical thinking. We talked about them briefly in this chapter and they are discussed throughout the book.

The consulting process covers all the steps in a consulting engagement. The engagement often begins with marketing services to clients. Marketing efforts may be *within* an organization—as is the case with corporate accountants. For public accountants, these efforts can be directed at new clients or current clients of audit and tax services. Consultants typically prepare an engagement proposal that details the work they recommend. Once a proposal is accepted, work begins in collecting and analyzing data. Providing deliverables is not the end of an engagement. Generally, follow-up work is necessary to ensure client satisfaction.

DISCUSSION QUESTIONS

1-1. Do you think accounting is more of a "tool of business" or a "partner to business"? Explain.

1-2. The Securities and Exchange Acts of 1933 and 1934 mandated independent audit opinions on financial statements of public corporations. How do you think the accounting profession might have evolved without this mandate?

1-3. Many early consultants were accountants. What other professions had the specialized expertise to offer advice to business organizations?

1-4. Harry Ballman began his business in the traditional service areas of audit and tax. Kevin Martin started his public accounting firm with the intent to specialize in nontraditional accounting services. If you were to start an accounting firm today, what services would your firm offer? In answering this question, think about market needs and your own skill set.

1-5. Imagine that you are a partner today in a small CPA firm (5–10 employees). Your firm has engaged in audit and tax work for more than 10 years but revenues do not appear to be growing. What services would you consider offering to clients that would ensure double-digit growth rates over the next decade?

1-6. Large professional service organizations such as Arthur Andersen and Ernst and Young are faced today with difficult decisions concerning the audit independence issue. Do you think it is possible for a public accounting firm to offer both audit and consulting services?

1-7. One interesting independence issue public accounting firms now confront concerns outsourcing. Many businesses are outsourcing their internal audit work to public accounting firms. Suppose that a company engages one Big Five firm to conduct its external audit and another for its outsourced internal audit work. What are some of the conflicts that might emerge from this arrangement?

1-8. The AICPA is running an advertising campaign to reposition the CPA. Do you think this advertising campaign can be successful in changing the image of an accountant from "bean counter" to "forward-thinking business advisor"?

1-9. Many management accountants today work on cross-functional teams. What do you think the role of a corporate accountant might be on a team choosing an enterprise-wide software solution for their organization?

1-10. Why is consulting an *imperative* for accountants?

1-11. This chapter described some of the obstacles faced by accounting consultants—the accounting consultant paradox. Can you think of some others?

1-12. Accountants are not typically known for their marketing skills, yet these skills are important to consultants. Why is marketing so important for accountants?

1-13. Several of the skills consultants need to be successful are the same skills that accountants have traditionally needed for their work. Which of the skill areas mentioned in the chapter do you think accountants particularly excel at?

1-14. Which stage of the consulting process do you think is most important? Why?

EXERCISES

1-15. Find some advertisements for CPAs and public accounting firms. What is the image of accounting the ads are attempting to communicate? Do the ads refer to consulting services? Which ones?

1-16. Visit the AICPA web site for proposed assurance services. One of the new assurance services that CPAs are offering is CPA Web Trust.^{SM} What are some of the other proposed assurance services?

1-17. The AICPA offers a variety of publications for sale. Visit the AICPA web site and document the consulting-related publications.

1-18. Evaluate your skill levels in: written communication, oral communication, team-building, diversity, conflict resolution, negotiation, marketing, project management, change management, critical thinking, and interpersonal relations. List each skill and indicate whether you are strong, moderate, or weak in that area. What are the skills you feel you need to develop further to be a consultant or business advisor? Are there any other skills, other than those on the list, that you think might be important in consulting?

REFERENCES, RECOMMENDED READINGS, AND WEB SITES

References and Recommended Readings

Barcus, S. W. III, and J. W. Wilkinson, *Handbook of Management Consulting Services,* 2nd edition (New York: McGraw-Hill, 1995).

Biech, E., *The Business of Consulting* (San Francisco: Jossey-Bass Pfeiffer, 1999).

Biswas, S., and D. Twitchell, *Management Consulting* (New York: John Wiley and Sons, 1999).

Block, P., *Flawless Consulting,* 2nd edition (San Francisco: Jossey-Bass Pfeiffer, 2000).

Bobrow, E. E., "Poof! You're a Consultant," *Journal of Management Consulting* (November 1998), pp. 41-43.

"Counting More, Counting Less," *A Research Project of the Institute of Management Accountants* (Montvale, NJ: The Institute of Management Accountants, 1999).

Crockett, R. O., "Next Stop, Splitsville," *Business Week* (January 18, 1999), pp. 100-102.

Emerson's 1999 Big Five Annual Report (Bellevue, WA: The Emerson Company, 1999).

Flesher, D. L., P. J. Miranti, and G. J. Previts, "The First Century of the CPA, *Journal of Accountancy* (October 1996), pp. 51-57.

History of Accounting (Dayton, OH: The National Cash Register Company, 1964).

Hollander, N., and S. Needle, *Handbook of Computer and Management Consulting* (Rockville, MD: Computer Training Services, 1997).

Koreto, R. J., "Bill Gates' Win-Win Scenario for CPAs," *Journal of Accountancy* (May 1997), pp. 59-61.

Kulesza, C. S., and G. Siegel, "It's Not Your Father's Management Accounting!" *Management Accounting* (May 1997), pp. 56-59.

McKenna, C. D., "The Origins of Modern Management Consulting," *Business and Economic History* (Fall 1995), pp. 51-58.

Siegel, G., and C. S. Kulesza, "The Practice Analysis of Management Accounting," *Management Accounting* (April 1996), pp. 20-28.

Siegel, G., C. S. Kulesza, and J. E. Sorensen, "Are You Ready for the New Accounting?" *Journal of Accountancy* (August 1997), pp. 42-48.

Thomas, J., "The Future—It Is Us," *Journal of Accountancy* (December 1998), pp. 23-26.

Washburn, S. A., "Challenge and Renewal: A Historical View of the Profession," *Journal of Management Consulting* (November 1996), pp. 47-53.

Whitford, D., "Arthur, Arthur...," *Fortune* (November 10, 1997), pp. 169-178.

Zarowin, S., "Finance's Future: Challenge or Threat?" *Journal of Accountancy* (April 1997), pp. 38-42.

Web Sites

www.aicpa.org

www.arthurandersen.com

www.dttus.com

www.ey.com

www.kpmg.com

www.pwcglobal.com

Chapter 2

Basic Skills for Consultants

No matter how much technical expertise you possess, if you cannot communicate messages effectively, clients will have difficulty understanding, interpreting, and relating to those messages.

> Steven P. Golen, "Effective Communications Skills," In *Handbook of Management Consulting Services,* 2nd edition (New York: McGraw-Hill, 1995), p. 5-1.

INTRODUCTION

Accountants are known for their strong technical skills. After all, preparing tax returns and performing audits are the hallmarks of the CPA's activities. Accountants, however, are not generally known for their "soft" skills—leadership, communications, team-building, and so on. Although these skills may not be technically demanding, they are vital to success in both accounting and consulting.

Chapter 1 introduced the *CPA Vision Project,* which was designed to identify how the accounting profession will adapt to the changing needs of the future. The project identified the "top fives." These are the five most important issues for the public accounting profession in each of the following domains: core values, core services, core competencies, and significant issues. Of particular importance for this chapter are the top five **core competencies,** along with an emphasis on *one* of the top five **core values**—continuing education and lifelong learning (see Figure 2-1).

The core competencies as identified by the *CPA Vision Project* are equally applicable to accounting consultants. This chapter discusses essential competencies for the accounting consultant, organized around the core competencies identified in the *CPA Vision Project.* These include: communications and leadership skills, strategic and critical thinking skills, customer, client, and market focus, interpretation of converging information, and technological expertise. The chapter ends with a discussion of the importance of a commitment to continuing education and lifelong learning.

COMMUNICATIONS AND LEADERSHIP SKILLS

As evidenced by the quote at the beginning of the chapter, communication skills are essential for the accounting consultant. In fact, they are vital for any professional dealing with the public. The ability to clearly express one's ideas is the foundation of consulting. Likewise, demonstrating leadership is crucial to a successful consultant. The ability to motivate others is necessary to work cohesively and efficiently together to achieve a common purpose. This section discusses the *Vision Project's* interpretation of communications and leadership, and how these qualities relate to the accounting consultant

Core Competencies	Core Values
Communications and Leadership Skills Able to give and exchange information within meaningful context and with appropriate delivery and interpersonal skills. Able to influence, inspire, and motivate others to achieve results. ***Strategic and Critical Thinking Skills*** Able to link data, knowledge, and insight together to provide quality advice for strategic decision-making. ***Focus on the Customer, Client, and Market*** Able to anticipate and meet the changing needs of clients, employers, customers, and markets better than competitors. ***Interpretation of Converging Information*** Able to interpret and provide a broader context using financial and non-financial information. ***Technologically Adept*** Able to utilize and leverage technology in ways that add value to clients, customers, and employers.	***Continuing Education and Life-Long Learning*** CPAs highly value continuing education beyond certification and believe it important to continuously acquire new skills and knowledge.

FIGURE 2-1   CPA Vision Project core competencies and core values as related to basic skills consultants need.

Communications

The object of communication, whether oral or written, is to convey thoughts, attitudes, perceptions, and opinions to an interested party.

Oral Communication   Let's start with oral communication. There are a number of factors to which the consultant should pay attention with respect to oral communication. They include: attitude traps, listening skills, credibility, first impression, organization and delivery of ideas, use of jargon, and nonverbal cues.

Attitude Traps   Always be aware that your attitude is showing! There are several pitfalls you must guard against to avoid alienating your client or audience. For instance, an inexperienced consultant sometimes falls into the defensive trap. This can happen when the client questions the consultant about a recommendation. A more experienced consultant knows that it is not merely acceptable to have your work questioned, but it is most likely going to result in a *better* project.

Another pitfall occurs when the consultant has a "know-it-all" attitude. Admittedly, CPA consultants are highly trained and skilled. However, many clients are too—but maybe not about the same subjects. The smart accounting consultant adopts a "down-to-earth" attitude and carries an attitude of quiet confidence. Nothing turns off prospective clients faster than an arrogant attitude. This is particularly problematic when the consultant is much younger than the client personnel.

Of course, a consultant can also encounter a "know-it-all" attitude in a client and should be careful in responding. Client arrogance is sometimes due to fear of change, uncertainty, or insecurity. You need to try to build a climate of support and trust. Reiterating to the client that you share a common goal—the successful resolution to the problem at hand—may be helpful. Some people simply need time to adjust to change and may mellow out over time. In others, arrogance is a personality trait that doesn't go away. If that's the case, you just have to do your best to cope.

Listening Skills   How many times have you been introduced to someone, only to immediately forget the person's name? Most of us have been guilty of this at one time or another. It's not only embarrassing, but in consulting, it can be lethal. People want to feel that they're important. To this end, an extremely important interpersonal skill consultants should master is remembering names, everyone from the client's secretary to the CEO.

The ability to listen attentively is an acquired skill. (We discuss listening during interviews in Chapter 8.) People usually forget names because they aren't listening effectively. It takes more than hearing the name. It takes focusing on the conversation, meaning, *really* listening. Repeating the name as you shake hands is helpful, as is writing down the name—if you can do it unobtrusively. In conversation, try to tune out extraneous details like the room surroundings or the person on the phone in the next room. Listen objectively, empathetically, and sincerely to your client. Ask yourself mentally if you are listening. You should not only focus your attention on the message being communicated, but also make sure that you understand the message correctly. One means of accomplishing this end is to rephrase what the client is saying.

Example   Client: We want to increase our profitability by 30 percent over the next three years. We aren't sure exactly how to do that but we have several ideas. One way might be to introduce a new product that has been in development for some time. Another way might be to cut our costs by trimming overhead expenses. We are also considering a merger with a competitor, but aren't sure exactly when or even if that will materialize.

You, the consultant, after nodding and listening, rephrase the client's statements.

Consultant: I see. So, to increase profitability over the next three years you have several possible ways in mind to accomplish this, including developing a new product, cutting costs, and a possible merger.

Rephrasing serves to let the client know that you are paying attention and that you understand what he or she is saying; reiterating the thoughts out loud helps to reinforce the ideas in your own mind.

Another useful habit is to take notes while listening. Note-taking, if not done properly, can be intimidating to a client. To avoid this, remember these rules for note-taking:

1. Don't write *everything* down that a client says. Write down only *key* items.
2. Take notes *unobtrusively,* without flourish or calling attention to the note-taking.
3. *Summarize* and fill in the details after the client meeting.
4. Refer to your notes as needed to *refresh* your memory, particularly with respect to names.
5. If *personal observations* are written down in your notes, don't leave them lying around for client personnel to read.

Taking notes can also help you identify future opportunities for the client's business. For example, if the client happens to mention difficulty in putting a child through college, you might make a note to discuss personal financial planning at the appropriate time.

Credibility   If you want your clients to take your advice, you have to be credible. You primarily establish credibility by being as knowledgeable about your subject matter as possible. Your client should have no doubts about your ability to provide a successful solution for their business problem. Your attitude should demonstrate confidence (but not arrogance) in your competence. At the same time, pretending you have all the answers can damage your credibility, so know your limitations. Even if you're sure you know the proper path to the solution, it's always a good idea to give yourself some time to think. Quick answers can be wrong, and will damage credibility in the long run.

First Impressions   It's a cliché, but it's true: you never get a second chance to make a first impression. Clothing, hairstyle, jewelry, perfume, handshake, voice, even your laugh, all communicate something about you. Although first impressions can be overcome, it's much easier to try to make a good impression the first time you meet client personnel. Your appearance and demeanor should be professional without being overbearing. Dress appropriate to the business. If you're working with a machine shop, you can dress more casually than if you are working with a bank. Jewelry should be tasteful, your perfume or cologne subtle. Your handshake should be firm, but not bone-crushing. Keep your voice modulation to an even pitch, but not monotone. Show interest with the inflection of your voice. Think too about any products you display versus products your client produces. If you're working with an American automobile manufacturer, don't show up in a foreign car.

Organization and Delivery of Ideas   It is essential to have a well-organized client presentation. The talk should flow logically, with visual aids arising naturally from the subject matter. You should be intimately familiar with your subject and avoid using any notes. If you need "prompts," put them on an overhead or Power Point slide. Practicing a presentation is extremely helpful in gaining familiarity with how the presentation will unfold. Inform the audience at the outset when you wish to entertain questions. Observance of these points will greatly aid in delivering a successful presentation. And keep your eye on the clock! Shorter is better and going over your time allotment is always a bad idea. (Presentation skills are covered in detail in Chapter 4.)

Use of Jargon   Jargon is sometimes intimidating and often annoying. Resist the urge to "show off" by using jargon. *Knowing* your audience will go a long way in determining what level of jargon you can use. An audience of systems analysts and system engineers will be completely comfortable with jargon regarding the implementation of a new computer system. On the other hand, low-level users of the systems such as bookkeepers and clerks will not. Modify your use of jargon accordingly. Also avoid acronyms. How many times have you heard someone use an acronym throughout a talk while you're sitting in the audience wondering what it means?

Nonverbal Cues   Learning to observe and read nonverbal cues is a useful skill for consultants. What attitudes do the client personnel display? Are they open, supportive, and interested in what you have to offer or do they appear hostile or resistant to your presence? Do they make eye contact? Do they maintain crossed arms? In general, nonverbal cues can give important insight into the climate and attitudes of the client's business. However, one word of caution: it's possible to misread verbal cues. Consider both verbal and nonverbal cues in your assessment, and give the client personnel time to adjust to your presence.

Written Communication   The consulting proposal is usually the first written document that comes from the consultant, and is the first evidence of your written skills. You should take care that the proposal is clearly written, logically organized, and free from grammatical and spelling errors. In today's age of word processing software, catching grammatical and spelling errors has become much simpler. But sometimes that makes it harder. Remember that a spell checker will catch spelling errors only when you use words that are not in a dictionary. It won't correct you when you use *their* instead of *there* and so on. Chapter 4 discusses the written proposal.

Leadership

There are many formal theories and models of leadership that regard it from various perspectives. This book takes a practical perspective. What leadership traits should accounting consultants seek to acquire and refine? The *CPA Vision Project* (see Chapter 1) defines leadership as the ability to "influence, inspire and motivate others to achieve results." The ability to influence others means that you can get others to not only see your point of view, but also *espouse* that point of view. It's getting others to come over to your side. Inspiring others means stirring emotions, while motivating means communicating a vision and then rousing others to action to realize that vision.

Undoubtedly, many great leaders are born with the ability to influence, inspire, and motivate. However, that doesn't imply that leadership skills cannot be acquired. Let's look at some other personality traits that might be fostered to develop leadership skills. First, leaders are able to command respect by giving respect. Leaders must be good listeners. They give weight and consideration to the views of their subordinates, and treat views offered sincerely with respect. They value and acknowledge the contributions of their subordinates.

> ***Case-in-Point 2.1***   Geoffrey A. Moore, a highly popular Silicon Valley consultant, is also known for his leadership skills. Says Peter West, a leadership consultant at Microsoft about Mr. Moore, "He teaches very much in the best way that college professors teach. He's challenging and provocative but never sarcastic, and he never puts people down." In an article on Mr. Moore, it is noted, "His gentle but engaging manner charms and energizes audiences of even the toughest managers."[1]

Client personnel should always be treated with courtesy and respect. Remember—they're paying the bill! A big part of your job is listening carefully to your client and eliciting the best information possible. While the consultant is an expert in consulting, recognize that the client is an expert at his or her business.

Effective leaders recognize that they can't do all the work themselves. They effectively delegate work to subordinates, as appropriate, and reinforce to them how important their role is in the successful outcome. For the consultant, this is often seen in the managing of teams. A project manager must be able to effectively delegate, and then coordinate, work performed by team members. Project managers must also be facilitators in communication between team members, helping a team to function as effectively and efficiently as possible.

Finally, a strong leader enjoys credibility stemming from a number of personal factors, including competency in domain knowledge, personal integrity, ability to accept criticism, and ability to work with diverse groups of people. These traits together might be called, "charisma." One thing is true: effective leaders have their own

---

[1] Faith Keenan, "Geoff Moore Goes Mainstream: The Best-Selling High-Teach Guru Is Trying to Take His Cyber-Management Ideas to Corporate America, *Business Week,* October 23, 2000, p. 66.

individual leadership styles that they have developed over time. In short, they have figured out what works for them. A consultant must do the same: figure out what works, while striving for complete competency and personal integrity.

Time/Project Management

Consulting projects are managed within a framework of project management. Careful management of the project is essential to maintain profitability on the engagement. The team leader typically is responsible for seeing that the consulting team adheres to budgeted time and expense costs where possible. In the case when it becomes apparent that a significantly larger amount of time is needed to complete a consulting engagement, it's important to discuss the situation as soon as possible with the client. Because project management is so important to consulting success, we discuss it in depth in Chapters 5 and 6.

Team-Building

A consulting team is just that—a team.[2] True teams function cohesively. Dysfunctional teams often cause inefficiencies and errors in the consulting process and/or solution. Of course getting a team to function cohesively is easier said than done. Corporate managers use several approaches to facilitate team-building. These include retreats, games, outdoor experiences, or any project that serves to bring people together for a common purpose. The goal is for the group to learn to trust and respect each other and work together to achieve a common purpose.

> **Case-in-Point 2.2**   Habitat for Humanity, a nonprofit organization that helps build homes for low-income people, is a popular philanthropic outlet. However, corporations such as National Gypsum are increasingly taking on construction of Habitat houses as team-building exercises for their organization.[3]

There are several considerations with respect to consulting teams, including: size of the team, team leadership, team goals, managing team-member roles and expectations, and managing conflict.

Size of the Team   Consulting teams may range from two to 30 personnel, depending on the scope of the engagement. Most experts put the upper limit on team membership at 10, with an emphasis on the smallest size possible. The bigger the team, the more risk there is for interpersonal problems to enter into the team process. Again, the nature and scope of the consulting engagement will dictate the specific size.

Team Leadership   The project leader bears a critical role in the success of the consulting project. An ineffective leader will demand personal credit and praise for a successful project outcome, while an effective leader will bear much responsibility

---

[2] John Schermerhorn, James Hunt, and Richard Osborn, "Teamwork and the Creative Use of Groups," *Managing Organizational Behavior,* 5th edition (New York: John Wiley & Sons, 1994), pp. 326–349.
[3] Geoffrey Brewer, "Building Team Spirit at National Gypsum," *Sales & Marketing Management,* June 1, 1994, p. 39.

for the lack of stellar results. The team leader should possess the abilities mentioned in the previous section, "Leadership," including the ability to influence, inspire, and motivate the team members. These include excellent communications, time management, delegation, and conflict resolution and negotiation skills. Additionally, project managers should facilitate management of team members' skills and expectations. An effective leader is a good coach.

Team Goals   Teams are formed to achieve a common set of goals. To be effective, the team leader should clearly communicate what the goals and priorities are and keep the team focused accordingly. Creating a sense of urgency, moving toward completion of the project, will facilitate proper functioning of the team.

Managing Team-Member Roles and Expectations   Stress and conflict may arise in the case of role ambiguity. This occurs when team members are uncertain as to what their roles are or where role boundaries lay. The team leader can head off role ambiguity by clearly defining each team member's responsibilities. Being open to questions in order to clarify what expectations are for each team member will also help eliminate role ambiguity. Role negotiation can also erase role ambiguity. In role negotiation, team members who are experiencing such ambiguity write lists directed at other team members to clarify what they want from the other group member. The other group member can then agree or disagree to modify behavior accordingly. The final result of negotiation is a written statement of what each team member agrees to do.

Managing Conflict   When working with people, inevitably conflicts will occur. Conflicts due to role ambiguity were already discussed. It is the consulting team leader's responsibility to manage conflict. Schermerhorn et al. (1994) identifies and defines several conflict management styles a team leader may adopt, including: avoidance, authoritative command, accommodation, compromise, and collaboration. *Avoidance* occurs when the team leader believes the problem is trivial and will go away on its own, or when the team members involved need time to cool down. *Authoritative command* is used when decisive action is called for or when unpopular decisions must be made. This method basically communicates, "Because I am the boss, that's why." *Accommodation* might be appropriate when the team leader wants to build goodwill for later, or when the team leader doesn't view the conflict as important. *Compromise* is important when a temporary settlement is needed or when it is important to make a quick decision. Finally, *collaboration* is the ideal conflict management technique, wherein the team leader works with team members to determine and implement the ideal solution. An effective team leader will use most or a combination of these techniques in many consulting engagements, as the situation and resources dictate.

Interviewing Client Personnel

An important part of gathering necessary data is to interview client personnel. (We discuss interviewing in depth in Chapter 8.) Interpersonal skills are extremely important in this process. A consultant's goal is to elicit the best quality information as possible. Establishing a rapport with the client is an important aspect.

When possible, the interview should take place in a private area, free from excessive noise or other disruptive influences. Be aware that when interviewing lower level client personnel, there may be a certain amount of resistance to the proposed change that may lead the person to be less than forthcoming. Your job is to make the client feel comfortable and nonthreatened. However, take care that in discussing the potential change with client personnel, you don't make any promises. For example, if the client company is contemplating installing a new computer system for which a lower level clerk is untrained, the consultant may be tempted to reassure a nervous clerk that his or her job will remain secure. Unless the client has specifically made that promise, the consultant cannot make such statements.

Cultural Considerations

Due to ever-increasing globalization, diversity in the workplace has become the rule, rather than the exception. Consultants very often have to deal with a variety of cultures, ethnic backgrounds, and traditions in the workplace. It is important for a consultant to recognize and respect these differences.

STRATEGIC AND CRITICAL THINKING SKILLS

Consulting involves the exercise of both strategic and critical thinking skills. Although these two skills are similar, they're not the same. Strategic thinking involves the ability to think *proactively*, not *reactively*. It is anticipating what future needs might be, as opposed to concentrating only on today's needs. On the other hand, critical thinking is the ability to analyze a problem from many perspectives and viewpoints in order to arrive at an optimal solution. This chapter section explains the consultant's need to acquire and refine both strategic and critical thinking skills.

In preparing to work on a consulting problem, one of the first things a consultant must do is figure out the underlying nature of the problem. Quite often, this is more difficult than it might seem. What appears to be the problem may only be a symptom of an underlying, unrecognized problem.

> **Example** You're the owner of First Class Consulting, engaged to install a new accounting system. The client tells you that the old system just isn't sufficient—reports are not only inadequate, but they often provide erroneous information. On its surface, the project seems clear-cut and unambiguous. However, the consultant should carefully evaluate and analyze the client's financial statements, as well as the complete transaction processing cycle, before forging ahead with the new accounting system. Maybe the stated problem is merely symptomatic of misunderstood interpretation, flawed information processing, or something else. Figuring out what is "really" wrong and how to fix it is the heart of critical thinking.

Definition of Critical Thinking

There is plenty of research in critical thinking, yet there is no universally accepted definition of the concept. When asked what critical thinking means, accountants and other professionals will often respond with a currently popular catch-phrase, "thinking outside the box." But what does that mean?

The Federation of Schools of Accountancy (FSA) Pedagogical Resources Committee (1995) has adopted Kurfiss's definition:

Critical thinking is a rational response to questions that cannot be answered definitively and for which all the relevant information may not be available. It is an investigation whose purpose is to explore a situation, a phenomenon, a question, or a problem, to arrive at a hypothesis or conclusion about it that integrates all available information, and that can therefore be convincingly justified.[4]

Two other definitions worth reviewing are provided by Paul (1990) and Stark (1988). Paul defines critical thinking as:

...disciplined, self-directed thinking which exemplifies the perfection of thinking appropriate to a particular mode or domain of thought.[5]

Baril et al. (1997) relate Stark's definition of critical thinking as:

...involving the examination of issues rationally, logically, and coherently; being able to acquire, evaluate, and perhaps produce information and knowledge and being able to make decisions in both familiar and unfamiliar circumstances.[6]

For the consultant, then, critical thinking involves evaluating and analyzing information before accepting it as fact. It means dissecting the stated premises and asking important relevant questions to ascertain the accuracy of those premises and the resultant conclusion(s). It requires generating rational hypotheses based on the available information and interpolating for missing information. It entails resisting the urge to form quick conclusions. And, finally, it means studying a problem from several perspectives.

Returning to our earlier critical thinking example, the client has stated two premises regarding the old accounting system: (1) the reports are inadequate, and (2) the reports often provide erroneous information. Let's examine these two statements carefully.

First, the consultant should question the client carefully and thoroughly as to exactly *why* she believes the reports are inadequate. In what way are the reports inadequate? What information is missing that the client believes is essential? Perhaps the information is available, but is simply not being requested properly.

Second, the client says the old accounting system often provides erroneous information. Again, the consultant should ask the client to elaborate and provide examples. A well-known axiom in systems states that the output of a system is only as good as the input. Thus, the erroneous output may be due to input errors. Perhaps

---

[4] J. G. Kurfiss, *Critical Thinking: Theory, Research, Practice, and Possibilities,* ASHE-ERIC Higher Education Report Number 2 (Washington, DC: Association for the Study of Higher Education, 1988).

[5] R. Paul, *Critical Thinking,* Edited by A.J.A. Binker (Rohnert Park, CA: Center for Critical Thinking and Moral Critique, Sonoma State University, 1990).

[6] J. Stark and M. Lowther, *Strengthening the Ties that Bind* (Ann Arbor: Professional Preparation Network, University of Michigan, 1988).

the data entry clerk hasn't been properly trained or supervised. Perhaps the input documents need refinement. There may be many alternative hypotheses as to why the output is erroneous. Each hypothesis should be carefully evaluated and discarded or accepted.

As you can see, it may be tempting to take the client's word and simply proceed to install the new system. However, the client may find that the same problems exist with the new system. This happens when you treat symptoms rather than problems. In the long run, the client will develop loyalty to a consultant who can be trusted to look out for the client's best interests, instead of simply generating consulting fees.

Components of Critical Thinking

In 1997, the Federation of Schools of Accountancy issued its research report on critical thinking entitled, "Critical Thinking Competencies Essential to Success in Public Accounting." This report, which was based on empirical evidence, identified nine major components of critical thinking important for accountants. These are: (1) recognizes problem areas or potential problem areas; (2) recognizes when additional information is needed; (3) fits details into the overall environment; (4) transfers knowledge from one situation to another; (5) exhibits initiative; (6) exhibits curiosity; (7) anticipates, thinks ahead, and plans; (8) exhibits confidence; and (9) communicates clearly and articulately. We will examine these components with respect to the consultant's view, as discussed in some detail in the following section.

Recognizes Problem Areas   A skill that fits into this area includes recognizing when the client presents conflicting evidence. Recognizing conflicting evidence is a skill especially highly valued by auditors who must seek to determine whether or not financial statements are fairly presented in accordance with GAAP. This is often referred to as "analytical ability." Overall, does the information presented fit together reasonably? Auditors sometimes refer to the "sniff test" as the ability to discern when one or more pieces of information are incongruent with the whole picture being presented. Analytical ability, or the ability to spot problem areas, is usually a skill that grows with experience. Less senior consultants may not have a fully developed ability in this area, while team leaders will possess strong analytical skills.

Recognizes When Additional Information Is Needed   The converse of knowing when information is incongruent is recognizing when relevant information is omitted. Notice here the inclusion of the word *relevant*. Inexperienced consultants may often waste time searching for missing data when the data will ultimately have no impact on the problem or solution. Again, experience is sometimes the best teacher to know what is relevant and what is not. If you identify missing data, you should ask "Will this missing information have any impact on my decisions?" If not, it is probably not worth pursuing. Consultants, however, should make this decision cautiously. Poor critical thinkers often simply ignore missing data. To do so may lead to costly errors in the ultimate solution.

Fits Details into the Overall Environment   Consultants must be experts at seeing not just the details of the problem at hand, but recognizing how this problem relates to the business as a whole. Proposed solutions must be appropriate for the holistic business so as to provide synergy among the components of the business.

What impact will your solution have on the interrelated components of the business? Consultants must be able to "see the big picture." Sometimes this is particularly hard for accounting consultants. Accountants are often accused of being wedded to their numbers—no matter what. Being able to step back and look at the whole picture means accepting that even the most laborious and detailed analysis might produce answers that don't make sense.

Transfers Knowledge from One Situation to Another   Transferring knowledge deals with the ability of a consultant to relate prior experience to the current problem. What similarities can be found among the current consulting job and prior consulting jobs? What did you learn on past jobs that can be related to this job? What other experiences have you had that you can draw on to apply to the current job? What mistakes did you make that you might be able to avoid this time? Transferring knowledge from past experience is key to the process of developing expertise.

Exhibits Initiative   Consultants must demonstrate that they are able to move forward without waiting for specific instructions. Of course, this must be tempered by prudent judgment. Does the client want you to proceed? How far should you go without touching base with your client? If you're missing information, can you reasonably locate the information without "spinning your wheels"? Ask questions like these to guide whether or not this is an appropriate time to exhibit initiative.

Exhibits Curiosity   "Learning to learn" is a popular phrase these days. Wanting to learn and demonstrating this desire is what is meant by "exhibiting curiosity." Successful consultants don't need to be told every detail. They will take steps to identify resources and learn on their own. This, of course, is closely related to exhibiting initiative.

Anticipates, Thinks Ahead, and Plans   This skill is also linked to being able to fit details into the whole environment. Identifying possible courses of action, competing hypotheses, and planning how to achieve the best outcome are elements of strategic thinking that all consultants should possess.

Exhibits Confidence   Confidence is not something that is taught. Rather, it comes from knowing you have the skills to bring a consulting project to successful end. If a consultant has the skills needed and has established a rapport with the client, gaining and exhibiting confidence is a natural by-product of such competence and client affinity. However, remember: there's a fine line between confidence and arrogance.

Communicates Clearly and Articulately   As we've explained, both oral and written communication skills are extremely important skills for the consultant to possess. Although the world's best ideas might reside between your ears, what good are they if you cannot convey those wonderful ideas and solutions to others?

A Roadmap to Thinking Critically

Although it is important to maintain an attitude of critical thinking throughout a consulting engagement, it is particularly important in the problem identification stage (refer to Figure 1-9) of the consulting engagement. This is the time when the consultant must guard against jumping to quick conclusions about the nature of the problem or form hasty opinions as to the best solution.

So, is there a *systematic* approach to thinking critically? One method is to ask a series of probing questions that evaluate the problem at hand. The questions in essence provide a type of roadmap to assist in the critical thinking process. Although the following list of questions is not comprehensive, it serves to give an idea of the type of questions you should consider.

What Is the Problem?   Identification of the problem is the first step in solving the problem. In this step, the consultant must identify the true nature of the issue(s) being communicated by the client. As already exemplified, sometimes the client may not know what the problem really is; rather, what the client believes to be the problem is often really only a symptom of deeper, underlying, systemic troubles.

A consultant, much like an auditor, should maintain professional skepticism in seeking to uncover the root of a problem. This is often difficult to do, as it is human nature to "rush to judgment." Consultants should resist the urge to form quick opinions about the nature of a problem. Interviews with client personnel should be conducted (see Chapter 8), background information should be sought and checked, and the problem should be studied from several different perspectives to gain clear insight.

Two main perspectives of critical thinking are people and technology. We will examine critical thinking questions related to both the people and technology perspective; however, the savvy consultant should realize that most often the problem is a combination of both.

Is the Problem a People Problem?   This question relates to the dynamics of the client's environment. A people problem is characterized by untrained or improperly trained employees, inadequate supervision, inadequate cross-training of employees, improper or inadequate segregation of duties among employees, unqualified or sometimes overqualified employees, or interpersonal conflicts between employees. A consultant must consider each of these possibilities in the process of identifying and understanding the problem. Again, what the client believes to be a technology problem is sometimes a people problem.

Is the Problem a Technology Problem?   With the ever-increasing role of technology in business today, the consultant must consider the client's technology issues. The questions in this regard are many. For instance, what type of computer system does the client have? What operating system does the client maintain? How much memory does the system currently have available? Who is responsible for backing up and system and how often is this done? Are offsite backups done regularly? What medium is used to back up the computer system? Is there a current disaster recovery plan maintained by the company? You need a full understanding of the client's technology to evaluate the role of technology in solving the client's problem.

What is the Scope of the Problem?   The scope of the problem is sometimes referred to as "ball-parking," that is, understanding the problem's dimensions. A consultant must understand specifically what the client wants done. Often consultants begin an engagement and somewhere along the way the client wants to add a requirement or two. This dilemma highlights the need for a signed project proposal or consulting contract (see Chapter 4) in which the client and consultant agree specifically as to what the engagement will consist of. The project proposal is a valuable tool in protecting the consultant from unreasonable additions by the client.

How Long Has the Company Had the Problem?   Asking this question will help trace the origins of the problem. In the introductory example, if the company has maintained the accounting system for several years and the problem just began with the hiring of a new accounting clerk, one might suspect the problem is directly related to the competency or training of the new clerk.

To What Does the Company Attribute the Problem?   Interviews with client personnel can be particularly helpful in uncovering the true nature of a problem. Employees who work closely in the areas in question will have firsthand knowledge and experience with the issues involved. Employees who work with the new data entry clerk will generally know if the clerk is not competent or not properly supervised.

Are the Premises Tainted by Personal Feelings?   It is important to remember that different people bring different perspectives to a problem. We are each influenced by our own backgrounds, attitudes, and experiences. Although the existence of differing perspectives is inescapable, it can certainly be dealt with in problem-solving. First, acknowledge the differing perspectives. If you are a part of a consulting team that contains an economist, an accountant, and a strategic manager, recognize that each will bring individual biases to the table. These biases, however, can be strengths in that each person has a specialty.

Are There Competing Hypotheses?   Development of alternatives is a crucial component to critical thinking. A consultant should attempt to generate as many reasonable hypotheses as to the cause of a problem as possible. This often happens in "brainstorming" sessions within a consulting team. The team leader can be responsible for throwing the question out, with the team members voicing possible causes.

Returning to our example, competing hypotheses to the computer system problem might be incompetent employees, inadequate knowledge of the computer application's capabilities, inadequate computer memory to do the tasks, inadequate hardware, inadequate software. You should be particularly careful not to accept the client's assessment of the problem and proposed solution until competing hypotheses have been generated, investigated, and either discarded or accepted.

What Would It Take to Solve the Problem?   This question is often one of resources. What additional computer hardware or software would be required? Would existing hardware need to be upgraded? Would additional employees be required to be hired? Would existing personnel have to be retrained? These questions, among others, should be considered in recommending a solution to a client.

Does the Organization Have the Resources to Solve the Problem or Can the Company be Reasonably Expected to Obtain the Necessary Resources?   In recommending a solution to a client, you should be mindful of the client's resources. In this regard, a consultant should consider both technical and economic feasibility. *Technical feasibility* involves examining whether the client can reasonably be expected to use the solution provided. Is the new computer system too complex for lower level employees to operate? Would it involve hiring specially trained employees? If so, can the company afford to hire these new employees? Questions of affordability are related to *economic feasibility.*

Example   Many companies today are contemplating installation of an enterprise resource planning (ERP) system. A consultant recommending implementation of an ERP system will undoubtedly have to consider questions of both technical and economic feasibility. Is the client personnel sophisticated enough to operate and maintain the system? Can the client's existing information technology infrastructure handle the ERP implementation? These are questions of technical feasibility. Is the cost of training existing personnel in the new system or hiring employees already experienced in the system manageable? Can the company afford to hire these new employees and upgrade necessary information technology components? These are questions of economic feasibility.

FOCUS ON THE CUSTOMER, CLIENT, AND MARKET

Specialization

We know accountants are increasingly becoming known as business advisors, and that this expanding role is not strictly limited to performing audit and tax planning and compliance work. Chapter 12 describes many areas in which accounting consultants have established areas of consulting expertise. Along with holding oneself out as an expert in a given business area, the consultant must be thoroughly competent in the intricacies of the area. For example, suppose you are engaged to perform litigation services consisting of advising a client in a bankruptcy proceeding. You have a duty to be thoroughly knowledgeable in the subject of bankruptcy in order to provide competent business advice. Remember, a consultant who poses as an expert in a particular business area will undoubtedly be open to costly and protracted legal action.

Living with Change

The CPA Vision Project makes the following statement, "The only constant is change at an unprecedented pace." A reality of living in the information age is that while we have increased information at our disposal, consultants must learn to make decisions much quicker than in the past. We are no longer afforded great amounts of time to perform research and develop solutions. Clients expect efficiency *and* quality in solutions. The consulting profession must move to a strategic, proactive stance in developing business. We must learn to identify business opportunities and possible solutions before the client has thought of them. And, we must be willing to commit to a process of continuing education. Let's face it: we'll never know it all! The rapid pace of technology change will not allow that. We must accept and commit to lifelong learning.

Negotiation and Marketing

A large part of the consulting process is getting the engagement in the first place. Learning to market your skills and negotiate a fair price for an engagement are valuable skills. A beginning consultant can often look to trade magazines and other industry sources for insight into how to negotiate the engagement price. Because marketing professional services is different from product marketing, and also due to its importance, Chapter 3 discusses the topic in depth.

INTERPRETATION OF CONVERGING INFORMATION

The Global Perspective

Consultants need to understand how increasing workplace globalization impacts business. There are many opportunities for accounting consultants to provide insight for businesses concerning the impact of the national marketplace on their business. For example, consultants can help businesses identify e-commerce opportunities (with almost limitless product markets) that did not exist 10 years ago. Increasing value-added services is the heart of consulting. Globalization only increases the consultant's opportunities to provide value-added services.

Timeliness

With respect to interpretation of converging information, the consultant should always focus on timeliness. Timing is everything in the business world, and speed to market is becoming an imperative if most businesses are to survive. Recognizing a unique opportunity and then acting on that opportunity—quickly—often establishes a company as a market leader. How many times have you seen new products in the marketplace that you had conceived of but did not act on? You should train yourself to recognize those opportunities and then act to make them happen quickly.

Essential Accounting Expertise

In order to interpret information from a wide variety of sources, an accounting consultant needs a strong base of domain knowledge in accounting. For example, generally accepted accounting principles (GAAP), SEC rulings, and FASB pronouncements are all technical areas with which most accountants will be familiar. Additionally, CPA consultants should be intimately familiar with the AICPA *Code of Professional Conduct* (see Chapter 11) as applicable to consultants, as well as the Statement on Standards for Consulting Services No. 1 (see Chapter 1) and the seven statements on consulting standards (SSCS) contained within Statement No. 1. Remember that the consultant should be able to spot problems as part of critical thinking. While you may be engaged to do one thing, you may come across another area in which the client could benefit from your knowledge and expertise.

TECHNOLOGICAL ADEPTNESS

The fifth core competency identified in the *CPA Vision Project* is technological adeptness. This refers to using technology, "not for technology sake, but when it can be leveraged to enhance performance and produce measurable results" (*CPA Vision Project,* p. 19). That is, the consultant should be able to identify and utilize the appropriate technology needed to facilitate completion of a consulting engagement in an efficient and effective manner. Many of the consulting specializations described in Chapter 12 require technological expertise.

IFAC Guidance

Depending on the nature of consulting service specializations, there are specific technologies accounting consultants should master. The International Federation of Accountants (IFAC) has provided specific guidance to the accounting profession on which competencies are important in IFAC International Education Guideline No. 11, *Information Technology in the Accounting Curriculum.*

IFAC identifies four roles that accountants play with respect to technology, including the accountant as user of information technology, manager of information systems, designer of business systems, and evaluator of information systems. See http://www.ifac.org for details on the four roles.

Additional Technology Considerations

Accounting consultants are finding themselves more and more linked with engagements that require significant hardware and software knowledge. For example, a common engagement is to evaluate a company's computer system and make recommendations for either customization or perhaps the implementation of a different system. The consultant should be familiar with most common accounting application packages commercially available. These usually include such packages as Quick-Books, Peachtree, Great Plains, Solomon, Dac Easy, and others. It is important also to know the market for each of these accounting packages, as well as their distinguishing features. Additionally, accountants must become familiar with the features and benefits of popular ERP packages, such as SAP, Oracle, Peoplesoft, and J. D. Edwards. Although it is unlikely that any single accountant can become proficient with an array of ERP packages, the consulting accountant should at least be conversant about them. If deeper knowledge and understanding are needed, the consultant should know where to find ERP domain experts.

Hackers are another risk to a company's investment in its proprietary intellectual capital. Software programs maintained on a computer network are vulnerable to sophisticated hacking techniques, wherein hackers attempt to steal or modify source code. Accounting consultants acting as IT auditors should be sure that clients are aware of and observe security measures to mitigate the possibility of compromised software.

> **Case-in-Point 2.3**   Microsoft Corp. was recently the target of hackers attempting to steal proprietary source code. Although Microsoft believes the hackers were discovered before they were able to download or modify the source code of Microsoft programs such as the Windows operating system and Office, Microsoft does believe the hackers were able to access and view source code for products designed for release several years in the future. This occurrence serves as a wake-up call to companies everywhere. If Microsoft is vulnerable to hackers, isn't everyone? And the intrusion resulted from the failure of a simple control. At least one Microsoft employee didn't update the antivirus software.[7]

Other computer competencies that are almost certainly a necessity include word processing, spreadsheets, databases, web page development, HTML (the language that

---

[7] "Microsoft Said Hackers Failed to See Codes for its Most Popular Product," *Wall Street Journal,* October 27, 2000; "Microsoft Says It Detected Hacker Quickly, Monitored Activities Throughout the Attack," *Wall Street Journal,* October 30, 2000.

web pages are written in), e-commerce knowledge, and presentation software such as PowerPoint. Sometimes consultants may even develop programming skills—Visual Basic and JAVA are also becoming highly sought-after programming skills.

CONTINUING EDUCATION AND LIFELONG LEARNING

The *CPA Vision Project* recognizes the importance of lifelong learning by listing it as the first core value (see Figure 2-1). As mentioned earlier, a popular lexicon that has come into usage in accounting education and practice is "learning to learn." We can't overemphasize the need for accounting consultants to be committed to lifelong learning. Particularly in today's technological environment, you can't know it *all.* Every day new technologies are introduced and old ones refined. To remain competitive, consultants must stay abreast of both technological as well as domain-specific changes. How does one do that? By committing to a goal of continuing education and lifelong learning.

Formal continuing professional education (CPE) is offered in many fashions. Many companies offer training sessions for their employees. On-line CPE is available from the AICPA on a variety of technical topics. The Internet also provides a wealth of self-education opportunities. For example, if you would like to learn web page design and development skills, simply type "web page design" into a search engine. The search engine will return a plethora of tutorials and resources for the novice web page designer.

> ***Case-in-Point 2.4*** John Butler is a CPA from Salt Lake City, Utah, who has been out of school for only 10 years. His eclectic work experience during that time has provided the knowledge base for a solid part-time consulting business, while keeping his full-time job for Call Business Systems. John attracts consulting clients mainly through his web site, for which he did all of the programming, designing, and writing. He taught himself HTML and then more sophisticated programming techniques for viewing the source code of other web sites.[8] Accounting consultants must be willing to continually acquire new technology skills, since the vast majority of consulting engagements will have a technology component.[9]

While remaining competitive by refining technology tools is very important, it is increasingly important for the accounting consultant to stay abreast of the current trends in technology. To accomplish this, you should commit to read current newspapers and trade periodicals. A casual reading of a computer trade magazine, such as *PC Magazine,* will keep the consultant knowledgeable about computer trends. It takes self-motivation and discipline to do so, but the rewards are great. Reading business newspapers such as the *Wall Street Journal* and trade periodicals such as the *Journal of Accountancy* and *Strategic Finance* will help you keep up with current domain-specific knowledge.

One caveat: Many consultants don't get the training they need because they're loathe to give up billable hours for education. But—failing to spend the time learning in the short run can impact revenues down the road.

---

[8] It's simple to view the HTML source code of any web site. While viewing the web site in the browser, click "View, source code" from the browser's menu. The source code can then be copied and pasted into another HTML document. However, users of this method are cautioned that a web site source code may be copyright-protected. If in doubt, the best solution (and the most ethical) is to e-mail the owner of the web site and ask for permission to copy and use the source code.

[9] Richard J. Koreto, "Consulting on the Side," *Journal of Accountancy,* December 1997, p. 81.

SUMMARY

The *CPA Vision Project* identifies the top five core competencies that CPAs of the future should possess. These competencies are particularly relevant to accountants who serve as management consultants.

Communication and leadership skills form the first core competency. Communications includes both oral and written communications. Oral communication skills include paying attention to one's attitude, developing and refining listening skills, establishing credibility with the client, making a good first impression, having a well-organized and well-delivered presentation prepared and practiced, using jargon as appropriate to the audience, and learning to read nonverbal cues. Written communications skills include writing clearly and in a well-organized manner and ensuring that the document is free from spelling and grammatical errors. Leadership skills are defined as the ability to influence, inspire, and motivate others to achieve a common goal. Additionally, strong leaders respect and acknowledge the contributions of subordinates, as well as the expertise of the client. They also delegate effectively and enjoy credibility among others stemming from competency, personal integrity, and interpersonal skills. Project team leaders have the added responsibility of managing the time and expense components of the engagement. Team-building is the process of strengthening the mutual trust and cohesiveness of a project team to achieve a common goal. The project team should be as small as possible, and the team should have a well-defined, well-communicated goal. Team members should understand their roles and what is expected of them. Role negotiation may help clarify responsibilities and deal with conflict effectively. Several conflict management techniques are available to project leaders, including: avoidance, authoritative command, accommodation, compromise, and collaboration. Most effective leaders employ a combination of these techniques. Interviewing skills are important to develop to interact successfully with the client. Finally, strong leaders recognize and respect the influence and blending of a variety of cultures and traditions in the workplace today.

The second core competency is the development and use of strategic and critical thinking skills. Although there is no one accepted definition of critical thinking, critical thinking involves evaluating and analyzing information before accepting it as fact. It means asking relevant questions to ascertain the accuracy of stated premises and generating rational hypotheses. It means resisting the urge to form quick conclusions, and studying the problem from many perspectives. This chapter details seven critical thinking competencies essential to success in public accounting and relates these competencies to the consulting profession. A roadmap to thinking critically is provided to illustrate the types of open-ended questions that consultants can ask to help figure out the solution to a business problem.

Core competency number three is the ability to focus on the customer, client, and market. For the consultant, this means being thoroughly competent in the area in which business expertise is claimed. It also means living with the fact that change is here to stay. The successful consultant will move to a strategic, proactive stance in developing business. Finally, it means learning the art of marketing to a broad customer base to provide value-added services.

The fourth core competency is the interpretation of converging information. This includes recognizing the increased globalization of business and adapting services to compete effectively in the global market. It also means that there is an increased emphasis on timeliness. That is, the consultant must see opportunities and act on those opportunities with foresight and vision. Lastly, in order to interpret and integrate information from a wide variety of sources, the consultant must be completely familiar with accounting standards, SEC rulings, and other authoritative literature of the profession. An intimate knowledge and practice of the AICPA *Code of Professional Conduct,* as well as the seven statements on consulting standards (SSCS) contained within the Statement on Standards for Consulting Services No. 1 is essential.

The fifth core competency stated in the *CPA Vision Project* is the possession of technological adeptness—that is, the ability to recognize and leverage the appropriate technology to enhance performance and produce successful results. The International Federation of Accountants

(IFAC) has issued helpful guidance regarding what specific information technology competencies are desirable in the accounting profession. The guidelines for IT competencies for user accountants and evaluator accountants are particularly relevant to the accounting consultant.

Finally, one of the *Vision Project's* core values, commitment to continuing education and lifelong learning, is highly relevant for the accounting consultant in order to remain competitive and competent in this technological age. This includes regular professional reading, online courses, CPE, and technology and trade magazines and periodicals.

DISCUSSION QUESTIONS

2-1. Describe the purpose of the *CPA Vision Project.* How do the findings of this project relate to the accounting consultant?

2-2. What are the top five core competencies for accountants according to the *Vision Project?* Can you think of any other core competencies for accountants?

2-3. What is meant by "attitude traps" that consultants can fall into?

2-4. What types of listening skills are important to a consultant? How can a consultant improve listening skills?

2-5. Suppose you are a new consultant—just out of your undergraduate program. How can you demonstrate credibility to a client?

2-6. What should consultants be aware of with respect to the first meeting with the client?

2-7. How does a consultant use jargon *appropriately* in dealing with client personnel?

2-8. What types of nonverbal cues should a consultant be aware of?

2-9. How does the *CPA Vision Project* define leadership?

2-10. Think of a leader you admire. What are some personality traits or interpersonal skills demonstrated by this person?

2-11. What is the team leader's responsibility with respect to managing the budget and expenses of a consulting engagement?

2-12. Describe some approaches corporations use to develop team-building skills.

2-13. What are some considerations the consultant should keep in mind when interviewing client personnel?

2-14. Why are cultural considerations increasingly important to today's consultant?

2-15. Name the nine major critical thinking competencies as identified by the 1997 FSA report. Describe how each of these competencies relates to the consultant.

2-16. What is an accounting consultant's responsibility with respect to offering specialized services to clients?

2-17. What types of accounting expertise should consultants possess?

2-18. Why is the commitment to continuing education and lifelong learning so important to accounting consultants?

EXERCISES

2-19. Locate an example from the popular press of a person who has shown great leadership. How did this person demonstrate leadership? Do you think these qualities can be learned or are they innate?

2-20. All the Big Five accounting firms employ team-building exercises in training sessions. Locate an example of a team-building exercise used by one of these firms and describe how it works.

2-21. Refer to Figure 2-1. List the IT competencies you think are the most important for a consultant to possess in order of importance (from most important to least important). What were your reasons for selecting your number one choice?

2-22. Visit the AICPA web site at www.aicpa.org. What types of CPE programs would you be interested in as an accounting consultant?

2-23. There are many IT tools available to consultants. Pick three of the following topical areas and locate the names and vendors of at least five tools available in this area: web page design; flowcharting; spreadsheet analysis, ERP systems, business graphics and presentation, virus software, utility programs, database programs.

REFERENCES, RECOMMENDED READINGS, AND WEB SITES

References and Recommended Readings

American Institute of Certified Public Accountants (AICPA), "CPA Vision Project, 2011 and Beyond" (New York: AICPA, 1999).

Baril, Charles, Billie Cunningham, David Fordham, Robert Gardner, and Susan Wolcott, "Critical Thinking in the Public Accounting Profession: Aptitudes and Attitudes," *Journal of Accounting Education* (Vol. 16, Nos. 3/4, 1998), pp. 381–406.

Browne, M. Neil, and Stuart M. Keeley, *Asking the Right Questions,* 5th edition (Upper Saddle River, NJ: Prentice-Hall, 1998).

Capaldi, Nicholas, *How to Win Every Argument: An Introduction to Critical Thinking* (New York: MJF Books, 1987).

Federation of Schools of Accountancy (R. Baker, B. Cunningham, P. Kimmel, and C. Venable), *A Catalog of Resource Materials for Teaching Accounting Students Critical Thinking* (The Pedagogical Resources Committee of the Federation of Schools of Accountancy, New York, NY, 1995).

Federation of Schools of Accountancy, "Critical Thinking Competencies Essential to Success in Public Accounting" (New York, NY, Report of the FSA 1997 Education Research Committee, December 1, 1997).

Golen, Steven P., "Effective Communications Skills," in *Handbook of Management Consulting Services,* 2nd edition (New York: McGraw-Hill, 1995), pp. 5-1–5-29.

International Federation of Accountants (IFAC), IFAC International Education Guideline No. 11, *Information Technology in the Accounting Curriculum* (New York: IFAC, 1996).

Laudon, Kenneth, and Jane Laudon, *Business Information Systems: A Problem-Solving Approach,* 2nd edition (New York: The Dryden Press, 1993).

Reeb, William, *Start Consulting—How to Walk the Talk* (New York: American Institute of Public Accountants, 1998).

Schermerhorn, John, James Hunt, and Richard Osborn, "Teamwork and the Creative Use of Groups," *Managing Organizational Behavior,* 5th edition (New York: John Wiley & Sons, 1994), pp. 326–349.

Web Sites

To access the AICPA website for Continuing Professional Education offerings: www.aicpa.org.

PART TWO

SELLING, DEVELOPING, AND MANAGING CONSULTING PROJECTS

Chapter 3

Marketing Professional Services

You must sell yourself to sell your firm.

Ford Harding, *Rain Making* (Holbrook, MA:
Adams Media Corporation, 1994), p. 9.

INTRODUCTION

Most accounting students take just one marketing course in college. They might think marketing has little to do with the technical competencies needed to succeed in the accounting profession. Not true. Although marketing may not help you analyze a financial statement or plan a client's tax strategy, it is important to the success of today's accountants and consultants. For instance, a staff member in a professional services firm might find her career stalled at some point without the ability to "get new business." Marketing involves a bit more than merely selling your views and analyses to corporate bosses.

This chapter is about marketing professional services. Marketing is not the same as selling, although many people confuse the two. Selling has direct impact on a company's revenues—it's the exchange of services for income, whereas marketing supports and generates these sales.

Service marketing is quite different from traditional marketing of products, like toothpaste or soft drinks. The customers are different, expectations are different, and even the "four P's" of marketing—price, promotion, place, and packaging—are different.

We start this chapter with some discussion about professional services marketing. We cover both the accounting consultant's market niche and the competitive consulting environment. We next look at the marketing process, beginning with identification of target markets, and ending with selling and contracting. Advertising and promotion are such important techniques for recruiting new clients that we discuss them separately. Lastly, the chapter describes professional service contracts and pricing.

MARKETING PROFESSIONAL SERVICES

Both accounting and consulting are professional services, as are engineering, medicine, and law. Professional services differ from products in many respects. It is important to understand these differences because they dictate alternate approaches to marketing and selling.

The Special Nature of Services

Customers *experience* services. These experiences are actions or performances within processes. Having your car washed is a process. Customers may choose between service levels, such as a wash versus a wash and wax. Machines and/or personnel perform certain actions within these process alternatives. The level, amount, and quality of service determine the price customers are willing to pay. In consulting, the attributes that create quality are mostly personal. These attributes include a consultant's intellectual capital, skill set, and personality. The nonpersonal qualities are whatever organizational resources the consultant can bring to the job.

Characteristics of Services   A primary distinguishing feature of services versus products is *intangibility.* A customer does not touch a service in the same way that you might touch a product. How can you touch the car wash process? Of course some services do have tangible components. There are water and other supplies involved in a car wash, just as restaurant service includes food and ambiance. There is a range of intangibility for various services, as shown in Figure 3-1. Note that consulting services are at the end of the intangible side of the spectrum.

Some services are *attached* to a product. Automobile dealerships, for example, sell both cars and services. Restaurants and stores also sell both products and services. For these businesses, the service portion of the package may be as important to consumer satisfaction as the quality of product.

Case-in-Point 3.1   Nordstrom, the retailer originally known for its footwear, is famous for its quality of services. From the moment a customer enters a Nordstrom store, evidence of superior service abounds. It is this service quality that distinguishes the chain from other retailers and allows Nordstrom to charge premium prices for its goods.

Although some products may be standardized, it is more difficult to produce homogeneous services. When you purchase a can of a particular brand of soup, you can be assured that it will taste exactly like the last can you purchased. But a steak dinner in a restaurant may be better some days than others. Restaurants and other service providers often compete based on their ability to provide some degree of standardization. It is difficult to achieve homogeneity in the service arena because so many variables are beyond control. A restaurant meal varies with the skill levels and even the mood of the individual involved in its preparation. It may also change with quality of supplies, timing, and other factors.

Standardization poses some risk because it invites *commoditization.* When a service becomes a commodity, its customers are unable to distinguish one service product from another—regardless of the service provider characteristics. This commoditization is one of the problems associated with financial audit services. Public companies require an audit opinion; they may believe that a favorable audit opinion from one CPA has the same value as a favorable audit opinion from any other.

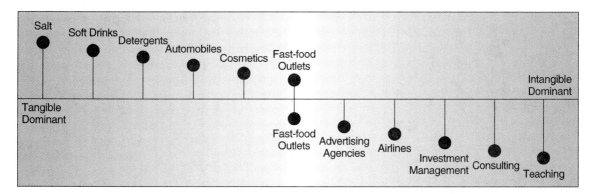

FIGURE 3-1   Scale of Market Entities. (Reprinted with permission from *Journal of Marketing,* published by the American Marketing Association, G. Lynn Shostack, April 1977, p. 77.)

Standardization is desirable *within* an organization but not *across* an industry. Service providers must find a balance in standardizing their services. They want to ensure that their own customers receive consistent quality, but if they can do it, perhaps so can their competitors. For instance, McDonald's wants to serve the same french fries in all its stores, but they do not want their competitors to serve McDonald's fries.

A service provider may choose a niche and try to standardize within that niche. The niche itself differentiates the service. To make sure that customers experience what has been promised and promoted, it is very important to provide a consistent level and quality of service within the chosen niche. A retail store, for example, might run a promotional campaign about its high level of service. A customer who visits the store and has difficulty finding someone to process a sale will be particularly unhappy because the promotion did not match the service delivery.

There are no inventories of services. Service providers produce services at about the same time that customers consume them. This makes them highly perishable and problematic with respect to supply and demand. Unlike a manufacturer, a service provider can't "stock up" on inventories to meet heavy demand periods. Public accounting firms have particular problems in this respect, because the demand for their services is highly cyclical. Accountants have a "busy season" that typically runs from January 1 to April 15. This season is a function of year-end closings and tax filing requirements. Most employees do not want to be hired on a seasonal basis, so accounting firms must cope with uneven demands in a variety of ways. Marketing services that an organization can perform at different times of the year is one way of coping with this problem. Because services are perishable, clients cannot return them. This makes service *quality* more important than product *quality*.

Service Quality   Quality is both real and perceived. The perception of quality is sometimes a function of a *created* image, rather than the *true* positioning of a service level. Perceptions are also relative. If you try several services or products, you can make comparisons on quality levels. However, if you are purchasing an expensive service, you will not have the option of multiple experiences. Because objective measures of service quality are difficult to construct, evaluators often use *perception* of quality to measure quality levels.

Perceptions of service quality are indicators of customer satisfaction. A satisfied client will use a service or service provider again. Satisfied clients will also recommend services and service providers to others. To satisfy a client, it is important that the job meets the client's expectations. It is also important to maintain a customer focus. This idea is the underpinning of the total quality management (TQM) philosophy. To maintain customer focus, you should constantly seek feedback from customers.

Marketing researchers have developed a model of perceived service quality that includes the following characteristics: reliability, responsiveness, competence, access or approachability, courtesy, communication, credibility, security or lack of risk, understanding/knowing the customer, and tangibles (see Figure 3-2). Accounting research has shown that this model applies to the management advisory or consulting services that accounting firms offer. Two of the most important dimensions of quality for accounting consulting services are responsiveness and reliability. *Responsiveness* means that consultants respond to client requests on a timely basis. *Reliability* means that actions match promises. Certain activities, such as intentionally underbidding on a project so that the actual cost of the service exceeds the bid by a wide margin and cost overruns, will impair perceived service quality.

RELIABILITY involves consistency of performance and dependability.
It means that the firm performs the service right the first time.
It also means that the firm honors its promises. Specifically, it involves:
  – accuracy in billing;
  – keeping records correctly;
  – performing the service at the designated time.

RESPONSIVENESS concerns the willingness or readiness of employees to provide service. It involves timeliness of service:
  – mailing a transaction slip immediately;
  – calling the customer back quickly;
  – giving prompt service (e.g., setting up appointments quickly).

COMPETENCE means possession of the required skills and knowledge to perform the service. It involves:
  – knowledge and skill of the contact personnel;
  – knowledge and skill of operational support personnel;
  – research capability of the organization, e.g., securities brokerage firm.

ACCESS involves approachability and ease of contact. It means:
  – the service is easily accessible by telephone (lines are not busy and they don't put you on hold);
  – waiting time to receive service (e.g., at a bank) is not extensive;
  – convenient hours of operation;
  – convenient location of service facility.

COURTESY involves politeness, respect, consideration, and friendliness of contact personnel (including receptionists, telephone operators, etc.). It includes:
  – consideration for the consumer's property (e.g., no muddy shoes on the carpet);
  – clean and neat appearance of public contact personnel.

COMMUNICATION means keeping customers informed in language they can understand and listening to them. It may mean that the company has to adjust its language for different consumers—increasing the level of sophistication with a well-educated customer and speaking simply and plainly with a novice. It involves:
  – explaining the service itself;
  – explaining how much the service will cost;
  – explaining the trade-offs between service and cost;
  – assuring the consumer that a problem will be handled.

CREDIBILITY involves trustworthiness, believability, and honesty. It involves having the customer's best interests at heart. Contributing to credibility are:
  – company name;
  – company reputation;
  – personal characteristics of the contact personnel;
  – the degree of hard sell involved in interactions with the customer.

SECURITY is the freedom from danger, risk, or doubt. It involves:
  – physical safety (Will I get mugged at the automatic teller machine?);
  – financial security (Does the company know where my stock certificate is?);
  – confidentiality (Are my dealings with the company private?).

UNDERSTANDING/KNOWING THE CUSTOMER involves making the effort to understand the customer's needs. It involves:
  – learning the customer's specific requirements;
  – providing individualized attention;
  – recognizing the regular customer.

TANGIBLES include the physical evidence of the service:
  – physical facilities;
  – appearance of personnel;
  – tools or equipment used to provide the service;
  – physical representations of the service, such as a plastic credit card or a bank statement;
  – other customers in the service facility.

FIGURE 3-2   Determinants of service quality. (Reprinted with permission from *Journal of Marketing,* published by the American Marketing Association, A. Parasuraman, VA Zeithaml, and L.L. Berry, Fall 1985, p. 47.)

Challenges in Marketing Services   Because you cannot see, touch, or try services, communicating the quality of professional services poses special marketing challenges. Not only is it difficult to manage the *perception* of services, it is even hard to *ensure* reliability and responsiveness.

A common approach to quality management in the realm of products is to tolerate zero defects. It is assumed that no defects means customers are satisfied. Unfortunately, zero defects is not a realistic goal for services. Delivery of services cannot be consistent, despite best efforts. Variables are not always controllable—employees are not machines and do not perform consistently over time and from person to person. Plus, the real-time delivery of services means that mistakes cannot be corrected in advance. Therefore, while professional service organizations can and should strive to achieve some consistent level of quality in service delivery, they should also be able to recover well when defects occur. Service recovery can lead to even higher customer satisfaction than "doing it right the first time."

Most people have had some experience with service recovery on a personal level. When you tell your waiter that your meal is cold, the restaurant must make a service recovery. Levels of service recovery in this instance may range from an apology to a free meal. The airline industry, because it has so many variables to control in service delivery, has frequent opportunities for service recovery. Late arrivals, lost luggage, and bumpy fights are all possible defects in airline service delivery. How the airline compensates for these defects determines customer satisfaction and loyalty.

Customer loyalty is valuable beyond measure. Attracting new customers is many times more costly than retaining current customers. Service recovery can promote loyalty, but in instances when customers *do* leave, analyzing defections provides important information. Many service providers take customer satisfaction surveys aimed at understanding why customers defect to competitors. These surveys may be somewhat helpful, but they are usually limited in explaining the true reasons for customer defections. Analyzing defections requires examining failures, which is not the most pleasant undertaking. But talking to a customer who no longer does business with you is important in getting to the root of service quality problems.

Professional service firms profit when they can increase the amount of services they offer to customers. Customer defections may not just be customers leaving a firm entirely, but rather taking a part of their business elsewhere because one firm can't meet all their needs. This is one of the reasons why accounting firms have expanded their service lines. Businesses today want fewer, rather than more, suppliers. A risk, however, is that new services have more potential for failure than old services. Service deliverers should pay even closer attention to customer satisfaction when trying out new service offerings.

The Accounting Consultant's Market Niche

Consulting organizations often have a market niche. Some firms are known for their software implementation services, others for their work in value chain analysis, electronic commerce, or strategic planning. Accenture made its name in information technology consulting. Gemini (now Cap Gemini Ernst and Young) became famous for its business transformation solutions. Despite carving a niche, most consulting organizations offer a wide range of services in line with current business vogue, such as total quality management, business process reengineering, strategic planning, Year 2000 issues, and implementation of enterprise resource planning systems (ERPs).

Throughout the 1990s, consulting firms expanded in response to the need to help companies solve the Year 2000 problem. That issue caused many corporations to implement new software, rather than fix their legacy systems. ERP implementations accounted for a large portion of the revenues of the Big Five consulting practices throughout the decade. At the end of the millennium, this business slowed due primarily to market saturation and consultants were re-deployed to other arenas. Today, consulting firms are all trying to seize the niche for expertise in electronic commerce and e-business. The Internet age creates a real need for businesses to change rapidly and use the new technology to their best advantage. Consultants with expertise in supply chain management, customer relationship management (CRM), and Internet technologies are in greatest demand.

Diversification and the ability to see ahead are critical for the growth of consulting practices. To this end, professional service firms sometimes employ researchers whose job is to supply vision about future business needs for consulting services. Accounting consultants are carving out their own niches in the areas in which their particular skill sets lend expertise. Changes in financial reporting enabled by the Internet and new software languages, such as XBRL (extensible business reporting language), provide new consulting opportunities for accountants. Assurance services are a service line in which accountants can function without too many fears about independence issues. And, since accountants have moved from a control focus to a risk-based approach in audit and assurance services, they can provide businesses with more value-added services. With the increased risk brought about by online business exposures, assurance services in the form of real-time audits and privacy and security consulting are high potential growth areas for accounting consulting services today. Chapter 12 describes some of the consulting services that accountants are uniquely equipped to offer successfully.

Consultants create value by bringing a unique set of qualities to engagements. Specifically, these qualities are objectivity, dedicated resources, industry and functional expertise, skills such as project and change management, negotiation, facilitation, technical competency, and an orientation toward getting results. (See Figure 3-3.) Accounting consultants bring these skills and others. The stereotype of an accountant burdens accounting consultants with a few image problems. The "stuffy" image doesn't help when a client is looking for innovative, creative consulting help in effecting change.

Accountants today use marketers and advertising to communicate their value to prospective clients. The American Institute of Certified Public Accountants (AICPA) undertook a major advertising campaign in the 1990s to change the public's thinking about accountants. The message the AICPA wanted to send was that accountants were not just bean counters but that CPAs could add value to businesses. The slogan "The CPA—Never Underestimate the Value" appeared in advertisements in all types of media. One of the objectives of the AICPA's communications/public relations team is to "brand" the CPA designation and enhance its value. The recent AICPA image enhancement campaign is designed to accentuate the range of services available from CPAs. One of the print ads appears in Figure 3-4.

Competition in the Marketplace

Consulting can be a highly profitable business—and the barriers to entry are low. That's great in one sense, but it does create intense competition for client engage-

---

Consulting's Value-Added

Objectivity
- Independence lends credibility
- "Outsider" view

Dedicated Resources
- Ability to focus on the problem
- Temporary costs
- Expertise brought by experience with multiple clients
- Knowledge infrastructures such as Best Practices databases and distributed expertise

Industry and Functional Expertise
- Consultant's niche in industry and problem area
- Current and specialized expertise
- Knowledge of industry competitors, risk factors, and opportunities

Consulting Skill Set
- Project and change management skills
- Facilitation, negotiation, communication, critical thinking skills
- Technical competency

Results Orientation
- Responsibility for results
- Accountability for results
- Incentives tied to results

Professionalism

FIGURE 3-3 The sources of a consultant's value.

ments. The past decade has been a boom time for consultants, but competition is increasing. A significant downturn in the economy could mean that only some consultants survive. The largest consulting firms are merging and consolidating, finding that they need a global infrastructure to continue increasing revenues. Bigger firms are able to support larger overhead budgets for marketing and in-house technology investments in knowledge bases and intranets.

FIGURE 3-4 One of the print advertisements in the AICPA Image Enhancement campaign.

For traditional public accounting organizations, competition is intensifying and its nature is changing. These firms find themselves competing not just with each other, but also with IBM, McKinsey and Company, EDS, the Boston Consulting Group, and other established consulting groups. They are even competing with law firms. The Big Five rank among the biggest law firms globally in terms of the number of lawyers they employ. They compete for legal work with dedicated law firms. Smaller professional service firms, or "boutiques" specializing in niche areas, are another source of competition. And, as the traditional accounting consulting organizations spin off or sell their consulting practices, they may find themselves competing with their own incubated organizations.

Case-in-Point 3.2 Accenture and Arthur Andersen began segmenting the market by size of client. Today, they compete for jobs with clients wanting ERP systems or e-business help.

As illustrated in the next Case-in-Point, accounting work itself has new competition too.

Case-in-Point 3.3 American Express, hoping to grow a consulting practice, and noting the link between audit and tax work and consulting, bought mid-size accounting practices and expanded its financial services business accordingly. American Express now competes with public accounting firms for audit and tax business, and also for the human resources (i.e., accounting majors) they need to grow their business.

Accounting firms did not accidentally grow into large consulting organizations (see Chapter 1). Public accountants have always had an edge over other consultants in the marketing area. The edge is that they already have a client—the company they audit. During the course of an audit, the auditor gets to know a business well and in a fairly objective way. This knowledge makes auditors natural agents for advising management on problems. As managers turn to their auditors for advice, the auditors become consultants. Knowing what services the audit firm or internal audit organization can offer management, such as help in protecting the security and privacy of information systems, is an important aspect of marketing. Of course auditor independence issues can limit these services.

It's not just public accounting that has competition issues. Management accountants are facing some new competition within their companies. As management accountants and corporate financial officers have evolved from cost accountants and internal control experts into strategic management advisers, other managers with finance and marketing backgrounds compete with the accountants. Increasingly, accountants have to prove their value to their internal organizations—and show that they can think more broadly than just in terms of the numbers. Internal accounting groups, such as internal audit, also face competition from outside consultants as businesses outsource more of their business outside their core competencies. Company accountants, since they do not contribute to revenues, need to demonstrate their value or risk having their work outsourced.

The Services Marketing Mix

The traditional marketing mix is the group of product elements that satisfy customer needs. These are known as the "four Ps" of marketing and they are: price, product, promotion, and place. A later section of this chapter discusses pricing services. Products are physical goods and their packaging. Promotion includes advertising, public relations, and sales activities. Place refers to the distribution channel or site. Place could be a retail store or a warehouse. Transportation is also a part of place and an important one. On-line retailers make decisions about how their products are to be delivered to customers. This decision could be the most important part of the marketing mix for e-commerce businesses.

The services marketing mix includes the traditional elements, plus three others. And the traditional elements change a bit for services versus products. For example, "product" assumes the characteristics of services. The three additional "P's" in the marketing mix for services are: people, physical evidence, and process.

People   The people are employees and customers. Employees perform services. This element of the marketing mix can be controlled—with training, motivation, and appropriate reward systems. Customers are not as easy to control as employees, except that service providers do have the ability to walk away from customers they do not believe they can satisfy.

Physical Evidence   Physical evidence in the services marketing mix is the tangible service component. As we said earlier, you cannot see or touch a service, but there may be some physical manifestations of it. The way a consultant dresses is an example. Casual business attire sends one message; a business suit signals another. Equipment is another example of physical evidence in service delivery. Consultants with state-of-the-art computer equipment appear to a client to have technological competency. The *appearance* of deliverables, such as client presentations and reports, is yet another variable of physical evidence in professional services.

Process   The delivery of services is a process that takes place over time. The *number of components* in that process, (i.e., how many people are involved in delivering the consulting project) and the *time period* covered by the process (i.e., how long does the project take) are both part of this marketing mix element. Another factor is the *level of customer involvement.* The perception of service quality may increase or decrease as a customer participates in the process.

Processes may be standardized or customized to an individual or engagement. The degree of customization or personalization can increase or decrease satisfaction. For instance, you can customize your traditional software implementation model to fit your client's business. But the customization effort may delay the project so much that the client is ultimately less pleased.

The Marketing Mix as a Whole   Elements of the marketing mix are interdependent. Changing one part of the mix may impact another. For instance, changes in many of the mix elements affect price. More personalized service processes and higher quality physical evidence characteristics are more expensive. The marketing plan should consider all these elements and the relationships among them.

THE MARKETING PROCESS

Marketing is a process. For services, that process includes both external and internal marketing efforts. The real-time delivery of services makes marketing *interactive* as the employees market continuously as they perform their service functions. In this section, we look at key components of the marketing process: the marketing plan, target market identification, marketing to new clients, and recruiting new clients.

The Marketing Plan

Developing a consulting practice requires a plan. A sample marketing plan appears in Figure 3-5. The marketing plan grows out of an organization's overall strategic planning process. The plan describes the specific promotion and marketing steps needed to achieve organizational objectives. Wherever possible, the plan should include quantifiable goals and targets such as number of new clients.

Identify the Target Market   The first step in a marketing plan is to identify a target client market. This means developing a profile of your current and potential client base. For example, if your main strength is helping clients to select and implement middle market accounting software, your clients are companies with approximately $10 to $50 million in revenue. On the other hand, if you are specializing in high-end, enterprise software, potential clients are likely to be Fortune 500 companies. We discuss target markets in more depth later in this chapter.

Conduct Competitive and Demographic Analysis   Once you know your target clients, you need to determine the size and demographic characteristics of the market, analyze the competition in that market, and estimate how much market share you might expect to capture. This is done to find a market niche. In analyzing the competition, you should learn as much as you can about the two or three major players in that market. Be sure you understand also how you compare. For example, if the consultants who dominate the market space are known for their level of service or for especially creative solutions, but are expensive, you may decide to compete on price. Or you may be able to offer more technical help, more specialization, more depth, and so on.

A word of caution about market niche: in today's business environment, the nature of consulting services desired is changing rapidly. Consultants must be careful not to simply ride a "new wave" of consulting services, only to see it disappear or go

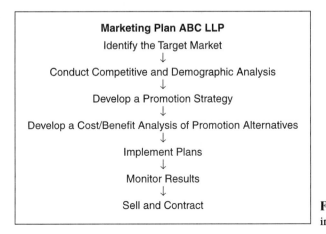

FIGURE 3-5   A sample marketing plan.

out of vogue. An example to think about is how many of the Year 2000 consultants had to be retrained in other areas when that problem was solved. Another example is a current shift in information systems consulting from ERP implementations to e-commerce business models.

Develop a Promotion Strategy   After you identify your market and conduct competitive and market analysis, next develop a list of various promotion approaches to target that market. How will you make target clients aware of the services you offer? In part, this depends on the market niche. If you are a value-added reseller for software, as in the previous example, you can promote your firm through vendor contacts. Making clients aware of other types of services may require more effort. New dot.com businesses spent a lot of money advertising their business in Super Bowl 2000. Running a commercial in that venue is not likely to be cost-effective for a consultant who is targeting a certain business market segment. But perhaps an advertising campaign in professional and business journals would be more worthwhile.

Develop a Cost/Benefit Analysis of Promotion Alternatives   Promotion can be expensive, whether it involves spending billable time obtaining feedback from existing clients or running an image campaign. As a result, cost/benefit analysis is an important part of a marketing plan. You can calculate costs more easily than benefits, but an attempt should be made to capture both to help in selecting among alternative marketing strategies.

Implement Plans and Monitor Results   Implementation of marketing plans is not the final step in the marketing process. Marketers monitor results of strategies to learn which approaches are successful and not successful. Feedback is important in making this determination so there should be mechanisms for capturing this information. You might collect feedback in terms of number of inquiries based on an advertisement or by asking current clients to complete a survey or interview regarding their level of satisfaction.

Sell and Contract   The final stage in a marketing plan is selling and contracting. Sometimes people confuse marketing with selling, but selling is actually the end of the marketing process. It is closing the deal, a critical step. Once you attract a client, you will probably need to make a presentation about what you can do for them. It is likely that you will be competing with other consultants for the new business. We discuss proposal writing, contracting and pricing, and presentation skills in this chapter and future chapters. All these topics are components of selling. Perhaps the most important piece, however, is personality. Consultants need to impress clients with their personality so that the client will truly want to work with a particular consultant or professional service firm.

Identifying Target Markets

Target markets are people or organizations in need of consulting services. In general, it is best to define a target market as narrowly as possible. It is easier to work within a narrow niche than to try to appeal to a large base of businesses. Within a niche, you can make your specialization known widely. Word of mouth and reputation also travel better in a small market space. The elements of a target market include industry, geographic region, client size, and functional specialization.

Specific target client audiences vary, depending on whether you are an internal or external consultant, and also depending on the market niche chosen. Basically, however, there are three sources of business: (1) management (for internal consultants), (2) current clients (particularly in the case of audit and tax professionals), and (3) new clients (who may be generated through cold calls or referrals).

Internal accounting consultants have a natural audience for their services. Internal auditors, for example, are in an optimal position to advise management on internal control systems. This is, in fact, part of their job description. Internal consultants do not have to advertise their services in the same way that external consultants do, but they do have the same job of convincing their clients of the value of the services they are offering.

Marketing to Current Clients

Current clients are the best source of new business. External auditors used to refer to their clients as "annuities" because they typically represent repeat business. This situation is still likely, but less so today, when audit clients are much more willing to switch auditors, particularly if the price is right. Still, the mentality of repeat business makes it difficult sometimes for auditors to appreciate the time and effort it takes to cultivate new business. Remember, hours spent marketing are not billable. Marketing to new clients is likely to be more time-consuming than selling additional services to current clients. This makes current clients the best and most natural target of consulting services.[1]

New Services for Old Clients   It is impossible to overstate the importance of retaining clients. That's why consultants need to pay constant attention to service quality and service recovery. Current clients must be pleased with the services you provide. This means that a consultant shouldn't market any services to a current client if the consultant is not certain of delivering the same quality as the current level of service. Any uncertainty about the effects of new services on a client, particularly an "annuity" client, should be part of the equation in deciding whether or not to market to a client.

Listening to Your Client   Listening to clients may be the most important action consultants can take in practice development. Sometimes consultants are wary of asking a client how they are doing for fear they will get an answer they don't want to hear. It is much better, however, to get that answer when problems can be remedied, rather than at the end of an engagement. This is like a teacher asking a class for feedback periodically, rather than on the evaluation form at the end of the semester. Listening is an ongoing part of the consultant-client relationship. Not only can listening help you learn early on of any problems in ongoing engagements; it can also lead to identifying other client needs and wants.

There are many ways to listen to clients. Social activities may put clients at ease so that they feel free to talk about their business. Focus groups are a more formal listening process. In a focus group, a small group of client personnel meet with a facili-

---

[1] Although current clients may represent the biggest and easiest target for consulting services, accountants must be careful about the services they offer to audit and tax clients, taking into account SEC and professional regulations.

tator who presents them with consultant-developed questions. The facilitator is a third party who shares the focus group comments with the consultants. Alternatively, the consultant can watch the group interact through special glass or on videotape. Feedback questionnaires are yet another tool in the listening process. These surveys should not be used alone, but distributing them as an engagement progresses shows clients that you are serious about your relationship.

Cross-Selling   There are times when clients almost market your services to themselves as a current project progresses. This occurs when clients make requests that are "outside scope." Consulting contracts (discussed later in the chapter) should clearly define the parameters of an engagement. As engagements progress, clients often find that they would like additional services or features. For example, you may be designing a database system for a specific client process. When the client previews a prototype of the database, they might realize that they would like other processes or activities to be included. Sometimes additional client requests are minor, but if they are not, and are not specifically covered in the contract, they may be an expansion of the project. At other times, the consultant will see opportunities for additional services as an engagement progresses. This type of client cultivation requires consultants to be very familiar with their organization's or team's skills and service offerings. For instance, in the 1990s, auditors often saw that an audit client's information system was not Y2K compliant. If their firm had specialists in the Y2K problem, this was a natural service to offer. This is known as "cross-selling" additional services to current clients.

Cross-selling is how the Big Five grew to become among the largest consulting firms in the world. An audit provides external auditors with the opportunity to understand a client's business needs, which naturally leads to suggestions for improvement. Accounting firms see client business needs before anyone else and can develop consulting services to meet those needs. A word of caution: cross-selling can backfire. Overselling may deteriorate a client relationship and tarnish a consultant's image.

Your Firm's Alumni   Strategic placement of firm alumni, a practice started with McKinsey, is both a way to sell more business to existing clients and to "get in the door" at prospective clients. Turnover in professional service firms is high. Those who leave and go to work for clients are in a position to refer business back to their old firms. If they enjoyed their work experience at their former employer, they will always have a bias when judging competing proposals for consulting work. That favorable bias can be a big edge.

Attracting New Clients

New clients are those you have not served previously. Attracting new clients is hard work. But a consulting business cannot grow without constantly building on its current client base. In his book *Managing the Professional Service Firm,* David Maister describes actions for recruiting clients in a hierarchy based on their effectiveness. Figure 3-6 lists these marketing tactics that range from demonstrating your expertise to cold calling. We now discuss a few of these strategies in more detail.

Current Client Referrals   Satisfied current clients are a valuable source for new clients. The most valuable asset a consultant has is reputation. Each job that is com-

---

Marketing Tactics in Descending Order of Effectiveness

The first team
Seminars (small-scale)
Speeches at client industry meetings
Articles in client-oriented (trade) press
Proprietary research

The second string
Community/civic activities
Networking with potential referral sources
Newsletters

Clutching at straws tactics
Publicity
Brochures
Seminars (ballroom scale)
Cold calls
Sponsorship of cultural/sports events
Advertising
Video brochures

FIGURE 3-6   A hierarchy of marketing tactics. (Reprinted with the permission of The Free Press, a division of Simon and Schuster, Inc., from *Managing The Professional Service Firm,* by David H. Maister, Copyright 1983 by David H. Maister.)

pleted successfully enhances that reputation and creates potential new business. The beauty of current client referrals is that they probably require no action on your part.

Showing Off Your Expertise   The first set of marketing actions you might take concerns developing a reputation for expertise. Consulting firms do this by holding seminars, making speeches, and conducting and publishing research. To inform the business community about the potential of e-business, you might hold a seminar on the subject in a local hotel. Speaking engagements are easy to get. Professional organizations such as the Institute of Internal Auditors, the Institute of Management Accountants, and the Information Systems Audit and Control Association are frequently looking for speakers for their meetings.

As for publishing, accounting and consulting professional journals are excellent tools for establishing expertise in a particular area. *The Journal of Accountancy,* for example, is a journal read by more than 300,000 professionals. Many professional service firms, small and large, publish newsletters that they distribute to current and prospective clients. These newsletters are a good forum for discussing new lines of service and showing what you know. Writing books is also a good way to establish expertise.

Case-in-Point 3-4   Partners at Arthur Andersen recently wrote a book, *Cracking the Value Code.* The book showed Arthur Andersen's expertise in understanding how organizations create market value in the knowledge age. The authors of the book gave speeches about it to clients and other groups of business professionals and academics. This was an effective strategy for positioning the firm as a provider of value-added professional services.

Networking   Other professionals and social acquaintances are also good sources of referral. Lawyers, bankers, and even competitors will refer you to clients seeking the types of services you can provide. People sometimes joke that golf should be a required course in a business school. It sounds funny, but sports and social activities are a great avenue for networking and building business relationships as well as social ones. Memberships in social professional organizations are also important for networking purposes. Participation in community activities is another marketing tactic for attracting new clients. Obtaining visibility is a very effective marketing approach in small communities in particular. Sponsoring a youth baseball team or offering to help a church implement new software are two examples of this type of client recruitment initiative.

Cold Calling   David Maister refers to cold calling as a form of "clutching at straws." It's a technique dreaded by most professionals, but it can be useful. One consulting firm specializing in implementing business strategy increased its revenues four times to more than $100 million a year between 1987 and 1990 with a cold-calling campaign as the source of most new clients.[2] Of course, cold calls made by professional consultants may not be all that cold. Usually, you begin with a referral or networking contact and call the prospective client to request a meeting. If you're trying to generate business without introductions or referrals, you may send a letter describing your business and announcing your intent to call. Again, while it may not be fun, cold calls are a powerful tool for communicating a message to a large population of potential clients.

Creating Awareness   Building referral networks takes time and a new business may need to attract clients more quickly than this allows. To establish or grow a consulting business you will likely need to undertake some promotional activities such as advertising, distributing promotional materials, establishing a web site, and attracting press. The next section of this chapter discusses these activities in some detail.

PROMOTION AND ADVERTISING

Consulting work rarely gets free press. It might happen when an engagement is extraordinarily successful; however, it's more likely to occur when the quality of work is so poor that it results in legal ramifications. As a result, consultants must blow their own horns and generate their own press. Otherwise no one will know that you managed to save a corporate department thousands of dollars due to better cost calculations or helped a company avoid choosing the wrong enterprise software solution. These jobs will enhance your reputation in small groups and they help to establish a network, but you will need to develop a promotion strategy in order to reach a larger audience.

Where to Promote Yourself

As we discussed earlier, marketing strategies vary, depending on whether you are hoping to retain clients and generate additional business with them or attract new clients. They also vary with the size of a consulting organization. Advertising and promotion strategies for attracting new consulting clients are not likely to include advertising in the general media, unless you're a large firm trying to establish your brand.

---

[2] Ford Harding, *Rain Making* (Holbrook, MA: Adams Media Corporation, 1994), p. 89.

Print and Other Media   Promotional and advertising strategies include placing an ad in print media, investing in radio and/or television commercials, sending advertising materials to target clients, engaging a public relations firm to help create an image, generating press through unusual or pro bono activities, and establishing a web site. A public relations consultant can help an organization choose the optimal promotion strategies to create your desired image in the marketplace. Press releases, like the one in Figure 3-7, should be addressed to a specific individual and describe a current event.

The Internet   Internet web sites have become important advertising tools. You can advertise at your own or at someone else's web site. Consulting organizations use their own sites to convey messages about the services they offer and the industries they serve. They may advertise at other sites too. If you choose to invest in Internet advertising, you might first do so at a web site of a partner or a company that has an image you would like to have rub off. For instance, if your image is high-tech, you would advertise at web sites of technology-related companies, journals, or professional sites.

Accountants and Advertising

The accounting profession, along with other professional service professions, including the legal and medical professions, resisted advertising for most of their history. The AICPA banned advertising in the accounting profession from 1922 until 1978. In 1977, a Senate report critical of the accounting profession's oversight and disciplinary structures prompted the Federal Trade Commission to investigate impediments to increased competition within the industry. It was also at this time that the

---

To: Allison Kline, Software Editor
The Daily News

October 1, 2000

For Immediate Release:

Woodworth and Associates Announces New Strategic Alliance
Mason, Ohio. Woodworth and Associates announced today that they are partnering with *JD Edwards* to implement its *One World* software in client businesses. Woodworth and Associates will offer implementation, training, and customization of the software to organizations in the construction industry.

Woodworth and Associates will host a reception and seminar to describe the software and details of their new alliance on Wednesday, October 24 in the ballroom of the Mason, Ohio Hyatt Regency hotel, from 5:00–8:00 p.m.

Bob Woodworth started Woodworth and Associates in 1981. Today, the firm employs 24 professionals and offers accounting and accounting and enterprise software consulting services. The firm's clients include Cincinnati area businesses such as CyberNet, Ohio Construction, and The Montgomery Brothers.

For more information, contact: Sherry Center, Director of Public Relations, at 1-800-555-2212 or scenter@woodworth.com.

FIGURE 3-7   Sample Press Release.

Supreme Court granted lawyers the right to advertise in their profession. These events prompted the AICPA to allow advertising within the accounting profession—with limitations. It wasn't until 1990 that the AICPA lifted virtually all of its advertising restrictions.

Increasing competition and growing consulting revenues led the large professional service firms to increase their advertising budgets dramatically in the 1990s. In 1993, for example, Coopers and Lybrand launched an advertising campaign with a commercial spot on the television broadcast of the Super Bowl. In 1995, Coopers and Lybrand and KPMG spent millions of dollars branding their corporate images in news and sports magazines, in television advertisements, and through sponsorship of sporting events. Smaller firms used newspapers and radio media to advertise their services. When Price Waterhouse and Coopers and Lybrand merged, the new firm, PricewaterhouseCoopers, spent between $30 and $50 million on television and print ads to brand the new name. Andersen Consulting advertised its new name, Accenture, at the 2001 Super Bowl – and, everywhere else. As professional service firms vied for the e-business consulting market, advertisements highlighting this expertise appeared virtually everywhere.

CONTRACTING

When competing with others for a consulting job, consultants will often develop and present a proposal to the client. (Chapter 4 will describe the details of writing and presenting a client proposal.) The result of a successful marketing effort, proposal, and subsequent negotiation is a consulting contract. The contract describes pricing, along with the nature and schedule of deliverables as promised in the proposal. The contracting process is important, both because it determines profitability and also because it protects both the client and the consultant. Case-in-Point 3.5 describes an unfortunate result of poor contracting.

> **Case-in-Point 3.5** *UOP vs. Andersen Consulting*, a multimillion dollar lawsuit settled in 1998 for an unspecified amount, resulted from ill-specified contract terms. Consulting industry watchers say the contract on which the lawsuit is based contained promises and also implied promises of results they could not be assured of delivering on.[3]

What's in the Contract?

Contracts for professional services have three major sections. The first describes project requirements, the next outlines the terms and conditions, and the final details the legal issues.

The project requirements section of a contract begins with the objectives of the consulting project. Clients hire consultants for a variety of reasons. If the consultant is to solve a particular problem, such as implementing a software problem or designing a security and privacy system of internal controls, the contract may be fairly specific in its objectives. When a consultant is hired for "fuzzier" reasons, say to help a

[3] James O'Shea and Charles Madigan, *Dangerous Company* (New York: Penguin Books, 1997), pp. 98–104.

company improve its business processes or enhance its use of resources and systems, the contract language describing objectives and results is naturally less precise. In either case, this section of the contract defines the engagement deliverables.

The terms and conditions section of the contract lays out the boundaries of the consultant's analysis. Specific language helps here, in defining what the consulting team is and is not expected to do. Almost any consulting engagement requires access to client personnel and data. The contract should specifically describe the support and involvement the consulting team expects from the client. Time schedules are another part of the terms of the contract, as are any warranties the consultant chooses to offer. Warranties and guarantees are risky, but they do provide clients with confidence about the work they will receive.

Lawyers design contracts; hence, any contract is likely to contain some legalese. Promises of consultant confidentiality are one legal aspect of a consulting contract. Both the client and the consultant want to protect their interests. Again, clients want to have legal recourse for unmet promises. Consultants wish for ways to void the contract if the client does not provide them with the support needed to complete the engagement. The legal language in the contract represents negotiation of these and other rights and privileges. Chapter 11 covers the thorny legal problems arising from contract disputes.

How Much Should You Charge?

The price consultants charge for their services balances costs and profit margin versus what the market is willing to pay. In setting price, consultants choose from among a variety of schemes. These include: time and materials contracts, cost-plus or fixed-price contracts, and value-based pricing. In addition, prices may be set conditionally, with bonuses and penalties attached to certain performance measures.

Pricing Strategies   Time and materials contracts call for payments as work progresses. The consultants are paid by the hour or by the day, and reimbursed for direct expenses. This pricing arrangement places most of the contracting risk on the client unless there are built-in ceilings. For that reason, it is likely to be used mostly for smaller projects and generally, the client will stipulate a limit to the billable hours covered. Consultants using this pricing strategy build the profit margin into the billing rate directly.

Cost-plus or fixed cost contracts explicitly build a profit margin on top of costs. The costs include billable hours times rates, plus overhead charges and direct expenses such as travel. Many times a request for proposal (RFP) will ask consultants to bid a price. This may well be a fixed price, with perhaps some caveats. While a time and materials contract poses most risk to the client, fixed cost contracts are risky for consultants. Client management and employees, to say nothing of unforeseen circumstances, can cause cost overruns that the consultant has to "eat." If the consulting contract has a fixed price, there's not so much incentive for the client to work as hard to ensure a project is completed most efficiently. As a result, these pricing arrangements usually include a list of assumptions or qualifications that allow the consultant to earn more than the fixed fee in the case of exception conditions.

Few consultants use value-based pricing, although it may provide the most profitability to them. Value-based pricing calls for the consultant to be paid for the perceived value of the services rendered. A number of measures are usually agreed on to calculate the profit-sharing. This means that the technique will only work in the case where the results of the consulting service can be clearly seen and evaluated. One example is a business process reengineering engagement where the price-sharing is tied to specific cost reduction targets.

Regardless of the pricing approach, many consultants collect a retainer or up-front payment of some percentage of the contract price. Otherwise, a consulting firm that bills monthly could invest two or three months of work with no payment. And sometimes, payment might be made in stock or services, rather than cash. This arrangement might make sense, for instance, when a large consulting firm is doing work for a small start-up company with high growth potential.

The Ethics of Pricing   Pricing ethics require similar pricing for similar work. Sometimes a consultant will "low-ball" a price for good reasons—such as a desire to break into a new service line offering. But prices typically should not vary by client, only with tasks or engagement type. An exception is work performed for not-for-profit organizations. Consultants might offer a discount to this type of client. Consultants should not offer to reduce their price simply because it does not fit within the client budget. If the client's budget for the engagement does not cover the bid for the job, the conventional wisdom is to either reduce the work or walk away from the job. As we explained earlier, once on an engagement, clients often think of additional work they would like the consultants to do. Consultants must keep a tight rein on project scope—reminding clients that additional work means additional cost to them. Chapter 11 elaborates further on ethical issues regarding fees and expense reimbursement.

SUMMARY

Marketing of professional services differs from traditional product marketing. Unlike products, services are largely intangible. Their intangible nature makes it difficult to standardize them. Sellers of professional services do not keep inventory. Customers consume services in real time, as they are produced. The inability to store services for use or standardize them makes consistently high service quality difficult to attain. How professional service organizations recover from poor service quality is important. A good recovery can make a client even more loyal than an initial high-quality service experience.

In addition to the "four Ps" of product marketing, the services marketing mix includes people, physical evidence, and process. People are both employees and customers. Intangible services may have a tangible dimension. Consultants, for example, have offices, wear certain business clothing, and use technological equipment. The process of delivering services takes time. How this process progresses is a final element of the service marketing mix.

The marketing process for professional services, or practice development, begins with identifying target customers. Next, a marketing plan should estimate the potential size and nature of the target market. Consultants should also analyze their competition in the market space, recognizing that not all competition is obvious. Marketing plans include detailed strategies for promoting and advertising. To invest marketing dollars optimally, consulting organizations should monitor the results of various promotional strategies and pay attention to cost/benefit projections. Selling and marketing are not synonymous. Selling a service or closing the deal is the final stage in a marketing plan.

Consulting firms, particularly those offering accounting services, will likely find it most efficient to grow revenues by courting current clients for continued and additional business.

Cross-selling, the practice of selling additional services to an existing customer, is a delicate and difficult process, but one with high potential payoffs. Attracting new clients is costly and likely to take time. Approaches to recruiting new business include advertising, writing articles and giving speeches, various networking activities, and cold calling. Advertisements for professional services may appear in print media, billboards, radio, and television. When Price Waterhouse and Coopers and Lybrand merged, airports were filled with posters branding the new PricewaterhouseCoopers name.

Closing the deal means that the client signs a contract. Consulting contracts contain specific data about the objectives of a consulting engagement, the scope, support to be given by the client, timing, legal matters, and pricing. There are several approaches to pricing consulting work, including time and materials, cost-plus, and value-based pricing.

DISCUSSION QUESTIONS

3-1. What are the marketing implications that stem from the intangible nature of services?

3-2. Identify two poor service experiences in your past. How did the service purveyor attempt to recover from the quality failure?

3-3. What marketing issues do internal consultants face?

3-4. Accountants have a client base for their audit and tax services. Should they leverage that base by selling consulting services to existing accounting clients? What are the risks of doing so?

3-5. Think of a recent service experience you had. Identify the people, physical evidence, and process associated with it.

3-6. Consulting is a lucrative profession and competition is therefore intense. Suppose you are a marketer for a mid-sized consulting firm with a niche in e-business. Identify your competition.

3-7. What are the different strategies to employ when marketing to existing versus new clients?

3-8. Do you think that professional service firms should hire marketing staff or train their accounting and consulting staff in marketing and rely on them to develop new business?

3-9. During the past few years, the Big Five have mounted significant television and print advertising campaigns to brand their firm names. What are the benefits they can expect from this investment?

3-10. Contracts are important in defining the terms and scope of an engagement. What are the risks that stem from being too specific in terms of engagement objectives versus being too general?

EXERCISES

3-11. Think of a consulting service you might offer in the e-commerce niche. Develop a marketing plan for the new service that includes: (1) identification of target markets, (2) competitive analysis, and (3) a promotional and advertising strategy.

3-12. Imagine that you have a client who is dissatisfied with your work. You believe that you have fulfilled the engagement contract requirements, but the client thinks you have done poor quality work and that the solution you developed is suboptimal. Describe the service recovery options available at this juncture.

3-13. Choose a well-known consulting firm from the list of the 50 largest firms shown in Chapter 1. Visit their web site and gather print materials from business and computer magazines. What message is the organization trying to send? Have they chosen a relatively aggressive marketing or advertising strategy? What sales market are they targeting?

REFERENCES, RECOMMENDED READINGS, AND WEB SITES

References and Recommended Readings

Allred, Sam M., "Making It—As a Consultant," *Journal of Accountancy* (September 2000), pp. 71-74.

Barcus, S. W. III, and J. W. Wilkinson, Editors in Chief, *Handbook of Management Consulting Services* 2nd edition (New York: McGraw-Hill, 1995).

Biech, E., *The Business of Consulting* (San Francisco: Jossey-Bass Pfeiffer, 1999).

Biswas, S., and D. Twitchell, *Management Consulting* (New York: John Wiley and Sons, 1999).

Blumberg, Donald F., "Marketing Consulting Services Using Public Relations Strategies," *Journal of Management Consulting* (Spring 1994), pp. 42-49.

Brownlow, B. R., "The Importance of Customer Focus," *Journal of Accountancy* (April 1997), pp. 63-65.

Harding, Ford, *Rain Making* (Holbrook, MA: Adams Media Corporation, 1994).

Hart, Christopher W. L., James L. Heskett, and W. Earl Sasser, Jr., "The Profitable Art of Service Recovery," *Harvard Business Review* (July/August 1990), pp. 148-156.

Hollander, N., and S. Needle, *Handbook of Computer and Management Consulting* (Rockville, MD: Computer Training Services, 1997).

Hulbert, Jack E., and Vanessa S. Lawson, "The Status of Advertising in the Accounting Profession," *The National Public Accountant* (July 1996), pp. 22-29.

Maister, David H., *Managing the Professional Service Firm* (New York: Free Press Paperbacks, 1993).

O'Shea, James, and Charles Madigan, *Dangerous Company* (New York: Penguin Books, 1998).

Parasuraman, A., V. A., Zeithaml, and L. L. Berry, "A Conceptual Model of Service Quality and Its Implications for Future Research," *Journal of Marketing* (Fall 1985), pp. 41-50.

Reeb, W. L., *Start Consulting—How to Walk the Talk* (Jersey City, NJ: American Institute of Certified Public Accountants, 1998).

Reichheld, Frederick F., "Learning from Customer Defections," *Harvard Business Review* (March/April 1996), pp. 56-69.

Shepherd, C. David, and Marilyn M. Helms, "Advertising the Accounting Firm: A Review with Managerial Suggestions," *Journal of Professional Services Marketing* (1996, Vol. 15, Issue 1), pp. 147-156.

Simon, Gerald A., "What to Share?" *Journal of Management Consulting* (November 1997), pp. 2, 79.

Turner, L. D., G. R. Aldhizer III, and M. D. Shank, "Client Perceptions of MAS Quality as Measured by a Marketing-Based Service Quality Model," *Accounting Horizons* (March 1999), pp. 17-36.

Wiegers, Eric., "CPA Firms Are Aggressive about Marketing," *The CPA Journal* (April 1995), pp. 69-71.

Web Sites

www.ama.org (The American Marketing Association)

Chapter 4

Writing and Presenting the Client Proposal

Writing is among our most ancient arts, the mark of civilization, in fact, and despite our best efforts, it has remained far more art than science.

Herman Holtz, *The Consultant's Guide to Proposal Writing,* 3rd edition (New York: John Wiley & Sons, 1998), p. 145

INTRODUCTION

Once the consultant attains an understanding of the client's business and the problem at hand, the next step is to draw up a proposal to perform the work. When signed by the consultant and the client, the proposal becomes a legally binding contract between the parties for the work to be performed. Alternatively, a consulting contract may be drawn up that contains an engagement letter spelling out the terms of the work to be performed. In any case, the consultant and the client both sign the document affirming the details of the agreement.

THE PROPOSAL AS A MARKETING TOOL

The purpose of the proposal is to clearly spell out what work will be done, what the client can expect as a final product, when the client can expect the project to be completed, and the fee schedule. In the event of a disagreement on any of these points, the client and consultant can look to the proposal to clarify what was agreed on originally.

The proposal is the first written evidence a potential client has of a consultant's marketing skills. You use it to sell your expertise to the client. It says, "Here's why you should hire me to help solve your problem." Very often several consultants are competing for a project. The purpose of the proposal is to persuade a client that you're the best one to help solve the company's problem. This chapter discusses the intricacies of the consulting proposal: how to organize it, how to present it, and what happens after the presentation.

The Request for Proposal (RFP)

Many companies who need consulting services decide to put the proposal out for bid. This is done by putting together a document called a Request for Proposal (RFP) and sending it to consultants identified as having the qualifications and experience necessary to do the job. An RFP specifies what the problem is and what the company's time frame for response is, along with any specific requirements relevant to the project. Figure 4-1 shows a sample RFP for an example that will be used throughout this chapter.

A consultant is not prohibited from submitting a proposal, even if he hasn't received the RFP. Most companies welcome as many proposals as possible, since it

August 5, 2001

Request for Proposal #01–07

Shenandoah Financial Planning Services, Inc.
1517 Devon Lane
Shenandoah, VA 22849

I. Company: Shenandoah Financial Planning Services, Inc. (hereafter *Shenandoah*) is a mid-sized financial planning firm in Shenandoah, Virginia. The company has approximately 500 employees and has been in business since 1961. The company offers individual and business financial planning for clients all over the nation.

II. Proposed Project: Shenandoah is seeking proposals to aid us in developing a virtual private network, or corporate intranet. The intranet will be used by the company to facilitate sharing of information within the company, including among other things, current developments relevant to company employees, benefits information, training program schedules, and the company calendar of events.

III. System Requirements: The intranet should be designed to run on a Novell NT platform (see III (a) for additional specifications), preferably using Front Page web authoring software (see III (b) for additional specifications). The proposal should include the design and implementation of the intranet, including establishing proper security such as firewalls and any other security measures necessary to ensure security of the intranet (see III (c) for additional specifications). Additionally, training of the company's network administrator should be factored into the cost (see III (d) for additional specifications).

IV. Time Schedule: Shenandoah would like to have the intranet in place and working by January 1, 2002. Please include in your proposal your estimates for implementation of the intranet. The closing date for proposals is August 31, 2001. Proposals must be postmarked no later than August 31, 2001 to be considered.

V. Submission of Proposal: Send three copies of your proposal to:

Mary Smith
Chief Information Officer
Shenandoah Financial Planning Services, Inc.
1517 Devon Lane
Shenandoah, VA 22849

FIGURE 4-1 Sample request for proposal (RFP) for design of a corporate intranet.

leverages risk somewhat for the company by giving them more choices. A consultant who believes his or her firm has the requisite qualifications and experience to do the job may submit an unsolicited proposal. Many times, it is the unsolicited proposal that wins the job.

Writing Skills

How important are writing skills? We talked about them a bit in Chapter 2 and discuss them again here. Accountants in particular are expected to be able to not only crunch the numbers, but communicate the results effectively and articulately.

We can't overemphasize the importance of writing skills. The executive in Case-in-Point 4.1 explains why.

Case-in-Point 4.1   Several executives recently participated in a roundtable about doing business and managing people in an era of rapid technological change. Said Jonah Shacknai, chairman and CEO of Medicis Pharmaceutical Corporation, "I'm convinced that with the technology rage in the United States, we are teaching kindergartners to be fluent with computers and how to access the Internet. But we are not teaching them how to read and write and do basic analytical skills, not to mention the humanistic aspects of education. ... And the same people who can spin a spreadsheet and do all sorts of tricks that would dazzle any one of us from a programming standpoint can't speak English appropriately, (and) their writing skills are at a level that I think is a national embarrassment."[1]

The next case-in-point also points out the importance of communications skills.

Case-in-Point 4.2   A recent survey of 150 executives of the largest U.S. companies asked, "Other than job-related skills, which of the following skills is hardest to find in job candidates?" Thirty percent responded that leadership and management were the number one hardest skills to find in job candidates. Writing skill was a close second at 29%. Others listed included problem solving 14%; interpersonal skills 11%; organizational skills 7%; and oral communications 5%. While leadership and management skills were first, note that communications overall, including both writing skills and oral communications, is the overall most difficult skill to find in job candidates.[2]

The basic rules for proposal writing are that the proposal should be clearly written, well organized, and free from spelling and grammatical errors. Although spellcheck is a useful tool for ferreting out spelling errors, spellcheck can also lull users into a false sense of security. That's because spellcheck doesn't identify all errors. For example, a correctly *spelled,* but incorrectly *used* word will not be identified with spellcheck. And then theirs the problem of ... oops—there and their. You also want to avoid sentence fragments, using passive voice, and making other grammatical errors.

Standardization

The name of the game in consulting is profits. Consulting firms are in business to make a profit by leveraging their expertise to aid businesses in solving problems. To maximize profits, a consulting firm should be as efficient as possible. One way to increase efficiency is to standardize some of the administrative work. Many proposals have standard material included in every proposal—for example, company information, experience, and letters of reference, attesting to the skills and qualifications of the consulting firm. These "boilerplate" paragraphs can be maintained in a template for a proposal, with information unique to a particular consulting project inserted to customize the proposal. Such standardization can significantly reduce the administrative burden involved in preparing a consulting proposal.

Organization

The proposal should be divided into several constituent parts, with each part clearly stating the terms therein. The parts include: the up-front material, a description of the proposed project, management of the project, the fee structure, a statement of

---

[1] "Special Report: Pace of Change Keeps Execs Running Keeping Up with the Technology Advances Not Easy in Internet Era," *The Arizona Republic* (May 14, 2000, S4).
[2] *Journal of Accountancy,* April 1998, p. 13.

confidentiality, the consultant's qualifications and references, and any necessary appendices. These components can be used or not as appropriate to the nature of the project and size of the company. A larger company typically requires a more formal proposal, while a less formal proposal might work best for a smaller company. Most consulting contracts will have specialty details that relate to the project at hand. The consultant should feel free to include anything in the proposal believed necessary to clarify the work to be done. We'll discuss each of the components below.

COMPONENTS OF THE PROPOSAL

Let's say your firm, First Class Consulting, has received an RFP to design a virtual private network, or corporate intranet, for a client (see Figure 4-1). Your firm is putting together a proposal to bid on the project.[3] This section provides detail and sample documents to show how the proposal might be assembled.

Up-Front Material

The first section of your proposal contains the "up-front" material, including the letter of transmittal, the title page, the executive summary, the response matrix, and the table of contents.

Letter of Transmittal   The letter of transmittal is usually the first item in the proposal. Often consultants include a copy bound inside the proposal's front cover. The purpose of the letter of transmittal is to confirm that the submitted proposal meets or exceeds the requirements of the project as stated in the RFP. It is provided on company letterhead and is addressed to the party who made the request for proposal, usually the party indicated on the RFP. The letter of transmittal only speaks to technical requirements as stated in the RFP. Cost considerations are withheld to a separate section of the proposal. The letter states how long the offer is firm for, perhaps giving an expiration date. Lastly, the letter of transmittal makes an offer to provide further details upon request, including a formal presentation if asked. Figure 4-2 provides an illustration of a letter of transmittal.

Title Page   The title page is presented on company letterhead. It states who the proposal is meant for and, if applicable, references an RFP number. If the proposal is unsolicited, the RFP number is omitted. The title page should also say that the proposal may contain proprietary information that shouldn't be divulged to outside parties. By putting a copyright notice at the bottom of the title page, the consultant obtains a common-law copyright privilege. You don't have to register the copyright formally with the U.S. Copyright Office unless litigation arises. In that event, you should go ahead and formally register the copyright. Figure 4-3 shows a sample title page.

Executive Summary   The main purpose of the executive summary is to provide a concise overview of the proposal. But it's more than that. Just as the entire proposal

[3] The components of the proposal were adapted from Herman Holtz, *The Consultant's Guide to Proposal Writing,* 3rd edition (New York: John Wiley & Sons, 1998), pp. 219–237.

First Class Consulting, Inc.
334 Main Street
Washington, DC 20017
Telephone: (202) 341-0384
Fax: (202) 341-3222

September 10, 2001

Letter of Transmittal
Request For Proposal #01-07

Mary Smith
Chief Information Officer
Shenandoah Financial Planning Services, Inc.
1517 Devon Lane
Shenandoah, VA 22849

Dear Ms. Smith:

   This letter of transmittal is in response to your request for proposal #01-07 to design and implement a virtual private network, or corporate intranet for your company. Our proposal meets or exceeds all requirements stated in the RFP.

   This will serve to confirm that I am an authorized representative of First Class Consulting, and authorized to make this offer to Shenandoah Financial Planning Services. Further, this offer is a firm offer, not subject to revocation until October 31, 2001, at which time the terms contained in this proposal and the proposal itself will expire.

   We would welcome the opportunity to speak with you further regarding the terms contained in this proposal. Upon your request, we would be happy to make a formal oral presentation regarding our proposed services. If you have any further questions or would like to schedule a conference or presentation, please contact me at (202) 341-0384.

Sincerely,

Mark Jones, CPA
Partner

FIGURE 4-2   Sample letter of transmittal.

is a marketing tool designed to sell your firm's services, the executive summary is critical as a *selling* tool. In fact, the executive summary may be the most important part of the entire proposal simply because, for many people, the executive summary may be the only part of the proposal that they read. This is especially true for busy executives, which is where the executive summary gets its name. Most firms have staff people who read and analyze the technical components of the proposal from beginning to end. The highest-level executives don't usually read all the technical matter. They are more interested in the "big picture." Who is this company, what do they claim to be able to do for us, and how do they plan to accomplish that? Those are the details the high-level executive really cares about, and the executive summary should aim to provide them.

First Class Consulting, Inc.
334 Main Street
Washington, DC 20017
Telephone: (202) 341-0384
Fax: (202) 341-3222

September 10, 2001

CONSULTING PROPOSAL

Prepared for:

Shenandoah Financial Planning Services, Inc.
Mary Smith
Chief Information Officer
1517 Devon Lane
Shenandoah, VA 22849

Note regarding confidentiality: The information contained within the proposal is proprietary and may not be disclosed to anyone except the recipient reviewer of the proposal.

Copyright September 1, 2001 by First Class Consulting, Inc.

FIGURE 4-3   Sample title page.

An executive summary should be as brief as possible while also conveying the necessary information. One rule of thumb for length is two to three pages of executive summary for every hundred pages. Use a dynamic style in writing the summary. Remember—you want to be concise. Many consultants use bullets to convey main points. This can be an effective way to get the main points across as efficiently as possible. Keep one overriding question in mind when writing the executive summary: if the client reads nothing else but the executive summary, have you conveyed all your *main* points as efficiently and effectively as possible? That's the ultimate goal.

Response Matrix   A response matrix is a document that, like the letter of transmittal, provides a confirmation that the submitted proposal meets or exceeds the specifications of the RFP. It differs from the letter of transmittal in that it provides this confirmation by technical specification as specified in the RFP. The response matrix facilitates the comparison of multiple bids by the company initiating the RFP. The response matrix does not refer to costs. Again, costs are discussed in a separate component of the proposal. Figure 4-4 shows a sample response matrix.

Table of Contents   Just about every proposal has a table of contents, no matter how small or how informal. You can use various formats for the table of contents, but in any case it lists the major headings along with subheadings and page numbers. Every page in the body of the proposal is given a page number. While it's not necessary for every page of the appendices to be numbered, they're usually numbered or lettered in some logical manner. For example, a proposal containing four appendices may have the appendices labeled "A," "B," "C," and "D." The pages within the appendices may be numbered at your discretion. However, because the appendices usually consist of extraneous matter, many proposals don't number these pages. Figure 4-5 provides a sample Table of Contents.

Response Matrix
RFP #07-01

Specification

Paragraph	Subject	Compliance	Exceeds	Page Number in Proposal
II. (a)	Design of all pages named	Yes	Yes	3
III. (a)	Novell network software	Yes	—	3
III. (b)	NT operating system	Yes	—	3
III. (c)	Front Page	Yes	Yes	3
III. (d)	Security	Yes	Yes	5
IV.	Dates	Yes	—	7

(Source: Adapted from *The Consultant's Guide to Proposal Writing,* 3rd edition [John Wiley & Sons, 1998], p. 235.)

FIGURE 4-4   Sample response matrix.

Proposed Project

The technical components of the project are presented in a separate section of the proposal. You can title this section if you want. You need to clearly indicate that this is where the details are spelled out about what you'll do and how you'll do it. Specifically, this section of the proposal includes an overview of the work to be performed, the scope of the project, objectives of the project as understood by the consultant, deliverables to be provided on completion of the engagement, a clarification of the roles and responsibilities of the consultant and client, and what follow-up the client can expect to receive after the engagement is completed. Let's take a look at these components individually.

Overview of the Work to be Performed   The proposal should begin with a broad overview of the work to be performed. This section does not present details such as *who* will collect data, *how* the data will be analyzed, and so on. It's just a paragraph that describes the project objectives and deliverables. Returning to our example consulting project, the overview section of the proposal might look something like the one in the following example.

> **Example**   First Class Consulting will design a corporate intranet for Shenandoah Financial Planning Services, Inc. The intranet will be designed using Front Page 2000. The intranet is expected to consist of from 400–500 links and 50 separate web pages. JAVA and JAVA Script will be used to customize the intranet, as directed by the client. First Class will install the intranet on the client's NT Novell server and train Shenandoah's network administrator in the maintenance of the intranet. Appropriate security considerations will be included in the design.

As you can see, the overview by definition is generally short. You aren't trying to spell out all the details. Rather you are providing a concise description of what the client can expect to end up with.

FIGURE 4-5   Sample table of contents.

Scope of the Engagement   An essential component to the proposal is the description of the engagement's scope. This is called "scope creep." We've witnessed many consulting projects in which the client attempts to "add on" work. This usually happens when the client innocently asks, "Would you mind just taking a look at one thing for me? It won't take but just a minute." Be wary of these words! What the client thinks will take a minute usually doesn't. You have to be careful not to be distracted from the work you've been engaged to do.

The purpose of the scope section is to clarify what you, the consultant, *will* and what you *will not* do. A consultant should be as comprehensive as possible in this section, as any future conflict as to scope may be resolved by a well-written scope paragraph in the proposal.

Returning to our corporate intranet engagement, the scope paragraph might look something like this.

Example   This engagement involves designing a corporate intranet web site for Shenandoah Financial Planning Services, Inc. It does not involve the corporate Intranet for Shenandoah's subsidiary, ABC Company. The project will involve using Front Page 2000 and JAVA and JAVA Script. No other web authoring tools will be used. The engagement involves training Shenandoah's network administrator. Shenandoah is responsible for training its other employees.

Again, a consultant should include any terms needed to clarify the boundaries of the engagement.

So, how do you handle the client who attempts to add on extra work? This can be awkward for the consultant and requires the consultant to use those interpersonal skills discussed in Chapter 2. Here's an example of how you might approach this situation as a consultant.

Example   *Client:* "Would you mind taking a quick look at our accounts payable program? I don't think it's anything serious. You seem to have such a grasp of computer software. I think you could take one look and tell us what's wrong. Could you help us out?"

Whew, that's tough! The client is so nice and you would really like to help them. And you *are* pretty good with application software. *Stop!* This problem is outside the scope of the engagement.

Consultant: "I would really like to help you with that problem, but honestly, my job is to work on your intranet. I really need to stay focused on this problem."

The keys to the response are sincerity, empathy, and honesty. You don't want to seem brusque or uncaring. To do so only unnecessarily alienates the client. A consultant should communicate sincerity and empathy, but must be honest. Inexperienced consultants will often agree to help the client with the new problem, only to find themselves three hours later mired in a problem completely outside the scope of the engagement. Then it becomes even *more* difficult for them to extract themselves from that problem since they have invested three hours in it.

Another approach that some consultants use in this situation is what we call the "Five-Minute Solution." Here the consultant offers to give five minutes to the problem, at which time if the problem is not solved, it reverts to the client. Given our experience, we do not recommend this approach. Experience has taught us that it almost always takes considerable time to stop what you are working on, have the problem explained to you, look at the data, figure out the answer, relate the solution, and return to your original assignment. However, in some cases very experienced consultants do use this technique successfully.

The consultant should always be alert to new consulting opportunities. Sometimes such opportunities present themselves as follows.

Example   *Client:* "You know, our accounting program just doesn't seem comprehensive enough. We are using a very low-level program, and I think we could be better served by upgrading to a more comprehensive program."

Now, granted, this is outside the scope of the *current* engagement. However, a smart consultant will realize that this may be a golden opportunity to be hired for a whole separate engagement. The consultant might reply:

Consultant: "Really? We have considerable experience in evaluating accounting application software. After this current job is over, why don't we sit down and discuss that?"

This reply lets the client know you are interested in that work and sets a plan for when you will next discuss that with them.

Objectives   This section describes the overall objectives of the consulting engagement. For example, is the objective to provide a solution to some business problem? Is it to train the employees in some technique or software? Is it to improve operational efficiency by a certain percent? Be as specific as possible.

Example   "The objectives of this engagement are to:

- design and implement a complete corporate intranet;
- incorporate security considerations for the intranet as appropriate; and
- train Shenandoah's network administrator to maintain the intranet."

Deliverables   This section of the proposal explicitly states what the client can expect to receive on completion of the project. This includes the type of report you'll deliver to the client on completion, a description of a presentation, if any, that you plan to make, and type of written documentation you expect to leave with them, and disks, if applicable.

Type of Report   Do you plan to submit a formal, written report at the completion of the project? If so, how long do you expect it to be? Keep in mind that you don't have a crystal ball to give you all the answers. You don't know *exactly* how long the report will be. However, based on your experience, you can give a ballpark estimate of the length of the report. Most of the time, a range of the number of pages will suffice.

Description of the Presentation   Your client should know if you're planning to make a formal oral presentation on completion of the work. Most consulting projects do culminate in a meeting at which the consultant makes a formal oral presentation of the findings. If you created a product as part of the engagement (e.g., a software program), this is where you'll demonstrate it. The proposal should state if this is your intention. Also, be sure to state to whom the presentation will be made. For example, if you plan to make the presentation at the monthly Board of Directors' meeting, say so in the proposal.

Documentation   Often in engagements in which the deliverable is a customized software package or a similar product, the consultant puts together a user manual for the client. The proposal should spell out any documentation you plan to provide with a product.

Disks   Again, in software development engagements, web page development, spreadsheet analysis, database analysis, or similar projects, it's customary to provide the client with original disks containing the programs. Even in cases when the work is uploaded on the client's system, you should still give the client the original disks.

Management Letter   During the course of the engagement, a consultant will often discover errors or inefficiencies in the client's business. You might keep a running list of these and incorporate suggestions as to how to improve or correct these problems into the final product. However, the client should be aware that you're planning to do so.

Example   "On completion of this project, First Class Consulting will deliver the following:

1. Formal written report, approximately 100–150 pages, to include diagrams of each page of the corporate intranet.
2. Complete HTML source code for the intranet.
3. All class files and applets needed to run the JAVA script.
4. All inline graphics required by design.
5. One-hour formal oral presentation to be made at the January 2002 monthly Board of Directors' meeting.
6. User manual, approximately 50 pages, for specifics on how to maintain the intranet.
7. Uploaded and fully tested intranet on company servers.
8. Backup disks for the entire web site.
9. List of any management recommendations we wish to make relating to operational efficiency or accuracy of company operations."

Roles and Responsibilities   The proposal should clarify both a client's and a consultant's responsibilities. The client should know that their responsibilities include ensuring that employees fully cooperate with the consultant and that they provide the highest quality of data and information possible. The client should also provide any other information needed to complete the project.

At this time a consultant should reiterate his or her commitment to a quality product and should restate what the final product is expected to consist of.

> **Example**   "Our goal with this engagement is to design and implement a corporate intranet. We will interview your employees as previously stated, and develop the web pages and links. Your employees will assist in the testing and validation stage of the project. We will finalize the web site based on your employees' input. Finally, we will train your network administrator in the maintenance of the intranet. Your company will assume the responsibility for training its other employees. We are fully committed to designing a corporate intranet that will be a valuable tool in communication and marketing for your company."

Follow-up   It's common for consulting firms to provide some follow-up assistance. If you plan on it, state clearly the scope of the follow-up in the proposal.

> **Example**   "First Class will provide follow-up service in the following way: For the first week after completion of the project, a consultant will be available at no charge by telephone to answer questions from 9:00 a.m.–5:00 p.m. Monday through Friday. After the first week, our regular hourly rate of $75 per hour will apply for telephone or on-site visit."

Project Management

This section of the proposal describes how the project will be managed from an administrative standpoint, including who's on the project team, project team members' qualifications, how you'll collect and analyze data, and estimates of time frames to complete the project. Let's look at each of these components.

Project Team/Resumes   The composition of a project team is critical to the success of a consulting engagement. You should give the names of personnel expected to participate in the project, what their expected role will be in the project, and what each one's unique qualifications are. Never lose sight of the fact that the proposal is a selling tool. You're selling the fact that your firm has unique expertise and experience that makes it the best candidate to do the job. If the project team members have prior experience in similar engagements, emphasize that. Many consulting firms also include each project team member's resume.

Data Collection and Analysis   An engagement proposal should clearly state the type of data to be collected, where you'll get it, and how the data will be used or analyzed. Recognize that the client is often somewhat anxious about this particular phase of the engagement. The client (at the top level) wants to present the best possible picture of the organization. But the also client knows that lower level employees often aren't shy about expressing their dissatisfaction to outside consultants. Some employees view their time with consultants as a great opportunity to gripe! So your client may be a bit hesitant to give you access to some or all lower level employees. An experienced consultant can help to alleviate those fears using those same keys of empathy, sincerity, and honesty. The following two examples illustrate how you might do this.

Example "We will interview three marketing employees, including the marketing manager, four accounting employees, including the controller, and the managers of finance and sales. Additionally, we will interview four employees chosen at random to evaluate the completeness and efficiency of the intranet."

Example "We will use questionnaires and personal interviews to gather data from fifteen randomly selected individuals from each department. We anticipate we will spend approximately two hours per employee in the initial data-gathering phase. After designing the prototype intranet based on the initial data gathered, we will select five of the original fifteen individuals to evaluate the system. We anticipate another hour per employee for this phase."

Notice that these examples specify how many employees you expect to interview and, where appropriate, who you expect those employees to be. It's a good idea also to include an estimate of how much time the consultant intends to spend with each employee so that the client can plan accordingly. It's important to remember and respect that the client is still conducting a business while this consulting engagement is taking place.

Time Frame and Estimates This section of the proposal spells out when the work will take place and how long it will take overall to complete the engagement. To protect yourself, stress that these are estimates and subject to change as the work progresses.

Example "The following is an estimate of our time schedule to complete this engagement. Please note that this is an estimate only and, as such, this schedule is subject to change as the project progresses. Any significant deviation from the final date of delivery will be discussed as the project progresses."

Task	Estimated Time to Complete	Estimated Date of Completion
Initial interview of client personnel	15 hours	November 4, 2001
Analysis of data	30 hours	November 10, 2001
Prototype design of intranet	40 hours	November 17, 2001
Test and validation of prototype	40 hours	November 24, 2001
Refinement of intranet	20 hours	November 29, 2001
Training	8 hours	November 30, 2001
Total hours	153 hours	

Fee Structure

The most common fee structure is an hourly rate times an estimated number of hours. Under this method, be sure to discuss the contingency for a significant variation from the estimated number of hours. Some consultants estimate the number of hours and then charge a flat fee. Following this method, the consultant does not make provision for significant overage. That is, if the consultant's number of hours to complete the project are significantly underestimated, the consultant assumes the loss. This fee structure is rare in today's environment. See Chapter 3 for a detailed discussion of pricing.

Example "Based on the estimate of 153 hours provided, at our regular hourly rate of $75 per hour, we estimate the fee for this engagement at $11,475. This is only an estimate, as the total number of hours will likely vary. Any significant variance from the estimated number of hours to complete the job will be fully disclosed and agreed on as soon as known."

Chapter 3 discusses other fee arrangements.

Statement of Confidentiality

Confidentiality is no small matter for the client. The client will very often be divulging sensitive financial information, marketing information, or other proprietary trade secrets to the consulting firm. To this end, a statement of assurance of confidentiality is a "must" for consulting proposals.

Ideally, all members of the consulting team sign the confidentiality statement. However, if the consulting team is very large, it may be more practical for a representative of the consulting firm (a partner usually) to sign on behalf of the firm.

Example "First Class Consulting promises not to discuss any aspect of this consulting engagement with any party outside your firm unless we obtain your permission first."

_____   _____
Signed   Date

_____   _____
Signed   Date

_____   _____
Signed   Date

Qualifications and References

In addition to selling the qualifications of the individual project team members, a consulting firm will want to be sure to emphasize how the *overall* experience of the firm can contribute to the overall success of this engagement, should this firm be hired. This is especially important today, when consulting firms are leveraging their experience with technology such as Best Practices databases and artificial intelligence systems. Some of this information may have been captured in the section detailing the qualifications of the team members. However, it's worth reiterating from a firm-wide perspective the specific engagements the company has successfully completed to draw attention to and play up prior experience. References from client personnel on those successful engagements may be provided in this section. This includes names, job titles, and telephone numbers of happy clients, particularly if those engagements shared similarities to the proposed job. Of course, it goes without saying that the client's permission should be obtained in advance before listing them as a reference. The best time to receive such permission is at the end of a successful engagement. It is wise to obtain such permission in writing from the client.

Appendices

Appendices contain any extraneous material deemed important enough to give your client, but not important enough to put in the body of the proposal. For example, other firm background and history, samples of work to be performed, details about any firm technology you'll use, and relevant but not essential demographic data are examples of items that might appear in an appendix.

PRESENTATION OF THE PROPOSAL

Once the proposal has been drawn up and ready to present to the client, there are several points to keep in mind. What if the client doesn't agree with something in the proposal? How do you present the proposal and to whom do you present? This section covers these and other important details.

To Whom and by Whom

A formal presentation of the proposal isn't always necessary. Particularly on small projects, the presentation may simply involve the client and the consultant sitting down together and going over the proposal topic by topic. On a larger, more complex project, however, a formal presentation is customary.

On the more formal type of presentation, a consulting partner, the project team leader, and perhaps several team members with varying functional expertise may participate. The project team leader usually conducts the meeting.

The client, of course, decides who attends the presentation. Depending on the nature of the consulting engagement, a client may or may not want many people from the company to know about the project. A consultant must be aware that some projects are politically sensitive and respect the client's directions as to who inside the company is privy to the proposed project.

How Long Should the Presentation Be?   A common question we hear is "How long should the client presentation be?" The answer really depends on the scope of the consulting project itself. If the project is relatively small and narrow in nature, a 30-minute proposal might be appropriate. On the other hand, a complex project with multiple deliverables may require a more protracted presentation.

Overall, experience is the best guide. However, in the absence of either broad consulting experience or familiarity with this specific type of consulting problem, a good rule of thumb is 15 to 20 minutes per deliverable. The trick is to be thorough, but not to the point of boring the client. Most any client's eyes tend to glaze over after an hour. We tend to aim for no more than an hour presentation, with a formal question-and-answer session at the end for feedback.

Presentation Skills

The presentation to the client requires excellent presentation skills, including organization, articulateness, confidence, and facility with technology.

Organization   The team leader or consulting partner ideally should conduct the meeting. You should prepare handouts for each person in attendance and distribute them at the beginning of the meeting. A well-organized oral presentation demonstrates professionalism and acts to inspire confidence in the consulting team. The team leader should open by introducing him- or herself and then the remaining team members. If desired, team members may tell a little something about their professional experience or specialty. Remember that at this stage, the consultant is selling the product, which is the collective experience of the consulting team and the team's ability to solve the problem at hand.

Articulateness   Being articulate comes easier for some than for others. It seems that many people speak fluently, without noticeable nervousness in somewhat stressful situations such as in a client presentation. Others struggle to maintain a composed, professional outward appearance while knees are knocking. It may help to know that often articulateness comes with experience. Over time as you participate in more and more client presentations, you eventually gain confidence and with that comes clarity of expression.

For those people on this side of the learning curve, the best advice is practice. Practice your presentation individually and also as a team. Practicing and knowing your topic will go a long way toward diminishing presentation jitters and increasing your articulateness.

Confidence   A consultant should strive to project confidence in the presentation. This includes confidence both in the consulting team members individually and in the team's ability to solve the client's problem. Again, remember that you're selling your ability to help the client. The client will not have much confidence in a team that does not appear to have confidence in itself.

Technology   In today's business environment, it's common to present a proposal using presentation software such as PowerPoint. If your team is planning to use this type of technology, it is important to have at least two team members highly proficient with the hardware setup as well as the software. Find out ahead of time what facilities the client has available and what you'll need to furnish. We recommend a practice run with the client's technology if possible. This ensures that the technology will work as you anticipate and that there are no unforeseen glitches in compatibility between the client's facilities and your laptop.

It's also a good idea to designate one person in charge of running the technology. If you plan to alternate people at the computer, try to make the transition as seamless as possible. We highly recommend use of a wireless mouse if possible. This permits freedom from the keyboard and allows the speaker to control the presentation from anywhere in the room.

Finally, what do you do when the team is standing before the client's representatives and the technology fails? A smart consultant *always* has a contingency plan for the presentation in the event of technology failure. We recommend two contingencies. First, have an extra laptop battery as well as an extra laptop. It is fairly easy to occupy your audience while another team member makes the necessary changes to the technology. Second, if it becomes apparent that the technology is not going to cooperate, we recommend you have a set of color overhead transparencies for this contingency. Granted, this can be quite an expense; however, if you ever need to rely on them, you will consider it money well spent.

If you experience technical difficulty with the technology, how much time do you spend trying to get it to work? Our rule of thumb is five minutes. If you can't get the technology to work in that amount of time, chances are you never will. A technology failure does not in itself imply failure for the presentation if an inordinate amount of time is not spent struggling in front of the audience and if the consultant can produce a quality backup plan. On the contrary, showing such composure and planning for contingencies demonstrates your professionalism and the ability to handle a crisis with grace.

Visual Aids

You can use other visual aids besides presentation software such as PowerPoint. If you do, keep some basic points in mind regarding these visual aids. First, visual aids should be used appropriately and should flow from the presentation. As a point is being made, the visual aid is shown to reinforce that point. It might be a chart, a graph, a short film or movie, or any other device intended to help drive the point home. Bringing up the visual aid should be smooth and relatively invisible to the audience. That is, the audience should not observe the presenter fumbling or fiddling to make the visual aid appear. For computer aids, while the use of a wireless mouse is recommended, we caution that it takes a little practice to get used to. In selling your firm's expertise, a consultant who isn't able to manage the technology will not inspire the client's confidence.

The size of a visual aid is critical to the usefulness of the device. The aid won't work if the audience can't see the aid! Many presenters are guilty of making this mistake. If your audience is squinting to try to see what you're pointing to, it distracts them from what you're saying. Provide handouts when the print on the visual aid might be too small to comfortably read. It's a good idea to check the readability of your visual aids during the practice session at the client's place of business, assuming that is where you are making the presentation. Give yourself plenty of time to practice so that you can correct any problems. For visual aids the rule of thumb concerning writing is that less is more. Color can be used as appropriate to make your point. For example, a graph containing demographics by gender should show males in one color and females in another. The audience can quickly and with minimum effort catch on to the point of the visual aid.

Communication of Roles and Responsibilities

The presentation is an opportunity to again define the roles and expectations of both the consultant and the client. This reinforces the "Roles and Responsibilities" section of the written proposal and helps avoid potential areas of conflict.

AFTER THE PRESENTATION

Asking for Feedback

When the presentation is over, the presenter should warmly thank the client for the opportunity to present the proposal. Finally, you should open the floor for feedback and questions. If a more informal presentation has occurred with questions taken throughout the presentation, it may not be necessary to have the question-and-answer period at the end.

Negotiation

Now it's time to negotiate. It is possible that during or after the presentation, that the client expresses reservations about some aspect of the project.

> **Example**   *Client:* "I really like what you have presented here, but I need the intranet up and running within three weeks."

Thus opens a period of negotiation. It is important for the consultant to be honest in the negotiation. Can you reasonably work within the time frame?

> *Consultant:*   "I don't think that it is possible to have the intranet completed within that time frame unless you are willing to pay an overtime premium."

The consultant here has acknowledged the client's problem, given an honest answer, but still left the door open, if the client is willing to pay the price.

Impasses

Sometimes negotiations break down and you're at an impasse. Perhaps the client is making unreasonable time or quality demands. No matter what you're thinking, a consultant should stay true to the keys of empathy, sincerity, and honesty.

> *Step one: Recognize whether this is a major or minor impasse.* If all attempts at negotiation have still not brought an agreeable compromise, the consultant must consider whether it is a major or minor impasse. A major impasse occurs when the entire project is at risk. For example, if the client absolutely will not compromise on the proposed time frame and isn't willing to pay an overtime premium and you cannot negotiate a middle ground, the entire project is at risk of not proceeding. A minor impasse occurs when negotiation on a minor or secondary objective fails to reach compromise.
>
> *Step two: Reiterate to the client your willingness to find a middle ground along with your commitment to a quality solution, and ask the client for suggestions.* This communicates sincerity and authenticity and puts the ball back in the client's court to identify any area for middle ground.
>
> *Step three: Be prepared to say "no."* If it becomes obvious through conversation, negotiation, and body language that a major impasse is not going to be resolved, you must be prepared to turn down the engagement. Ethically, you can't accept a consulting engagement where you can't agree on major terms or conditions. As difficult as this may be, particularly if the engagement promised to be lucrative, the client will ultimately respect you for standing your ground, which may inspire the client to reconsider.
>
> *Step four: Verbally acknowledge a minor impasse as such and resolve it.* The last thing a consultant should engage in is a power struggle with the client.

The client is, after all, paying the bill. If it's ethically and practically possible to defer to the client, in most cases this is a reasonable course of action.

When to Walk Away

What do you, the consultant, need to get the job done efficiently and accurately? You must be honest about what your needs are. If the client cannot furnish these resources or is unwilling to do so, you have no ethical choice but to say no to an engagement. This may become apparent at any time up to the signing of the proposal. It's not uncommon for consultants to say "no" to an engagement. In fact, many consultants will tell you that they turn down as many projects as they accept. It is unethical to accept an engagement for which you know you do not have the requisite skills or experience to bring the job to a successful conclusion. It's also not good business.

Reaching Agreement

A client may be entertaining proposals from several consulting firms. In this case, agreement may not be reached immediately following the presentation. Judgment is called for in reading the client's body language and verbal and nonverbal signals. If it appears that the client is excited about the project and indicates that, you may ask for an agreement. If the client acknowledges the agreement of the engagement, the consultant may present the proposal for signature. Once signed, the client is given a signed copy and the consultant retains the original.

Subsequent Changes to the Contract

What happens when you have accepted a consulting engagement and, in the process of completing the job, it becomes obvious that some term or condition may not be met. For example, suppose you have agreed to complete the job in four weeks but due to your programmer's unexpected illness, you cannot meet the deadline. Again, it is not uncommon for such events to transpire.

Step one: Discuss the situation with the client. Make your client immediately aware of the situation. The longer you put that off, the more risk you run of the client being unhappy. Your client will appreciate being informed as quickly as possible of the circumstances and what you plan to do.

Step two: Have a plan! When you do discuss the situation with the client, be prepared with a contingency plan. What is the revised estimated delivery date? How will you compensate for the problem? Will it cost the client or will you absorb the loss? Again, a professional always has a backup plan.

Step three: Prepare an amendment to the contract if necessary. For major changes to the contract, such as scope changes, you should type up a formal amendment stating what the change is and any relevant details. Both you and the client should both sign and date the amendment and each should retain a copy.

Once you have convinced the client that you are the best consultant for the job and have a signed project proposal or contract in hand, the next step is to plan the project, including how you will manage it. The next two chapters discuss project management in detail.

SUMMARY

Writing and presenting a client proposal is an essential part of the consulting process. The proposal is, in fact, the most important marketing tool a consulting firm possesses. The purpose of the proposal is to clearly spell out what work will be done, what the client can expect as a final product, when the client can expect the project to be completed, and what the consulting fees are. The Request for Proposal (RFP) is often the invitation for a consultant to submit a proposal for the solicited services. Consultants may submit an unsolicited proposal in the event they do not receive an RFP directly. The proposal should be clearly written, well organized, and free from spelling and grammatical errors.

The proposal should be organized into several constituent parts, including the (1) up-front material, (2) the proposed project, (3) project management, (4) the fee structure (5) a statement of confidentiality, (6) qualifications and references, and (7) the appendices. The up-front material includes the letter of transmittal, the title page, the executive summary, the response matrix, and the table of contents. Details of how the consultant will complete the project are given in the proposed project section, including an overview of the work to be performed, the scope of the project, objectives of the project, deliverables, a clarification of the roles and responsibilities of the consultant and client, and what follow-up the client can expect to receive after the engagement is completed. The project management details how the consultant expects to manage the project. It includes the names of the project team, the qualifications of the project team members, how the data will be collected and analyzed, and estimates of time frames for completion of the project. The fee structure is contained in a section by itself or it may be disclosed in a completely separate document. The statement of confidentiality reaffirms the commitment of the consultant to keep all client information the consultant becomes privy to as a result of the consulting engagement completely confidential. The qualifications and references section of the proposal reiterates the qualifications and relevant experience of the bidding firm in order to convince the company that the consulting firm should be hired. Often letters of reference from past clients are included in this section. Finally, the appendices contain any information deemed important enough to be supplied to the client, but not important enough to be placed in the body of the proposal.

The presentation of the proposal is the selling of the consultant's ideas to the client company. The proposal is presented by the consultant to client personnel as chosen by the client and should last no more than an hour if possible. Presentation skills include being well organized, articulate, demonstrating confidence in presentation manner, and being proficient with the technology used in the presentation. Additionally, use of visual aids should flow from the presentation and enhance understanding of the material being presented. The roles and responsibilities of the consultant and client should be communicated to ensure the parties are in agreement with those roles and responsibilities.

Once the presentation has been completed, the consultant asks for feedback through a question-and-answer session. A period of negotiation may arise if the client asks for concessions on the part of the consultant. The consultant may or may not be able to meet the client's requests. If an impasse is encountered in negotiations, four steps should be kept in mind: (1) Recognize whether this is a major or minor impasse; (2) reiterate your willingness to find a middle ground along with your commitment to a quality solution, and ask the client for suggestions; (3) be prepared to say "no" if you cannot meet the client's requirements; and (4) verbally acknowledge a minor impasse as such and resolve it. Subsequent changes to the contract may be necessary if major changes in conditions arise. Three steps to follow regarding subsequent changes to the contract are: (1) Discuss the situation with the client immediately; (2) have a contingency plan; and (3) prepare an amendment to the contract if necessary and obtain the client's signature acknowledging the contract amendment.

DISCUSSION QUESTIONS

4-1. Why is the proposal such an important marketing tool?

4-2. What's the purpose of the proposal?

4-3. Explain what an RFP is and what it contains.

4-4. Describe what's contained in an executive summary. Why is it so important to keep it short?

4-5. What's the purpose of the response matrix?

4-6. What does a consultant need to do to obtain a common-law copyright?

4-7. How should a consultant respond if asked to perform services significantly outside the scope of the current consulting engagement?

4-8. Identify the types of deliverables usually included in a proposal.

4-9. Why is a statement of confidentiality important to include in a proposal?

4-10. What type of information is provided in an appendix as opposed to the body of the proposal?

4-11. How long should a proposal presentation be? Why is it important to have a definite time frame for the proposal?

4-12. What considerations regarding use of technology should be given?

4-13. What are the consultant's responsibilities during a period of negotiation following the proposal presentation?

4-14. What are some signals that might tell you it's time to walk away from a project?

EXERCISES

4-15. Many government entities regularly put out requests for proposal. Search the Internet to find a request for proposal put out by a government entity. Write a summary of what the requester needs.

4-16. You have a client whose parents are quite elderly. The client has asked you to provide a general review of the estate tax rules in order to engage in some estate tax planning. Write a business letter to your client outlining the basics of the estate tax.

4-17. You're the CPA for a small manufacturing company. The sales people often travel during the day and are gone from early morning to late evening. They routinely ask for reimbursement for meals while engaging in these activities. Research this issue and write a memo to the head of sales describing the appropriateness of the meal reimbursements and the options available to the sales people.

REFERENCES, RECOMMENDED READINGS, AND WEB SITES

References and Recommended Readings

Allred, Sam, "Making It—As a Consultant," *Journal of Accountancy* (September 2000), pp. 71–74.

Block, Peter, *Flawless Consulting, A Guide to Getting Your Expertise Used,* 2nd edition (San Francisco: Jossey-Bass Pfeiffer, 2000).

Gerber, Michael E., *The E-Myth Revisited* (New York: Harper Business, 1995).

Holtz, Herman, *The Consultant's Guide to Proposal Writing,* 3rd edition (New York: John Wiley & Sons, 1998).

Tepper, Ron, *How to Write Winning Proposals for Your Company or Client* (New York: John Wiley & Sons, 1990).

Web Sites

Texas A&M offers proposal-writing tips at: http://tlrc.tamu.edu/grants/grantpro/writprop.htm.

OpenAir.com is a web-based company that provides small companies with project management software assistance, including client billing and time and expense tracking, as well as help with proposal writing. See: www.OpenAir.com/.

Another company that maintains project management tools for small businesses is: www.iNiku.com.

Chapter 5

Managing the Project—Part One

The project manager of a troubled project was replaced with a new manager. On his way out the door, the departing manager gave three sealed envelopes to the new manager and said, "These envelopes are each marked with a "1," "2," and "3" on the outside. When you find yourself in a tough spot, open the envelopes in sequential order and perhaps you will find some helpful tips." Well, soon into the project, the new manager was faced with a serious crisis. The programmers found a bug in the software and fixing it could extend the whole project by at least four weeks. In his frustration over how to break the news to the client, the new project manager opened the first envelope. The message read, "Blame the prior project manager." The new manager followed the sage advice and it worked. A little later, the new manager was confronted with intrateam bickering and fighting so serious that the whole project was in jeopardy. Once again, he resorted to the envelopes for an answer. The message in the second envelope read, "Blame the prior project manager once again." The new manager abided by the advice and, to his shock, it worked again. A third crisis arose soon thereafter. The project team had ordered the wrong computer equipment and the switch-out would cost a lot of money and time. Despite the seriousness of the problem, the project manager was calm, as he was certain that envelope three would hold the answer to how he should divulge this terrible news to the client. He quickly found the envelope, ripped it open, and read the following: "Sorry you're having a tough time. Here is my advice. First, find three envelopes. . . ."

Source unknown

INTRODUCTION

On the surface, it seems a waste of time to teach accountants the essentials of project management. After all, accounting is part of the service sector of the economy, not the manufacturing sector. Accountants do not produce ships, buildings, bridges, or spaceships, so you may as well skip this chapter, unless of course you are an architect, engineer, or building contractor—right? Hold it! Before you tear the pages of this chapter out of the book, let's be sure that the conventional view of projects is accurate in today's economy. Could it be that project management is an essential skill set for contemporary accountants? Is it possible that accountants who acquire such knowledge are increasing the value of their intellectual capital? The answer to these questions is a definite YES. By reading this chapter, you will learn that the very nature of work in accounting is project-centric and accountants who acquire project management skills will gain a competitive advantage in the workplace.

In this chapter, you'll discover how to spot a project when you see one. You will also learn how to plan, schedule, monitor, and control project parameters, resources, activities, and deliverables. With respect to project activities, a considerable amount of the chapter will focus on two key concepts—developing a work breakdown structure (WBS) and utilizing the critical path method (CPM) of planning, executing, and controlling project activities, as these useful tools are integrated into most project management software packages. Finally, the chapter addresses an important topic that is often overlooked by project managers; that is, how to properly close a project.

THE ROLE OF A PROJECT MANAGER ON A CONSULTING TEAM

The key to successfully completing a project on time, within budget, and in accordance with quality expectations rests squarely on the shoulders of the project manager. Although the necessary skill set for an effective project manager varies, depending on the nature and extent of the project, talents that are common to all project managers include (1) possessing a strong technical background in the relevant area, (2) organizing people, processes, and resources into a cohesive framework, (3) leading multiple and simultaneous project team activities and change management processes, (4) guiding team members and client representatives through a minefield of unexpected issues and problems, and (5) controlling trade-offs among project scope, time constraints, and financial budget. While it may seem impossible for anyone to successfully orchestrate and execute a project, the project manager can significantly increase the probability of success by following sound, proven project management techniques, as next discussed.

OVERVIEW OF PROJECT MANAGEMENT

This section of the chapter discusses the nature of projects.

Characterizing the Project

At a fundamental level, the purpose of a project is to solve a problem. Each project is designed to resolve a unique situation whereby the world is transformed from a known state to a desired state. It is the prime objective of the project manager to lead and coordinate this often delicate change process in the most efficient and effective manner possible. To be successful in this regard, one must understand the fundamental nature of projects. In essence, a project is a system with a limited life span and defined outcome. The systems aspect of a project arises from its similarity to the general notion of physical and social systems. Specifically, a project has boundary conditions (work scope, time, and cost), a desired goal (the project outcome), and is comprised of a set of interrelated value-added processes (activities) each with their own boundaries (parameters), inputs (resources), and outputs (deliverables). These unique characteristics of projects differentiate them from routine workflow activities. Figure 5-1 graphically depicts project attributes and the project life cycle as a workflow system. This figure will be referred to again in upcoming sections.

Without a doubt, consulting is an extremely project-centric line of work, as there are little, if any, ongoing routine activities in the consulting world. For the most part, a consultant's work life is composed of client projects. Sometimes, a consultant is heavily involved with a single project, while at other times the consultant is simultaneously juggling multiple projects. The project-centric nature of work is also applicable to accountants in a wide array of other job positions. For instance, in the public accounting domain, auditors and tax preparers work almost exclusively on client projects. In the public, governmental, and not-for-profit sectors, most of the work performed by accountants, except for repetitive "close out" and reporting tasks, can be classified as projects. Developing a budget, analyzing the net present value of a

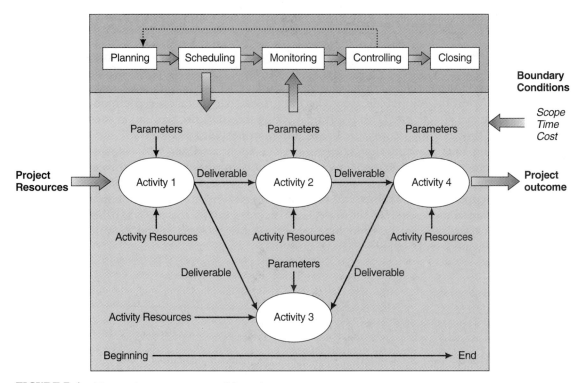

FIGURE 5-1   The project management life cycle.

proposed acquisition, deciding whether to outsource a certain organizational function, and implementing new or upgrading existing computer hardware and software are common work tasks performed by accountants. Such tasks can all be considered projects. Only recently has the accounting profession begun to recognize that the vast majority of accounting work involves projects. Accordingly, learning and utilizing solid project management skills are a great way for accountants to become valueadded players in their respective organizations.

Defining the Project

When defining a project, one must clearly articulate the project outcome and boundary conditions. Only after the project outcome has been clearly defined can the project boundary, which is composed of work scope, time, and cost, be established.

> **Example**   The outcome for Project A is defined as "the successful implementation of a microcomputer-based general ledger package for a Mom and Pop grocery store." The work scope of this project is considerably less than Project B in which the outcome reflects "the successful implementation of a large-scale enterprise resource planning (ERP) system for a Fortune 500 company."

Even within each project in this example, the work scope can vary considerably. For instance, what is meant by "successful" implementation? Does this mean that once the computer hardware and software are up and running, the project is deemed successful? Alternatively, might the project outcome also include employee training? What about converting the existing data from the old manual or computer files to the new system? Is that considered part of the successful project outcome? As indicated, the work scope of a project increases when more responsibilities are integrated into the definition of "successful." Therefore, the project manager must be very careful to make absolutely clear all the terms and conditions related to the desired project outcome in the client engagement letter.

As you can readily see, the project outcome and scope are inextricably linked. In a similar fashion, the next two boundary conditions, time and cost, are tightly coupled with the work scope. Specifically, a wider work scope generally translates into a longer time period and higher cost.

> **Example**   Assume for a moment that you are the project manager for a project where the outcome is clearly articulated (in writing) and, basically, the engagement involves the implementation of a commercially developed inventory tracking system for a client. Further assume that the project scope is restricted to installing and testing the new software on the client's existing computer hardware. For simplicity's sake, suppose that the project will consume 300 hours of work at a billing rate of $100 per hour, for an estimated project cost (EPC) of $30,000.
>
> At this point, the client has determined that the estimated project value (EPV) of installing the new inventory tracking system over its estimated life of five years is $40,000, yielding a project profitability index (PPI) of 1.33 (EPV/EPC). At about the halfway point in the project, the client realizes that converting the existing data from the old to the new inventory tracking system would be quite time consuming (about two weeks) and costly (approximately $5,000) if performed manually by client employees, yielding a revised PPI of 1.14 ($40,000/$35,000). So, the client has asked how much you would charge to convert the data from the old to the new system. After some reflection and calculation, you respond (in writing) that your project team could perform the conversion task more efficiently (20 hours; $2,000) by writing a specialized computer program that would automatically convert the data formats from the old to the new systems. As shown, the project manager's response to the increase in work scope includes revised time estimates and associated cost changes, which yield a revised PPI of 1.25 ($40,000/$32,000).

In this example, it is fairly obvious that the client should increase the scope of the project to include data conversion by the consultants. The determination of EPV, EPC, and PPI will be further examined in the next section.

The prior example brings up an interesting phenomenon in the project world known as "scope bloat." Once a project is under way, clients often keep changing the desired project outcome such that the scope of work continually expands. Let's assume that an initial engagement involves implementing the accounts receivable application of a general ledger package for a client. Assume also that the operational meaning of the word "implementing" is spelled out very clearly at the beginning of the engagement. Thus, based on initial expectations, the project's work scope, time, and cost boundary conditions are mutually established and understood. As the project moves forward, the accounting clerks and supervisors begin to realize that integrating the cash receipts application of the software package would also be very beneficial (oops, a scope bloat is in the making). The project manager readily agrees to do so, as the inclusion of this application involves no additional software expenditures since it is already built into the software package. At this point, the project manager should submit a revised time and cost budget to the client in writing. However, project managers typically are so caught up in project details and pleasing the client that they fail to clearly articulate the implications of such a change in work scope on the initial time and cost estimates. Instead, they often say, "No problem. The time and costs will go up a bit, but we'll deal with those issues later." At a subsequent point in the project, the client's chief accountant suggests that the project team integrate the sales order application (which is also part of the overall suite of applications built into the software package), as this would significantly enhance the speed and accuracy of the accounting information system. Once again, the project manager says, "No problem, I'll handle it."

Well, before you know it, the project is 55 days behind schedule and the costs have soared upward by 25 percent. The client becomes frustrated and the relationship begins to sour. Explanations of time and cost variances after the fact by the project manager are fruitless if the "meeting of the minds" was not clearly documented at each instance of scope bloat. The project manager will most certainly be blamed and condemned. Then the finger pointing begins and the relationship continues to decline. Guess who wins in these "he said/she said" blame game exchanges—the client, naturally. Unfortunately, the scenario just described is all too common. The lesson is obvious. Project managers should always be realistic, articulate, and forthright with the client regarding trade-off implications among the project outcome, work scope, time, and cost. The best way to avoid client misunderstandings of this nature and to ensure that the project will be delivered on time and within budget is to employ sound project management techniques, as next discussed.

Selecting the Project

From the client's perspective, decisions regarding which project(s) to undertake are quite complex. The client must analyze the costs and benefits of multiple project proposals and select those projects that are expected to add the most value to the organization. Because this textbook focuses on the project manager's viewpoint, the details of such organizational decision-making are, for the most part, outside our scope. However, it is nevertheless important to understand some aspects of the project selection process—specifically, the determination of estimated project value (EPV), estimated project cost (EPC), and project profitability index (PPI).

If firm managers are to understand the value-added potential of a given project within the framework of an organization's strategic goals, they must somehow develop a metric that provides a reasonably accurate estimated project value (EPV). Although there are various accepted methods of determining EPV, we will discuss only one for illustrative purposes.

Example Assume that a brick-and-mortar auto parts store, called Quick Parts, desires to establish a business-to-consumer (B2C) presence on the Internet with the objective of soliciting and fulfilling sales orders via a new company web site. Quick Parts management estimates that the implementation of the proposed B2C web site, referred to as "Quick Parts Online," will result in the following sales increases (Table 5-1):

Table 5-1	Estimated Sales Impact of the Quick Parts Online Project		
Sales Periods after Project Completion	Incremental Gross Sales	Incremental Sales Expenses	Net Sales Increase
Sales Year 1	$100,000	$50,000	$50,000
Sales Year 2	150,000	60,000	90,000
Sales Year 3	200,000	75,000	125,000
Sales Year 4	200,000	75,000	125,000
Sales Year 5	200,000	75,000	125,000
TOTALS	$850,000	$335,000	$515,000

At a glance, it appears as though the EPV of the Quick Parts Online project is $515,000. However, this example fails to consider the time value of money. That is, the value of a dollar earned at the end of Year Five is not equal to the value of a dollar earned at the end of Year One. This concept is called the "present value" (PV) of money. Because this textbook is not designed to teach PV principles, we will keep the following discussion fairly straightforward.

Assume it is January 1 and you want to calculate the PV of a dollar earned at the end of the year. In order to do so, you must first determine a rate at which money increases in value over time. For instance, assume that a typical bank savings account would pay a simple interest rate of 7 percent. This means that the future value (FV) of a dollar invested in the bank on January 1, Year One, will be worth $1.07 ($1.00 × 1.07) on December 1, Year One. However, our question addresses the PV as of January 1 of a dollar sitting in the bank account on December 31. Accordingly, the PV of a dollar at the end of the year, assuming an annual time value of money of 7 percent, is $0.9346 ($1/1.07).

Let's extend this example one more year. The future value of a dollar invested on January 1, Year One, is worth $1.1449 on December 31, Year Two ($1 × 1.07 × 1.07). Notice the mathematical formula at work here. To find the future value, *FV*, of a given sum of dollars, *d*, for a given number of periods into the future, *n*, at a constant interest rate, *i*, one can use the following formula:

$$FV = [d \times (1 + i)^n] \qquad [1]$$

Conversely, the value of $1.00 at the end of Year Two is worth $0.8734 at the beginning of Year One (1.00/1.07²). Accordingly, the formula for finding the present value, *PV*, of a given sum of dollars, *d*, for *n* periods into the future at a constant interest rate, *i*, is as follows:

$$PV = [d \div (1 + i)^n] \qquad [2]$$

Many finance and accounting textbooks provide PV tables, so you do not have to worry about calculating the PV of a given sum of dollars by hand. Such tables often present a discount factor (DF) for multiple periods, *n*, and interest rates, *i* (often referred to as discount rates). The DF shown on these tables is the inverse of $(1 + i)^n$, as shown:

$$DF = [1 \div (1 + i)^n] \qquad [3]$$

Thus, to find the *PV* of a given sum of dollars, *d*, over *n* periods at a constant interest rate, *i*, one would multiply *d* by the appropriate *DF* (representing the appropriate interest rate, *i*, and time periods, *n*), as shown in the following formula:

$$PV = [d \times DF_{(i,n)}] \qquad [4]$$

Rather than using the market rate of savings accounts as the basis for discounting future cash flows, most firms develop their own internal rate of return (IRR) metric, which reflects the minimum return they expect from projects. The calculation of a company's IRR can be quite complicated, for it considers a multitude of factors, such as inflation trends, interest rates, market risks, and opportunity costs. For purposes of simplicity, let's assume that Quick Parts' IRR is 7 percent.

The following partial table is relevant to the project example.

Table 5-2   Present Value Discount Factors at 7%

Present Value (PV) Discount Period	Present Value (PV) Discount Factor as of the End of the Discount Period at 7% Simple Interest
End of Year 1	0.9340
End of Year 2	0.8734
End of Year 3	0.8163
End of Year 4	0.7629
End of Year 5	0.7130
End of Year 6	0.6663

Referring to Table 5-1, assuming that the project will take one full year to complete, the first year that the company can expect to realize a net sales increase (reflected by Sales Year 1 in Table 5-1) is at the end of the second year into the future (reflected by "End of Year 2" in Table 5-2). Accordingly, the EPV of the proposed project is shown in Table 5-3.

Table 5-3   EPV of the Quick Parts Online Project

B2C Sales Year	Net Sales	Discount Year	Discount Factor	Present Value (PV)
Year 1	$50,000	Year 2	0.8734	$43,670.00
Year 2	90,000	Year 3	0.8163	73,467.00
Year 3	125,000	Year 4	0.7629	95,362.50
Year 4	125,000	Year 5	0.7130	89,125.00
Year 5	125,000	Year 6	0.6663	83,287.50
Estimated Project Value (EPV)				384,912.00

Note that the EPV represents the maximum project cost whereby the company can realize its minimum desired IRR (7 percent in this case). That is, if the project cost also happens to be $384,912.00, the company will realize exactly the desired 7 percent IRR. Once the EPV is determined, the organization must next assess the project cost.

As discussed earlier, the cost of a project is a function of how long the project will take to complete, which is a function of the work scope. At this point, firm managers often solicit a "request for proposal" (RFP) from internal parties who might tackle the project, external consultants, or both. The project outcome and scope should be clearly described in the RFP. However, the RFP typically does not include the EPV because providing such information to the RFP bidders might bias their cost estimates. For instance, a consultant might determine that the most likely cost to complete the Quick Parts Online project is $200,000. If the consultant knows management's EPV, she might "pad" her estimate upward to the point at which she determines that her bid will be competitive. Conversely, if she calculates a realistic project cost of $425,000, she might try to cut corners, which could sacrifice project quality, by submitting an RFP that is at or below the EPV.

Continuing with our example, assume that management has decided to solicit RFP's from three consulting firms. When the RFP's are returned, the cost estimates are as follows: ABC Consulting–$294,000; DEF Consulting–$305,000; HIJ Consulting–$318,000. Now, accepting the lowest bidder would be tempting; however, Quick Parts management must perform due diligence to ensure that ABC Consulting is honest and reliable. Assume that management's investigation in this regard finds that all three firms are known for submitting realistic bids, finishing projects on time, and delivering high quality results. Accordingly, Quick Parts decides to use ABC consulting firm's bid to calculate the net present value (NPV) of the project, as well as the project profitability index (PPI). Recall that the estimated time to complete the project is one year. Hence, Quick Parts must first discount the estimated project cost (EPC), using their desired IRR, and then they can determine the NPV and PPI of the Quick Parts Online project.

The discounted value of the EPC at the end of discount year one is $274,596 ($294,000 × .9340; see Table 5-2). Hence, the net present value (NPV) of the project is $110,316 ($384,912 − $274,596). Since the NPV is positive, management already knows that the project will yield the desired IRR of 7 percent. The PPI will tell management the extent to which the IRR is exceeded. The Quick Parts Online PPI is 1.402 ($384,912/$274,596), indicating that the project is expected to yield 40 percent over the desired IRR. At this point, management would compare the Quick Parts Online PPI to alternative project proposals within the company and decide whether this project should be undertaken. After reviewing the company's project portfolio, Quick Part's management has decided to pursue the Quick Parts Online project and hire ABC Consulting. Next, let's take a look at how ABC Consulting manages (plans, schedules, monitors, and controls) projects.

PLANNING THE PROJECT

Projects are not completed successfully by accident or luck; rather, they are successful because they are well planned and executed. Unfortunately, most projects are poorly planned, if planned at all. Under such circumstances, the seemingly "controlled" project can rapidly degrade into chaos. Once the project outcome and scope are established, the critical project factors that must be planned are time, quality, cost, activities, and resources. Without such planning, things can go terribly wrong.

Example The manager of the "Seal-O-Matic" project is summoned to the client's office. After briefly updating the client on the project's current status, the client yells, "What do you mean the project is running late? It must be completed on time–no excuses!" The project manager responds by saying, "Don't worry. You will have the Seal-O-Matic in your hands on the date we agreed. I guarantee it." Sadly, this is not an uncommon circumstance faced by project managers, nor is it an unusual response.

Tick, tick, tick; the clock is running and things are behind schedule. What to do, what to do? The project manager determines that there are three months of work left on the project, but the deadline is only two months away. Specifically, manufacturing of the Seal-O-Matic can be completed in one month, with another two months of testing planned thereafter. During the first test month, the Seal-O-Matic will be subjected to varying temperature extremes to determine the extent of contraction and expansion over an expected operating temperature range. During the second test month, the Seal-O-Matic will be exposed to temperature ranges that are 50 percent lower and 50 percent higher than normally expected as a way to assess the maximum "safety factor" inherent in the product. Out of frustration and stress, the manager decides to skip the last month of testing because the first test already has a 25 percent safety factor built into the temperature extremes and the client estimates that the probability of exceeding these extremes is less than 1 percent. As you might have guessed, in two months the project manager hands the

Seal-O-Matic over to the client. At this point, the project is successful, the project manager is happy, the client is ecstatic, and the world is a wonderful place.

Four months later, on January 28, 1986, the project manager is driving his car from one client site to another, listening to his favorite music station and singing along to the tunes. Suddenly, the radio announcer interrupts and reports that the space shuttle *Challenger* just exploded 73 seconds after liftoff, claiming the lives of all seven astronauts. The cause was determined to be an O-ring failure in the right solid rocket booster. Unusually cold weather prior to launch was a contributing factor. The O-ring vendor, Seal-O-Matic, has yet to issue any comments.[1]

As demonstrated, an undue emphasis on meeting the time schedule can result in disastrous consequences. The same can be said for insisting that the project be completed at or under budgeted costs. Many times, as the project progresses, good reasons surface for believing that initial cost estimates were incorrect and, in order to ensure the quality of the project outcome, budget overruns may be inevitable. Naturally, the opposite can also be said. That is, there are areas in which project time and costs can be reduced without negatively impacting the outcome. The delicate balance between project efficiency and effectiveness must be methodically managed throughout the project life cycle, as next discussed.

Examining the Project Life Cycle

A project is born to solve a specific problem and the project's life is over when the problem is resolved or the project is abandoned. Projects have a defined life span. This is an important distinction between projects and routine work tasks. Once the problem solution is clearly defined and the scope is meticulously circumscribed, the project must be judiciously managed. The project life cycle, as depicted in Figure 5-1, reflects four essential phases of project management: planning, scheduling, monitoring, and controlling.

The planning phase entails the process of coordinating and regulating activities, time, and resources toward the accomplishment of a specific goal or objective within a specified time period. The operative word in this definition is "process," implying that planning is not a one-time static event; rather, it is an ongoing dynamic force that continually shapes and adapts activities, time, and resources to internal and external environmental conditions.

Notice in Figure 5-1 that project planning details are sent to the scheduling phase, where the sequence and timing of project activities are placed into action. Next, key information regarding the current status of ongoing activities is continuously observed via the monitoring phase, where deviations from planned and actual performance are determined. If a corrective action is deemed necessary, through the controlling phase, the action is transmitted back to the planning phase, where plans are adjusted accordingly and the cycle begins once again.

The feedback loop just described reflects an essential component of sound project management. Without such feedback, the initial plan would be frozen and necessary adjustments to work scope, time, and cost would never occur. As a result, the project would likely degrade into confusion and turmoil. Unfortunately, the vast majority of projects do not make good use of the project management life cycle just described, particularly the feedback loop.

---

[1] The circumstances surrounding the *Challenger* explosion just described are for illustrative purposes only. The authors do not suggest that the events depicted in this text are factual or that the actual O-ring manufacturer was culpable or liable in any way for the shuttle accident.

The lower part of Figure 5-1 indicates that each project is composed of multiple activities, each with its own parameters (tasks, methods, time, and scope), resources, and deliverables. The activities are linked to each other in a predetermined sequence such that each predecessor activity adds value, through its deliverable, to its successor activity. You will learn more about the lower section of Figure 5-1 in upcoming sections. For now, let's continue on with the planning phase of the project life cycle.

Earlier in this chapter, we examined the following tasks constituting the planning phase:

1. Establish the outcome and scope of a project.

2. Determine the project's EPV.

3. Transmit RFP's to internal and external parties who wish to bid on the project, where time and cost boundary conditions are estimated.

4. Calculate the project's NPV and PPI.

5. Select one or more projects from a portfolio of proposals.

In some instances, a project manager is involved in all five steps. This is particularly true if management has already identified the internal or external project manager they want to spearhead the project. However, more often, company management performs these five tasks without the involvement of a project manager, with the exception of the third task in which the prospective project manager prepares the RFP response to management. In this situation, planning, from the project manager's perspective, begins with the third task.

Under either scenario, the chosen or prospective project manager must estimate the project's time and cost estimates by first subdividing the project's workflow into definable and manageable activities. This planning task can be methodically achieved by developing a work breakdown structure (WBS) for the project, as next described.

Understanding the Work Breakdown Structure (WBS)

One of the biggest reasons that "good projects go bad" can be traced to the lack of a detailed comprehensive work breakdown structure (WBS) at the beginning of the project. The WBS is the rock-solid foundation of effective project management, and most of us know what happens when we build a house on sand. The same goes for a project. The WBS helps to answer the critical question, "Precisely what activities must be performed during the project's life cycle?"

The WBS is a hierarchical representation of the project scope. Recall the importance of clearly articulating the project scope early in the planning process. The WBS can only be developed after all scope issues are completely identified and resolved in writing. Once the project scope is clearly defined, the WBS becomes the first step toward the determination of reliable time and cost estimates. In essence, a WBS is developed by subdividing the project into manageable "chunks" of tasks, whereby complicated tasks are broken down into less complicated tasks. The subdividing of tasks continues until the lowest level tasks reflect relatively simple work activities that can be easily defined, planned, scheduled, and monitored. Hence, a WBS is a *structured* way to *break down* the *work* required to complete a project.

Unfortunately, many project managers either do not develop a WBS or they are sloppy and incomplete when doing so. It is not unusual for a project manager to write down a handful of activities that need to get done during the project, assign project personnel and resources to the activities, and run with the project. This approach results in at least two key mistakes. First, the project manager identified the project activities in *isolation*. It is unlikely that any single project manager has intricate knowledge of every aspect of a project. Rather, project managers typically rely on the work of "area experts" to plan and perform most project activities. For instance, say that a project manager is responsible for implementing a large-scale enterprise resource planning (ERP) system for a client. The project will include both software and hardware considerations. How likely is it that a project manager has a firm grasp on all facets of a project of this nature? Instead, most managers will assemble a project team composed of area experts (e.g., performance testing, computer networking, application programming, and user training) and assign appropriate responsibilities to the experts. Since this is the typical *modus operandi* for project managers, why then do so many managers try to develop a WBS by themselves (a rhetorical question with unknown and, perhaps, unknowable answers)? Regardless of their reasons, the planning and development of a WBS should be a team effort, with area experts offering advice and assistance along the way.

The team approach just described helps to avoid the second mistake; specifically, the project manager identified "a handful" of activities to be performed. Since, for the most part, the manager is not an expert in every area of the project, it is highly likely that he or she will omit many critical activities. It is not uncommon for an ERP implementation project to include hundreds, or even thousands, of activities representing months of work and millions of dollars. The lesson learned here should ring loudly—if an activity is not represented on the WBS, it will not be reflected in either the time or cost estimates. Imagine how far off the project timeline and cost budgets would be due to the oversight of tens or hundreds of work activities! Once again, to make sure this does not happen, project managers should take the team approach to developing the WBS.

It is normally appropriate for the project manager to outline the upper-level tasks to be performed on a project, such as systems analysis, design, conversion, and implementation. Perhaps the manager is experienced enough to further break down these tasks one or two levels deeper. However, there comes a point where the manager must call in the area experts to plan the precise nature and work activities that must be accomplished. The involvement of area experts in this regard brings up another benefit of the team approach: the assignment of responsibilities to project team leaders. Since the area experts are often assigned to the project, they can be delegated the primary responsibility of ensuring that work activities falling within their area of expertise are performed efficiently and effectively. Accordingly, the WBS reflects a hierarchical representation of all activities composing the project scope *and* it facilitates the assignment of responsibility for each activity to a specific project team member.

Classifying WBS Types Assume that you have been assigned as the project manager for a software development project. The software applications you develop are expected to serve all functional areas across the entire business organization, much like an ERP suite of applications. The project is named "Completely Integrated, Regulated, Coordinated, & Linked Enterprise Software," or CIRCLES. You have already worked with team members who are experts in the areas of analysis, design, conversion, and implementation to develop the WBS depicted in Figure 5-2. Naturally, the actual WBS for a project of this nature would be much more detailed than the one shown; however, for simplicity's sake, let's assume that Figure 5-2 is the final WBS for the CIRCLES project.

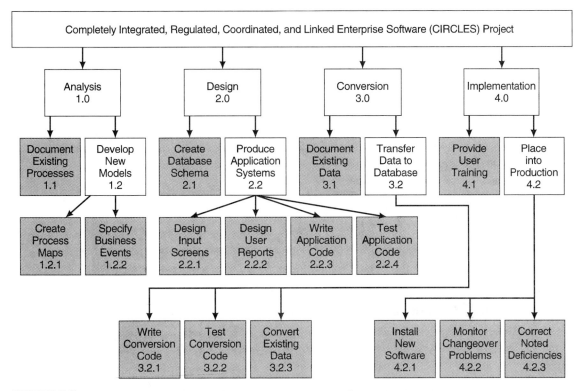

FIGURE 5-2   Function-based work breakdown structure (WBS) for CIRCLES project.

The first issue to think about is the hierarchical outline system used for the WBS. For this example, the outline system uses X.0 for the first level, X.X for the second level, X.X.X for the third level, and so on (where X represents sequential numbers from 1 to *n*). Although there are numerous acceptable outlining conventions (such as purely alphabetic or a mixture of alpha/numeric characters), make sure to choose one that is readily understandable and standardized across the project team. The next consideration is the type of WBS you wish to develop. Basically, there are two types: the function-based WBS and component-based WBS, as discussed in the upcoming two sections.

Profiling a Function-Based WBS   The type of WBS represented in Figure 5-2 is function-based, which represents the subdivision of work tasks by functional area of the project (i.e., analysis, design, conversion, and implementation). The advantages of a function-based WBS are that key functional activities are not likely to be omitted during the development of the WBS and team members in each functional area can focus their efforts solely on their defined areas of responsibility. However, the latter advantage can become a disadvantage, as the function-based WBS can lead to "activity myopia," whereby team members are so focused on their area(s) of responsibility that larger issues involving the project as a whole escape their radar screen.

Example   Referring to Figure 5-2, while working on Activity 3.1 (Document Existing Data), a couple of team members, who happen to be capable programmers in their own right, noticed several technical idiosyncrasies with the client's existing data file structure. However, dealing with the client's file structure was outside of the scope of Activity 3.1, as such issues belonged to

Team 3.2.1 (Write Conversion Code). Nevertheless, due to past experience, the team members knew that, unless the next team (3.2.1) had encountered these technical issues before, it would take a great deal of time to learn how to cope with these problems while writing the conversion code. The team members thought about documenting the file structure abnormalities and suggesting ways to "work around" potential problems in this regard, but doing so would take quite a bit of time, thereby "blowing" the time and cost budget for the 3.1 team. Since the 3.1 team was so intent on completing the deliverable in accordance with preestablished specifications and budgets, receiving a bonus, and moving on to the next activity, the two members who spotted the unusual file structure characteristics simply ignored the topic altogether (oops, activity myopia has struck!). Congratulations were in order, as the 3.1 team completed its activity on time and within budget and handed off the data specifications to the 3.2.1 team. Hooray ... the 3.1 team was rewarded with a bonus for doing such good work!

Meanwhile, as fate would have it, the 3.2.1 team encountered a great deal of difficulty with writing the conversion code, which caused a considerable time delay and cost overrun for activity 3.2.1. Also, the delay severely impacted the project deadline, as the remainder of the conversion activity and the entire implementation activity were waiting for and relying on the conversion code. The ripple effect led to an overall project delay, cost overrun, and, understandably, very unhappy client.

When activity myopia attacks, it becomes difficult to effectively coordinate work activities, provide smooth transitions from one activity to the next, and monitor the overall project quality. However, if the project manager establishes good communications with team leaders and incorporates a reward structure that embodies tactical and strategic considerations, situations like the one just described can be avoided.

Appreciating a Component-Based WBS For a moment, let's turn our attention to a component-based WBS. A simplified schematic of a component-based WBS for the CIRCLES project is shown in Figure 5-3. Notice that the central focus of the columns becomes an observable component of the project, rather than a function. With a component-based WBS, the functions are considered along the horizontal plane. For instance, one observable component of the CIRCLES project is the installation of a client-server computing system. In order to install a client-server system for this project, the client-server team must *analyze* the computing needs, *design* an appropriate client-server architecture, *convert* from the old computing system to the client-server system, and *implement* the client-server system.

This type of WBS works best in a cross-functional team environment, where activity teams are composed of component and functional experts. The advantage of this approach is that cross-functional teams tend to see the "big picture" from analysis through implementation. Thus, they are less likely to feel the insidious effects of activity myopia and more likely to be careful not to skip any steps throughout the process, as the team deliverable (an operating client-server system that will handle the computing workload) will be compromised. Another advantage is that this approach makes it easy to monitor time and cost budgets across project components. One disadvantage is that the management of cross-functional teams can be fragile, as there are team members with varied backgrounds who, many times, do not understand each other. Hence, team intracommunications can be difficult. A second disadvantage is that a project made up of cross-functional teams can result in a larger overall number of team members, as each area must have a variety of component and functional experts on board. Finally, a third disadvantage of component-based cross-functional teams mirrors a disadvantage noted with functional-based teams. That is, the project manager still needs to establish interteam communication systems and reward structures that facilitate cooperation and quality from one team to another.

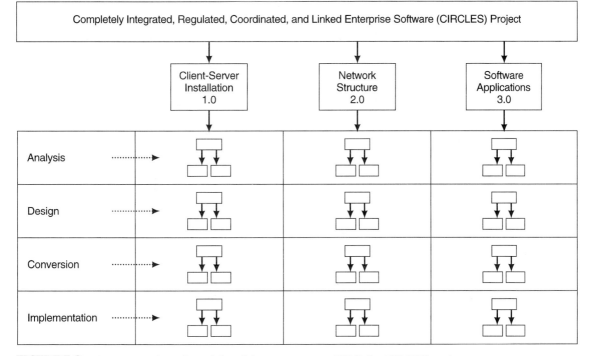

FIGURE 5-3 Component-based work breakdown structure (WBS) for CIRCLES project.

Developing a WBS Referring back to Figure 5-2, assume you have decided that the functional-based WBS is the best strategy for the CIRCLES project. After identifying four major functional areas [analysis (1.0), design (2.0), conversion (3.0), and implementation (4.0)], you call in the experts (i.e., team leaders). You learn from the Analysis' Team Leader that the two major areas of work to consider are "Document Existing Processes" (1.1) and "Develop New Models" (1.2). After discussing the first area of work (1.1), you and the team leader decide that the *parameters* (i.e., tasks, methods, time, and scope) are easily manageable, the *deliverable* can be clearly defined, and appropriate *resources* are available to complete the work. So, you conclude that 1.1 should be designated as an "activity." You now turn your attention to the next area of work "Develop New Models" (1.2). After some debate, you jointly determine that Work Area 1.2 is too complex to stand by itself. Thus, you decide that 1.2 should be further broken down into "Create Process Maps" (1.2.1) and "Specify Business Events" (1.2.2). After lengthy examination, you determine that the parameters, deliverables, and resources for each area of work are manageable and controllable. Therefore, you designate each as an "activity." Next, you go through the same process with the Design (2.0), Conversion (3.0) and Implementation (3.0) Team Leaders, resulting in the WBS shown on Figure 5-2.

A closer examination of Figure 5-2 reveals that shaded boxes represent project "activities" whereas the nonshaded boxes reflect "areas of work," which are intermediary steps leading to activities. As such, activities are considered to be at the *atomic level,* or the lowest level of decomposition. When to designate an area of work as an "activity" is a subjective matter. It depends on the complexity and risk inherent in the area of work. There is no hard-and-fast rule in this regard. Some project managers designate activities by the expected amount of time to complete the work. Depending on the nature of the project, one week, two weeks, or a month might be the dividing line. For instance, if the area of work involves writing computer programs and each routine takes about a week to write and test, the project manager might designate a programming activity by the amount of work that can be accomplished in a week. This way, he or she will insist on a fully functioning program routine as the deliverable on a weekly basis. In another area of work (e.g., documenting user procedures), the project manager might deem that monthly activity reports are sufficient to serve as deliverables. Accordingly, the manager would designate each documenting "activity" by the amount of work that can be accomplished in a month.

Other project managers might determine "activities" by the dollar amount of expenditure required. For example, a manager might decide that no area of work should exceed a given percentage of the total cost of the project. If it does, the area of work must be further subdivided into multiple activities. In this manner, the project manager may be trying to control the risk that the project cost will get out of hand. Thus, the determination of "how low you go" with respect to decomposing areas of work into activities, also referred to as the granularity of the atomic level, depends on the situation.

In determining the precise granularity of activities, the following guidelines are helpful [*note:* these guidelines deal with an activity's parameters (tasks, methods, time, and scope) and assigned resources, as illustrated in Figure 5-1].

1. Once an area of work has been broken down into activities, the project manager and area expert should list each activity's *tasks.* For instance, Activity 4.1 (Provide User Training) on Figure 5-2 might be composed of three tasks: develop training programs, write training materials, and conduct user training.

2. Next, the manager and expert should document preferred *methods* of accomplishing each task. For example, develop training programs might be accomplished by reviewing similar programs offered to other clients and adapting the methods used to the current project.

3. After the tasks and methods are understood, the project manager and area expert are in a good position to estimate the amount of *time* it will take to accomplish each task. Then, by summing the task times, they can derive an estimate of the total time to complete the activity.

4. The project manager and area expert should next list the required *resources* for each activity, delineated by human, equipment, and supply resources needed to accomplish each task. Along with this listing, the estimated dollar amount of expenditures in each area (human, equipment, and supplies) should be estimated on a task-by-task basis. In this manner, the total cost of the activity can be estimated.

5. If the control of overall *project time* is most critical, the time-related *scope* of a given activity should not exceed two times the progress-reporting period. Thus, if the project manager requires progress reports from all team leaders on a weekly basis, the amount of time allocated to any activity should not exceed two weeks.

6. If the control of overall *project cost* is most critical, the cost-related *scope* of a given activity should not exceed 5 to 10 percent of the overall estimated cost of the project.

7. If *both time and cost factors* are equally critical, a combination of the two *scope* guidelines should be used. For example, if the progress reporting period is monthly and an activity is expected to take three weeks to complete, it meets the

first guideline. However, assume that, due to the nature of the activity, it is expected to consume 20 percent of the overall project cost. In this instance, it violates the second guideline; therefore, the project manager should consider subdividing the activity into two or more smaller pieces.

One more observation should be made about the activities shown in Figure 5-2. Notice that each activity begins with a verb, which denotes that some action is taking place. This active documentation style makes it easier to read the WBS and understand what is happening within each activity.

Establishing Activity Deliverables Referring once again to Figure 5-1, we have learned how to plan a project and define an activity. We have also discussed the importance of establishing identifiable deliverables for each activity. Also, as shown in Figure 5-1, the deliverable from a predecessor activity (e.g., Activity 1) becomes a value-added resource input for a successor activity (e.g., Activity 2). As illustrated, it is possible for a single deliverable to become a resource input for more than one activity. For example, say the deliverable for Activity 1 is an architectural model of how the new information system will be built. Activity 2 (e.g., computer programming) would certainly need to know this information, as would Activity 3 (e.g., developing user-training sessions). Some activities also require the deliverables from more than one predecessor activity, as with Activity 4. In this case, the computer programs from Activity 2 and user manuals from Activity 3 are used during the system implementation (e.g., Activity 4).

Earlier in the chapter, we discussed the vital importance of clearly articulating and documenting the project outcome. There should be no ambiguity in this regard. The same can be said for activity deliverables. Naturally, the precise nature of a deliverable depends on the project and the activity. As with the decomposition of areas of work into activities, there are no steadfast rules. However, the guidelines shown below can be useful. Activity deliverables should be:

1. Mutually agreed on (between the project manager and the activity team leader)
2. Clearly defined
3. Fully documented in writing
4. Well communicated to all project team members
5. Delivered on time (unless there are mitigating or extenuating circumstances)
6. Handed off in writing from the predecessor team leader to the successor team leader, indicating a successful transfer of responsibility for the deliverable

We'll continue discussion of project management in the upcoming chapter.

SUMMARY

A project is a system with a limited life span, defined outcome, boundary conditions (work scope, time, and cost), and desired goal (the project outcome). Additionally, a project is comprised of a set of interrelated value-added processes (activities), each with their own boundaries (parameters), inputs (resources), and outputs (deliverables). When viewed through this lens, it becomes quite clear that the very nature of work for accountants is project-centric. As such, learning how to manage projects is a value-added skill set for practicing accountants.

The project management life cycle (shown in Figure 5-1) includes five phases: planning, scheduling, monitoring, controlling, and closing. This chapter focused on the first phase, project planning, which encompasses the following steps:

1. Establishing the outcome and scope of a project.
2. Determining the estimated project value (EPV).
3. Calculating the estimated project cost (EPC), net present value (NPV), and project profitability index (PPI).
4. Developing a work breakdown structure.

There is much more to be accomplished with respect to managing the project. Now that the activities have been identified, along with their deliverables, parameters, and required resources, the next step is to schedule, monitor, and control the activities. These, and other project management considerations, will be discussed and developed in the next chapter.

DISCUSSION QUESTIONS

5-1. Discuss why it is important to make absolutely clear all the terms and conditions related to the desired project outcome in the client engagement letter.

5-2. How does "scope bloat" impact project outcome and client relations?

5-3. Explain why EPV is not typically included in a RFP.

5-4. Explain why undue emphasis on meeting time schedules can result in disastrous consequences.

5-5. Why can the WBS only be developed after all scope issues are completely identified and resolved in writing?

5-6. Identify the two key mistakes project managers make whey they do not develop a WBS. How does the "team approach" avoid these pitfalls?

5-7. What are the advantages of a function-based WBS? Discuss "activity myopia."

5-8. When is the best time to employ a component-based WBS? Why?

5-9. Why is it important to consider the "granularity of activities" when developing a WBS?

5-10. Identify the six characteristics of activity deliverables.

EXERCISES

5-11. You are the general manager of a very large grocery store chain, called Groceries-R-Us. Your chain of stores is investigating the possibility of implementing an automated checkout system, called Quick-Scan, whereby customers merely pass their grocery cart through a scanner (which looks much like a metal detection machine at an airport) and the computer system detects every item in the cart and its price. The Quick-Scan system has the possibility of eliminating all cashiers in your stores. Because the new scanning system will be much faster and more accurate than using cashiers, you have determined that incremental grocery sales arising from new customers over the first five years of operation will be $300,000, $400,000, $450,000, $500,000, and $525,000, respectively. Additionally, Groceries-R-US will save $350,000 in cashier salaries/benefits during the first year of operation (for salaries/benefits savings in operational years two through five, assume that salaries/benefits would increase by 5 percent each year). The initial cost of the Quick-Scan system, which must be paid up front, is $1,500,000 and annual operating costs will be $300,000 for the first year of operation and are expected to increase by 5 percent every year thereafter. It is now November 1, 20XX. Should you decide to purchase the system on January 1, 20YY, the consultants can have it installed and operational by January 1, 20ZZ. The consultants will charge $425,000 to install the system, which would require a $200,000 payment on January 1, 20YY, and a final payment of $225,000 at year-end 20YY. At the end of five years of operation, your company guidelines are that new capital investments must yield a minimum 6 percent internal rate of return.

Required

Perform a quantitative analysis of the Quick-Scan system and write a proposal (in good form) to the board of directors that supports your position whether Groceries-R-Us should implement the Quick-Scan system.

5-12. Referring to Exercise 5.11, assume that your company has just increased the minimum internal rate of return to 7 percent on new capital investments.

Required

Perform a quantitative analysis of the Quick-Scan system and write a proposal (in good form) to the board of directors that supports your position whether Groceries-R-Us should implement the Quick-Scan system.

5-13. You have agreed to become the project manager for the Old Car Restoration project. The client wants you to draw a work breakdown structure (WBS) for the car restoration process, as next described. First, the project team will find a suitable car to restore by searching for a car, inspecting prospect cars, and purchasing the car to restore. Next, the team will separate the body from the frame, remove the drive train (which includes the engine and transmission as a single unit) from the frame, and disassemble remaining components from the frame. At this point, all major car components are now removed from the car's frame, which stands bare. The next step involves rebuilding the car components, which includes restoring the interior, rebuilding the drive train (which involves three separate steps: rebuilding the engine, rebuilding the transmission, and coupling the engine and transmission back together as a single unit), replacing electrical components, repairing the car body, and restoring the car frame. Finally, the car is reassembled by installing the drive train back on the frame (the engine and transmission are a single unit once again), bolting the body on the frame, installing remaining components, and painting the exterior.

Required

Draw a functional work breakdown structure (WBS) for the scenario described above. Use the X.X.X coding structure and highlight the work activities or atomic level tasks.

REFERENCES, RECOMMENDED READINGS, AND WEB SITES

References and Recommended Readings

Baguley, P., *Project Management* (Berkshire, UK: Hodder & Stoughton Educational, 1999).

Betz, K. W., "Communication Is Crucial to Planning," *Energy User News* (April, 1999), pp. 16–19.

Bruns, A., "Taking off and Staying on Track: The Art and Science of Effective Project Management," *Lessons in Leadership* (November, 1999), pp. 23–25.

Cleland, D. I., and L. Ireland, *Project Manager's Portable Handbook* (New York: McGraw-Hill, 2000).

Forsberg, K., and H. Mooz, *Visualizing Project Management* (New York: John Wiley & Sons, 2000).

Gido, J., *Successful Project Management: A Practical Guide for Managers* (Cincinnati, OH: South-Western College Publishing, 1999).

Hutchins, G., "Project Management—The Next Big Thing," *Quality Progress* (November, 1999), pp. 8–11.

Kleiman, C., "Project Management Comes Into Its Own," *Chicago Tribune* (February 14, 1999), pp. 6, 12.

Laufer, A., and E. J. Hoffman, *Project Management Success Stories: Lessons of Project Leaders* (New York: John Wiley & Sons, 2000).

Lewis, J. P., *Fundamentals of Project Management* (New York: American Management Association, 1997).

Lientz, B. P., and K. P. Rea, *Guide to Successful Project Management* (San Diego, CA: Harcourt Brace Professional Publishing, 1999).

Peterson, A. H., "The Evolution of the CFO," *Credit Union Magazine* (May, 1999) pp. 13–14.

Raskin, A., "Task Masters," *Inc. Technology* (March, 1999) pp. 14–15.

Veeneman, B., "Teaching Project Management," *Inside Technology Training* (May, 1999), pp. 4–5.

Wysocki, R. K., R. Beck, Jr., and D. B. Crane, *Effective Project Management* (New York: John Wiley & Sons, 2000).

Web Sites
www.pmi.org (The Project Management Institute)

Chapter 6

Managing the Project—Part Two

Project management has been described as the ability to create the impossible, with the unwilling, against insurmountable odds, under budget, on time, while singing the Battle Hymn of the Republic and drinking a glass of water.

> Ron Black, *The Complete Idiot's Guide to Project Management with Microsoft Project 2000* (Indianapolis, IN: Que, 2000), p. 7

INTRODUCTION

In the last chapter, we discussed the project life cycle and learned how to plan a project. In particular, we emphasized the importance of developing a detailed work breakdown structure (WBS). We discovered that the WBS helps to answer the critical question: "What activities must be performed during the project's life cycle?" We were also able to obtain a reasonable estimate of activity and project costs from the WBS. In this chapter, we will continue to answer key project management questions such as, "In what sequence must the activities be performed?" "Precisely how much will each activity and the project cost?" and "How much time will it take to complete each activity and the project?" Answers to these questions and more can be obtained via critical path analysis.

SCHEDULING THE PROJECT

Although there are several established methods one can use to schedule projects, we will focus on critical path analysis (CPA), which represents an effective technique of scheduling complex projects that include sequential and parallel activities. In essence, CPA determines the maximum length of time it will take to complete a project. It also identifies which activities fall along a path, from the beginning to the end of the project, representing the maximum timeline. This path is referred to as the *critical path.* If time slippage occurs in any of the activities along the critical path, the project will be delayed. Armed with such information, project managers are in a position to continually refine activities, resources, and scope such that the project's timeline and costs are properly controlled. Before taking an in-depth look at CPA, let's step back and briefly review a predecessor to CPA—the Gantt chart.

Understanding the Gantt Chart

In 1908, Henry Laurence Gantt began using horizontal bar charts to graphically display time relationships among work activities. Gantt charts are easy to read and represent an intuitive way to visualize the planning, allocating, and scheduling of work activities and resources. Today, there are various mutations of Gantt's original work, but they all have one thing common—they represent work activities as horizontal bars on a chart.

Example   A sample Gantt chart is shown in Figure 6-1. In this example, the objective of the project is to purchase new computers for a business office. Notice that project activities are listed down the left- hand column and the timeline (in weeks) is shown across the top row. Horizontal bars represent the expected amount of time to complete each activity. It will take over one week to analyze the client's needs (1.0). Afterward, the project manager will purchase the computer equipment (2.0). Since Activity 1.0 must be performed before Activity 2.0, there is a sequential dependency between these activities, such that the former (1.0) must be completed before the latter (2.0) can begin. This type of dependency is called a *finish-to-start* relationship. Next, the computers are installed (3.0). Once again, we see a finish-to-start relationship between *sequential activities* 2.0 and 3.0. User training (4.0) can begin after some computers have been installed, but there is no need to wait until all computers are in place. Hence, there is a sequential dependency between activities 3.0 and 4.0, but the former (3.0) does not have to be completed before the latter (4.0) can begin. This is called a *start-to-start* relationship; the successor activity (4.0) can begin after the start but before the end of the predecessor activity (3.0). Activity 5.0 (test computers) begins after all computers are installed (3.0) but during user training (4.0). However, user training (4.0) and computer testing (5.0) must end simultaneously. Accordingly, Activity 4.0 has a finish-to-start relationship with Activity 3.0. However, Activity 4.0 has no dependent relationship with Activity 5.0. That is, computer testing (5.0) is dependent on computer installation (3.0), but independent from user training (4.0). As such, Activities 4.0 and 5.0 are considered to be independent *parallel activities*. Finally, when the business office transitions from the old to the new computers (6.0), user training (4.0) and computer testing (5.0) must be completed. As such, Activity 6.0 has a finish-to-start relationship with Activities 4.0 and 5.0.

As shown, Gantt charts are easy to read and intuitively appealing. However, there is one serious drawback to Gantt charts. If the schedules of one or more interdependent activities vary from the plan, it is very difficult to determine the impact of such time slippage and cost on subsequent activities and the project as a whole. The remedy for this problem can be found in a scheduling technique known as critical path analysis (CPA). Note, though, that some project scheduling software packages, such as *Microsoft Project*, have incorporated the features of CPA into Gantt charts, as shown in Appendix A.

Introducing Critical Path Analysis (CPA)

CPA was born in the late 1950s as a sophisticated way to plan and control projects. CPA is based on a network portrayal of project activities whereby the sequence of activities and their duration are used to determine a project's most critical path. This identifies the interdependent activities that make up the longest timeline through

Activities	Week 1	Week 2	Week 3	Week 4	Week 5
1.0 Needs Analysis					
2.0 Purchase Computers					
3.0 Install Computers					
4.0 Train Users					
5.0 Test Computers					
6.0 Use New Computers					

FIGURE 6-1   Schematic representation of a Gantt chart.

the project. Two such network techniques, the **C**ritical **P**ath **M**ethod (CPM) and the **P**rogram **E**valuation and **R**eview **T**echnique (PERT), emerged nearly simultaneously. Both techniques fall under the CPA umbrella.

CPM was developed in 1957 in the construction industry. PERT surfaced in 1958 in the defense industry. Use of both techniques is common in all types of construction and civil engineering work, as well as for controlling other large-scale projects such as aircraft, ships, mainframe computer systems, and missiles. For all intents and purposes, the two terms are used interchangeably today. One commonality between the two methods is that they are both designed to handle finish-to-start relationships among activities, as well as parallel activities. However, neither method can deal with start-to-start relationships.

There is another project scheduling method designed to cope with alternate relationship types, such as start-start relationships, called the **P**recedence **D**iagram **M**ethod (PDM). Due to the limited scope of this book, we will not investigate the PDM further in this chapter. However, the PDM is referred to in Appendix A, where we explain how to use a project management software package called *Microsoft Project.*

There is a significant difference between CPM and PERT that you should note. CPM is deterministic, such that the estimated elapsed time for each activity is considered fixed and invariant. For example, during project planning, a project manager might determine that a given activity should take 10 days to complete (CPM does not allow a project manager to say $10 \pm X$ days). On the other hand, PERT introduces variability into the equation by estimating the optimistic, pessimistic, and most likely time it will take to complete each activity based on probability theory. Thus, PERT might calculate that an activity could take 14 days (pessimistic), 10 days (most likely), or 8 days (optimistic) to complete. In this chapter, we will focus on CPM rather than PERT for several reasons. First, it takes a considerable amount of time to explain and absorb the underlying probability theory and *beta* distribution associated with PERT. Second, there is some question regarding the extent to which real-world events can be accurately predicted by the *beta* distribution. Finally, project managers are constantly updating and changing time estimates as projects unfold. Therefore, the incremental value of knowing pessimistic, most likely, and optimistic activity times may be too small to warrant an in-depth study of this technique.

Employing the Critical Path Method (CPM)

The first step in CPM is to develop a work breakdown structure (WBS) for the project.

Example In order to keep the CPM lesson manageable, let's work with the fairly simple WBS shown in Figure 6-2. The project depicted in Figure 6-2 concerns the development of a sales transaction accounting register (STAR) for a small business. In essence, the objective of the STAR project is to develop and install a computer application that will keep track of sales transactions. The project manager and area experts have decided that the project can be easily subdivided into five controllable activities: design prototype (1.0), build system (2.0), train users (3.0), convert data (4.0), and install system (5.0). Once the WBS is created, the next step is to draw a *network diagram* of the activities, which shows the sequence and dependencies of all project activities. However, before doing so, we should standardize the way in which we draw activities, as next discussed.

Designing the Activity-on-Node Network Diagram Although there are many acceptable techniques for illustrating activities in a network diagram, we will use the

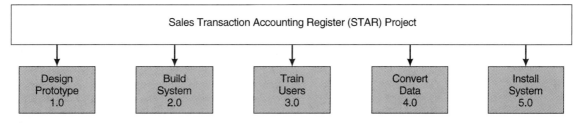

FIGURE 6-2   Abbreviated work breakdown structure (WBS) for the sales transaction accounting register (STAR) project.

one shown in Figure 6-3. Activities will be drawn as rectangles, with the *activity name* and *activity ID* (as reflected by the WBS number) shown in the middle of the rectangle. At the top and bottom of the rectangle are placed the estimated *duration period* and *slack time,* respectively. The activity's *early start* and *early finish* times are entered in the upper left-hand and right-hand corners, respectively. Finally, the activity's *late start* and *late finish* are shown in the lower left-hand and right-hand corners, respectively. The definitions of each italicized term used in this paragraph will become clear as we use CPM in conjunction with the network diagram.

In this chapter, we will focus on an intuitive network diagramming technique called activity-on-node (AON). The STAR project activities have been placed on the AON network diagram shown in Figure 6-4. The rectangles are called nodes, which represent activities; hence, activities are represented on the nodes (AON). The arrows reflect relationships among nodes.

The STAR project begins with Activity 1.0 (Design Prototype). Once the prototype is designed, the system can be built (2.0) and user training (3.0) can begin. Thus, Activities 2.0 and 3.0 are *sequential activities* with respect to Activity 1.0 and they share a *start-to-finish* dependency with Activity 1.0. Activities 2.0 and 3.0 are independent *parallel activities* with respect to each other. Recall from our earlier discussion that CPM can only handle start-to-finish and parallel activity relationships. Activities 3.0 and 4.0 (Convert Data) are sequential with a start-to-finish relationship. Finally, the system can be installed (5.0) only after it is built (2.0) and the data is converted (4.0). Accordingly, Activity 5.0 shares a start-to-finish relationship with both Activities 2.0 and 4.0.

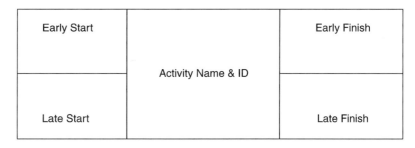

FIGURE 6-3   Standardized template for illustrating activities.

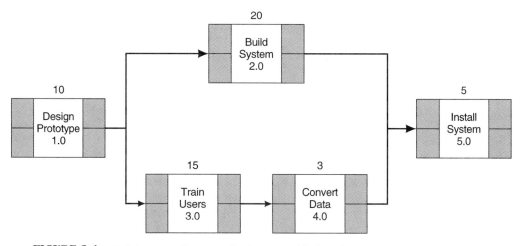

FIGURE 6-4 Activity-on-node network diagram with durations.

The estimated number of days it will take to complete each activity (Duration Period) is placed at the top center of each node. For example, the project manager estimates that it will take 10 days to complete the first activity (1.0). The duration period can be stated in terms of minutes, hours, days, weeks, and so on, depending on the nature of the project.

Calculating Early Start and Early Finish Times The next step in building the AON network diagram is to calculate early start and early finish times, which reflects the earliest times that each activity must start and finish if the entire project is to be completed on time. This can be accomplished using a technique called "Forward Pass," as illustrated on Figure 6-5.

The forward pass technique begins with the first activity in a network (1.0) and proceeds from the left side to the right side of the diagram, following the arrows

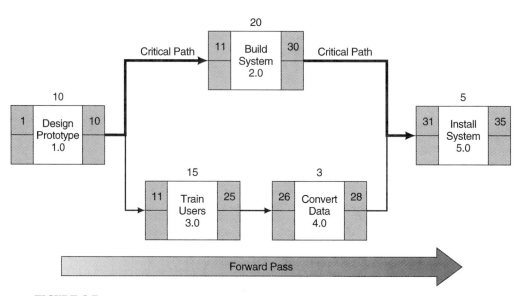

FIGURE 6-5 Activity-on-node network diagram with early starts and early finishes.

from predecessor activities to successor activities. In the first node (Activity 1.0), the early start begins with the first day of the project (Day 1) and should be completed on Day 10 (early finish), since the duration period of the activity is expected to be 10 days. The formula for determining an early finish is as follows:

$$\text{Early Finish} = \text{Early Start} + \text{Duration Time} - 1 \qquad (1)$$

Next, we will assume that if a predecessor activity ends on a given day, the successor activity can't begin until the next day. Moving from Activities 1.0 to 2.0, we find that Activity 2.0 can begin as early as Day 11 (early start). Thus, the following formula is used:

$$\text{Early Start} = \text{Predecessor's Early Finish} + 1 \qquad (2)$$

Since the duration of Activity 2.0 is 20 days, it should end on Day 30 (early finish). Now, let's turn our attention to the relationship between Activities 1.0 and 3.0. Activity 3.0 can start as early as Day 11 (early start) and finish as early as Day 25 (early finish), as its duration is estimated to be 15 days. Moving from Activity 3.0 to 4.0, since the early finish for 3.0 is Day 25, the early start for 4.0 is Day 26. The early finish for Activity 4.0 is on Day 28, since the elapsed time is three days.

At this point, we must determine the early start and early finish for Activity 5.0 (Install System). To determine the early start for nodes having more than one predecessor, such as Activity 5.0, one must determine the longest path to the node. For example, it will take 30 days to complete both Activities 1.0 and 2.0 (10 days + 20 days), while it will take 28 total days to complete Activities 1.0, 3.0, and 4.0 (10 days + 15 days + 3 days). Thus, the longest path to Activity 5.0 runs through Activities 1.0 and 2.0. Focusing on the longest path, we can determine the early start of Activity 5.0 by using the early finish of its predecessor node on the path (2.0). This means that Activity 5.0 can't begin until Day 31 (early start) and could end as early as Day 3 (early finish), based on its duration of five days. (See Figure 6-6.)

The critical path has now been identified. That is, barring any time slippage, it will take 35 days to complete the STAR project. The critical path represents all activities located along the path that constitutes the maximum expected completion time. In our example, Activities 1.0, 2.0, and 5.0 fall on the critical path. This means that if any time slippage occurs in these activities, the project will be late. However, Activities 3.0 and 4.0 could slip somewhat without compromising the project's deadline, as next discussed.

Determining Late Start and Late Finish Time   You use the backward pass technique to calculate the latest times at which activities might start and finish, while holding the total project time constant. As the term backward pass indicates, we begin with the extreme right-hand node and follow the arrows (or paths) backward through the network diagram. It's easiest to first calculate the late start and late finish times for activities along the critical path.

Starting with Activity 5.0, the latest time this activity can start and finish happens to be the same as the early start and early finish times. This is not a coincidence; rather, it occurs because Activity 5.0 must be completed on Day 35. So, the first step in the backward pass is to set the late finish of the final activity equal to the early finish. In our example, the late finish of activity 5.0 will be Day 35. Then, you can calculate the late start using the following formula:

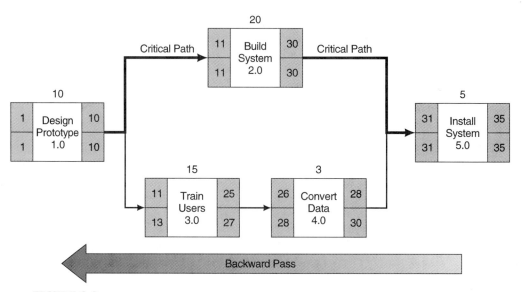

FIGURE 6-6 Activity-on-node network diagram with late starts and late finishes.

$$\text{Late Start} = \text{Late Finish} - \text{Duration Time} + 1 \qquad (3)$$

Hence, the latest day on which Activity 5.0 can start must be Day 31 (35 – 5 + 1). There is a pattern emerging. Specifically, for all activities along the critical path, the early start and late start times will be the same, as will the early finish and late finish times. Once again, this indicates that there is no room for time slippage for any activities along the critical path if the project is to be completed on time.

Now, let's move along the noncritical path from Activities 5.0 to 4.0. If the late start time for Activity 5.0 is Day 31, the latest finish for Activity 4.0 is Day 30 (one day before the late start of 5.0). Hence, the late finish of predecessor activities can be determined accordingly:

$$\text{Predecessor's Late Finish} = \text{Successor's Late Start} - 1 \qquad (4)$$

Since the duration of Activity 4.0 is 3 days, its late start time is Day 28 (30 – 3 + 1). Moving backward to Activity 3.0, its late finish falls on Day 27 (since the late start for 4.0 is Day 28), and the late start for Activity 3.0 is on Day 12 (27 – 15 + 1), since its duration is 15 days. We have now determined that there is some slippage built into activities that do not fall along the critical path, but no slippage for these activities on the critical path. The next step is to better understand the concept of time slippage, or slack.

Investigating Slack Time and Contingency Time As with the determination of late start and finish times, it's easy to calculate slack along the critical path, since there is none. Accordingly, slack time is always zero (0) for activities along the critical path, as shown in Figure 6-7.

To determine the amount of slack associated with noncritical path activities, subtract the late finish from the early finish. In our example, the slack built into Activity 3.0 and 4.0 is two days each. The calculation of slack time is reflected in the formula shown below:

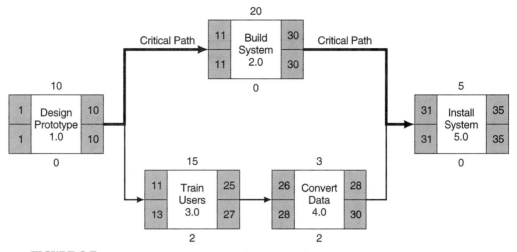

FIGURE 6-7   Activity-on-node network diagram with slack.

$$\text{Slack Time} = \text{Late Finish} - \text{Early Finish} \qquad (5)$$

Let's examine the interpretation of slack time at the activity and project levels. The slack time built into Activities 3.0 and 4.0 does not mean that both activities could slip by two days and the project will stay on track. Assume that Activity 3.0 slips by exactly two days. This means that Activity 4.0 will begin on its late start day (28) and there is no longer any slack left for this activity. Accordingly, slack time used by a predecessor activity (not on the critical path) is deducted from slack time for all successor activities on the same noncritical path. If Activity 3.0 is completed on time, then Activity 4.0 could be finished in five days, rather than three days, without harming the project's timeline. This should not imply that any excess slack should be absorbed by the last activity on the noncritical path. Rather, any slack time gained can be used to allocate idle resources to activities on the critical path or to another project.

This brings up an interesting issue. How precise are the estimated duration times provided by area experts? This topic deals with a cousin of slack time—*padded duration time* (a.k.a. contingency time). Assume that you're an area expert and a project manager asks you how long it will take to complete an activity for which you are responsible. Let's say that you really believe the activity could be completed in 11 days. However, because you can't predict exactly how long it will take, due to unanticipated delays, you "fudge" by telling the project manager that the activity will take 15 days. By doing so, you've padded your estimate by an extra four days of contingency time. If every area expert incorporates this type of "padding" into all activities, think of how much inefficiency is built into the entire project! Not only will the project time become inflated, so will the associated costs. Also, if the area experts pad their estimates for contingencies at the activity level, *Parkinson's Law* (work expands to fill available time) is bound to flourish. Meaning, if an activity is scheduled to take 15 days, even though it could be completed in 11, it will likely take 15 days—regardless of the circumstances.

One way to avoid the "padding" problem is to develop an incentive/reward system that fosters honest reporting. This way, if an activity is delayed for some reason, the area expert will not be afraid to tell the project manager. Rather, both individuals would work together to resolve the problem and revise the plan. Naturally, with such a tight timeline, if something does go wrong in one or more activities, the project manager could be in trouble with the client. To avoid this situation, a project manager should include a "dummy" activity at the end of the network diagram that anticipates a certain amount of contingency time. In this manner, the project manager, project team, and client all know how much contingency time is built into the plan and can monitor its usage as the project unfolds. Even though the project's time and cost estimates are still inflated using this method, at least all parties are aware of the extent to which such contingency time is adding to the project and, if things go well, time and cost saving could result by the end of the project. In this manner, if the project is completed on time (including the built-in contingency time), the project manager, project team, and client are satisfied because there is no negative surprise. However, if the project is finished ahead of time, due to unused contingency time, the positive outcome leaves everyone ecstatic.

Back to our example—assume that activity duration estimates for the STAR project each include an extra day of "padding" by area experts for contingencies. After the project manager explains the importance of honest reporting and incorporates an inventive/reward scheme that induces truthfulness in this regard, the area experts admit to their padding. The project manager then revises and recalculates the network diagram as shown in Figure 6-8.

Notice that the noncritical path activities (3.0 and 4.0) are now reduced to a single day of slack. This means that either Activity 3.0 or 4.0 (but not both) could slip by one day on their duration estimate without negatively impacting the project's completion on Day 35. If things go as planned with respect to Activities 1.0, 2.0, and 5.0, the project could finish ahead of schedule on Day 32. However, if unexpected delays occur along the critical path, three days of lag would still bring the project in on Day 35. Building contingency time into the project in this manner provides a great deal of control with respect to the management of unexpected delays.

There are many more intricacies and nuances associated with fine-tuning a CPA-based network diagram. However, due to the limited scope of this book, we will not go deeper into these areas. If you are interested in furthering your understanding of CPA, many project management books are devoted specifically to the CPM, PERT, and

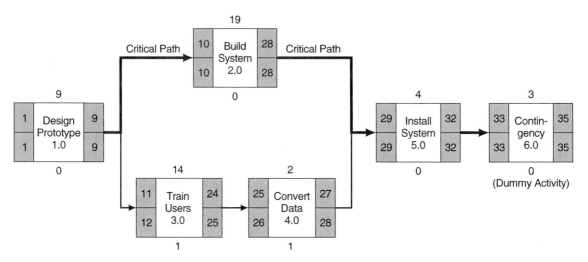

FIGURE 6-8 Activity-on-node network diagram with slack and contingency time.

PDM. There are also many project management software packages that include CPA. As shown in Appendix A, *Microsoft Project* incorporates components of CPM, PERT, PDM, and Gantt charts into its project management software. At this point, we will turn our attention to the resource side of the equation.

Assigning Activity-Level Resources

In the last chapter (Project Management—Part I), we discussed activity-level parameters (tasks, methods, time, and scope). Also, we emphasized the importance of preliminarily identifying activity-level resources while developing the WBS as a way to estimate the project cost. At this point, we'll refine our method of allocating resources and determining costs at the activity-level by preparing an activity-level resource allocation sheet detailing the types of resources needed for the project, along with the cost of using the resources. A sample allocation sheet is shown in Figure 6-9.

In Figure 6-9, the top of the activity-level resource allocation sheet includes the project name, project manager, activity name, activity WBS number, and the activity team leader. Also notice that the activity is subdivided into two tasks: analyze client needs and build prototype. For some projects, these two tasks might represent two activities. However, given the restricted scope and complexity of the STAR project,

Project Name:	STAR Project				
Project Manager:	Never Late				
Activity Name:	Design Prototype		Activity WBS Number:	1.0	
Activity Team Leader:	Honest Abe				

Resource Name	Resource Type	Unit of Measure	Unit Rate	Allocated Units	Resource Cost
Task: Analyze Client Needs					
Systems Analyst	Labor	Hourly	$45.00	50.0	$2,250.00
Computers	Equipment	Hourly	$5.00	50.0	250.00
Other	Supplies	Box	$25.00	1	25.00
Task Total					$2,525.00
Task: Build Prototype					
Programmer	Labor	Hourly	$30.00	100.0	$3,000.00
Computers	Equipment	Hourly	$5.00	100.0	500.00
Other	Supplies	Box	$25.00	2.0	50.00
Task Total					$3,550.00
Total Activity Cost					**$6,075.00**

FIGURE 6-9 Activity-level resource allocation sheet.

the project manager and activity team leader (a.k.a. area expert) decided that both tasks could be easily managed and controlled in this manner.

The first column shows the resource name. The sample sheet doesn't indicate specific names of individuals; rather, it reflects general categories of human resources. For example, systems analysts and programmers are represented as distinct human resource categories. Naturally, if the project manager and activity team leader wish, they could enter the specific names individuals assigned to the activity rather than generic categories. Computers have been identified as another needed resource. Inclusion of the computer category suggests that computer equipment is allocated to activities on a charge-back basis. Finally, the "other" category reflects miscellaneous expenditures.

The next column, Resource Type, specifies whether a resource is labor, equipment, or supplies. The Unit of Measure column reflects the allocation basis of the resource, such as hours, gallons, pounds, and so on. In our example, supplies are allocated by the box, which includes a predetermined amount of pens, paper, staples, and so on. The Unit Rate column shows the dollar amount that will be charged for the resource per unit. The Allocated Unit column reflects the estimated amount of resource units needed for the activity. For instance, the first task associated with Activity 1.0 (Analyze Client Needs) will require 50 hours of systems analyst time. Additionally, 50 hours of computer time and one box of supplies are allocated to this task. The final column, Resource Cost, is obtained by multiplying the unit rate times the allocated units. After activity-level resources have been identified and estimated, the sum of the Resource Cost column represents the total activity cost. Naturally, other resource cost factors might be added to activities, such as overhead. When all activity costs have been estimated, they can be summed to obtain an estimated cost for the entire project.

Rather than keeping manual sheets for each activity, it would much more efficient to set up an electronic spreadsheet that automatically updates activity and project totals each time a change is made at the activity level. Additionally, there are a number of project management software applications that include asset allocation features. As illustrated in Appendix A, *Microsoft Project* neatly automates the resource allocation and tracking process.

Once a project has been initially scheduled, the work begins and the project must be constantly monitored, as we explain next.

MONITORING THE PROJECT

Now that the project is under way, the project schedule we just developed serves as a guideline to steer actual events as they unfold. At this point, the project manager must be fully cognizant of reality, such that the plan is not viewed as a fixed model, but a fluid framework. Too many times, plans become frozen and project managers either lose control of their projects as time marches on, or they try to force the initial plan into future events (does the concept of a square peg and a round hole come to mind?). Either course of action or inaction is a recipe for disaster.

> **Example** Think about the intense planning and training that goes into a sports team prior to the start of the season. The coaches and players develop a "play book" filled with perfectly choreographed movements. The offensive and defensive coaches string together a series of con-

secutive plays that are bound to result in scoring—nothing can go wrong because the plan is flawless! Soon, the season begins and the hometown crowd is excited. The lights are dimmed and each hometown player is introduced. The crowd is super-energized and the players are confident. Next, the opposing team enters, the lights go up, "Boos" can be heard from the stands, and the play begins. The hometown starts on the offense. The first play is perfectly performed. Yeah, the second play worked marvelously. Wow, the third play is fabulously executed; *oh no*, the defending team didn't respond in accordance with the "plan" and things went terribly wrong. Suddenly, the hometown team is confused. "How could this happen?" yells the offensive coach. "I had the perfect plan. Our next play won't work now because the situation has changed and I didn't count on things turning out this way." The coach can ignore what just happened and run the next play in the "planned" sequence or modify the upcoming play to accommodate for the new situation. As you can imagine, making the former choice would likely be a costly mistake.

Project managers constantly face similar situations. They must prudently and timely respond to real-world circumstances and complications. The first step in determining the extent to which actual events are operating in accordance with plan is to *monitor* the project. Referring to Figure 5-1, which shows the project management life cycle, notice the arrow pointing from the activities to the monitoring phase. This arrow represents a continuous flow of information from project activities as time and work progress. Monitoring involves two basic steps:

1. Information regarding the "actual" status of activities must be *collected* on a periodic basis.
2. The "actual" information must be *compared* against the "plan" to determine the nature and magnitude of variances.

The questions at this point are: "How often should monitoring take place?" and "What should be monitored?" We will not provide answers to these questions.

Establishing the Monitoring Cycle

Let's tackle the first question. The determination of how frequently monitoring should take place follows a fairly simple rule:

> **Guideline**   The period of time it takes to *collect* and *compare* activity information (i.e., the monitoring cycle) must be compressed to the point at which the project manager has adequate time to *analyze* the situation and *respond* appropriately.

As stated, the term "cycle" refers to the period of time it takes to *collect* and *compare* activity information. The subject of *analyzing* and *responding* after each monitoring cycle will be dealt with in the next section. For now, we will focus on the monitoring cycle only.

The cycle time granularity depends on the nature of the project.

> **Example**   Take, for instance, a missile guidance system. Suppose a ground-based missile is shot into the air with the objective of hitting a fast-moving jet fighter. As the missile is fired, the fighter is moving away, taking evasive action. The missile guidance system must monitor the jet by *collecting* information pertaining to the fighter's current state (e.g., time, speed, distance, altitude, and location) and *comparing* this information to the missile's current state (e.g., time, speed, distance, altitude, and location). The question is "How often should such monitoring take

place?" The answer depends on the relative speed, acceleration, location, and agility of the jet and the missile.

Say the missile is five miles away from the jet fighter and closing on the fighter at a rate of one mile per second. In five short seconds, the missile could impact the jet fighter, unless the fighter changes something in the meantime. Now suppose that the fighter begins to accelerate at a rapid rate while performing evasive maneuvers. Under these circumstances, the missile guidance system might need to monitor the fighter every nanosecond in order to *collect* and *compare* relevant information quickly enough that the missile's computer system can analyze the situation and react in sufficient time to overtake the jet.

Let's now assume that the missile is aimed at a building, rather than a fighter jet. Because the building is stationary, the guidance system need only monitor the missile's movement. Thus, the monitoring cycle (*collecting* and *comparing* flight information) could be reduced to, say, every second. Since the objectives and circumstances changed in both scenarios just described, the monitoring cycle for the former scenario was one *billion* times smaller than the latter scenario.

As illustrated by this example, project managers need to monitor project activities frequently enough that they can effectively analyze and respond to changing conditions. For a three-year bridge construction project, the monitoring period might be monthly, because the construction firm has built several bridges like this in the past and knows that events are not going to get so far out of hand in a month that the project will be compromised. However, for a three-year space vehicle construction project, the monitoring period might be weekly, because too many complications can arise within a month that could cripple the entire project.

As just discussed, the exact frequency of the monitoring period is highly contextual in nature—it depends on the situation. Thus, there are few rules in this regard. However, the following guideline can be helpful:

Guideline A common way to set the monitoring period is to establish milestones (based on certain dates, events, or both) that are used to mark the progress of the project over time. Often, milestones are set at the end of each activity along the critical path. Therefore, projects needing more frequent monitoring should set the granularity of activities small enough that the duration of each activity coincides with the monitoring cycle time.

Measuring Activity Performance

The second aspect of monitoring concerns "what" to monitor. In essence, a project manager should be able to make at least three determinations at each milestone:

1. The *cost* incurred by the activity.
2. The *quantity* of work performed.
3. The *quality* of work performed.

The first factor (cost) is relatively easy to determine at any given point in time. Referring once again to Figures 6-8 and 6-9, the planned duration of Activity 1.0 is 9 workdays. Assume a monitoring cycle of every five workdays. Also assume that the first task, Analyze Client Needs, can be completed in five workdays, according to plan. Thus, the planned cost at the end of the monitoring period is $2,525. At the end of the first monitoring period the activity leader tabulates the following actual costs to date: Systems Analyst = $2,500, Computers = $250, and Supplies = $25.00 (Total = $2,775). No other activities have begun at this point and the project is already $250 over plan ($2,525 plan less $2,500 actual).

The second factor (quantity) can be determined by assessing the amount of work that should have been accomplished during the monitoring period, based on prespecified metrics. For instance, if the monitoring period is every five workdays and each programmer is expected to write 100 lines of code per day, three programmers should produce 1,500 lines of code during the monitoring period (3 programmers × 100 lines per day × 5 workdays). If they wrote only 1,200 lines of code instead, the manager could determine the following with regard to the quantity of work performed:

1. Plan = 5 days (the duration of the monitoring cycle)
2. Actual = 4 days (1,200 lines of code divided by 300)

   (3 programmers at 100 lines each per day)
3. Variance = –1 day (4 actual days of work less 5 planned days of work)

The third factor (quality of work) can be quite difficult to measure. Although there are numerous ways to assess quality, one technique is to determine the "best practices" or "benchmarks" against which activity work will be evaluated. Then, the difference between actual and planned quality can be assessed. For instance, assume that programming quality is determined by the *completeness* of program documentation and the *speed* at which the programs run. An independent party (judge) who, through experience, understands the best way to document programs (best practices) could assess the first aspect of quality. The second quality aspect could be determined using a known standard, such as the speed (measured in mega bits per second or mbps) at which similar programs should process data in the client's computing environment based on extensive pilot testing (benchmarking). Then, using 100 percent as the highest quality level, the judge might score the documentation at 90 percent and performance test might assess the processing speed at 95 percent (actual speed of 190 mbps second divided by benchmark speed of 200 mbps). Assuming that each aspect of quality is equally important, programming quality is deemed to be 97.5 percent (90 percent + 95 percent) divided by two.

For activities on the critical path, the activity deliverable, established while developing the WBS, can be used to evaluate the quantity and quality of work during the monitoring cycle, particularly if the duration of the activity and the monitoring cycle are congruent. However, not all activities neatly end at the marking of a milestone, especially activities located on noncritical paths. With regard to such activities, milestone deliverables become *progress reports,* which should be specific enough that the project manager can assess the activities' costs, quantity of work, and quality of work during the monitoring period.

Documenting the Monitoring Cycle

After collecting activity information, a project manager can use a form similar to the one shown in Figure 6-10 to document the information collected and compared. In Figure 6-10, the project name, project manager, and monitoring period are shown along the top (the monitoring period for the STAR project was determined to be five working days). Since the monitoring report reflects Days 11 through 15, there must have been two prior reports (Days 1 through 5, and Days 6 through 10), as reflected by Monitoring Report Number 3 (also shown on top of the form).

Project Name:	STAR Project		
Project Manager:	Never Late		
Monitoring Period:	Day 11 through Day 15	Monitoring Report #	3

WBS #	Activity Name	Cost (Dollars)			Quantity of Work (Days)			Quality of Work (Percentage)		
		Plan	Actual	Var	Plan	Actual	Var	Plan	Actual	Var
1.0	Design Prototype	6,075	7,859	−1,784	9	11	−2	100	97	−3
2.0	Build System	2,495	2,086	409	5	6	−1	100	110	0
3.0	Train Users	1,892	1,948	−56	5	5	0	100	90	−10
4.0	Convert Data	−	−	−	−	−	−	−	−	−
5.0	Install System	−	−	−	−	−	−	−	−	−
6.0	Contingency Time	−	−	−	3	−	3	−	−	−
Period Status		4,387	4,034	353	10	11	−1	100	95	−5
Project Status		10,462	11,893	−1,431	22	22	0	100	96	−4

FIGURE 6-10   Monitoring comparison of actual and planned performance report.

The columns reflect WBS numbers assigned to activities, activity names, cost dollars, quantity of work measures, and quality of work assessments. The rows list all activities constituting the STAR project. The shaded row associated with Activity 1.0 indicates that the activity had been completed throughout the monitoring cycle reported. The "Contingency Time" activity (6.0) is always shaded, as it represents a dummy activity. The "Period Status" row sums the performance metrics associated with the current monitoring period (Days 11 through 15), while the "Project Status" row reports cumulative performance results from first day of the project (Day 1) through the end of the monitoring period (Day 15).

The columns labeled "Var" denote the variance from plan to actual performance. For example, Activity 2.0 should have spent $2,495 over the monitoring period; however, actual spending for the period was only $2,086. Accordingly, the result is a positive variance (i.e., actual expenditures were less than planned) of $409. The other columns can be interpreted in a corresponding manner. The period status row shows the summation of Activities 2.0 and 3.0, since these were the only activities engaged in project work during the monitoring period. For instance, actual expenditures for the period were **under** plan by $353 ($4,387 planned − $4,034 actual). The project status row sums all data in each column. Notice that the variance for "quantity of work" in the project status row is zero. This means that all contingency time has been consumed at this point in the project.

The next phase of the project management life cycle involves *analyzing* and *responding* to the current situation. If certain actual-to-plan variances are beyond prespecified limits, the project manager must decide what to do, as next discussed.

CONTROLLING THE PROJECT

The next phase in the Project Management Life Cycle (see Figure 6-1), after monitoring, is the Controlling Phase. When unacceptable actual-to-budget variances occur, responsive actions taken can impact the project's time, cost, and scope. The number and nature of alternative courses of action available to the project manager are often dictated by circumstances. Hence, identifying and making the "correct" choice is seldom easy.

The term "unacceptable" needs some clarification. Suppose an activity's planned cost is $150,000 and the actual cost is $151,000. Is this unfavorable variance ($1,000) acceptable? The answer is likely YES; however, the acceptability, or tolerance level, of time, cost, or scope variances depends on the circumstances. This issue receives a great deal of attention in the area of financial auditing, when the question is "How *material* must a variance be before the auditor insists on an adjusting entry?" As with auditing, the acceptability, or materiality level, of actual-to-plan variances in a project setting is highly subjective and contextual. The following guideline might help:

> *Guideline*   The project manager and client should jointly establish tolerance levels with respect to time, cost, and scope variances before the project begins. This way, as the project unfolds, a project manager will know when to attend to such variances during the controlling phase of the project management life cycle.

Deciding What to Do

There's a natural tug-of-war going on among the project's time, cost, and scope factors, such that a change in one factor generally impacts one or both of the other factors. For instance, referring to Figure 6-8, assume that Activity 1.0 of the STAR project (Design Prototype) finished five days over budget (on Project Day 14), while the activity's cost and deliverable fell within planned specifications. Since this activity is on the critical path, the unfavorable time variance will impact the entire project; thus, it demands attention. The project manager has built in three days of contingency time at the end of the project. Therefore, the net impact on the project's timeline is reduced to two days (five-day unfavorable time variance less three-day contingency time).

The first choice available to the project manager is to do nothing. If this inaction is taken, the whole project is likely to slip by two days. Perhaps the client is more concerned about the project's cost and scope than the deadline. If so, the "do nothing" option might be appropriate. Let's look at other alternatives.

Another choice is for the manager to add more resources to Activity 2.0 (Build System). Currently, assume that Activity 2.0 includes three (3) programmers working eight (8) hours per day for 19 workdays. This equates to 456 programming hours. In order to trim two days off from Activity 2.0, either one or more of the current programmers could work a total of 48 hours overtime (2 days × 8 hours × 3 programmers) by the end of Project Day 28. Alternatively, you could add a fourth programmer for six workdays (6 days × 8 hours) by the end of Project Day 28. Of course, if the project manager wants to trim more than two days off from Activity 2.0 (to gain back some contingency time), the overtime hours or additional programmer hours go up accordingly. The overtime option might work, but then again it might not due to the added stress and marginally diminished productivity of the programmers during overtime. The second option might also work, but once again it might not because the nature of the programming activity may not be conducive to adding another programmer in midstream due to a steep learning curve. Besides, there may not be another qualified programmer available. In the final analysis, if the overtime option works, the activity and project costs will rise. If the additional programmer option works, a project manager might be able to recover from the lost time at no additional cost (because the activity would still consume a total of 456 hours of programming). However, the additional programmer option would likely increase costs somewhat due to "learning curve" effects; a new programmer likely would not be as productive as the other three programmers in the beginning.

Once again, it should be noted that merely adding more resources to an activity might not compress activity time, depending on the nature of the activity. In fact, more resources might slow things down or harm the quality of the activity's deliverable. For instance, adding another programmer to Activity 2.0 might trigger serious coordination, control, and morale problems among programming team members such that their accuracy and speed deteriorates.

Yet another choice facing the project manager involves cutting the project's scope. For instance, suppose the project manager, once informed of the five-day time delay by Activity 1.0, informed the client. After some consideration, the client told the manager that the project's deadline of 35 days was immovable and, further, that cost overruns must be kept to no more than 10 percent. After calculating the impact of a 10 percent cost overrun on Activity 2.0 (the project manager decided that the overtime option was the only viable choice), the project would still finish one day beyond the deadline, on Day 36. After a briefing by the project manager, the client was willing to cut the scope in order to finish on time. At this point, the project manager can either cut the scope in Activity 2.0, 5.0, or both, since they fall on the critical path. After conferring with area experts, the project manager decided to eliminate some of the more elegant programming features initially designed into the software application, which saved another day from Activity 2.0. Further, by adding another installer to Activity 5.0 (Install System), the activity's duration could be cut from four to three days. After another client briefing, everyone agreed to the changes. However, it is important to recognize that the scope was reduced and project costs rose in order to meet the project's initial deadline.

As illustrated in this example, when the project begins to deviate from plan, nearly all choices impact the project's scope, cost, and time. Hence, the client must become involved at this point because, ultimately, the client must determine priorities among scope, time, and cost.

> *Guideline*   The nature and number of alternative choices available to project managers with respect to taking corrective action depend on the circumstances. Accordingly, there is no formula-based method for anticipating the nature and extent of problems and solutions that may arise during a project. However, one thing is clear: corrective decisions nearly always involve tradeoffs among the project's time, cost, and scope.

Viewing the Feedback Process

Finally, referring to Figure 5-1 (The Project Management Life Cycle), notice the dashed line from the Controlling Phase to the Planning Phase. This line represents a *feedback loop,* whereby corrective actions are reintroduced through the Planning

Phase, such that the WBS and CPA-based network diagram are changed accordingly. The revised plan and schedule then become the new baseline on which future performance is compared. This observation leads to the following definitions:

> ***Feedback Loop*** The process of monitoring (*collecting* actual information and *comparing* to plan information) project activities, controlling (*analyzing* the situation and *responding* appropriately) unacceptable variances, adjusting the project plan to accommodate changes, and revising the activity schedule accordingly.

> ***Feedback Cycle Time*** The feedback cycle time is a period sufficient to allow the project manager to monitor actual conditions, control unacceptable variances, adjust the project plan, and revise the activity schedule such that the project remains manageable at all times.

As indicated in the definitions, managing a project is a living process, not a static display. The last phase in the Project Management Life Cycle is discussed next.

Closing the Project

All projects end! Many projects fail, some die of benign neglect, and a few are completed. However, regardless of the nature of the project's termination, remember, "It ain't over till it's over." Meaning, after the partying has stopped and the guests have gone home, the cleanup begins. The major issues to be resolved pertain to project personnel, project assets, client acceptance, project evaluation, and information archive.

Project Personnel Consulting project team members are typically reassigned to other projects or duties with the project's completion. Before disbanding the team, a project manager should debrief all personnel who worked on the project—even those who came and left *during* the project. The debriefing should include a recapitulation of the project from beginning to end. The good, the bad, and the ugly should be exposed because it is often very instructive to learn from mistakes as well as successes. A suggested forum for such a debriefing might be an informal dinner or an afternoon outing of some nature. During the debriefing, awards could be handed out, the project and team leaders could be "roasted," and other fun activities could take place. This is a great way to bring some closure to project personnel who have formed relationships with one another during the course of the project. Let's not minimize the importance of such affairs to people who worked on the project, as the human relation side of the equation is immensely important to all projects.

Project Assets During the course of a project, assets may be borrowed, purchased, leased, or rented. These assets need to be returned, sold, or reassigned on the project's completion.

Client Acceptance The client should sign off on a project's deliverables, thereby formally accepting ownership. If the client and project manager have worked together throughout the project, a formal acceptance of this nature signifies that the client agrees to accept the deliverable, however compromised it may be from the initial plan.

Post-Project Evaluation The post-project can be executed on two fronts. First, an independent third party, such as a peer reviewer, can audit the project. The auditor would be looking to see how such issues as cost overruns, scope changes, and timeline revisions arose and were resolved. The auditor could summarize "best practices" for future reference, as well as areas of improvement. Second, the project manager could request "360-degree" evaluations from the project team. That is, superiors would evaluate the subordinates, subordinates would evaluate superiors, and peers would evaluate peers. An all-encompassing review process of this nature is beneficial for all involved. Consulting firm management can use the information gleaned from post-project evaluations to improve the firm's operating, evaluating, training, and recruiting methods.

Information Archive The project's history should be preserved for future reference. In the beginning, the project manager should establish a project database to chronicle the life and times of the project. For instance, one might use groupware, such as Lotus Notes, to keep track of all correspondence, meetings, plans, revisions, and so on. At the end of the project, the project manager should make sure to include last-minute notes, the client's formal acceptance, and the post-project evaluation. Then, the information archive should be stored in an easily accessible location so future project managers can learn from the incidences and events that took place during the project.

SUMMARY

The objective of this chapter is to understand the scheduling, monitoring, controlling, and closing phases of the project life cycle. Most of the chapter is devoted to the scheduling phase because the method used to schedule and track project activities is the key to sound project management. In particular, the chapter focuses on critical path analysis (CPA), which is a scheduling technique that allows project managers to determine early start and finish times, late start and finish times, slack time, and contingency time. The chapter also emphasizes the critical importance of implementing a continuous feedback loop into the project management cycle, such that activities are continuously monitored to facilitate timely plan revisions and schedule adjustments, if necessary. Finally, the chapter highlights steps to be taken at the close of each project.

DISCUSSION QUESTIONS

6-1. Compare and contrast the following activities: "finish to start," "start to start," and "parallel activities." How does the use of a Gantt chart aid in the scheduling process?

6-2. We have defined two project scheduling methods, CPM and PERT. Discuss their differences and appropriate uses.

6-3. How does padded duration time effect project time and costs? How does Parkinson's Law come into play?

6-4. Why must the project schedule serve as a guideline rather than a fixed model?

6-5. How frequently should monitoring take place? Why?

6-6. Discuss quality-monitoring techniques, including the use of benchmarks and known standards (a.k.a. best practices). Give examples of their appropriate uses.

6-7. The acceptability, or materiality level, of actual-to-plan variances in a project setting is highly subjective and contextual. How should this be addressed between project manager and client?

6-8. Discuss the advantages and disadvantages of adding more resources to an activity.

6-9. Discuss the terms "feedback loop" and "feedback cycle time." Why are these concepts important to project management?

6-10. Explore the major issues to be resolved in closing a project. Why is it important to address them?

EXERCISES

6-11. Your client has just bought a house that needs a little fixing up on the outside. After looking around, the client decides that it needs a new coat of paint, new gutters, and a new birdbath on the front lawn. Your client has asked you to plan and manage the house improvement project. Accordingly, you have decided to develop a CPM diagram for this project so that you know how long the project will take and can identify the critical path. The activities (duration times in hours) involved with this project are as follows:

The following activities can be performed simultaneously:

1. Pressure wash the house (3)
2. Scrape the house (19)
3. Select the bird wash (3)

   Once the bird wash is selected, the project team can:

4. Install the bird wash on the lawn (complete with watering system) (10)

   Once the house is pressure washed and scraped, the following activities can be performed simultaneously:

5. Paint the front of the house (5)
6. Paint the back of the house (6)
7. Paint the sides of the house (10)

   Once the sides of the house are painted, the project team can:

8. Install new gutters on the sides of the house (8)

   Once the house is painted (front, back, and sides) and gutters are installed, the next activities can be performed simultaneously:

9. Paint doors and door trim (4)
10. Paint window trim (8)

    Finally, after doors and trim are painted, the project crew can:

11. Clean up (2)

Required

Draw a CPM diagram for the House Improvement Project and, for each activity, identify the following:

1. Duration time
2. Early start time
3. Early finish time
4. Late start time

5. Late finish time

6. Duration time

7. Slack time

8. The number of hours it should take to complete the project

9. All the activities along the critical path

6-12. You have been hired as the project manager to implement an accounting software package in a medium-size company. Client management has already selected the package. Your first task is to develop a CPM diagram for the systems implementation project. The activities (duration times in days) involved with this project are as follows:

The following activities can be performed simultaneously:

1. Review existing computer hardware (5)

2. Analyze existing business processes (11)

Once the hardware and business processes have been reviewed and analyzed, the project team can perform the following simultaneous activities:

3. Purchase computer hardware (2)

4. Conduct a gap analysis [where the project team and client management determine "gaps" between the capabilities of the old and new accounting systems] (16)

5. Convert existing data to the new format (4)

After the computer hardware is purchased, it must be installed at the client's site. Plus, once the gap analysis is completed, the project team must modify the new applications to "fit" with existing business practices. These activities can be performed simultaneously:

6. Install computer hardware (6)

7. Modify new applications (20)

Once steps 5, 6, and 7 are complete, it is time to train users:

8. Conduct training sessions for users (8)

Finally, after all training is complete, the transition from the old to new systems can proceed:

9. Transition from old to new system (2)

Required

Draw a CPM diagram for the Systems Implementation Project and, for each activity, identify the following:

1. Duration time

2. Early start time

3. Early finish time

4. Late start time

5. Late finish time

6. Duration time

7. Slack time

8. The number of hours it should take to complete the project

9. All the activities along the critical path

REFERENCES, RECOMMENDED READINGS, AND WEB SITES

References and Recommended Readings

Biemesderfer, S. C., "Thin Ranks, Fat Opportunity," *Contract Professional* (December, 1999), pp. 6-7.

Buckler, G., "Back on Track," *Infosystems Executive* (June, 1999), pp. 1-3.

Devaux, S. A., *Total Project Control: A Manager's Guide to Integrated Project Planning, Measuring, and Tracking* (New York: John Wiley & Sons, 1999).

Jacobs, P., "Recovering From Project Failure," *Infoworld* (September 27, 1999), pp. 14-15.

Kerzner, H., *Applied Project Management: Best Practices on Implementation* (New York: John Wiley & Sons, 2000).

Kiser, K., "Working on World Time," *Training Magazine* (March, 1999), p. 7.

Kunde, D., "Project Management Training on Increase," *The Dallas Morning News* (August 8, 1999), pp. 4-6.

Leach, L., *Critical Chain Project Management* (Boston: Artech House, 2000).

LeRouge, C., "Managing by Projects," *Strategic Finance* (November, 1999), pp. 3-7.

Lientz, B. P., and K. P. Rea, *Breakthrough Technology Project Management* (San Diego, CA: Academic Press, 1999).

Reid, A. P., *Project Management: Getting It Right* (Boca Raton, FL: CRC Press, 1999).

Roetzheim, B., "Customized Process Improvement," *Software Development* (March, 1999), pp. 21-22.

Swanson, D., "Planning, Projects, and Control," *CIO Canada* (February, 1999), pp. 18-20.

Tavares, L. V., *Advanced Models for Project Management* (Boston: Kluwer Academic Publishers, 1999).

Weglarz, J., *Project Scheduling: Recent Models, Algorithms, and Applications* (Boston: Kluwer Academic Publishers, 1999).

Web Sites

www.microsoft.com/office/project (Home page for *MS Project*)

PART THREE

THE CONSULTING PROCESS

Chapter 7

Documenting the Consulting Project

INTRODUCTION

THE ROLE OF DOCUMENTATION

GRAPHICAL DOCUMENTATION TOOLS

Flowcharts

Process Maps

Decision Tables

Special Tools for Information Systems Consulting

Storyboards

SOFTWARE TOOLS FOR CREATING DOCUMENTATION

SUMMARY

DISCUSSION QUESTIONS

EXERCISES

REFERENCES, RECOMMENDED READINGS, AND WEB SITES

Art does not reproduce the visible; rather, it makes visible.

Paul Klee, *The Inward Vision*

INTRODUCTION

Visual imagery provides a powerful means of recording, interpreting, and presenting information throughout the consulting process. Documentation is not unlike the work of a fine artist whose skills go far beyond a reflection of the obvious. And, like the artist, consultants rely on special tools—the brushes, paint, and canvas—to fully express themselves. These tools include a variety of graphical documentation techniques and software tools. The goals of documentation are to enhance the consultant's grasp of the project throughout its life cycle and, in the end, present findings and recommendations in an understandable format.

Consultants begin documenting a particular project with the engagement letter or consulting contract, which outlines the work to be done and the deliverables. Consultants use a variety of documentation tools as they engage in data collection and analysis. These tools include graphical documentation aids such as flowcharts, process maps, and information systems design tools.

Flowcharts have been part of the accountant's tool set for many years. Auditors have long used them to document their understanding of business processes and information flows. This type of documentation allows them to pinpoint strengths and weaknesses in the internal control system. Similar to flowcharts, process maps focus on the events that comprise business processes. Consultants use them to both document an understanding of existing processes and explain process changes or reengineered processes. Consultants involved in the design and development of information systems may use other graphical documentation tools, such as data flow diagrams, entity relationship diagrams, and Computer-Assisted Systems Engineering (CASE) tools.

Given the importance of documentation to consultants, we discuss the topic in several other chapters. For example, marketing efforts, discussed in Chapter 3, require documentation in the form of marketing plans. Chapter 5 introduces the role of documentation in project management. Chapter 4 discusses the engagement letter and client proposal. Chapter 8 describes questionnaires and worksheets used for collecting and analyzing data, while Chapter 9 covers reports and deliverables. Although we talk about documentation frequently throughout this book, this particular chapter focuses on the tools consultants use during the data collection and analysis phase of the consulting engagement. In particular, we discuss graphical documentation tools. *It is a well-known fact that a picture is worth more than a thousand words.* In fact, the *right* picture may be worth *much more* than a thousand words. Appropriate pictures as part of consulting documentation provide this same value.

This chapter begins with an explanation of the role of documentation in the consulting process. We then discuss the value of different forms of documentation, in particular text versus graphics. The chapter next describes flowcharts and process maps, two of a consultant's most important tools. A brief discussion of special tools for information systems consultants follows. The final section is devoted to documentation media, including voice tapes and videotapes. Yet another medium consultants use are computer databases, typically consisting of issues and their resolution and recommended best practices.

THE ROLE OF DOCUMENTATION

Documentation is invaluable for communication, analysis, and preservation. Various forms of documentation allow consultants to communicate their understanding and their findings with respect to projects or processes. Documenting a client's processes sometimes provides a near epiphany in terms of understanding. One of the true values of consultants is the objective view they provide. Typically, people involved in activities within a process have a difficult time viewing the entire process, particularly seeing it without prejudice. A consultant studying a process in its entirety and documenting each step along the way provides a service in presenting that documentation to a client. Finally, documentation preserves a consulting project. Each *task* a consultant completes should be well documented—in the same sense that a computer programmer should document every line of programming code. Poor documentation results in conflict, missed opportunities, failure to meet objectives, and, sometimes, legal conflicts.

GRAPHICAL DOCUMENTATION TOOLS

Most consultants recognize the value of pictures. Sometimes capturing a "picture" of a process is the critical step in solving a problem.

> ***Case-in-Point 7.1***   One of the authors of this book was once involved in a consulting project to help a company create an audit approach for their computer tape backup and recovery process. The system was quite complex and the consulting team spent many hours interviewing those involved in the process *and* observing the process in operation. After several weeks, the team met in a classroom to create a process map of the various backup and recovery activities. One team member drew the map on a blackboard as the team walked through the process. At the end of the day, the consultants had created a detailed picture showing all the activities involved in the backup and recovery process. Creating the audit system was easy at that point. The consultants also presented the process map to the client as a project deliverable.

Process maps and flowcharts are valuable to client organizations because businesspeople themselves don't always understand how the various activities within the major processes of their organizations connect and work together.

This section of the chapter discusses several graphical documentation tools consultants might use. The recommended tool for a particular consulting project varies, depending on the project. Flowcharts, along with a special kind of flowchart called a process map (as in the previous example), are probably the most commonly used graphical documentation tools. Flowcharts are often most useful for describing document flows and computerized information systems. Process maps are valuable in many kinds of consulting projects and are particularly valuable when a consultant is engaged in reengineering or project redesign work. In addition to flowcharts and process maps, which are discussed in some detail, information systems consultants have other graphical documentation tools available. We describe each of those briefly.

Flowcharts

There are many types of flowcharts. These include program, system, document, and internal control flowcharts. Information system designers use program flowcharts to outline specific steps in systems and application programs. Consultants may use system flowcharts to document either a current or proposed information system. Use of these tools is not limited, however, to *computerized* information systems. A consultant may prepare a flowchart to describe *any* type of system. Document flowcharts, for example, are a special kind of system flowchart oriented toward manual documents. The document flowchart shows the origin and distribution of all copies of a specific document type, such as a sales or purchase order. Internal control flowcharts are also a form of systems flowchart. Auditors may use an internal control flowchart to pinpoint strengths and weaknesses in controls over processes. An example of its use would be in pinpointing weaknesses in the sales order process.

Case-in-Point 7.2 emphasizes the value of flowcharting tools to consultants. We then describe some of the mechanics for developing flowcharts.

> **Case-in-Point 7.2** As part of the MBA degree program at the University of California at Davis, students must complete a consulting job for a company. The students begin the consulting project by developing a master flowchart. They then design more flowcharts as they work through the consulting process. The school believes mastery of flowcharting is an important skill to attain.

Symbols for System Flowcharts   General system flowcharts are physical descriptions of a system. They show the physical media in the system, such as documents and storage devices (e.g., disks). They also differentiate between process types—for example, manual versus computerized. Use of a standardized set of symbols allows for better communication in a systems flowchart. Figure 7-1 illustrates some of the symbols, described in some detail, used in drawing systems flowcharts.

Document   The document symbol shows a manual or paper document, such as a sales order or a sales report. Text within the symbol describes the type of document. Placing multiple copies of the symbol on top of one another indicates that a document has multiple copies. Numbers or letters in the upper right-hand corner of each symbol indicate document copies.

General Input/Output   Consultants prepare system flowcharts in decreasing levels of detail. A very high-level systems flowchart may include only one process symbol, along with general symbols indicating inputs and outputs. There is no attempt to describe the form of the input or output. Instead, a parallelogram shows the general inputs and outputs, with the text within the symbol defining the types. For example, inputs to a billing process would be sales orders, shipping notices, and other billing data. As flowcharts display more detail, the general input/output symbol is sometimes used for records and master files, or in accounting, journals and ledgers.

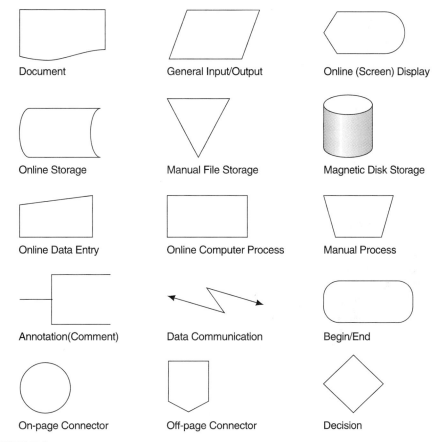

FIGURE 7-1 Systems flowchart symbols.

Online (Screen) Display   When a computer process outputs information to a computer terminal, the online display symbol shows the screen output.

Online, Manual File, and Magnetic Disk Storage   There are many types of storage in manual and computerized information systems. The online storage symbol indicates storage of data online. This is likely to be temporary storage. The manual file storage symbol shows paper files. These may be copies of documents stored in a file cabinet. Alphabetic characters indicate whether the file is organized chronologically (D for date), alphabetically (A), or in numerical order (N). Magnetic disks are popular for storing data permanently. You can use the outline of a magnetic disk to depict this type of storage device.

Online Data Entry   Data entry clerks enter data into a computerized information system through a keyboard terminal. The online data entry symbol represents this process.

Online Computer and Manual Processes   The online computer process symbol appears in most system flowcharts. You may use the symbol to indicate a computer operation, such as updating files or printing reports. Although the computer performs many of the processes shown in system flowcharts, manual operations are also likely. For example, an accounting clerk might perform a cursory check of vendor invoices, even though the computer system also checks these for accuracy. Management approval of accounts payable checks is another example of a manual process.

Annotation (Comment) Flowcharting convention is to describe a symbol on the face of the symbol itself. For instance, you would indicate purchase order or sales order on the face of a document symbol to explain the document type. Sometimes, however, there is not enough room on the face of a symbol for a full explanation. As an example, if a manual process symbol represents several activities, you cannot show them all without using an annotation or comment attached to their related symbol with a straight line.

Data Communication More and more often today, communication occurs between multiple computers or information system sites. When communication is electronic as, for example, with the electronic data interchange (EDI) of source documents, you indicate this with a zigzag line.

Begin/End The Begin/End symbol shows the terminal points of the flowchart. You may use this symbol to indicate the source of data into the system and information about the next system or destination of reports. The terminal symbol sets limits on the flowchart scope.

On-page Connector and Off-page Connectors Rather than crossing lines, or cluttering a flowchart with long connecting lines, you may use an on-page connector to show a starting and stopping point in the system flow. By entering a number or alphabetic character, you can direct the flowchart reader's attention to the connection. Off-page connectors are needed when the system flow is outside the particular system described in a flowchart. For example, if documents are going to customers or vendors, you may indicate this with an off-page connector.

Decision The decision symbol is more common to program flowcharts than to system flowcharts, but it may be used when alternative paths exist in the system flow.

Flowcharting Guidelines Creating a useful flowchart is more art than science. There is no one "right" diagram of a system or process. Most important is that a flowchart correctly communicates what you intend. Before starting to draw the flowchart itself, it's helpful to identify the documents, processes, and files that the flowchart should include. Make a list of these and then begin to create the diagram.

In drawing a flowchart, you can observe a few rules to make the diagram more efficient and communicative. First, you should make sure that the diagram flows from top to bottom and left to right, as the reader will naturally follow it. Using the standard symbol set shown in Figure 7-1 will ensure that there are no interpretation problems. You should also observe the "sandwich rule"—that each process in a system flowchart is located between an input and output symbol. Make liberal use of descriptions and comments to avoid misunderstandings and ensure completeness. Finally, a good flowchart designer makes many drafts before settling on a final diagram. Use of erasable media such as a blackboard or white dry-erase board, or documentation software, facilitates drawing multiple versions of any type of graphical documentation.

Depending on the nature of the engagement, consultants may use flowcharts to describe or evaluate a specific process. Flowcharts are an extremely useful tool for showing work processes and the activities within those processes. Figure 7-2 is a system flowchart for the sales process. This is a relatively *high-level* system flowchart. The highest level, or most general, flowchart shows only one process—that is, one symbol for a computer or manual process. More detailed flowcharts break the process into more detailed steps or activities within the process. The lowest level flowchart shows the most detailed breakdown of tasks.

Process Maps

Many consulting jobs involve the analysis of business or work processes. An understanding of these processes often points to ways of doing them better, thus making

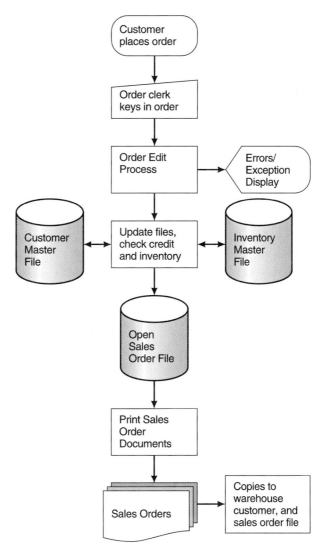

FIGURE 7-2 A system flowchart of the sales process.

organizations more efficient and profitable. System flowcharts are a tool consultants can use to map or diagram processes. Many consultants also employ another type of flowchart for that purpose: a process map or process flow diagram. Although system flowcharts show the *physical* nature of a business process, such as manual and computer processes, process maps simply outline the processes and, in various levels of detail, the activities within those processes. A visual diagram of business processes can make it clear where there are problems such as redundant activities, excessive documentation, and nonvalue-added tasks. Process maps are analytical documentation tools that detail every step in current and proposed business processes. Case-in-Point 7-3 describes the origins of process maps.

Case-in-Point 7.3 General Electric (GE) created the technique of process mapping, which has now become a widely used documentation technique of consultants and managers. GE managers developed the tool primarily for use in reengineering business processes. Reengineering, or redesigning business processes, requires, first, an examination of current processes. (We will revisit reengineering in Chapter 12.) GE successfully used process mapping to reengineer its inventory acquisition process at its Louisville appliance plant. In a reengineering effort, management found that some of their inventory parts could be stocked, while others could be placed on a just-in-time delivery schedule. The process maps helped in sequencing the delivery of parts to the assembly line.[1]

Creating Process Maps Developing a process map, or any documentation for that matter, requires first collecting data. The next chapter in this book will explain various collection techniques for data, including interviewing, questionnaires, and observation. Process mapping may include another approach: a group interview. A helpful first step in creating a map is to gather those involved in a particular process at a meeting and "map out" the process as a group. You may use a chalkboard, continuous paper rolls taped to the room's walls, or sticky note paper to diagram the process step-by-step. At the same time you are drawing the map, one person in the group might serve as the recorder, using a laptop computer and the documentation software described later in this chapter. The consultant needs to act as facilitator in this group interview, ensuring that the final diagram represents the best input of all parties involved in the process being mapped. Creating a process map requires gathering data about responsibilities, activities, inputs, and outputs.

Process maps are diagrams consisting of relatively few symbols. Some maps may include only rectangles for processes or process activities and arrows indicating process or activity flow. Other process maps may use many of the symbols shown earlier in Figure 7-1. For instance, they may include the diamond shape to indicate decisions and the terminal symbol to show starting and stopping points. Process maps showing sequences of events sometimes use an arrow type of symbol to indicate sequencing of activities. Expanding an arrow allows you to show a hierarchical representation of the activities within a step. Figures 7-3 and 7-4 show this type of symbol usage in process mapping.

There are several different types of process maps, including cross-functional maps, transactional maps, and relationship maps. Some indicate the parties or people involved in the activities described. Process maps indicating the constituents involved in activities and processes are *cross-functional maps.* Figure 7-5 is a cross-functional process map for a sales/collection process. Note the use of the four symbols and how this diagram shows clearly *who* is involved with each activity.

---

[1] V. D. Hunt, *Process Mapping* (New York: John Wiley & Sons, 1996), p. 2.

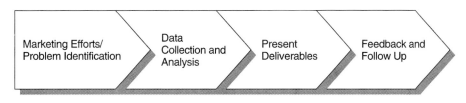

FIGURE 7-3 Process map with arrow symbol.

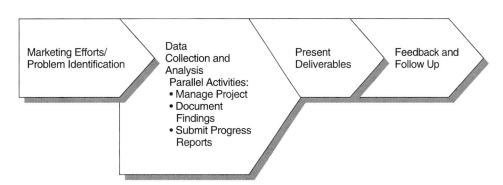

FIGURE 7-4 Detailed process map with arrow symbol.

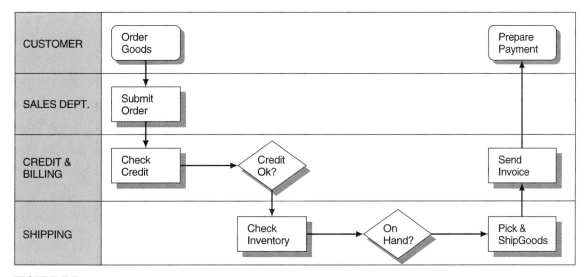

FIGURE 7-5 A cross-functional process map for a sales/collection process (Source: S. A. Moscove, M. G. Simkin, and N. A. Bagranoff, *Core Concepts of Accounting Information Systems* [New York: John Wiley and Sons, 2000].)

Horizontal bands indicate *where* and *who* performs a set of activities. The diagram makes a process easier to follow by taking a reader through a process step-by-step. A business process reengineering consultant may prepare a process map showing a business process before and after it is redesigned. The *transactional map* is similar to a cross-functional map. You would usually use this diagram at the beginning of the process mapping effort. It shows each activity in a process. Another type of map is a *relationship map,* which focuses on relationships among the major business functions both within and outside an organization. Relationship maps illustrate an entire supply chain, the major constituents within the organization being studied, as well as its vendors and customers.

Process Mapping Guidelines   As with flowcharts, there are no hard-and-fast rules that will help you create a "perfect" process map. However, there are guidelines to assist you in developing these diagrams.

A complete process map includes more than a single diagram. As with other types of flowcharts, maps are built in hierarchical levels, moving from the most general to successively more detailed diagrams. Process mapping is both top-down and bottom-up. Consultants identify the major processes in an organization at the top. They then work at the bottom level to decompose the processes into their individual tasks and activities.

> **Example**   The two process maps shown in Figures 7-6 and 7-7 for a health care company illustrate this hierarchy. Figure 7-6 is a process summary map for the process of arranging health care.[2] Figure 7-7 takes the registration process and breaks it down into specific tasks. Note the numbering on the document symbols. In the first diagram, the registration process is shown as Process 1.5. Figure 7-7, the detailed map for the registration process, covers steps 1.5.1 through 1.5.3. Numbering schemes indicate the successive levels of detail in a set of maps and allow users to navigate easily throughout the diagrams. Figure 7-7 also illustrates another feature of hierarchical process maps. The chart uses connector symbols, in this case inverted triangles, to link the pages in the map set.

A well-designed process map is balanced in terms of the level of detail in each area. The first map should be one of a high-level process, based on your data gathering. To ensure balance as you progress through the map hierarchy, limit the number of steps to five or six for each map. Most important, maintain focus by carefully defining the beginning and end of each process or subprocess. Verify the accuracy of the diagram by allowing everyone involved in the activities described by the map to review it and identify any missing activities. You may need to draw and redraw a process map many times. As with flowcharts, the first draft is not likely to be the final drawing. When a map appears too "busy," it may be time to start fresh.

Many methodology and software tools are available to help create process maps. One such tool is ICAM (Integrated Computer Aided Manufacturing) DEFinition language, or IDEF. The defense industry has used this process mapping standard for some time. IDEF is complex, and models based on this method are difficult and time consuming to develop. We discuss software tools for creating IDEF maps and other types of graphical documentation later in this chapter.

Process Value   Developing flowcharts and process maps is important, but their use does not end once the diagram is complete. With process mapping, consultants use the drawings to undertake a process value analysis. In this analysis, you classify each activity on a map as "value-added" or "nonvalue-added," primarily based on its perceived value to customers. This process value analysis, when used as part of process mapping, can lead to process improvements. Consultants use the analysis to ensure that value-added activities constitute a much larger percentage of a process than before the redesign effort.

---

[2] Figures 7-6 and 7-7 are based on diagrams prepared by Ernst and Young LLP for a client engagement. The graphs have been altered to fit a fictional health care organization. Ernst and Young LLP has given permission to the authors for use of the diagrams.

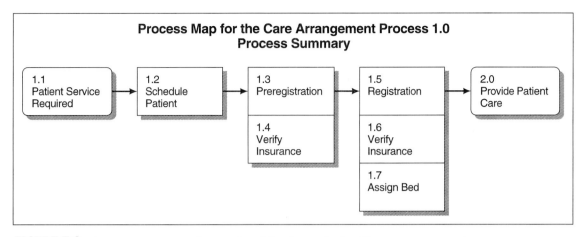

FIGURE 7-6   A process summary (transactional flow) map for health care arrangement.

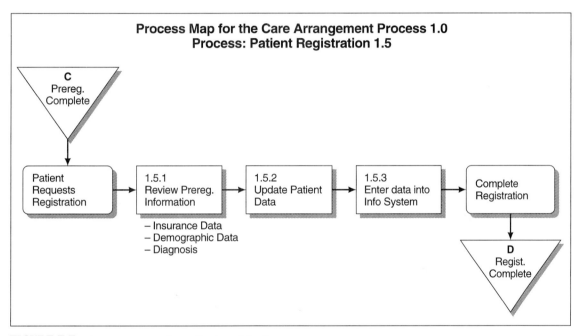

FIGURE 7-7   A process map for patient registration.

Example   As an example of value analysis, suppose you are preparing process maps for the accounts payable (vendor payment) procedure. After mapping the activities in the process, value analysis may indicate that steps such as routing invoices for approval and managing files, add no value to the process. These and other nonvalue-added activities are possibilities for elimination as you redesign the process.

In addition to allowing identification of nonvalue-added activities, process maps also highlight excessive control points, unnecessary handoffs, and superfluous documentation. An example of an excessive control point might be a supervisory approval. If approval by a supervisor is included in a process, it may be because the process itself is not designed appropriately to guard against risks. As an example, an accounts payable process requiring supervisory approval of all checks over a particular dollar amount is unnecessary if appropriate controls are in place to prevent duplicate or fraudulent payments.

Handoffs occur each time an activity moves from one player to another. Handoffs always have costs associated with them if for no other reason than that they introduce the possibility of information loss and other communication problems. For example, an order process that includes 10 handoffs is difficult to make responsive to customer inquiries. No one person in the process is responsible overall or has all the information available to provide to a customer.

Many processes are *over*documented. The ease of producing information often results in creating unnecessary documentation. Process maps, by highlighting outputs of a process, may indicate when this is the case.

Another feature of process value analysis is to include the time it takes to complete each activity within a process. When a consulting project's objective is to reduce process times, this is important, as illustrated in Case-in-Point 7.4.

> ***Case-in-Point 7.4*** Brooktree Corporation used process mapping, combined with process value analysis, to reduce time in its wafer (part of the computer chip) ordering process. The company first developed process flow maps of the current process, indicating the time required for each step. After conducting process value analysis, they reduced the time it took to commit wafer orders from 15 days to just 6 days.[3] The company's process value analysis identified steps that required too much time or cost, bottlenecks, critical relationships, loops in the flow (steps being repeated), and value-added versus nonvalue-added activities.

Decision Tables

Decision tables are useful when a system includes complex reasoning or logic. Some decisions have many conditions and outcomes, depending on the particular circumstances. For example, a decision to admit a student to a graduate degree program may depend on test scores, undergraduate grades, and work experience. Further, in evaluating grades, an admissions department might consider the rigor of the undergraduate program and enrollment trends. Decision tables list conditions and actions associated with a decision. The tables show conditions as "if" statements. The actions are possible outcomes, based on a set of conditions, which are the rules in the decision table.

There are two main sections in a decision table. The top section, the condition stub, lists the conditions or if statements. The bottom portion, the action stub, details the possible alternative actions. Rules are the combinations that may occur, along with the action based on the rules.

> **Example** In the decision table shown in Figure 7-8, a grade point average of less than 2.75 would result in the action to deny admission to the graduate program. A student who has a grade point average of more than 2.75 but less than 3.0 would be considered for conditional admission. According to Figure 7-8, a student who has the combination conditions of between a 2.75 and 3.0 grade point average and a General Management Admission Test (GMAT) score of less than 475 is denied admission. The decision table may contain many other combinations of conditions and rules for actions based on those conditions.

---

[3] D. D. Pattison, J. M. Caltrider, and R. Lutze, "Continuous Process Improvement at Brooktree," *Management Accounting*, February 1993, pp. 49–52.

	Rules:	1	2	3	4...	
Condition Stub	**Conditions (IF)** Grade Point Average <2.75 Grade Point Average <3.0 GMAT Score <475 GMAT Score <500	Y – – –	N Y – –	N Y Y –	N N N Y	**Condition Entries**
Action Stub	**Actions** Deny Admission Hold for Further Evaluation Accept Applicant	X	X	X	X	**Action Entries**

FIGURE 7-8 A decision table for evaluating applicants to a graduate degree program.

Decision tables may be useful for consulting purposes because they allow you to document and summarize many possible tasks within a process. Information systems programmers frequently use them, primarily in deciding how to handle conditional statements and decision points within a computer program. They can be helpful to a decision maker since they clearly show the decision to make given a set of conditions. A consultant who is redesigning processes may construct a decision table to assist the people who will be working in the newly designed processes.

Special Tools for Information Systems Consulting

A variety of special graphical documentation tools are available to the information systems consultant. This type of consulting work typically requires the *development* of a new system or a plan for a new system. Designing and developing new systems require documentation of system inputs, processes, and outputs. Graphical documentation software such as data flow diagrams and entity relationship diagrams can assist the system developer.

Data Flow Diagrams A valuable documentation tool for systems analysis is the data flow diagram. System developers and analysts use data flow diagrams to indicate the data and information flows for a business process. This type of graphical documentation shows the sources and destinations of data used by an organization.

There are two major categories of data flow diagrams: physical and logical. Physical data flow diagrams represent some of the physical attributes of a system, similar to system flowcharts. For example, they may indicate a type of data storage. Most data flow diagrams, however, are of the logical variety, omitting descriptions of the physical nature of processes, and data storage and display. Since they do not try to provide specific information about the media associated with inputs, processes, and outputs, logical data flow diagrams require only a small symbol set. Figure 7-9 shows the four symbols system developers and systems analysts use to create these diagrams. Circles represent processes where data is transformed. A square depicts the source or destination of a data flow. For example, sales order data flow from a customer source. Two parallel lines indicate the data store or file where data reside. Some data flow diagrams use an open-ended rectangle as the symbol for the data store. Finally, lines with arrows show the data flows. Data flows in flowcharts are usually indicated with straight lines; data flow diagrams often have curved lines.

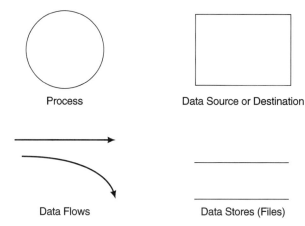

FIGURE 7-9 Data flow diagram symbols.

Data flow diagrams sometimes show a current system; at other times they describe a proposed system. As with many other documentation tools, they show increasing levels of detail. A context diagram is the highest level of data flow diagram. Figure 7-10 is a context diagram for the sales process. A context diagram shows only one process bubble, in this case indicating the sales process, which is the boundary of the system described. Subsequent levels of data flow diagrams decompose the process into subprocesses or activities, just as the system flowcharts and process maps described earlier do. Level 0, Level 1, Level 2, and further diagrams if needed, continue to break down the process "bubbles" into increasing detail. For example, a Level 0 diagram for the sales process might include three processes: the sales order, shipment of goods, and payment processes. A numbering system, similar to the one used for process maps, ties the documentation together.

Entity Relationship Diagrams Another graphical documentation tool available to systems consultants is an entity relationship diagram. The primary use of this tool is in data modeling. System designers creating a database or enterprise resource planning system for a company will use entity relationship modeling to identify the entities about which to capture data in the new system. An entity is a resource, event, or agent; examples are customers, sales orders, inventory, and cash. Entity relationship diagrams also show how entities relate to one another. A straight line connecting customer and sales order entities would indicate the direct relationship between the two and the need for the database to contain a link for the data.

Entity relationship diagrams require two symbols. Rectangles denote entities and connecting arrows show relationships between entities. Sometimes a diamond shape may appear in the relationship connection, with a description of the relationship.

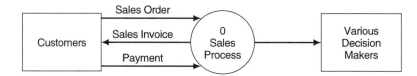

FIGURE 7-10 Context diagram for a sales process.

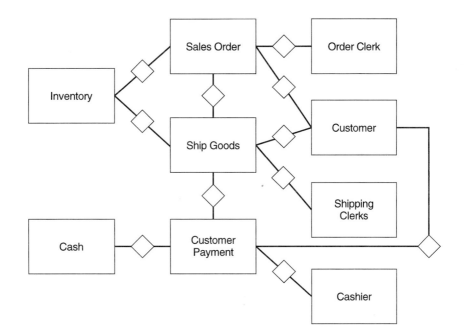

FIGURE 7-11   An entity relationship diagram for the sales process.

Example   Figure 7-11 shows an entity relationship diagram for the sales process. A relational database built on this model would contain a table or relation for each entity (rectangle) in the diagram. There might also be other tables with data about certain relationships.

Storyboards

The film industry uses storyboards to lay out the scenes in a movie. Advertisers use them to explain the story behind a commercial. Consultants can use this tool to outline the individual pieces of a client deliverable or tell a story about business processes. The next case-in-point describes the origin of storyboards.

Case-in-Point 7.5   The concept of storyboards originated with Walt Disney. Disney's animated cartoons required thousands of drawings and many more frames per second than animators previously used. By pinning the drawings sequentially on a wall, the studio could keep track of the progress of each project, and discard any unnecessary scenes.[4]

Creating a storyboard is a creative, structured exercise. It allows group members to express creative ideas and solve complex problems. Consultants may use storyboarding to outline client deliverables soon after they present a proposal, or they may wait until data analysis is complete. The storyboard provides a visualization of the outline of the deliverable in a chronological fashion, using symbols, images, and other graphics to support presentations or problem solutions. Accounting consultants sometimes use storyboard techniques for certain types of projects, such as activity based costing (ABC) projects.

---

[4] J.M. Higgins, "Storyboard Your Way to Success," *Training and Development,* June 1995, pp. 13–17.

Storyboards come in many forms. Some storyboards, particularly those used in creating films or advertising, are a graphical set of frames. Storyboards used in business presentations are generally about four feet square. One technique for creating a storyboard is to use a series of foam core or poster boards and attach index cards outlining the story in "scenes" or summarizing content. If you're creating a storyboard for a client report, you might develop a storyboard as a "grid" (described in the following paragraph). Some consulting organizations, such as Arthur Andersen's Business Consulting group, have developed their own tools for creating storyboards.

Each grid on the storyboard outlines the individual pages in the report. Each page has a headline or header that summarizes the page's main idea. The page also includes either textual or graphic support for the idea. This is called the storyboard's "subber" or subheading set. The story behind the storyboard of a consulting engagement may be laid out in terms of what is known and what is needed. For example, the first few pages explain the problem, the next few pages describe the actions to deal with the project to date, the next pages discuss what the consultants will do, and so on. You may create a storyboard in presentation software like PowerPoint. When you create a set of presentation slides, viewing them in the Slide Sorter tells the story of the entire presentation. Figure 7-12 shows a storyboard about storyboarding.

Apart from their use in presentations or organizing consulting projects, storyboards are useful for reengineering and ABC projects. Storyboards can show the work done by various people within processes. Workforce Activity-Based Management (WABM) combines ABC and process analysis concepts to help improve processes. Storyboards for this purpose can be created with poster boards and index cards, in addition to yarn or string, and other materials. Storyboards serve as the communication tool that shows the work done by various workers or work teams. Each index card identifies an activity. The final storyboard combines all activities to show the overall process. In WABM, the storyboard also identifies cost drivers associated with the process.

SOFTWARE TOOLS FOR CREATING DOCUMENTATION

A variety of software tools are available to assist in creating documentation for consulting projects. These include the documentation tools available in project management software (e.g., *MS Project*), graphical documentation software, and Computer-Assisted Systems Engineering (CASE) tools that combine graphical documentation with other system development aids.

Graphical Documentation Software   Consultants can create flowcharts, decision tables, process maps, entity relationship diagrams, and data flow diagrams with simple word processing or presentation software. For example, the authors of this book drew most of the figures in this chapter with *MS Word* tools. Within this word processing software is a toolbar that includes a drawing bar. The drawing toolbar in *MS Word* shows various shapes and has templates (see AutoShapes) available with flowcharting symbols.

While consultants can use general office productivity software to create graphical diagrams, the need for highly sophisticated or complex diagrams warrants special graphical documentation software. These specialized software tools include many

A Storyboard on Storyboarding
Storyboarding

Purpose	Major Uses of Storyboards	Types of Storyboards	Types of Sessions for Each Storyboard	The Project Team	Materials Needed	Rules for a Creative-Thinking Session	Rules for a Critical-Thinking Session	The Leader's Role	Miscellaneous
Solve problems more effectively	Strategic problem solving	Planning	Creative thinking	Five to eight people	Wall boards	No criticism	Be objective	Choose topic and team	Background: Walt Disney, Mike Vance
Raise levels of creativity	Operational problem solving	Idea	Critical thinking	Composition of group	Cards (sizes and colors), pins, and tape	Quantity; not quality	Be critical	Choose type of storyboard and brief the team	Visual
Improve planning and communications		Communication: who, what, when			Wide-tipped markers	Piggyback ideas	Attack ideas, not people	Warm up; review rules	Flexible
Increase participation		Organization: how, what tasks, who			"Stickie" notes	The wilder the better		Create topic header, other headers, and subbers	Symbols
					Scissors	Quick and dirty		Conduct creative-thinking session	
					Table			Conduct critical-thinking session	

FIGURE 7-12 Storyboard on Storyboarding. (Reprinted with permission from James, M. Higgins, "Storyboard Your Way to Success," *Training and Development,* June 1995, p. 14 ASTD, astd, www.astd.org.)

"smart" tools or wizards that actually guide consultants through their diagram development. They have templates with literally thousands of symbols available to create everything from a flowchart to room design layouts. You can attach files and other documents to diagrams and it is easy to use this software to create a hierarchy of documentation. Some of these graphical documentation software packages have the ability to convert text documentation into flowcharts. Graphical documentation software is generally inexpensive, with packages such as *SmartDraw* available for less than $100. Even the high-end packages, *MicrosoftVisio, Igraphx,* and *allClear,* are available at about $500. Consulting organizations, including Arthur Andersen's Business Consulting group and Ernst and Young's Information Systems Assurance and Advisory Services group, train their consultants in the use of this software.

CASE Tools Some of the high-end graphical documentation tools include application development capabilities similar to computer-assisted systems engineering (CASE) tools. CASE tools are software programs offering a wide variety of documentation and application development features. They assist system developers in maintaining and developing software solutions. Many of these packages include diagramming tools for creating flowcharts and data flow diagrams. Many CASE tools incorporate a data dictionary, a repository of data about data. The data dictionary documents every data item in an information system, including information about its source, its characteristics such as size, its type (e.g., text or number), security, the reports that use it, and so on. Today's more sophisticated CASE tools generate program code and incorporate artificial intelligence for system development. Consultants use CASE tools only when a project requires design of a new information system.

SUMMARY

Documentation is vitally important to consultants. Because images frequently convey a richer message than words, graphical documentation is particularly important. This chapter describes several of the graphical documentation tools available to consultants, focusing on flowcharts and process maps. Most accountants are familiar with flowcharts as a tool for analyzing an organization's processes and internal controls. Consultants may use them for these purposes as well as for capturing a systems' current state and proposed changes. Good system flowcharts use the standardized set of symbols described in this chapter. Process maps are a type of flowchart that focus on an organization's processes and activities. These graphical documentation tools are particularly useful in reengineering projects.

Other graphical documentation tools described in this chapter are decision tables, data flow diagrams, entity relationship diagrams, and storyboards. Decision tables describe decisions in the form of conditions and alternative actions. Data flow diagrams and entity relationship diagrams are two tools that information systems consultants in particular use to plan or evaluate information systems. Data flow diagrams describe the inflows and outflows of data associated with an information system. Entity relationship diagrams show tables in database systems and the relationships among them. Storyboards are helpful for describing projects and analyzing complex problems. Accountants may find them useful for activity-based costing and reengineering projects in particular.

Consultants may create some graphical documentation manually. For example, an initial storyboard may be best developed using poster board and index cards or sticky notes. There are many software tools available, however, that allow consultants to create professional looking graphical documentation easily. The simplest graphical documentation software helps in drawing diagrams. More sophisticated programs, such as CASE tools, assist the development and organization of the documentation. These tools even include features for developing software applications.

DISCUSSION QUESTIONS

7-1. Why does documentation have such an important role in consulting?

7-2. This chapter discussed many graphical documentation tools and software available to consultants. Consultants also use documentation features in project management software to manage consulting projects. Discuss the documentation features available in *Microsoft Project.*

7-3. How might a consultant use a system flowchart in a business process reengineering engagement?

7-4. Discuss the differences and similarities between system flowcharts and process maps.

7-5. How do you know when you have created a good process map?

7-6. Explain how process value analysis can improve an organization's profitability.

7-7. What are some applications of decision tables in a consulting project?

7-8. Explain the difference between data flow diagrams and entity relationship diagrams.

7-9. Storyboards are commonly used in the film industry and for creating advertising copy. How can a consultant use them?

7-10. Describe the features you would look for in selecting graphical documentation software.

EXERCISES

7-11. Create a system flowchart, similar to the one shown in Figure 7-2, for the following process:

Baker, Inc. is a medium-sized automotive parts manufacturer, located in the midwestern United States. When personnel in the various departments need supplies or equipment, they complete a purchase requisition form that is available on the company's intranet. After completing the form, the employee routes it by e-mail to his or her supervisor for approval. Supervisory personnel approve or reject the request and route it to the purchasing department. Purchasing clerks review requisitions daily and create purchase orders, working from a list of authorized vendors. Baker, Inc.'s accounting software updates the appropriate files with purchase order information and adds purchase transactions to the Open Purchase Order file. The system then prints multiple copies of the purchase order for distribution to vendors, the receiving department, and accounts payable.

7-12. Create a cross-functional process map, similar to the one shown in Figure 7-5, for a typical purchase/payment process. Assume that the parties involved in the process are vendors, employees requesting goods or services, a centralized purchasing department, an accounts payable department, and receiving.

7-13. Suppose a company's purchasing department uses the following rules in determining whether or not to place an order:

All employees have an annual discretionary supplies budget of $200. Any request for goods or services that does not exceed that budgetary amount is approved automatically, so long as the item requested has a reasonable work-related purpose. Requests for supplies that are over $200 but less than $500 or that would cause the employee's requests for the year to exceed the discretionary budget are held for supervisory approval. Only employees at staff level 12 and higher may order goods or services for more than the $500 ceiling.

Develop a decision table for this scenario.

7-14. Draw a context data flow diagram for an organization's purchasing process.

7-15. Visit the web sites for at least two of the graphical documentation software products described in this chapter. What types of documentation tools does the software allow you to create? If you were choosing a program for this purpose, how would you make your choice?

REFERENCES, RECOMMENDED READINGS, AND WEB SITES

References and Recommended Readings

Bagranoff, N. A., and M. G. Simkin, "Picture That," *Journal of Accountancy* (February 2000), pp. 43–46.

Barcus, S. W. III, and J. W. Wildinson, *Handbook of Management Consulting Services,* 2nd edition (New York: McGraw-Hill, 1995).

Boehringer, R., and P. King, "Process Mapping Gives Great Direction," *www.odgroup.com,* Orion Development Group.

Booth, R., "Process Mapping," *Management Accounting* (March 1995), p. 32.

Brown, A., "Use Storyboards as Visual Guide for Powerful Presentations," *Presentations* (August 1997), pp. 33–36.

Damelio, R., *The Basics of Process Mapping* (New York: Quality Resources, 1996).

Hagerty, M. R., "A Powerful Tool for Diagnosis and Strategy," *Journal of Management Consulting* (November 1997), pp. 16–25.

Higgins, J. M., "Storyboard Your Way to Success," *Training and Development* (June 1995), pp. 13–17.

Hunt, V. D., *Process Mapping* (New York: John Wiley and Sons, 1996).

Langham, B. A., "Drawing It Out," *Successful Meetings* (January 1994), pp. 114–118.

Mason, F., "Mapping a Better Process," *Manufacturing Engineering* (April 1997), pp. 58–68.

Moscove, S. A., M. G. Simkin, and N. A. Bagranoff, *Core Concepts of Accounting Information Systems,* 6th edition (New York: John Wiley and Sons, 1999).

Pattison, D. D., J. M. Caltrider, and R. Lutze, "Continuous Process Improvement at Brooktree," *Management Accounting* (February 1993), pp. 49–52.

Selander, J. P., and K. F. Cross, "Process Redesign: Is It Worth It?" *Strategic Finance* (January 1999), pp. 40–44.

Stewart, J., "Flowcharting Software Selection for CASE Tool Simulation in an AIS Course," *The Review of Accounting Information Systems* (Winter 1998–99), pp. 35–42.

Turney, P.B.B., "Beyond TQM with Workforce Activity-Based Management," *Management Accounting* (September 1993), pp. 28–33.

Web Sites

The following are web sites of graphical documentation software vendors:

www.micrografx.com/igrafx
www.microsoft.com/office/visio
www.smartdraw.com
www.proquis.com/allclear

Chapter 8

Data Collection and Analysis

Discovery is seeing what everybody else has seen, and thinking what nobody else has thought.

Albert Szent-Gyorgi

INTRODUCTION

The proposal's accepted, the contract's signed, the project is planned and it's time to do the work. Most consulting work begins with some type of data collection. You may have *begun* this process while preparing the proposal, but it is time now to collect data in earnest. There are likely to be both internal and external data sources. Internal data are collected through interviews, survey questionnaires, and observation. These same techniques may be useful for collecting data from external sources, but you can also research databases of information on the Internet and in libraries.

Sometimes merely collecting the data and documenting it (with some of the tools described in Chapter 7), is enough. Many times, however, consultants need to analyze data in some fashion. In analyzing data, you are likely looking for patterns or inferences. The data may be a guide to the consulting solution. Sometimes analyzing data is as easy as reading the data. Usually, though, visual inspection of the data isn't enough. Statistical tools such as regression analysis and analysis of variance will help to identify patterns among the data.

DATA—THE HEART OF THE ENGAGEMENT

Consultants collect some data while defining the problem at hand. Solving the problem requires assimilating more facts and data, then analyzing it. For instance, during a reengineering engagement, consultants may need to collect cost and time data for current processes. We use the term "data" here to include both facts and information. To an information systems specialist, *data* means unorganized or raw facts, whereas information reflects data that has been transformed in such a way that it is *useful* to the decision-maker. In any event, finding a solution to a client problem necessitates gathering data and information from both internal and external sources.

Internal data sources can be found within the client organization. Depending on the nature of the engagement, a variety of functional areas and management levels will provide data. The marketing department, for example, is the source of sales and customer data; accounting can provide most of the financial data.

Apart from people, internal documents are sources of data. These include management reports, minutes of meetings, budgets, worksheets, source documents, and plans. Figure 8-1 summarizes the types of documents available from a client organization.

Consultants collect some data from sources external to the client. These data sources consist of books, journals, industry reports, research organization reports (e.g., Gartner Group), governmental reports, other professionals, Internet sites, and data and knowledge bases. Many consulting organizations today maintain intranets with knowledge repositories, such as Arthur Andersen's *KnowledgeSpace.* These

Documents describing how the client's organization is run	Documents describing what the client plans to do	Documents describing what the client organization does
Policy Statements	Business plans (long-and short-	Annual reports
Methods and procedures	range)	Performance reports
manuals	Budgets	Internal staff studies
Organization charts	Schedules and forecasts	Legal documents, including
Job descriptions	Minutes of board of directors	copyrights, patents,
Performance standards	Statements of goals and	franchises, trademarks
Charts of accounts	objectives	Reference documentation
Delegations of authority		about customers, employees,
		products, vendors
		Transaction documentation,
		including purchase orders,
		time sheets, and expense
		records

FIGURE 8-1   Documents available in most business organizations. (Source: John G. Burch, Jr., and Gary Grudnitski, *Information Systems: Theory and Practice,* 5th edition, Copyright 1989. Reprinted by permission of John G. Burch, Jr.)

knowledge bases contain news reports, journal articles, best practices data, case studies, and other resources. Customers and suppliers can also provide data that may be relevant. For example, a survey of the client's customers may reveal that although customers like the company's product, they are dissatisfied with service and/or delivery times.

DATA COLLECTION TECHNIQUES

Although some data are readily available in client documentation, you will usually need to actively collect data. Interviews, questionnaires, observation, and research are all good sources of internal and external data. Consultants typically interview people at all levels of the client organization for different kinds of data. For instance, top management is a good source of data about plans and strategy, middle management can provide budget and operating data, and clerks and supervisors are the source of data about day-to-day operations. To get the whole picture, consultants also talk to people outside, but associated with, the client organization. For instance, customers and suppliers can provide data from different perspectives. Interviews are terrific sources of data, but they are not enough. Consultants supplement interviews with questionnaires and observation both for verification and enhancement purposes. A combination of data collection techniques results in the best set of objective data. To be a good consultant, you need to be good at interviewing and research.

Interviews

Interviewing is perhaps the most critical and valuable data collection technique. Interviews are personal exchanges of data. They're flexible and let a questioner probe sensitive topics. Most consulting interviews take place between the consultant and client personnel. These interviews are key to defining and solving an entity's problems because client employees are most familiar with the business and its processes. An effective interviewing technique that encompasses both questioning and listening is an invaluable consulting skill.

Preparing for the Interview   For an interview to be most successful, you need to do some homework beforehand. This preparation includes establishing objectives for each interview session, conducting some research, informing the subject of the interview, choosing an interview format, and designing a set of interview questions.

What Are the Objectives?   The interviewer needs to set objectives for each interview session. A distinguishing characteristic of interviews is that they not only provide factual data, but the interviewer can also use them to glean perceptions and ideas. A good interviewer can learn about interview subjects by watching how they respond to certain questions. For example, if the interview subject is ill at ease, you might guess that he or she is concerned in some way about the consulting project. A probing interviewer may learn whether an employee is fearful about job security or simply uncomfortable with one or more consulting team members.

Another objective of the interviewing process might be to extract problem solutions from interview subjects. Many times employees look forward to the chance to tell a consultant about problems they experience in their work, and to share opinions about how to solve them.

Finally, consultants can use the interview process not just to ask questions, but also to communicate messages. Perhaps you want to reassure workers that their jobs are not at risk or that the changes you will propose should make their work easier. The personal interview is a great chance to convey these assurances.

What Research Should You Do Beforehand?   Effective interviewing requires research about both the interview subject and the interview topic. As interviewer, you should know the job position and description of the interview candidate. In addition, you might find out from the subject's co-workers whether the candidate is likely to be cooperative or resistant to the interview process. (Do this subtly—you don't want to encourage disharmony!) This information will help in structuring the interview.

When interviewing client employees, consultants need to be especially careful to learn about the interview candidate's job and the work processes they are studying. Consulting engagements generally bring about change. Employees are often fearful of that change and can start out with a negative opinion of a consulting team. Lack of knowledge on the part of the consultant in an interview will only confirm that view.

> **Example**   Imagine interviewing an accounts payable clerk in this scenario. The consulting team is brought on to design a new process for paying bills. The new process is likely to make most of the current accounts payable staff redundant. While the interview is supposed to help the consultant better understand current processes, ignorance about the client company or accounts payable processes will confirm the employee's negative opinion of the consultants and can make the consulting work more difficult.

What Do You Tell the Interviewee?   Before the interview, the consultant and client should contact the interview subject, either by phone, memo, or e-mail. The client should set the stage, letting the interviewee, whether an employee, customer, banker, or supplier, know that it is all right to talk to you. The client should also explain the purpose of the interview and how the information will be used. The consultant should make any pre-interview contact personally, rather than delegate the task. Asking someone for their time so that you can interview them—via a subordinate—may offend the interview subject.

Depending on the interview objectives, you should let an interview candidate know what the interview is about—at least in general terms. In the pre-interview contact, you can encourage the interviewee to give some preliminary thought to their opinions and ideas about the subject of discussion.

What's the Interview Format? Some interviews are over the phone, but the most effective are in person. While nuances in a voice may assist an interviewer's perceptions, body language is even more telling. The interview format, like other interview variables, depends somewhat on the objectives. A fact-gathering interview calls for a *directive* format. With this format, the interviewer works through a series of predetermined questions and notes the responses without embellishment.

A *nondirective* interview is good for "fishing." If the interview objective is to go on an exploration to learn about unidentified problems, then a nondirective format may be needed. With this format, the interviewer may begin with a set of questions, but will allow the interviewee to direct the interview through his or her responses. The interviewer purposefully cedes control.

Most interviews fall somewhere in the middle of the directive and nondirective format. Structure is important at times, but the interviewer should allow for exploring areas not in the script when they appear important. As you might guess, spontaneous comments are often more important than cut-and-dried factual data.

What Questions Should You Ask? The questions you ask depend on the type of engagement and the interview format. Many questions should be developed *before* the interview, but you should leave room to add others *during* it. An interview should begin with a series of questions that are readily answerable, such as what is your job, background, and so on. These questions are icebreakers and their purpose is more to put the interviewee at ease than to elicit information. The structure of interview questions should proceed from easy, neutral questions to more difficult ones about sensitive issues. Early questions may call for quantifiable responses or yes/no answers. Later, more sensitive questions elicit opinions and ideas. Figure 8-2 provides an example of this progression.

Quay suggests designing interview questions around hypotheses (i.e., hunches) associated with interview topics. With this approach, the interviewer first lists the topics the interview should cover and then some hypotheses about the topic. For example, if the client problem is declining sales revenue, interview topics for a sales person might be customer satisfaction, competitive climate, and product array. Hypotheses regarding customer satisfaction could be that customers are unhappy with product quality, customers are experiencing delivery time problems, or customers feel prices are too high. The interviewer then develops a set of questions to test each hypothesis.[1]

---

[1] John Quay, *Diagnostic Interviewing for Consultants and Auditors* (Cincinnati, OH: Quay Associates, 1994), pp. 16–17.

1. What is your job title?
2. To whom do you report and who reports to you?
3. What are your job responsibilities?
4. Have you experienced any changes in your sales patterns over the past few years?
5. What do customers tell you about their experiences with your products?
6. If sales are off, do you have any ideas about the cause?
7. What do you think could be done to increase sales?
8. Do you feel that your boss listens to your input on this issue?
9. Are there any particular things that you believe hamper you in your ability to sell your company's products?

FIGURE 8-2 Sample interview questioning sequence.

A consultant should keep in mind that the questions asked let the interviewee know something about the work you are doing. On sensitive engagements, balancing the information you get with the information you give can be tricky.

Questions are good for collecting facts, but statements can elicit more information than direct questions. Statements like, "Tell me more about…" or "Let's talk about such and such for a few minutes" can encourage some interviewees to share their perceptions and ideas more freely. Usually a mix of questions and statements will gather the most information in an interview.

The Interview Process   Interviewing is both an art and an acquired skill. A consultant's interviewing technique is likely to improve with experience. There are three important parts of an interview process that affect its success: control of the interview, documentation of the interview, and "really" listening to the interviewee.

Controlling the Interview Process   Consultants need to establish a climate of trust and rapport with an interviewee at the outset. The lead statements for the interview serve this purpose. First, the interviewer explains the purpose of the interview and provides assurance of confidentiality. During the interview you can give some personal anecdotes to show empathy with the interviewee. These actions promote maximum cooperation.

An interviewer's facial expressions and body language provide clues to the person being questioned about how you perceive their answers. If you appear impatient or hurried, it sends the message that what the interviewee is saying is not important. And, while you wish to establish a feeling of trust, becoming *too* friendly might encourage the subject to wander too far from the subject at hand. Nods or verbal expressions of agreement encourage an interviewee to continue along in a vein. Occasionally, you may want to probe a response in a sensitive area. Gentle probing is more likely to elicit the information you want. Playing hardball may invite the interview subject to "shut down." You can probe gently by using the techniques described in Figure 8-3.

As an interview progresses, you can use a variety of techniques to move the process along and also to maintain control. One technique is summarizing or restating what you have learned about one particular topic as a lead-in to the next set of questions. Restating the points covered lets you validate what you've learned. It also gives the interviewee the chance to correct you or to expand on a salient point. Because time is valuable for both the interviewer and the interviewee, you need to make sure it's used wisely. Some time spent on irrelevant issues may improve trust

---

Interview Softening Techniques

Sound Tentative:
Might
Perhaps
Would you say that…
Is it possible that…
…or not so much so

Minimize:
A little bit
To some extent
Some
Somewhat
Fairly

Save Face:
What might have accounted for…
What prompted your decision to…
How did you happen to…
Has there been any opportunity to…

Be Indirect:
Let's talk a *little bit* about … (something related to the sensitive issue)
Let's talk about *some of your ideas about* or *some things that can go wrong with…*

Use a Balance Sheet Approach:
List some good things … and perhaps a few things that could be improved?
(Provide some reassurance or empathy as the negatives are mentioned)

FIGURE 8-3 Techniques and language to soften interview questions. (Adapted from J. Quay, *Diagnostic Interviewing for Consultants and Auditors* [Cincinnati, OH: Quay and Associates, 1994].)

and cooperation. Too much time spent on side trips may not leave the opportunity for covering important issues. You can control timing with gentle reminders about how time is limited, or by mentioning that you recognize the value of your subject's time and do not want to take up too much of it. As the interview draws to a close, remind the subject that he or she should feel free to contact you if they think of anything to add to what they have said during the interview.

Documenting the Interview To document an interview you can either record it or take notes. Tape and video recorders can provide a perfect record of everything said during an interview. Video recorders are best because they show body language and facial expressions; however, tape and video recorders can inhibit the interviewee. You must ask permission up front to record the interview. But you run the risk that the recording process will make the interviewee self-conscious and guarded about saying anything controversial. Recording equipment also requires some maintenance. For instance, having to change tapes or batteries during a crucial part of the interview might disrupt the interviewee's train of thought, thereby tainting the moment—one that you may never recapture.

Note taking *during* an interview is probably the most effective and most common approach to recording an interview. With notes you can record not only responses to questions, but also comments about the interviewee's nonverbal messages. As with tape and video recorders, you must make sure the interviewer understands the intent to take notes during the interview. A good way to reassure the person being questioned about this process is to let him or her review your transcribed notes at some point afterward. This allows some follow-up communication and also puts the interviewee more at ease. Another plus with note-taking during the interview is that it provides the interviewer with an excuse to ask for clarification. Although consultants don't want to appear ignorant, you should take care to make sure you ask questions thoroughly enough to get the level of understanding you need. Interviewing novices often make the mistake of not asking enough questions for fear of appearing unknowledgeable. When the time comes to transcribe notes, these interviewers usually find that they've traded off appearances for a poor understanding of problems or processes.

Note-taking *after* an interview can either supplement or supplant other documentation techniques. If you want to appear more casual or encourage maximum cooperation from an interview subject, taking notes immediately following an interview may be the optimal way to record it. Human resource personnel often use this approach when interviewing job candidates, allowing themselves 15 minutes or so after each interview to record the session. The downside to this approach is that you may leave something out and cannot capture full quotes.

Listening   One of the most important skills a consultant or accountant can use is the ability to listen. Interviewers need to listen to both what is said and what is perhaps unspoken. For instance, you should listen for signs of boredom, defensiveness, hostility, stress, fear, and other emotions. During an interview, the questioner must be alert also to nuances and implications. Skilled interviewers know which side trips are productive to follow and which are not. They listen for clues that indicate the next question to ask. Always remember that the best interviews are those where the interviewee does most of the talking.

Focus Groups

Most interviews take place one-on-one, but sometimes it is more efficient to interview people in groups. Focus groups are a popular data collection approach in marketing and politics. Consultants can use focus groups to generate a collective understanding or consensus. A focus group is an organized discussion and usually invited participants are told about the topic beforehand. The group consists of about 10 or fewer participants and at least one moderator. The moderator has to keep the discussion moving and on topic. Consultants may use focus groups to identify issues and problems. Sometimes the interaction that takes place in groups provides insights that individual interviews or surveys cannot. You can supplement a focus group discussion with individual interviews, surveys, and other data-gathering approaches.

Surveys

Consultants use interviews to gather data and opinions from small numbers of people. To collect data from a large group, you need to use paper or e-mail surveys, or questionnaires. Surveys, properly constructed, can be a very efficient data-gathering approach. You can use them to explore for areas to study in more depth or to verify other findings. Accountants use them for many purposes. For example, auditors use internal control questionnaires when analyzing an internal accounting control system.

Survey Design   Designing a useful survey isn't easy. Because you use a survey to collect data from a large number of respondents, making sense of the results requires data analysis tools. Poorly designed surveys don't lend themselves well to neatly organized results or valid inferences. Thus, while designing a questionnaire, you should always think about how you plan to interpret the data and calculate results.

The two potential pitfalls in survey design are choosing the wrong sample and measuring results incorrectly. Usually, you won't survey everybody, since surveying an entire population is costly, both in terms of a respondent and consultant's time.

Choosing an appropriate sample is a learned skill. (Of course, most accountants know this from their auditing classes!) Most important in selecting your sample is to make sure you give the questionnaire to the right *group* of people and the right *number* of individuals for meaningful results. Random sampling is important to make sure that the sample you choose does not have an inherent bias. Not everyone responds to a questionnaire. To avoid a nonresponse bias (i.e., a bias introduced because those who answered the survey did so because they shared a common opinion that was different from the opinion of those who didn't respond), you should follow up with some individuals who chose not to return the survey. The point is to make sure that these individuals do not have characteristics different from those who did respond. For example, if you're asking employees about job satisfaction, it may be that only those who are unhappy respond. Consequently, interpreting results from that group alone will not provide the whole picture.

It's possible that no one has ever designed a perfect survey, and certainly not on the first try. New surveys should be pilot tested or distributed to a small group at first. The results of the pilot test can be used to refine the survey. Some consulting firms may have a set of proven, standard questionnaires available for specific situations. Consulting firms that take advantage of knowledge sharing may categorize these questionnaires and post them on the organization's intranet. The internal control questionnaires used by auditors are an example of a standardized questionnaire of this sort.

Survey Questions   Good survey questions are essential for avoiding measurement error or misreading results. Survey questions should be unbiased and contain no emotional slant. They should also be specific and understandable. Writing good survey questions is an acquired skill. Practice makes, if not perfect, at least competent!

There are several types of questions consultants use in surveys. Figure 8-4 provides examples of each type. Objective or close-ended questions are easy to analyze. Questions are close-ended when the survey provides a limited set of possible answers. You can extract means and variances easily from this type of question. It is also simple to develop charts from these questions, showing the numbers or percentages for each response type. Close-ended questions can be most easily tallied, yet you will still want to leave room for "other" options or comments. Some close-ended questions are multiple choice, with letters or numbers indicating possible responses. Choices may be ordered in some way, for instance, increasing ages or levels of agreement. Alternatively, they may be unordered when the possible responses do not fall on a continuum.

Another approach to close-ended questions is to use Likert scales. This approach pairs statements with a choice of responses on a consistent scale. For example, survey respondents indicate where they strongly agree, somewhat agree, are neutral, disagree, or strongly disagree with a statement. Likert scales work well when you are asking questions involving beliefs or attitudes. A final type of close-ended question-

---

Close-Ended Questions

Multiple Choice:

1) On a weekly basis, approximately how many complaints do you receive from customers about Product X? (Circle the best answer)

      a. Rarely any

      b. 1–3 complaints

      c. 4–6 complaints

      d. 7 or more complaints (please indicate amount) _____

Likert Scale:

Please circle your response for each statement below where SD means strongly disagree, D means disagree, U indicates undecided (you neither agree nor disagree), A means agree, and SA means you strongly agree.

1) Customers rarely complain about Product X.	SD	D	U	A	SA
2) Customers are satisfied with Product X.	SD	D	U	A	SA

Rank Order:

Which of the products sold by your division appears to be most satisfactory to customers? Please rank order the following products in order of customer satisfaction, beginning with "1" for the product customers appear to like best. In your response, consider customer satisfaction with both the quality of the product and its usefulness to them.

Rank (1–5)

Product A	_____
Product C	_____
Product G	_____
Product X	_____
Product Y	_____

Open-Ended Questions

1. About how often do customers complain about Product X?
2. Do you believe customers are satisfied with Product X? If no, why not?

FIGURE 8-4   Types of survey questions.

ing is a rank-order approach. The survey asks respondents to rank order a group of concepts, usually in terms of their importance, preference, or likelihood.

    Consultants use open-ended questions—questions with no answer set provided—to discover new information. If you are on a consulting engagement in which the problem has yet to be identified, you won't know the range of responses to provide for a question. In this case, questions may be open-ended. Consultants might use this approach for a pilot survey and then, based on responses, construct a new survey using responses to the first questionnaire in close-ended questions.

    Sometimes open-ended questions are used together with close-ended questions. For example, a survey might ask respondents to explain their answer to a close-ended question. Open-ended questions are difficult to summarize or code for analysis. For this reason, surveys should use them sparingly.

    A final point about survey questions—make sure the questions you ask are unambiguous. If questions aren't clear, the person answering your survey won't know how to respond. Sometimes the terms used in the questions or answer categories require further definition. For instance, what does "usually" mean with respect to errors in processing invoices? Providing those surveyed with operational definitions, such as "In this survey example, the term 'usually' means two or more times per week" will help to avoid measurement error and provide accurate results.

Observation

As in life, it's often true in consulting that "seeing is believing." Direct observation can be the most effective way to gather facts or data for analysis. Being a keen observer requires sensitivity to nuances, facial expressions, and other "hints." In some cases, the best way to gather data is to watch how things are done. Consider, for instance, a reengineering consulting engagement. The purpose of this type of job is to tear down old processes and create new ones. While reference to best practices will help in configuring the new processes, the consultants also need to have an understanding of the processes they are replacing. The best way to learn about current processes and procedures is to observe them. Follow the involved workers as they perform their tasks within the process. While watching, make sure you understand what's being done. Ask questions to clarify any uncertainty. Document each task as the work progresses. Figure 8-5 lists some rules that will help you get the most out of your observations.

DATA ANALYSIS AND INTERPRETATION

Throughout an engagement, consultants collect data from many sources, using the approaches we just described. But raw data is useless. In order to use data in a mean-

---

1. **Plan observations carefully.** This includes making sure that the time you have scheduled for observation has been chosen so that you'll learn the most. Sometimes, when observing processes, you will want to make multiple observations to see if the process is performed the same way consistently, by the same or different people.

2. **Be appreciative and candid with the people you are observing—and be on time!** Being observed is not always comfortable for the subjects under scrutiny. Assuming that people are aware you're watching, you should be open and honest about your intent, express your thanks for their cooperation, and show good manners and respect. Be on time—people cannot wait for you when they need to do their work.

3. **Document your observations thoroughly.** The same rules regarding tape recording and note taking in interviews apply for observations. The difference is that when you're observing, you have less control of the data collection. You want to make sure that you allow the process to continue in a normal way, but at the same time you need to walk away with an understanding of what you have seen. Ask questions for clarification when needed.

4. **Keep your opinions to yourself.** It's natural sometimes to want to empathize with those you are observing, particularly when you are watching someone perform a difficult task. Some empathy is o.k., but consultants must be careful not to express opinions or to make judgements about what they are seeing. That's for later.

5. **Validate your observations.** Sometimes our eyes deceive us and sometimes they miss things. To make sure you have noted in full what you observed, share your write-up of each observation with those involved.

FIGURE 8-5 Rules for effective observations.

ingful way, consultants have to summarize and/or code it, analyze it, interpret it, and perhaps report it as information.

Summarizing and Coding Data

Suppose you're on a consulting engagement to help a client choose a new accounting software package. You've spent an eight-hour day observing various employees enter data into the old system. Unfortunately, your workday isn't over until you document your observations. You know you should arrange your observations in a meaningful fashion while your memory is still fresh. Preparing the summary or documentation such as flowcharts and process maps will help you determine what you didn't understand completely. This task will also direct your next steps in data collection.

Consultants typically need to summarize the data they collect from interviews, focus groups, and observations. They might even code the data. Both summarizing and coding are challenging tasks because you want to make sure that biases don't enter the process. Summaries, drawings, and coding schemes should be as neutral as possible.

Summarizing data from interviews and focus groups requires some editing or "cleaning up." You'll be taking notes or tape recording these sessions and there are likely to be redundancies and off-the-point comments. Transcribing notes and recordings requires removing all but the important points. Deciding *which* points are important is a skill acquired through practice. When you have a question about whether or not to delete a point, it's best to err on the side of including too much rather than too little. Again, make sure you are neutral in deciding what to cut and what to keep. Opinions and biases have no place in data summarization. If you have a question about a note or comment, return to the interviewee or person surveyed for clarification. There is no shame in admitting that you did not understand a point—particularly when weighed against the risks of solving the wrong problems!

Coding is the process of assigning numbers or quantifying responses to interview or survey questions. Consultants most often reserve coding for surveys, but sometimes structured interviews can be coded for statistical data analysis too. You should always develop your coding scheme *before* you administer a survey or interview questionnaire to minimize bias. Conducting a pilot test with a few respondents will let you refine the scheme and correct any errors. Coding schemes are easier to devise for close-ended versus open-ended questions. For example, you may assign the numbers 1–5 for responses to questions, with scaled responses ranging from strongly agree to strongly disagree. Rank-ordered questions already have assigned numbers and require no scheme other than to note the number the respondent assigned to each answer choice.

You may have an idea for a coding scheme you will use for open-ended questions but the final scheme depends on the responses. Remember that consultants use open-ended questions to gather data in areas in which they're not confident they know the range of likely responses. For example, if you're asking for a response about the number of times something occurs, but don't know what ranges are typical, you might use an open-ended question. Another use of an open-ended question is when you are trying to learn about the reasons or causes for a problem. For instance, you might ask why a group of employees believes that company sales of Product X are declining. In these instances, you do not want to construct a questionnaire or interview that limits responses. This limitation could keep you from learning the "real" answer. As a result you'll need to review your completed surveys or interview notes to develop a coding scheme. Usually this review will reveal a pattern of responses. For the example question that asks for reasons for a product's declining sales, you might find four or five responses that repeat themselves.

Sometimes respondents use different phrases to describe the same answer. This is another feature that makes open-ended questions difficult to code. Experience will help. It's also a good idea to use two coders for open-ended questions. Each person independently codes the responses and then you meet to resolve discrepancies. This approach helps to eliminate individual biases that can unintentionally affect results.

Data Analysis

Consultants collect data because they want answers to a problem or they need direction in making change. Data analysis is a necessary step in converting data into useful information. You analyze data to discover patterns that can guide you toward helping clients find solutions to problems or better ways of doing what they do.

Advances in computer technology make data analysis an increasingly useful tool in both accounting and consulting work. Consultants not only use data analysis techniques to analyze the data *they* collect on an engagement, but they also use it to analyze data their *client* collects. For example, consultants use data mining (see Chapter 12) to help clients use the data they collect from customers and suppliers to improve their operations. This section of the chapter discusses several statistical approaches to data analysis for multiple purposes, including measures of central tendencies and regression analysis.

Statistics—In Brief   Because all business school students usually have to take at least one statistics class, we offer only a brief review here of the statistical techniques used in data analysis. There are several statistics books referenced at the end of this chapter that you can refer to for more information. The data analysis approaches discussed here are: (1) calculating averages and variances, (2) finding meaningful differences, and (3) discovering relationships in data. Figure 8-6 summarizes the applicable statistics for each of these data analysis types.

Measurement Scales   The statistics you use and their level of precision depends in part on the scale used in data collection. Nominal and ordinal scales capture *qualitative* data. Nominal scales have no implied order and are typically used to code "groups" of data. For instance, coding female employees with a "0" and male employees with a "1" reflects a nominal coding scheme. The 0 and 1 codes have no intrinsic numerical value. Rather, they are used to distinguish data by some defined clusters or groups. The group codes can then be used by a spreadsheet or statistical program to sort and summarize statistics (e.g., count, sum, mean, median, mode) within and across groups. For example, adding up the number of female versus male employees is an example of information one can glean using a nominal scale.

Ordinal scales provide more precision than nominal scales, as they imply order. However, with ordinal scales, intervals between scale points may be uneven. The most common use of an ordinal scale is to have respondents indicate relative rankings. For example, a consultant might ask client employees to rank a set of issues in terms of their importance, where 10 represents the most important and 1 reflects the least important issue. Since ordinal scales represent only relative positions, they do not connote fixed intervals between and among responses. The psychological dis-

---

Calculating Means and Variances:
  Mean – the true average score. Best used to calculate averages of interval and ratio data.
  Median – the score in the middle. Half the scores are equal to it or larger, and the other half are equal or smaller. Best for ordinal data.
  Mode – the most frequent score. Best with nominal data.
  Variance – measures the distribution of scores around the mean.
  Standard deviation – the square root of the variance, it also measures the distribution of scores around the mean.

Finding Meaningful Differences:
  Nonparametric tests – for data where the distribution is not a normal one. Tests include Kruskal-Wallis and Friedman.
  Chi-square test – for nominal data samples.
  z-test – for interval and ratio data where sample sizes are larger than 30.
  t-test – for interval and ratio data where sample sizes are 30 or smaller.
  ANOVA – analysis of variance tests are used for finding differences among more than two samples.

Discovering Relationships Among Data:
  Regression analysis – finds relationships between data variables. Can also be used to predict a dependent variable, given the value of the independent variable. Multiple regression implies more than one independent variable.
  Discriminant analysis – predicts the data group based on data characteristics.
  Cluster analysis – identifies data groupings or clusters.
  Factor analysis – condenses data into factor groupings.

FIGURE 8-6   A summary of statistical techniques used in data analysis.

tance between issues marked 3 and 4 may not be the same as the psychological distance between issues 8 and 9, even though the mathematical distances (or fixed intervals) are 1 in both instances. The lack of fixed intervals does not make statistical analysis impossible, but it does indicate the appropriate type of analysis to use—generally nonparametric statistics. It also suggests using caution when interpreting the data. It would be acceptable to say that "Concerns over excessive overtime" was the highest rated employee issue and "Concerns over parking spaces" was the lowest rated issue. However, it would be inappropriate to infer that the highest rated issue was 10 times more important to employees than the lowest rated issue.

Likert-type scales, in which survey responses are coded from, say, 1 through 5 or 1 through 7, are also ordinal in nature and thus qualitative. However, from a statistical perspective, they are often treated as interval scales (where the assumption is that the distances between scale points are even across the entire scale), since rather severe "interval" departures do not seem to affect Type I or Type II errors dramatically. For example, a respondent might be asked the following question and provided with the following coding scheme: "How do you feel about your boss?" (1 = Very much dislike, 2 = Somewhat dislike, 3 = Neither like nor dislike, 4 = Somewhat like, 5 = Very much like). An interval violation arises, to some degree, because it is highly unlikely that the psychological distance between "Somewhat dislike" and "Neither like nor dislike" (which is 1) is precisely the same as the psychological distance between "Somewhat like" and "Very much like" (which is also 1) within and across respondents. Social scientists recognize that attaining such interval perfection is nearly impossible, yet careful wording and pretesting of survey items can help to validate Likert-type ordinal scales so that they can be statistically treated as interval scales. Thus, a great deal of information can be obtained via the use of these scales. For instance, if the mean rating for the above scale was 4.2 for male and 2.3 for female employees, and the means were statistically significantly different from each other, the consultant might draw some valid inferences about the boss, male employees, female employees, or some combination thereof. There are a wide variety of parametric and nonparametric statistical tests that can be used with data collected via Likert-type scales, depending on the distributional properties of the underlying data.

The third type of scaled data is called an interval, where there is order, equal distance between scale points across the entire scale, and an arbitrary zero point. For example, counts are instances of interval data, such as counts of income, years education, and weight. Assume that we weigh two married couples: Julie weighs 100 pounds and Sam weighs 150 pounds; Gretta weighs 110 pounds and Dan weighs 160 pounds. What inferences might we draw? We could say with certainty that Sam and Dan both outweigh their spouses by 50 pounds, and we would know that each point increment on the scale (one pound) has the same meaning across the scale *and* that each individual was weighed against a reference point of zero pounds. We could also say that Sam outweighs Gretta by 40 pounds. But could we say that Sam weighs 36 percent more than Gretta (40/110 pounds)? The technical answer is "no," since we do not have ratio-scaled data; hence, we can only use addition or subtraction operators on interval scaled data (where Likert-type scaled data is assumed to have sufficient interval properties), whereas we can also use multiplication and division operators on ratio-scaled data. Let's take a quick look at ratio-scaled data next and then come back to this example.

The fourth type of scale is called a ratio scale, which is much like the interval scale, except that a known zero reference point exists. There are few, if any, instances of "true" ratio-scaled data in social sciences. One example from the physical sciences would be temperature, where *absolute zero* (not zero as we know it on the typical Celsius or Fahrenheit scales) reflects the zero reference point. Although ratio-scaled data is all but absent from the social sciences, we often treat interval-scaled data as if it were ratio scaled, meaning that we use the multiplication and division operations on such data. Normally, the use of such arithmetical operations is deemed acceptable with interval data collected in the social sciences. In our example, it would be practically, though not technically, accurate to say that Sam outweighs Gretta by 36 percent.

However, the same degree of precision generally does not hold for a Likert-type scale, even though we often treat such scales as if they were interval from a statistical perspective. Say that employees rated their attitude toward the company's profit-sharing plan as: 1 = Very Poor, 2 = Poor, 3 = Acceptable, 4 = Good, 5 = Very Good. If warehouse employees recorded a mean response of 2 and accounting employees recorded a mean response of 4, one should be careful to interpret that the accountants' attitude was 50 percent more positive than warehouse employees. By doing so, the consultant would presume equal intervals (which might be somewhat close across the scale) *and* an arbitrary zero reference point (which would imply that all respondents started at a common psychological baseline). The former assumption may be acceptable, while the latter is not. Hence, the best one might conclude with the interval scale is that the accounting employees' attitude is significantly more positive (if the statistical difference in means meets some defined minimum criteria) than the warehouse employees' attitude.

It would behoove all consultants to brush up on their statistical prowess, as data collection, analysis, and interpretation can be vitally important indicators of underlying issues, attitudes, processes, and so on. A very brief overview of statistics is next provided.

Calculating Averages and Variances.   The simplest forms of data analysis make use of basic arithmetic as the following example shows.

> **Example**   Suppose you want to learn about customers' attitudes toward a particular client product. The response categories range from very dissatisfied to very satisfied, and are coded 1–5, respectively. The first step in analyzing this data is to add up the number of people who answered the question. Next you sum the coded answers. Dividing the summed answers by the number of respondents gives you the *mean* or average response (score).

A caution about means: Consultants and data analysts often use means because they can help in interpreting the data. However, means relate to populations versus samples. Consultants are most likely to collect data from a subset of a total population, as one usually doesn't have the luxury of gathering data from everyone involved in an engagement. But statistical formulas are different when applied to entire populations versus samples. We won't discuss sampling techniques here since accountants, particularly auditors, should be familiar with the notion of samples. However, beware that unless the sample is representative of the population, any inferences drawn from means can be invalid and misleading.

The mean is one type of average, or measure of central tendency. Others are median and mode. The mean represents the true arithmetic average, as previously illustrated. The median is the score where half the data is equal to or above it and the other half is equal to or below it. The mode is the score that occurs most frequently.

> **Example**   Suppose you're interviewing client employees to find out how many times their computer locks up when they're entering accounting data. The scores or numbers they report range from twice a week to 20 times per week. The mean appears to be six times. To learn more about the distribution (i.e., the pattern of data around the mean), you calculate the median too. It turns out to be five, indicating that half the workers have it happen less than five times a week and for the other half, the occurrence is more frequent. You may also want to calculate the mode. Perhaps four is the mode here; thus, you know that four times per week is the most reported frequency of personal computer failure.

Sometimes the variance, or difference around the mean, is as important as the mean itself. In our customer satisfaction example, a consultant might interpret the data one way if nearly all respondents felt neutral about the product (represented by a tight clustering of scores around the mean of 3). However, the interpretation might be different if the response distribution was somewhat evenly spread across the entire scale, meaning approximately the same proportions of customers were dissatisfied, neutral, and satisfied with the product—even though both situations would result in a mean of 3! Lesson learned: You should calculate the range of scores to get some clues about the distribution of occurrences before making any inferences.

In our second example the range of reported computer lock ups was between two and 20 times per week. But maybe only one person reported experiencing the problem 20 times and the next closest score was 12. Again, you should calculate differences from the mean and also prepare a frequency distribution to learn more about the data set.

The standard deviation is the most commonly used measure of variability around the mean. It provides an analyst with a good indication of the amount of variation in the scores. Perhaps the scores are all close to the mean (with the exception of an outlying data value or two like the score of 20 in our example). To calculate the standard deviation, you take the square root of the variance. In narrative terms, the standard deviation is equal to the square root of the variance, which is the sum of squared deviations from the mean divided by the number of scores. A large standard deviation would tell us that there's lots of variability in the data. In this example, that could mean that the problem isn't systemic, but rather relates to a characteristic about the employees who experience frequent personal computer failures. Maybe their computers just aren't as powerful, or perhaps these employees tend to keep several programs open at the same time.

Finding Meaningful Differences   Sometimes consultants need to find differences between groups and determine whether these differences are meaningful. For instance you might be looking at differences between stores, divisions, products, suppliers, and so on. Usually when you're looking for differences, you are comparing averages and/or the distribution of the data. For example, we may be interested in finding out whether customer satisfaction levels are different in, say, New York versus California. Maybe the means are different, but you're not sure that the difference is statistically significant—that is, not due to chance.

The statistical tool you will use to find meaningful differences depends on the data you're measuring. In any case, you will need one random sample from each of at least two different populations. The samples must be independent. You also need to know if the data follow a normal (bell-shaped) distribution. If they don't, you may need to use nonparametric tests (see Figure 8-6). Once again, you also need to consider if the scale of measurement is nominal, ordinal, interval, or ratio.

For nominal or qualitative data you should use a chi-square test. The chi-square test measures differences between the number of instances or occurrences of a nominal occurrence (e.g., the number of male versus female customers who return products). The chi-square statistic, χ^2, tells you whether or not there is really a relationship between gender and returned products, or whether that difference is due to chance.

Two popular parametric tests for interval, including Likert-type scales and ratio data, are the z-test and the t-test. Once again, you should be careful in relying too heavily on results when you use these tests with ordinal data, remembering that the intervals between the variables are not fixed. The z and t statistics are used for two-sample tests. If you want to find differences among more than two samples (e.g., customer satisfaction compared among more than two states), you will need to use analysis of variance (ANOVA) or F-test statistics.

The z-test of significance between sample means works when you have sample sizes larger than 30 (a general rule of thumb). The t-test applies for samples of 30 or less. Both tests rely on probability theory. Any two samples are likely to be different—what a consultant or researcher wants to know is whether that difference is *real* or due to chance. Since samples are just subsets of a population, the mean of a sample isn't necessarily the same as the mean in the population. And any randomly picked sample may have a different mean. The sample mean depends on which data are included in the sample. Difference tests determine the probability that the sample means are different due to some characteristic associated with the sample. For instance, maybe New York customers are less satisfied because service support is not as good in that region as in California. Formulas for z-tests and t-tests are beyond the scope of this book. We suggest you refer to one of the statistics books listed at the end of this chapter for more information.

Discovering Relationships in Data   Data can tell a story. Consultants, using computer programs that incorporate statistical techniques such as regression analysis, look for patterns in the data. Advances in computer technology, and the richness of data in databases and data warehouses allow consultants and managers to find all sorts of patterns or relationships among data. Some of these tools are used in "mining" data. Many consultants today offer data mining services to their clients. The service is popular because data mining can uncover important relationships between customer characteristics and sales patterns.

Regression analysis is one technique employed in data mining. When you "run a regression," you are looking for a relationship between an independent (causal) variable, X and a dependent variable, Y. That is, you want to see if X correlates or changes with changes in Y. Sometimes, there are many causal variables, in which case you need to use multiple regression analysis. Why is a consulting client's sales revenue decreasing? Perhaps it is due to decreased advertising expenditures, lower product quality specifications, or other factors.

Regression analysis produces a correlation coefficient, R, that indicates the strength of the relationship between the independent and dependent variable. The square of this coefficient (R^2) tells you how much of the variation is explained by the relationship between the two variables. For example, if you know that the relationship between the PC model and the number of screen freezes an employee experiences per week is .8, there is a positive relationship between the two variables. R^2 is 64 percent in this instance, meaning that the PC model explains 64 percent of the variance. The higher the R^2, the stronger the causal relationship between X and Y.

Other statistical techniques related to data patterns are discriminant analysis, cluster analysis, and factor analysis. Discriminant analysis differentiates groups from each other, based on a set of measures. For example, in discriminating between one PC model versus another, if you knew how many computer failures an employee experienced per week, you might use discriminant analysis to determine what PC model he or she has.

Cluster analysis is a technique for organizing "like" individuals or objects into groups. You group entities that have similar characteristics into clusters. In discriminant analysis, the groups are predefined and you try to fit data values or instances into the group. With cluster analysis, you are forming the group based on the data characteristics.

Factor analysis is similar to cluster analysis in that it groups similar data together. Factor analysis reduces a data set by condensing the information in a large number of variables into a smaller set by identifying the underlying dimensions or commonalities in the interrelationships among the variables. It can be useful in paring a questionnaire to a shorter instrument. For example, you might ask 100 questions in a pilot survey. Conducting factor analysis of the pilot results, you might identify five or so dimensions or factors in the data. Perhaps you can then develop a questionnaire with only that number of questions and yet lose a minimal amount of information.

Regression, discriminant, cluster, and factor analysis are all statistical tools most appropriate for interval and ratio data. Researchers also use them frequently with ordinal data.

Software Tools for Data Analysis

Today's computer software tools make it fairly easy to perform complex statistical data analyses. The click of a mouse in spreadsheet software, such as *Microsoft Excel,* lets you perform regression, sampling, analysis of variance, and other statistical tests. (See Figure 8-7.) Specialized statistical software like *SPSS, SAS,* and *Minitab* lets you

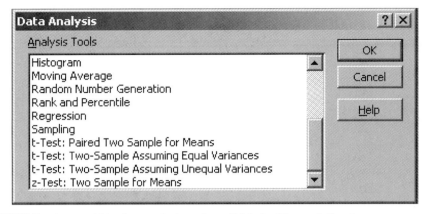

FIGURE 8-7. Some add-in data analysis tools available in *Microsoft Excel.*

do even more. Consultants can use these tools to analyze data collected from client interviews and surveys. You can also use them in the consulting work itself. The SPSS web site lists stories about customers who have solved problems with their statistics software. Some examples in data mining use include Dayton Hudson Corporation's selection of new retail store sites and customer satisfaction measurement, First Union's identification of new target markets and more cost-effective channels for delivery, and Deloitte Touche Tohmatsu International's improvement of information quality for their clients.[2] Apart from data mining, more consultants and companies are using statistical software tools in customer relationship management (CRM), e-business consulting, fraud detection, market research, and process analysis and improvement. Consultants (and accountants) today need to master these software tools to be competitive.

Turning Data into Information

So what does it all mean? Complex math equations and sophisticated statistical software provide you with an analysis of data that may run to the hundreds of pages. Interpreting the results, or turning the data into information you can use, is a human process.

Once you've performed data analysis of interview or survey data, you should go back through the original data, one interview or survey at a time, to see if the analysis results make sense. Errors are possible at each stage of data analysis so a visual check is a good idea. Revisiting the data will also help you in formulating your interpretation of the data results. As one researcher[3] put it, "Usually I can see a path through the data. Sometimes it's muddier than others, but by looking at it and thinking about it over time, a path emerges."

Pictures can help—not just in terms of the consultant's own understanding of the story behind the data, but also for communicating the story to others. Bar charts, pie charts, graphs, and tables are useful data interpretation and communication tools.

---

[2] www.spss.com/spssatwork/search.cfm.
[3] Keith Houghton, Fitzgerald Professor of Accounting, University of Melbourne.

Demographic Characteristics of Client Employees Who Responded to August 2000 Job Satisfaction Survey				
	Office			
Years of Service	Columbus	Dayton	Cincinnati	Cleveland
Less than 1	2	0	3	5
1–4	6	3	5	10
5–10	10	2	12	10
10–20	15	2	10	12
More than 20	25	0	8	13

FIGURE 8-8   An example of a data summary table from a consulting engagement.

Example   Figure 8-8 highlights some important characteristics about the employees who re-turned a job satisfaction survey to a consulting team. Figure 8-9 depicts the same data in bar chart form. Looking at the data in table or graphic form raises questions not readily apparent from individual data or averages. Is the Dayton office relatively new or did older employees choose not to respond for some reason? Are most employees in the Columbus office older, or did just the more experienced employees choose to answer the survey–perhaps because they are the most dissatisfied?

Finally, now that you have some information, revisit your original questions to evaluate the importance of what you've learned. Has the data collection and analysis process answered the questions intended? Consultants should also ask themselves at this time whether the results are meaningful or important and what additional, data if any, need to be collected. Frequently, answers raise more questions, so you may need to get more information, based on what you learn. It may also happen that while collecting data, you discover other issues a client needs to address. Sometimes the data collection and analysis phase of consulting work provides opportunities for cross-selling services (as discussed in Chapter 3).

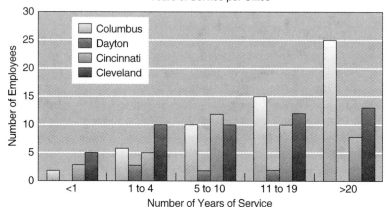

FIGURE 8-9   Bar chart for table in Figure 8-8.

SUMMARY

Consultants cannot walk into their client's business and implement a preformulated solution to the problem at hand—and live to tell about it. Each consulting engagement requires some data collection and analysis. Data comes from both inside the client firm and from external sources like publications and the Internet.

There are several ways to collect data. In this chapter we discussed interviews, surveys, and observation in some depth. Interviews are a particularly rich source of data. To maximize the effectiveness of interviews, you need to do some advance research and planning. There is an art to developing a good interview and also to carrying it out. There are advantages and disadvantages to tape or video recording interviews versus taking notes during or immediately following the interview. An interviewer must take control of the interview, not allowing the subject to wander too far off the topic. At the same time, a good interviewer's most important skill is the ability to listen carefully. Consultants often use focus groups to collect data. These are essentially group interviewers, requiring a facilitator to ask the questions and moderate the session. Surveys are useful in gathering data from large numbers of people. Constructing good surveys is both art and science. There are many resources available to help data collectors in creating a survey that will yield useful results. Consultants need to study these to avoid collecting the wrong data or data that tell a different story than the reality. Sometimes direct observation is the best approach to data collection. A consultant can learn more about how things are done by watching, rather than having someone report on a process.

Sometimes data analysis merely involves transcribing notes from interview sessions. At the other extreme, it can require complex statistical analysis, assisted by statistical computer software packages. All data must be summarized or coded in some way for analysis purposes. In the chapter we briefly discuss data analysis techniques for measuring central tendency, finding meaningful differences, and discovering relationships or patterns in data. Consultants use statistical analysis for analyzing data collected about a client engagement, and also frequently as part of the engagement. Data mining is one example of the latter use.

Thanks to statistical computer software, consultants don't need to memorize and apply formulas for regression and analysis of variance calculations. They do need to grasp the statistical techniques well enough to be able to interpret the analysis results correctly. Sometimes data interpretation is assisted by using table or graphical summaries. At its best, the data collection and analysis stage of a consulting engagement will point to problem solutions.

DISCUSSION QUESTIONS

8-1. Explain why this chapter refers to data as the "heart" of a consulting engagement.

8-2. Interviews require preparation. Imagine that you are planning to interview the chief information officer (CIO) of a client organization about information systems security. How would you prepare for the interview? How would you structure your interview questions?

8-3. During an interview, the interviewer must maintain control of the questioning process. Suppose you are interviewing someone who answers questions with 20 minutes or so of conversation that strays far off the subject at hand. What are some things you might say to move the interview along and steer it back to the topic?

8-4. In Discussion Question 8-2, you were planning to interview a client's CIO about the firm's information systems security processes and procedures. Would you tape record the interview or take notes? Why?

8-5. In an interview, listening is as important as questioning. Why? What are some nonverbal signals for which you might listen?

8-6. What preparation might you do prior to facilitating a focus group discussion with client employees?

8-7. Describe some problems that can result from improper survey design.

8-8. What are some important reasons to pilot test surveys?

8-9. What are the advantages and disadvantages of open- versus close-ended questions?

8-10. Why is it important for consultants to have a thorough understanding of statistics?

8-11. When might a consultant use tools for finding significant differences between two samples?

8-12. How could you use regression analysis in a client engagement?

8-13. Visit the web sites of one or more of the statistical software vendors mentioned in this chapter. What kinds of data analysis do they advertise? Does the web site discuss only statistical test features or does it describe applications?

8-14. Discuss the virtues of tabular versus graphical formats in interpreting data analysis results.

8-15. Data mining uses a variety of statistical tools. What are some of the most common?

EXERCISES

8-16. Suppose that you have a client with the following problem. The company is constantly increasing its inventory levels to improve delivery times to customers, but the delivery times keep going up anyhow. Devise a set of interview questions for the production manager, based on your hypotheses about the problem.

8-17. Conduct a role-playing exercise. One role is that of a production supervisor in a manufacturing plant in which product quality levels are falling off. The truth of the matter is that the supervisor is not doing a good job in managing workers. Because the workers have no respect for the supervisor and also because they believe that their performance evaluation scheme does not reflect the work they do, they could care less about improving quality. The supervisor believes the problems are not his fault. He blames his boss for pretty much everything and during your interview with him he tries to bring up this sore subject at every opportunity. He is also prone to going off on tangents; he wants to tell you about his recent gall bladder surgery in graphic detail. The other role is the interviewer with limited time in which to collect information about the problem.

8-18. You have been hired to help a client select a new accounting software package. You have interviewed the chief financial officer (CFO) and she has told you management's objectives for the new package. You plan to collect data primarily through interviews and observation, but you would like to first send a survey to the accounting clerks in the company's five offices to try to get a better handle on the problems with the current software and also learn about what the employees would like to see in the new package. Design a two- to three-page questionnaire for this purpose.

REFERENCES, RECOMMENDED READINGS, AND WEB SITES

References and Recommended Readings

Barcus, S. W. III, and J. W. Wilkinson, Eds., *Handbook of Management Consulting Services,* 2nd edition (New York: McGraw-Hill, 1995).

Block, Peter, *Flawless Consulting,* 2nd edition (San Francisco: Jossey-Bass Pfeiffer, 2000).

Gravetter, F. J., and L. B. Wallnau, *Statistics for the Behavioral Sciences,* 4th edition (St. Paul, MN: West Publishing Company, 1996).

Hair, J. F. Jr., R. E. Anderson, and R. L. Tatham, *Multivariate Data Analysis,* 2nd edition (New York: Macmillan, 1987).

Kerlinger, Fred N., and Howard B. Lee, *Foundations of Behavioral Research,* 4th edition (Fort Worth, TX: Harcourt, Brace, and Johnson, 2000).

Quay, John, *Diagnostic Interviewing for Consultants and Auditors* (Cincinnati, OH: Quay Associates, 1994).

Reeb, W. L., *Start Consulting—How to Walk the Talk* (New York: American Institute of Certified Public Accountants, 1998).

Salant, Priscilla, and Don A. Dillman, *How to Conduct Your Own Survey* (New York: John Wiley and Sons, 1994).

Web Sites
www.knowledgespace.com
www.microsoft.com
www.minitab.com
www.sas.com
www.spss.com

Chapter 9

Feedback, Implementation, and Follow-Up

The consultant's primary task is to present the picture—this is 70 percent of the contribution you have to make. Trust it.

> Peter Block, *Flawless Consulting*
> (San Francisco: Jossey-Bass/Pfeiffer 2000), p. 217

INTRODUCTION

Chapter 8 presented the fundamentals of collecting and analyzing data. This chapter continues with detail on how to solicit feedback from the client on the findings of data collection and analysis, including how to elicit a decision to proceed and what to do if major hurdles to the project's success are encountered. Next, we will discuss strategies for implementing the solution once the client gives the green light to proceed with implementation. We will outline a method we have found particularly successful for implementation, which we call the "step-check" method. We will revisit documentation in the context of implementation of the solution and offer tips for the final presentation. Finally, we will discuss following up with the client after the project is completed, including how to counsel the client for continued success and how to lay the groundwork for future business. Figure 9-1 shows what happens from presenting the results of data collection and analysis through the end of the engagement.

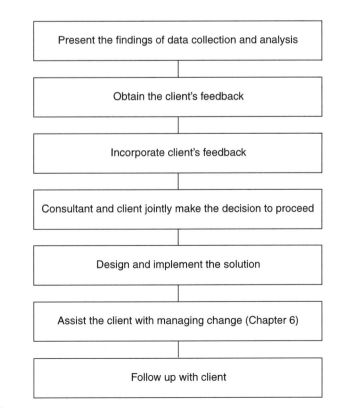

FIGURE 9-1   The feedback, implementation, and follow-up process.

THE FEEDBACK PROCESS

It's important to keep the client in the loop at each step of the consulting engagement. You'll likely work very closely with all levels of employees from upper management to line managers to mailroom personnel. The client will undoubtedly be anxious to know what your interviews and other data collection procedures have revealed. Now that you've gathered and analyzed data relative to the consulting engagement, you'll want to inform your client as to the preliminary results before proceeding with implementation.

Some consultants skip this step in the engagement—this is a big mistake. It's vital to give the client the opportunity to correct any misinterpretation of data you may have made or other errors in collection of data. Perhaps you didn't interview a key employee. Perhaps you interviewed a disgruntled employee whose input was consequently biased. In any case, proceeding with implementation before sharing the preliminary results with the client can cause later work and cost overruns. How much simpler to correct errors before implementation.

Presenting the Findings

The first step in the process is setting up a meeting to present the results of the data collection and analysis. The presentation may be formal or informal, as appropriate to the company and the project itself. All members of the project team and client personnel should attend the meeting. The project manager should be in charge of conducting the meeting and should at least present the introduction and conclusion. The intermittent details may be delegated to project team members as appropriate. Guidelines for presenting to the client were discussed in detail in Chapter 4. A brief review of the main points of presenting to the client is outlined below. See Chapter 4 for more detailed information on presentation skills.

How Long Should the Presentation Be?   The one-hour rule presented in Chapter 4 is a good rule of thumb to follow at this point, although an hour may not be needed. Allow enough time to comfortably convey what you've found.

Formal or Informal Presentation?   The type of presentation that is needed depends mainly on the type of business. A large, conservative corporate office may call for a formal, "blue-suit presentation," while a welding shop would not require nearly that level of formality. The objective is to aim to make the client feel comfortable. A blue-collar company will likely feel more comfortable if the consultant dresses in a manner similar to the company's formal or informal dress code.

Technology and Visual Aids   The consultant should use technology as appropriate to present the results of the data collection and analysis. In today's technological age, this will likely be a PowerPoint presentation complete with charts and graphs. A word about charts and graphs: they are invaluable visual aids and can convey summary information and conclusions at a glance. Be sure any charts and graphs are in color and labeled correctly. A descriptive title and legend also contribute to a thorough understanding of the picture. Be sure the visual aids are large enough to be comfortably seen, including chart legends. You'll lose the client if the visual aid can't be seen. It's a good idea to do a practice-run in the room where the presentation will take place. This helps the consultant develop familiarity with the room's layout, while allowing an opportunity to check the clarity and size of the visual aids.

Sensitivity

The presentation skills presented in Chapters 2 and 4 are applicable here and need not be repeated. However, one particular quality that is highly valued at this stage is sensitivity. Often you have had access to confidential company information, including company trade secrets and financial data. You also have conducted in-depth interviews with client personnel at all levels. The wise consultant realizes that certain sensitivity is required in discussing the results of interviews and other data collection.

What happens when the information gathered is not favorable to the client? What is the best way to convey the unfavorable information? For example, what if interviews with client personnel reveal underlying hostility toward the company? Should you convey this to the client? The question here is one of relevance. Ask yourself, "Is this finding directly relevant to the project at hand?" This is the easy case. If the answer is yes, you should inform the client immediately. Practice tact, diplomacy, and sensitivity. Tell the client that you have uncovered some issues, *why* this problem is relevant to the consulting engagement, and *how* it affects the data and implementation of the solution.

How about a problem that is only *indirectly* related to the consulting engagement? For example, if you are designing a corporate intranet and the disgruntled employee will not have any responsibilities associated with the new intranet, does this need to be disclosed? Here discretion must be exercised. Does the employee have a reasonable opportunity to sabotage the project at any level? Has the employee expressed an inclination to engage in such action? Remember that this is an employee's future at stake. If the threat is only indirect, and there is no opportunity and/or verbal explicit or implied threat, the best course of action is probably to refrain from mentioning it to the client at this point. Rather, you might instead include a suggestion or recommendation in the management letter presented at the end of the engagement. The management letter is discussed later in this chapter. The bottom line is to let experience and common sense guide your decision to disclose or not disclose.

What to Present

The primary items to include at this stage are results of data collection and analysis. Who did you interview? What are your overall conclusions based on those interviews? What statistical or other tests did you perform? What analytical procedures did you use? The client wants to know what you have found out. Does the data analysis change how you planned to implement the solution? Are there other significant changes from what you presented in the proposal as a result of the data collection and analysis? If so, this is the time to inform the client.

Getting the Client's Input—Feedback

OK, so now you've presented your findings, including any problems that may need the client's attention. The next step is to get the client's input. The consulting process is a collaborative partnership. The client knows the intricacies of his business better than you. After presenting the results of your data collection and analysis, ask the client for input. What are the client's thoughts about your findings? In particular, how does the client think problems you have identified should be dealt with? For example, returning to the disgruntled employee scenario, the client may have insight into this employee's behavior and may know better what type of risk this employee really is.

The client may seek your advice regarding a problem you have identified during discovery and analysis. You should be prepared to offer such solutions based on your knowledge and understanding of the situation.

The Client/Consultant Decision to Proceed

After presenting your findings and agreeing on tactics for handling problems, you should elicit from the client a firm directive to proceed. If the client has any stipulations arising from the discussion, they should be specifically stated and agreed on. A period of negotiation may be entered into in which the consultant and client work out any areas of confusion or disagreement as to how to proceed. If major changes in the consulting proposal need to be made, major amendments to the contract should be written and signed by both the consultant and the client and serve as amendments to the contract. Minor amendments do not necessarily need to be written out; however, to be on the safe side, all changes to the contract can be written up and signed by the parties. As discussed in Chapter 4, what is major and what is minor requires a judgment call on the part of the consultant.

It is possible that the client may decide not to proceed with the engagement. This may happen if the consultant identifies significant problems that may prevent or inhibit the success of the project. For example, suppose the consultant discovers through data collection that the client personnel are not significantly experienced or skilled to use the new system. Although training may go a long way to help get employees up to speed, if the employees are extremely resistant to change, successful implementation of the overall project may be in doubt. Another example might involve economic feasibility. For example, perhaps the consultant uncovers information about the client's existing resources that indicate the cost of completion of the project may turn out to be significantly higher than originally estimated. The client may not be willing or able to commit to a higher cost figure. If the costs cannot be negotiated or another compromise reached, the client may not be willing to proceed with the project.

Restatement of Commitment

A final component to presenting the findings is for the consultant to reiterate commitment to the success of the project. Restating your commitment reassures the client that the project will be completed as mutually agreed on and in a timely manner. As always, remember to thank the client for the opportunity to assist them with this project.

IMPLEMENTING THE SOLUTION

The "Step-Check" Method

There are various paths to design and development of the solution. One method is a stepwise approach that we term the "step-check" method for development. Following this approach, the solution is prepared a step at a time and confirmed with the client at major points in the design/development.

Note that we said, "major points." The client will not have confidence in you if you are constantly verifying your work with him or her. Ideally, you will have no more than two major points in the development in which you run the interim work by the client. These are crucial points at which the client's input is needed to affirm that the solution is taking shape as envisioned. These crucial points will likely have been identified as milestones in the preliminary planing. The client should know ahead of time that you will need him or her to look at the interim work to affirm the progress and as well as at approximately what stage of the work you need their input.

Prototypes

In the event the project involves development of a customized application, you may wish to develop a prototype before proceeding with a full-scale application. A prototype is a scaled-down, "bare-bones" version of the full model. The purpose of a prototype is to permit the client a preview of what the final model will look like. However, the prototype is not fully functional at this point.

For example, let's say you have been engaged to develop an expert system for a bank to determine whether a loan should be given.[1] The "guts" of the expert system consists of a series of "if-then" rules that lead to a decision, yes or no, to make a loan to an applicant. Many "shell" programs are available to facilitate development of expert systems. A full-scale model for the loan program may well require 100 or more "if-then" rules to cover all decision paths. However, this will take significant time to fully develop. A prototype model may consist of, say, 30 rules that cover a portion of the decision process, but not all paths.

This abbreviated version of the full model can often be put together in a fraction of time that the full model would take. This permits the consultant to preview the system with the client and obtain the client's input before hundreds of hours are invested in the project.

Prototypes are applicable for any customized application, including specialized spreadsheets, customized databases, Visual Basic applications, web internets and intranets, and customized accounting modules.

Is there any time when a prototype is not practical? The answer is "yes." A prototype is not needed when the application is relatively small. For example, an expert system that will only require 30 rules in the full model obviously doesn't need a prototype with 5 rules, since it doesn't take much longer to create a system with 30 rules.

---

[1] An expert system is an artificial intelligence technology that can make decisions similar to a human expert.

Resistance to Change

Change management is fully covered in Chapter 10. Suffice it to say that it is normal to experience some internal resistance to change. Employees do not like moving out of their "comfort zone." Perhaps they have invested many years in a particular way of doing things. Their security lies with their feeling confident about their jobs. The changes you are enabling may threaten that security. The consultant should assess the nature and extent of resistance, and employ the methods detailed in Chapter 10 to facilitate implementation and to help the employees feel less threatened.

Documentation

In the process of developing customized applications you will generate a great deal of paper. This includes analytic, program, and system flowcharts, run manuals, and other documentation. It is important to retain copies of all documentation, but it is equally important for the client to receive copies of appropriate documentation.

For example, let's say your consulting team developed a customized accounts payable program. Such a project would have involved analyzing the company's current accounts payable program for strengths and weaknesses, and would have likely used analytic and program flowcharts to do so. The source code for the program is also a vital part of the documentation process. Without the source code, the company cannot make subsequent changes to the program. Finally, the consultant would have written a run manual for operation of the new accounts payable application. Which of these documents is furnished to the client?

Not all documentation generated should be given to the client. The flowcharts used to analyze the old accounts payable system are internal to the consulting firm. The consultant retains the results of interviews with client personnel, as well as other internal documentation. Only documentation that the company needs to make subsequent changes or to use the new application is given to the client. Thus, the source code and the run manual are the two types of documentation that in this case should be furnished to the client.

"Going Live"

You've done the legwork, gathered and analyzed data, and prepared the solution. Now you must actually implement your solution. This is what you have worked for—it's the culmination of all of your work to date. What's the best way to proceed? The answer depends largely on the type of project.

One of the most common consulting projects involves the design and development of some type of customized software application, as previously discussed. Implementing a customized application can be accomplished in one of three methods: immediate cutover, parallel operation, or phased implementation. Each of these approaches is detailed.

Immediate Cutover In this approach, use of the old application is discontinued simultaneously with the use of the new application. One day you're using the old system ... the next day you're using the new one. This implementation strategy is often referred to as the "big bang" approach and this method of going live requires significant faith in the new system. It's generally used when modifications to an existing system are relatively minor or when there is a compelling reason to switch over immediately from the old to new systems. Implementation of a completely new application or major changes to an important accounting module, such as payroll, do not usually occur using immediate cutover due to the significant risks involved.

Parallel Implementation Parallel implementation is the most common type of implementation for major projects and/or modifications to sensitive programs. In this method, both the old and new applications are run simultaneously, with the output from the new program compared to the output from the old program for accuracy. This allows the client a period of time to reach a level of comfort with the new application before being "cut loose." This approach is popular with clients simply because many people are nervous about trusting a new application right off the bat. They need time to adjust and develop confidence in the new program. A parallel implementation procedure allows time for a smooth and orderly adjustment period.

The length of time that the two applications are run simultaneously depends largely on how long the client needs to develop confidence in the new program. If the new application proves to be as accurate as the old system, it may take only a couple of cycles for the client to feel comfortable with the new system. On the other hand, if the two outputs do not agree, the source of the disagreement must be located and resolved. Usually two cycles with no problems are considered a minimum.

Phased Implementation Phased implementation is another piecemeal method to implement a new system. This method provides that an application is implemented in stages or phases. For example, let's say you were hired to convert a company from one accounting software package to another. Phased implementation may involve implementing first the general ledger module, troubleshooting that module, and moving to implement subsequent modules one at a time. Once the consultant and client are satisfied with the accuracy of a module, the next module is installed, tested, and debugged. This continues until the new system is entirely installed.

Combination Strategies In some instances, the consultant might use a combination of immediate cutover, parallel, and phased implementation strategies. For example, assume that a client, with offices throughout the United States and Europe, just made major changes to its human resources applications. The consultant and client might decide to use a phased approach with respect to locations; offices in eastern Europe will be the first to receive the new applications, with western Europe and eastern United States and western United States to follow. Each "block" of offices will be fully implemented before moving on to the next. The consultant and client next decide that the existing human resource applications used in eastern Europe are so unreliable that an immediate cutover approach to the new applications is appropriate. Finally, because existing systems are more stable in the remaining office locations, a phased approach is used. Combined strategies of this nature can be considered for large companies with many subsidiaries, product lines, manufacturing plants, and so on.

Backups It's extremely important that when installing a new system, the consultant maintain backups of the client's system. In the event of a failure at any point of the new system or a portion of the new system, you can restore the system to the point prior to the point of failure.

Why Systems Implementations Projects Fail

Many consulting projects experience significant implementation problems, even to the point of partial or complete implementation failure. Why do these projects fail? What can consultants do to mitigate the possibility of failure? Let's take a closer look at those issues.

Client Failure to Monitor the Project   One reason systems implementation projects fail is the failure of the client to adequately monitor the project. Although a consultant may be employed to perform the implementation, this doesn't mean the client has no responsibilities for the implementation. The client must adequately monitor the consultant's progress and work to coordinate the participation of client personnel. A major systems implementation project at Blue Cross suffered from this type of problem and ultimately failed. Case-in-Point 9.1 describes the problems encountered at Blue Cross.

> *Case-in-Point 9.1*   After six years and more than $120 million invested in a new information system termed "System 21," Blue Cross and Blue Shield of Massachusetts abandoned the project and ultimately outsourced its computer operations to Electronic Data Systems. A main reason cited for failure of the project was the company's inability to properly supervise the project. While an independent vendor was hired to develop the software, the company failed to appoint someone to coordinate and manage the project.[2]

Premature Reliance on New System   It's essential that the consultant fully test the new system before live implementation. Failure to do so will invite implementation problems that will likely interfere with the company's services and/or operations, at a high cost to the company who may likely sue the consultant. Case-in-Point 9.2 provides recent examples of this problem

> *Case-in-Point 9.2*   SAP AG, the German company that makes the popular R/3 enterprise resource planning (ERP) software has suffered several highly publicized systems implementation problems. One problem was experienced by Hershey Foods in their new $112 million R/3 ordering-and-distribution system. Although SAP said its software wasn't at fault, it appears the problems were apparently due to relying on the system before it was fully tested. The costs to Hershey were high since the problem occurred immediately prior to the Halloween season. As a result of the computer system problems, distributors reported candy shortages plus trouble getting orders filled or receiving information about future orders related to the Halloween season. As if these problems weren't enough, Whirlpool also experienced similar problems with its new R/3 system, which led to shipping delays in five countries in which it used the system. Both of these systems failures were at least partially the result of failure to fully test the new system before going live.[3]

Inexperienced Consultant Personnel   Consultants must strive to assign personnel to consulting engagements to the best of their ability, balancing the client's best interests against a goal of allocating resources as efficiently as possible. When the consultant has named specific personnel to the project team and presented these

[2] Geoffery Smith, "The Computer System that Nearly Hospitalized an Insurer," *Business Week,* June 15, 1992, p. 133, in *Core Concepts of Accounting Information Systems,* 6th edition (John Wiley & Sons, 1999), pp. 412–413.
[3] Jason Fry, and Megan Doscher, "Tech Week in Review: SAP, Siebel Systems, IBM," *The Wall Street Journal Interactive Edition,* November 8, 1999.

personnel and their qualifications to the client in the consulting proposal, the consultant is ethically obligated to use these personnel in carrying out the engagement. Indeed, some companies have complained about a "bait-and-switch" tactic employed by some consultants who use the "big dogs" to secure the engagement and then bring in less experienced junior employees of the consulting firm to do the actual work. Less experienced personnel will naturally take longer to complete components of the engagement and will likely not posses the analytical ability and judgment necessary in a consulting engagement. Case-in-Point 9.3 provides two examples of consulting firms that have been sued for just this reason.

> ***Case-in-Point 9.3***   Deloitte & Touche LLP and Deloitte Consulting are currently being sued by W. L. Gore & Associates. The company hired Deloitte to install PeopleSoft software that would tie together Gore's personnel, payroll, and benefits departments. Gore claimed that Deloitte used the project to train inexperienced consultants ultimately leaving its HR department in chaos. Gore cited an example of the inexperienced consultants work, saying that the consultants had entered fictitious employees into the company database and then couldn't figure out how to remove them. As a result, Gore ended up cutting checks to, among other fictitious names, Donald Duck. Gore also charged that the Deloitte consultants were constantly on the phone with People-Soft asking for directions. The case has not yet been decided.[4]

These are just a few of the reasons for systems implementation failures, but consultants can learn a great deal from these examples. Let's turn now to the final presentation, including key points to remember in the presentation and the management letter.

FINAL PRESENTATION

Presenting the final product to the client requires use of many of the skills and tools described in earlier chapters. We'll leave it to the reader to review those passages to refresh the memory here. The purpose of this section is to emphasize how the consultant should proceed with the final presentation.

A sample timetable for the final presentation is provided in Figure 9-2. You should tailor the timetable to the individual project; however, in any case, the emphasis in the presentation should be on demonstrating your solution. Aim for about an hour for the entire presentation.

Key Points

There are several key points to keep in mind with respect to the final presentation. These include: focusing on the end product, being organized in the final presentation, giving handouts as appropriate, and turning out a professional product. Let's look at each of these key points individually.

---

[4] Ibid and Dean Foust, "First Sue All the Consultants: Malpractice Actions Against Them Are On The Rise," *Business Week,* July 17, 2000, p. 96.

Presentation Element	Estimated Time Allotted
Introduction of team, including the role of each team member	2 minutes
Overview of the engagement	5 minutes
Data collected and analysis of same	3 minutes
Presentation of solution	20–30 minutes
Discussion of documentation provided to client	2–3 minutes
Questions	15 minutes
Follow up	2–5 minutes

FIGURE 9-2   Sample timeline for final presentation.

Focus on the End Product   At this stage, this is an unveiling of the final product or service that you have developed. Thus, the majority of time here should be devoted to presenting your solution. If a product was developed, you should demonstrate the product. If you developed a customized software application, show how to use it. Refrain from a detailed discussion of how you internally managed the project. At this point, the client is eager to see what you have come up with and how the company will benefit from the client's services.

Be Organized   After introducing the project team and telling briefly how each team member contributed to the success of the project, give a brief outline of how the presentation will proceed. Include an estimate of how long the presentation will be, and whether questions should be held until the end or if they may be posed intermittently during the presentation.

Handouts   Handouts should be prepared when their use will enhance the client's comprehension of the presentation or when overhead projected information may be somewhat small. Handouts should be distributed at the beginning of the presentation. Ideally, if possible, have the handouts in place at the conference table when the client personnel arrive.

Turn Out a Professional Product   It seems like a no-brainer, but we have seen many unprofessional products provided to clients. What do we mean by "professional"? We mean how the product looks visually. Any written materials provided to the client should be appropriately labeled, professionally bound, and free from smudges or other detractors. The same goes for diskettes provided to the client. Label the disks with the content and the date. Use color as appropriate. It may be expensive, but it contributes to the overall professional look of the final product.

Remember That Your Reputation Is at Stake   The most valuable asset that a consulting firm has (besides of course the intellectual capital of its employees) is its reputation. A botched engagement at any phase, but especially in the implementation phase, will undoubtedly have a ripple effect. For the companies discussed in the cases-in-point in this chapter, the consequences were severe, including bad press and lawsuits. No one wants to hire a consulting firm that cannot bring a successful end to an engagement. Work hard to ensure that the contract is fulfilled to the best of your firm's ability. Don't be afraid to ask the client if he or she is happy with the results. If there are small things you can do to make the client happy, it is usually in the consultant's best interest to do so.

The Management Letter

Often you will wish to provide the client with a letter with recommendations on either the operational efficiency or accuracy of the client's operations. Auditors usually refer to this letter as a "management letter." These recommendations may be either directly or indirectly related to the project engagement. Sometimes they relate to peripheral observations that the consultant has made in the course of the engagement and for which the consultant feels a professional obligation to comment on to the client. Keep in mind that the consultant should inform the client if a management letter will be forthcoming at the end of the engagement. The client should not be surprised by the appearance of a management letter on completion of the engagement.

For example, let's say that in the course of your engagement to develop a customized accounts payable application, you observe serious problems with segregation of duties with the accounts payable clerk. You may well want to bring this internal control problem to the attention of management, who may or may not be aware of the problem. That's where the management letter comes in. You can communicate these concerns to the client in a management letter. Note that the letter is optional and is provided at the end of the final presentation. You may chose to present the management letter formally as part of the presentation or give the letter to the client informally at the end of the engagement. If you present the management letter formally, be sure to inform the client and give him or her the opportunity to review the letter before the presentation. Recognize the possible sensitive nature of any recommendations. Phrase the comments objectively and propose solutions for each item on which you comment. A sample management letter that continues the corporate intranet example used in Chapter 4 is provided in Figure 9-3.

FOLLOW-UP

The presentation should end with a few follow-up topics, including advising the client how to be successful in the long term and how to solicit future business.

Fulfilling Contractual Obligations

An essential part of the consulting proposal states what the consulting firm promises to do on completion of the engagement. Often this deals with providing technical support to the client as promised in the engagement. Particularly in systems implementation engagements, the client will need some sort of technical support for a time after the consultant leaves. Consultants usually build provisions for technical support into the proposal in two stages: Free technical support for a limited time, followed by support provided for a fee. Whatever you agree to in the contract, be sure to follow up and provide the services and support as promised. To fail to do so not only may cause legal problems for you, but it is unethical and will cause you to lose credibility with the client.

First Class Consulting, Inc.
334 Main Street
Washington, DC 20017
Telephone: (202) 341-0384
Fax: (202) 341-3222

October 30, 2001

Management Letter

Mary Smith
Chief Information Officer
Shenandoah Financial Planning Services, Inc.
1517 Devon Lane
Shenandoah, VA 22849

Dear Ms. Smith:

This management letter is designed to provide you with recommendations we hope will assist your company in improving its operational efficiency and effectiveness. These recommendations are a result of our having recently completed the design and development of your corporate intranet. The recommendations are divided into two categories: internal control, and operational efficiency.

Internal Control Recommendations

1. Shenandoah appears to maintain no regular schedule for backing up its network regularly. Rather the backup appears to be sporadical and no backup log is maintained. *Recommendation:* We recommend you institute a policy of daily backups of the company's network to be performed by the network administrator. The network administrator should also establish and maintain a backup log.
2. The company's software programs appear to be kept in an unsecured location. *Recommendation:* Maintain original software programs in the company's fireproof vault for maximum security.

Operational Efficiency Recommendations

3. The network administrator appears to be undertrained for the responsibilities he must assume. *Recommendation:* Invest in additional training for the network administrator. We can assist you in identifying the specific areas in which he can greatly benefit from additional training.

We would welcome the opportunity to speak with you further regarding the items covered in this letter. If you have any further questions, please contact me at (202) 341-0384.

Sincerely,

Mark Jones, CPA
Partner

FIGURE 9-3 Sample management letter.

Counseling the Client

It is important to provide some guidance to the client as to how to ensure the project's long-term success. One of the most important aspects is the handling of the client's core project team. The core project team is composed of personnel who worked integrally with the consulting team to implement the solution. Large-scale projects, such as implementation of an ERP system, require significant client personnel involvement. These are the people responsible for maintaining the new system after the consultants have packed up and moved on.

One of the biggest problems in a systems implementation engagement is maintaining the quality of personnel on that client's core project team. Often, the incidence of burnout is quite high. These people have worked extremely hard to ensure that the project goes live successfully. However, they are so burned out after the consultants leave, they are unable to maintain motivation to continue and thus leave.[5] The consultant can help mitigate this problem by making the client aware of this danger. Valuable client employees should be recognized and rewarded commensurate with their individual contribution to the success of this project. It's crucial that the client value the intellectual capital of their employees in order to enjoy their continued loyalty to the client and the success of the project.

Soliciting Future Business

The lifeblood of the consulting business is referrals. Happy clients tend to pass on your name to corporate friends. Likewise, happy clients will remember you next time they need a project done. Here are some steps to consider in soliciting future business.

Be Observant During the Engagement   Items in the management letter often provide a springboard for discussion of future projects. If you observed significant problems with internal control, perhaps the client could benefit from a complete analysis of internal control. You might tactfully mention this to the client, assuming, of course, that the client is happy with the work you did on this engagement.

Leave Business Cards   An oft-used tactic to solicit business is to leave a few business cards with the client and give the client permission to pass the cards on to contacts. Be sure to employ tact in doing so.

Be Open to New Ideas   Sometimes the client expresses an interest in your firm performing a service or developing a product for which your firm does not have an expertise. While it would certainly be unethical to accept an engagement for which your firm is not qualified, it is perfectly appropriate to hear the client out and take some time to think about it. Perhaps you can hire someone with expertise to complete the engagement. Perhaps you can outsource certain components of the engagement. In short, consider broadening your company's experience where practical.

This chapter summarizes what happens after the data have been collected and analyzed, through project implementation and follow-up with the client, after the engagement is completed. The next section of the book discussed some special issues for the accounting consultant including managing change, legal and ethical issues, and special service lines for the accounting consultant.

SUMMARY

This chapter discusses what happens after the consultant has completed the data collection and analysis stage of the consulting engagement. It includes managing the feedback process,

---

[5] "Planning for Success After "Go-Live," *Strategic Finance*," April 2000, pp. 55–58.

implementing the solution, making the final presentation, and following up with the client after the engagement is completed.

During the feedback process, the consultant presents the results of the data collection and analysis, including who was interviewed, what the results were of those interviews, what data were collected and how those data were analyzed, what conclusions and recommendations the consultant has for proceeding as a result of this component of the engagement. The client is undoubtedly anxious to know what the consultant found in this part of the engagement. Presenting the results to the client at this point serves two purposes: it allows the client the chance to clear up any misinterpretations in the data that may have been made and provides a checkpoint at which the client and consultant can decide whether to proceed with the next stage of the engagement. The meeting with the client can be either formal or informal, depending on the nature of the client's business. The presentation should last no more than an hour. You may use technology and visual aids as appropriate in the presentation. Keep in mind that the data gathered may be of a proprietary nature and you should therefore exercise tact in discussing the findings. Once you have presented the results of data collection and analysis, elicit the client's feedback. How does the client think the problems identified should be dealt with? What advice does the client have at this point for proceeding? The client knows his or her business better than the consultant, and the wise consultant recognizes that wisdom and capitalizes on it. Ultimately, the consultant and client in partnership make the decision to proceed or not. If significant changes need to be made in the consulting contract, an amendment to the contact should be prepared and signed by all parties.

The step-check method is one means for developing the consulting solution. Using this method, the consultant completes the design and development in stages and checks with the client at major points to ensure that the client approves of the direction of the solution development. A prototype may be developed before proceeding with a full-scale application. A prototype is a small-scale version of the full version to be developed. The advantage of developing a prototype is that it can give the client insight into how the full version will run well before the time and cost are spent on developing the full version. During implementation the consultant generates a great deal of documentation, including flowcharts, manuals, and other documentation. The consultant retains all documentation, furnishing copies as needed and appropriate to the client. For a systems implementation project there are various approaches to going live, including immediate cutover, parallel implementation, and phased implementation. Whichever method is used, it is essential to maintain a backup of the client's system in the event of an implementation problem. Systems implementation projects fail for a number of reasons, including inability of the client to adequately monitor the project, the consultant's failure to fully test the new system before going live, and using inexperienced consultant personnel for key implementation areas.

The final presentation requires the use of many skills and tools described in earlier chapters. Several key points to remember during the final presentation including: focus on the end product, be organized, use handouts as needed, turn out a professional product, and, above all, remember that your reputation is at stake. A management letter may be supplied to the client, at the consultant's discretion. The purpose of the management letter is to convey any recommendations the consultant has regarding either the operational efficiency or effectiveness of the client's operations. The client should know in advance if you are planning to provide a management letter.

Follow-up involves counseling the client as to how to ensure the long-term success of the project. The consultant must fulfill any contractual obligations with respect to follow up, including providing technical support or on-site help, as specified in the consulting contract. The consultant should also reinforce to the client the importance of valuing the client project team. Finally, the consultant should seek opportunities to generate future business, including being observant for opportunities during the engagement, tactfully leaving business cards, and being open to new ideas that the client may suggest for future projects.

DISCUSSION QUESTIONS

9-1. Explain why it is important to conduct a feedback meeting at the end of the data collection and analysis stage.

9-2. How should the feedback meeting be conducted? Who should attend? Who should present the main findings? Explain.

9-3. What is the role of technology and visual aids in the feedback meeting?

9-4. Explain why the consultant should exercise sensitivity in discussing the results of the data collection process.

9-5. What is presented in the feedback meeting?

9-6. Why is it necessary to elicit a decision from the client to proceed? Do clients ever back out of projects at this point in the engagement? What does the client do in this case?

9-7. Explain how the step-check method works in implementing a consulting solution. What are the dangers of using this method? Give an example of improper use of the step-check method.

9-8. What is a prototype? What is the advantage of using a prototype in a consulting project? When would a prototype be appropriate and when not? Give an example of a project that might benefit from a prototype.

9-9. What is the role of documentation in implementing a consulting solution? Is all documentation given to the client? Give an example of documentation that might not be given to the client.

9-10. What are the three main methods for implementing a new system? Describe when each is appropriate. What types of precautions should the consultant take to mitigate problems in systems implementations?

9-11. What are some main reasons why systems implementation projects fail? What can the accounting consultant do to minimize the change for systems failure?

9-12. Is using inexperienced personnel a legal or ethical problem for consultants? How do you think consultants can best balance the need to serve the client's best interest against allocating scarce resources?

9-13. What are some key points to remember in making the final presentation to the client?

9-14. Do you agree that the consultant's most valuable asset is its reputation? Explain and give an example to back up your reasoning.

9-15. What is the role of the management letter in a consulting engagement? Is the management letter always provided? How does one decide what to include in the management letter?

9-16. What are the consultant's responsibility with respect to counseling the client?

9-17. What can the consultant do to generate future business? Is there an ethical component to generating future business?

EXERCISES

9-18. There are many instances in the popular press of systems implementations failures. Obtain a recent article highlighting a systems failure. Write a summary of the problem the company experienced. Give your thoughts as to how the company might have proactively dealt with this problem.

9-19. Suppose you have been hired to evaluate the internal controls of a small manufacturing company. During the course of the engagement, you become rather well acquainted with the company's bookkeeper, Julia. You know she has been there for a number of years and is considered completely trustworthy by upper management. However, you are concerned that Julia is handling several incompatible (from a control perspective) tasks. For example, she opens the mail, receives the checks, prepares the deposit slips, brings the deposits to the bank, and makes the journal entries to the general ledger. You are concerned about this and not sure how to proceed.

Required

Write a short paragraph discussing the implications of this problem. Is it a big problem or a small one? Explain what the consultant's responsibilities are in this situation. How would you approach this problem?

9-20. You have been engaged to design and develop a new payroll system for a small company. Based on your data collection and analysis, you have determined that the project will take substantially more time to complete than you originally estimated. This is due to two problems: first, the client's existing system is inadequate to support the new software. The existing system runs on a low-level Windows 95 network with insufficient disk space and random access memory. As it turns out, the client will need an entirely new system, in addition to purchasing the software. Second, the client's personnel will need to undergo significant training to become proficient after the new system is installed. Given these concerns, prepare a discussion of how you would approach the problem in the feedback meeting. How would you present these concerns? What recommendations or options would you offer to the client? At what point would you feel the need to turn the project down?

REFERENCES, RECOMMENDED READINGS, AND WEB SITES

References and Recommended Readings

Barcus, Sam. W. III, and Joseph Wilkinson, *Handbook of Management Consulting Services,* 2nd edition (New York: McGraw-Hill, 1995).

Biswas, Sugata, and Daryl Twitchell, *Management Consulting, A Complete Guide to the Industry* (New York: John Wiley & Sons, 1999).

Block, Peter, *Flawless Consulting, A Guide to Getting Your Expertise Used,* 2nd edition (San Francisco: Jossey-Bass/Pfeiffer, 2000).

Hollander, Anita, Eric Denna, and Owen Cherrington, *Accounting, Information Technology, and Business Solutions,* 2nd edition (New York: McGraw-Hill, 2000).

Laudon, Kenneth C., and Jane Laudon, *Business Information Systems,* 3rd edition (Fort Worth, TX: Dryden Press 1996).

Moscove, Stephen A., Mark Simkin, and Nancy Bagranoff, *Core Concepts of Accounting Information Systems,* 6th edition (New York: John Wiley & Sons, 1999).

Rasiel, Ethan M., *The McKinsey Way* (New York: McGraw-Hill, 1999).

Reeb, William C., *Start Consulting—How to Walk the Talk* (New York: American Institute of Certified Public Accountants).

Web Sites

The AICPA provides guidance to accounting consultants at:
www.aicpa.org/members/div/mcs/pubs/index.htm
www.aicpa.org/members/div/mcs/index.htm

More information on prototyping can be found at:
floyd.os.kcp.com/home/catalog/rapproma.html

PART FOUR

SPECIAL ISSUES FOR THE
ACCOUNTING CONSULTANT

Chapter 10

Managing Change

The only constant is change at an unprecedented pace.

CPA Vision Project (New York: AICPA)

INTRODUCTION

Change is a necessity. As stated in the quote at the beginning of the chapter, the only constant, especially in the knowledge age, is change. Organizations must be visionary in anticipating what the market will dictate. When changes are contemplated, consultants not only help clients develop solutions to problems, but also facilitate change within the organization. The best-laid consulting plans will not succeed unless the client company is thoroughly committed to the change and upper management is able to communicate its vision for change throughout the organization. This chapter discusses change management and the consultant's role in facilitating change. Case-in-Point 10.1 drives home the need for change.

> *Case-in-Point 10.1*   In the 1960s and 1970s IBM was the king of the hill in computing. Their reputation was built largely around their mainframe expertise. However, in the 1980s something happened—IBM became complacent. Instead of capitalizing on opportunities, IBM lost out on more than one chance to remain at the forefront of the PC market. Despite pioneering computer chips that could increase processing speeds dramatically, the management of IBM did not support or pursue the continued development of this technology. IBM lost another opportunity when Glenn Henry, an IBM Fellow, came out with the multimedia PC in 1987, which the CEO of IBM promptly turned down. Of course, when the multimedia PC became a big hit in the marketplace, it became apparent that IBM had once again missed out in a big way.[1]

In Chapters 5 and 6, we presented the fundamentals of project management. You can apply the tenets of project management to change management, such that change management is approached as a project itself. Thus, the material presented in Chapters 5 and 6 can be directly applied to this chapter.

THE ROLE OF THE CONSULTANT IN MANAGING CHANGE

Change agents play a critical role in facilitating change within a company. A change agent is any person who acts to facilitate change within an organization. He or she may be an employee of the company or an outside consultant hired for this specific purpose. In this book, the emphasis is on the accounting consultant (often a CPA) who is acting as a change agent.

When Does the Consultant Become Involved?

A flowchart of the consulting process was presented in Chapter 1 (see Figure 1-9). Although this diagram depicts the management of change as occurring toward the

---

[1] Victor Tan, "Seven Stages of Managing Change," *The New Straits Times,* November 13, 1996, 11.

end of the consulting process (during implementation), the change agent may become involved at various points in the process. In fact, the consultant may be of assistance in any or all of the steps outlined by Lewin (unfreezing, change, refreezing), depending on when the consultant enters the picture.

Ideally, a consultant can best help facilitate change when he or she is involved from the very beginning, at the problem definition stage. That's because the consultant will become intimately familiar with the workings of the client company and the personnel involved in the proposed change. This intimate knowledge enables the consultant to anticipate problems and develop a business strategy for dealing with those problems. A consultant may still be very effective in facilitating change if he or she enters the process during the "change" phase. A consultant usually doesn't control the point of entry in the change process. The client company hires a consultant at some point, and the consultant must then deal with entering the process at that particular point in time.

Technical versus Interpersonal Role

The accounting consultant's role may be either technical, interpersonal, or more often than not, a mixture of each. A consultant assumes a *technical* role when assisting with the actual implementation process. For example, if accounting consultants are engaged in implementing a new ERP system, they're responsible for physically making the change from the old system to the new system and ensuring that the new system provides the proper output.

A consultant assumes a pure *interpersonal* role when hired to strictly facilitate the change, but *not* participate in effecting the change. In this case, the consultant is primarily concerned with managing the people aspect of the change. How can the transition be made easier for the employees who are affected? What are the impediments to change? How can the consultant help overcome employees' resistance to change? And how can the consultant help assure the long-range success of the change? These are the types of questions a change agent faces when concerned strictly with the interpersonal components of the change. More often than not, a consultant assumes both a technical and an interpersonal role.

> **Example**   In implementing the new ERP system, the consultant will have undoubtedly spent much time up front on preparing for the new system. During data collection and analysis, the consultant would have determined what level of resistance existed in the company at that time. This information would have been communicated at the time the results of the data collection and analysis were presented to management. The consultant would have also prepared and discussed alternative plans for dealing with employee resistance. In this example, the consultant plays a hybrid role, and has both technical and interpersonal objectives. As previously noted, the interpersonal role can be the most difficult aspect of facilitating change. This is because it is human nature to be somewhat resistant to change.

Resistance to Change

First, let's note that while overcoming resistance is a primary goal of change management, not *all* resistance is bad. Resistance can be useful in that it gives management pause for thought and, in fact, management may step back and rethink the change.[2]

---

[2] Gregory Moorehead and Ricky W. Griffin, *Organizational Behavior,* 3rd edition (Boston: Houghton Mifflin Company, 1992).

Is this change needed? Will the company be better off either economically or operationally when the change is implemented? In some instances of strong internal resistance to a proposed change, management may decide not to go forward after all.

Why are people issues the thorniest for consultants to deal with? Because it is the people within the organization who will either make or break the change process. If the company cannot get its people collectively on board with the change, the process is doomed to failure. Therefore, it's crucial for a consultant to recognize why people are resistant to change and develop strategies for dealing with that fear and resistance.

Let's take a closer look at some of the reasons why people are resistant to change. In identifying these barriers to change, the consultant can deal proactively to mitigate fear-related problems.

Why People Fear Change

When a client engages a consultant, the inescapable fact is that some change is most likely going to occur. People fear change, and thus may be less than cooperative with the consultant on the proposed changes. To be effective, the consultant must work to mitigate such fear.

The first step toward mitigating this fear is to recognize that there are psychological reasons people fear change. Although there are a myriad of reasons people fear change, most change boils down to three things: loss of financial security, loss of identity, and loss of control.

Loss of Financial Security   For most people caught up in corporate change, their first concern is for their job. For example, for business process reengineering engagements, employees may worry that their jobs may be phased out with the newly reengineered work structure. If their jobs are not phased out completely, they may worry that their hours or their benefits such as health insurance may be drastically reduced. One prevalent trend today is to replace expensive full-time employees with significantly cheaper part-time employees for whom the company usually does not pay benefits. Therefore, this fear is very real to employees, with the result that employees with little financial security may be reluctant to cooperate with consultants implementing major changes.

Loss of Identity   A second reason people fear change is that they are afraid they will lose their identity in the work environment. For example, an employee who has developed a reputation for being an expert in a given area may feel devalued with changes that minimize the contribution of his store of expertise and knowledge, since his self esteem may likely be hinged on his role as an expert. If he believes his role will be diminished in the future as a result of the consultant's proposed changes, he may view the change as a threat to his personal security and understandably be less than enthusiastic about the changes.

Loss of Control   Finally, much fear can be attributed to a feeling of losing control, either of one's future, or of one's everyday routine. Many people are "creatures of habit." They derive security from being good at their jobs and knowing what is expected of them on a daily basis. To some, change threatens to take away their control. New policies and procedures can cause a great deal of uncertainty on an employee's behalf, since they may feel they are no longer in control of their daily lives or even of the future. Thus, these employees will be resistant to change.

Understanding the reasons why people resist change is invaluable to the consultant. Once the consultant understands the psychological reasons why people fear change, he or she can advise management on effective strategies for mitigating overall resistance to change. Note that, overall, the most effective strategy for dealing with resistance to change is open and honest communication. When employees have access to quality information, they can make appropriate decisions with respect to their own lives and goals and can adjust gradually to the new ideas. Additionally, soliciting employees' input is another tried-and-true approach for assisting employees in developing ownership of the new ideas.

Tools and Techniques Used in Change Management

There are a variety of tools and techniques consultants use to facilitate change. These include: questionnaires, surveys, interviews, flowcharts, and graphs. In determining the level of resistance to proposed changes, consultants often use questionnaires to benchmark the current climate within the company. Just as each consulting project is customized to the particular needs of the company, the tools used to gather information must be customized to the particular company. If the company anticipates strong resistance, questionnaires may help pinpoint where the main resistance lies and what possible courses of action are available. Figure 10-1 shows a sample questionnaire.

---

1. How do you feel about the new ERP system the company is planning to implement?

_____

_____

_____

2. What changes do you foresee in your own job duties as a result of the new ERP system?

_____

_____

_____

3. Do you feel you have received adequate training in the new system? Explain.

_____

_____

_____

4. What suggestions do you have for helping this change occur in a smooth way?

_____

_____

_____

5. Do you have any suggestions regarding timing of the change?

_____

_____

_____

FIGURE 10-1   Sample questionnaire.

Like questionnaires, surveys are designed to determine the general climate and attitudes of employees toward change. Questionnaires and surveys can be of a variety of formats, including open-ended questions, Likert scale, or any other appropriate measurement scale (see Chapter 8). Formal or informal interviews may also be conducted with employees to gain insight into their attitudes toward change. The consultant usually formulates a written narrative based on the interviews. Flowcharts and graphs may also be generated to provide insight into factors affecting the company and the proposed change. All these methods are valid approaches to documenting existing attitudes and gaining insight into how the consultant can facilitate the change process.

The Company's Culture

A key consideration for the consultant is the existing culture within a company. The company's culture includes such items as organizational politics, history, communication policies, organizational structure, expectations, and reward structure. Politics and history are closely related, and include the dynamics of past events, power struggles, and organizational structure. The consultant is wise to pay attention to the company's culture in considering how to best implement changes within the organization. For example, consider the following scenario.

> **Example**   You have been hired by the company to develop a new executive compensation tool. In your interviews with client personnel, you discover that a high-level financial employee is upset at the company's choosing to use outside consultants to develop this tool. The consultant must pay attention to this information and decide how to proceed. The consultant may consider how this potentially impacts the project.

Leadership and Change Management

Leadership is an important aspect of change management. Leaders have the strength of vision and personality to persuade others to follow them. Leaders also know when to quit. A rule consultants in change management might follow is the 25/50/25 rule. In the face of significant organizational changes, you may find that about 25 percent of the people embrace the change, 50 percent more are at least open to the change, and the last 25 percent will resist any changes kicking and screaming. Effective leaders recognize that their chances of converting the most resistant group are slim. Rather than expending their limited energies trying to do the near impossible and spinning their wheels, change managers should focus on the 75 percent who are waiting to be convinced and led. These 75 percent may then convince the others. Knowing what you can and can't do in terms of change management is the key to effective change leadership.

Change Teams

The change process can be facilitated with the use of *change teams*. The change team may be a separate team of individuals assembled specifically to facilitate the change, or it may be a continuation of the consulting project team that has worked on the engagement from the beginning. Again, every company is different and so is every project. The dynamic nature of business requires that the consulting process be customized to be responsive to each company's unique needs. The change team is made up of consultants, as well as company personnel. It's essential that the change be embraced and accepted at the top of the company. Employees will often judge management's commitment to the change by the highest level of management to serve on the change team.

The breadth of the team varies directly with the breadth of the change. For example, a change that takes place within one division of a company would be made up primarily of people from that division, whereas an change that affects the entire organization would have a change team made of up representatives from the divisions affected. This type of organization-wide change often requires a special committee called a "steering committee" whose purpose is to guide the overall change effort. The steering committee often consists of representatives from all levels of management.

The change team has one priority—to assist the company with the transition to the new process. The team may choose to adopt a project management approach. That is, the change process will be treated as a project in itself. This is not an uncommon approach to change management. To this end, the mission, goals, objectives, and milestones are drawn up, and an implementation strategy such as critical path analysis may be used. This approach is quite effective in managing change, as it provides a structure from which to plan and efficiently effect the change. The consultant may not choose to work within a project management framework. Rather, he or she may adopt an alternative approach. The professional service firm of Coopers and Lybrand, now part of PricewaterhouseCoopers, developed such and approach. We discuss their framework in detail next.

A GENERALIZED FRAMEWORK FOR MANAGING CHANGE

Case-In-Point 10.2 KPMG recently surveyed 59 Colombian companies that had implemented significant change in the past five years. KPMG found that the companies that had adopted an integrated managerial approach were the most successful in managing change. Successful companies also had the following factors:

- Communication of a vision
- Identification of potential risk factors at the beginning of the change process
- Consideration of the organization's history of change
- Management commitment to the change
- Building synergy among work teams
- Planning structured involvement of all individuals affected by the change
- Ensuring that motivating mechanisms were in place
- Establishing follow-up procedures

Overall, KPMG found that companies that had a comprehensive methodology for the transformation process were the most successful in the change process.[3]

---

[3] www.latin.america.kpmg.net/virtual_library/1998/july/story_1.htm

Case-in-point 10.2 illustrates the need to have a structured plan for how to implement change in a company. There must be a well-thought-out approach for *integrating* the changes into the company. While some companies attempt to implement the change without outsourcing to consultants, many other companies outsource the change plan to consultants. These consultants will undoubtedly each have their own method for facilitating change in the client company. We offer a generalized framework that consists of five steps for facilitating change that consultants and companies can easily adapt to meet their specific needs.

> **Step One: Recognize the Need for Change** Step one is usually taken by the client's management. The consultant may or may not be involved in this step. If there is a prior relationship between the consultant and the client, the client may solicit the consultant's help at this point. In this step, the client recognizes that there are inefficiencies or inaccuracies in their current system that must be addressed. Perhaps work structures need to be redesigned, or perhaps the computer system must be updated or replaced. The need is often identified during strategic planning by steering committees or upper management.

> **Step Two: Decide How to Implement the Change** During this phase, the client and the consultant will work together to design and plan for the expected change. The consultant often will develop flowcharts and other graphical aids to deconstruct the company's work processes and study them for ways to improve operations. Cost-benefit analysis may also be conducted during this phase to determine the feasibility of the proposed change. Management and the consultant will also identify the key players in the change process and may establish the change team during this phase.

> **Step Three: Communicate the Change** Management must attempt to communicate the details of the anticipated change as soon as practical, since the company grapevine can often be counted on to relay inaccurate and incomplete information. Much fear and confusion about proposed changes can often be traced back to unfound rumors circulating through a company. The sooner management acts to disseminate accurate and complete information, the sooner employees can adjust to the idea of change. The company may engage the consultant to help with this phase. For example, the consultant may be hired to determine employees' attitudes towards the change. Management will want to know what employees' initial reaction is and what they can do to help allay employees' fears. The consultant will often interview employees either singly or in focus groups to determine these attitudes. (See Chapter 8 for more information on interviewing and data gathering.)

> **Step Four: Implement the Change** As discussed previously in the chapter, consultants are involved in this step in either of two ways: either they are technically involved with the change implementation or they are helping to manage the interpersonal dynamics involved at this stage. If technically involved, the consultant is concerned with the actual implementation of the change. For example, in a systems implementation engagement, the consultant will be going live with the new system. The pressure here is on the successful conversion from the old system to the new system. The consultant should have a detailed plan for the change and should communicate that plan with the client. If the consultant is serving in an interpersonal capacity, the role is

primarily to facilitate acceptance of the change by client personnel. In this capacity, the consultant closely monitors employee personnel for attitudes and behaviors that might be cause for action on management's part.

Step Five: Follow Up Following up is almost always the final step in any life cycle, whether it be the systems development life cycle, the consulting process life cycle, or change management. No change is successful without careful follow up by management and if needed, by the consultant. The consulting contract will often dictate what the responsibilities of the consultant are in following up after the change has been successfully implemented. In any case, the consultant should make sure that the client company has a plan for periodically reviewing the change to ensure employee commitment is strong and the new system is working as intended. Because change team burnout is a very real danger in major change projects, management should also make provisions to review and revise employee compensation plans to reward employees who are helping to ensure the long-term success of the new system. Such changes to the compensation system should be clearly communicated early enough so as to mitigate employee turnover as much as possible. Figure 10-2 displays a flowchart of the change management process.

Consultants may choose to use preplanned questionnaires to facilitate the change management process. A sample of the types of questions consultants might ask at each step of the framework is provided in Figures 10-3 through 10-7.

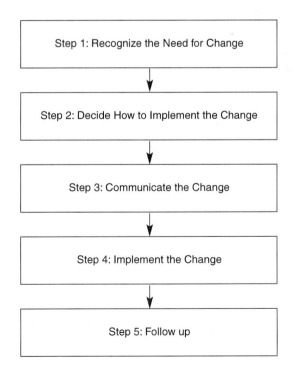

FIGURE 10-2 A Generalized Framework for Change Management.

---

1. What is the reason for the change?
2. What is the culture of change and history of change within the company?
3. Where does the company wish to end up in the future?
4. What principles will be used to facilitate the change process?
5. How does this change fit in with other projects the company is currently involved with?
6. How does the proposed change affect long-term strategic planning for the company?

FIGURE 10-3   Questions consultants ask during step 1 (recognizing the need for change) of the Generalized Framework for Change Management.

---

1. What outcomes does the company envision?
2. Who are the key employees with respect to the change?
3. What roadblocks might keep the vision from being realized?
4. What strategy will be employed to deal with the roadblocks identified?
5. How will the proposed change impact employees?
6. Who will be responsible for what task with respect to implementing the change process?
7. How will the company measure progress toward realizing a successful change process?
8. How will employees' fears be mitigated?
9. Has the project been examined and approved from a cost-benefit standpoint?
10. How can management be coached to model the behavior necessary to successfully implement the change?
11. How can the whole organization be involved in the change?

FIGURE 10-4   Questions consultants ask during step 2 (deciding how to implement the change) of the Generalized Framework for Change Management.

---

1. How will desirable employee behaviors be rewarded?
2. How will undesirable employee behaviors be dealt with?
3. How will those changes with respect to the compensation/incentive plan be communicated to employees?
4. What provisions have been made for training employees in the new process?
5. What provisions for receiving and addressing feedback are in place?

FIGURE 10-5   Questions asked during step 3 (communicating the change) of the Generalized Framework for Change Management.

---

1. How will the company measure progress toward realizing a successful change process?
2. How will employees' fears be mitigated?
3. What provisions has the company made for successful implementation?
4. What backup or contingency provisions are in place in the event of failure?
5. Does the client want the consultant to play a technical role or interpersonal role with respect to the implementation?

FIGURE 10-6   Questions consultants ask during step 4 (implementing the change) of the Generalized Framework for Change Management.

1. What can the organization do to reinforce commitment on the part of the employees and managers?
2. How can the organization keep from reverting back to the old culture?
3. What type of monitoring should be done to ensure continued success?
4. How is feedback incorporated into the process?
5. Has management restated its commitment to the new system via the employee compensation/incentive plan?
6. Has management communicated those changes to employees?
7. Has management made provisions for thoroughly testing the new system?

FIGURE 10-7   Questions asked during step 5 (follow up) of the Generalized Framework for Change Management.

SUMMARY

This chapter presents the fundamentals of change management from a consultant's perspective. Change management has not yet evolved into a clearly definable discipline. Rather, it comprises studies from a psychology, organizational behavior, or business administration perspective.

The accounting consultant acts as a change agent within the company to help bring about change in the most efficient manner possible. A consultant may be present from the beginning of the project or may enter it after an implemented change for the specific purpose of facilitating acceptance of the change by company employees. The earlier you're called in, the easier it will be to work the problem, since you'll know more about the company. A consultant may serve in a technical role, an interpersonal role, or a combination. Consultants who serve in technical roles are interested in physically bringing about change, whether it's a new ERP system or an e-business initiative. Consultants who serve in an interpersonal role generally come on the scene after the physical change has been effected, and work to help overcome employee resistance. Many times consultants serve in both capacities—simultaneously effecting the change and facilitating worker acceptance of the new system.

Resistance to change isn't always bad. It may serve a useful purpose when there is significant employee resistance in that it may cause management to rethink the value of the change. Dealing with employee resistance is one of the most difficult tasks a consultant has. It may be helpful to understand why employees are resistant to change so you can work proactively to mitigate those fears. Keener (1999) identifies 10 reasons why people fear change, including: the element of surprise, self-doubt, loss of control, debilitating uncertainty, disruption of routines, loss of face, increased workload, the real danger of losing out, institutional memory, and personal disruption.

There are a variety of tools and techniques that consultants use to facilitate change, including questionnaires, surveys, interviews, narratives, flowcharts, and graphs. Use of these tools aids the consultant in identifying sources of resistance to change and insight into how to deal with that resistance.

The use of change teams may also facilitate the change process. A change team may be the consultant's project team, or a separate team of individuals formed for the explicit purpose of facilitating the change. A change team may adopt a project management approach, treating the change as a separate project within itself, or it may choose any other structured approach. Whatever approach is used in change management, it is imperative that companies have a structured plan for implementing the change.

DISCUSSION QUESTIONS

10-1. When does an accounting consultant usually become involved in a change process? When is the optimal time for the consultant to become involved and why?

10-2. Consultants may play a technical or interpersonal role in change management. What's the difference between the two roles? Does the consultant ever do both?

10-3. Explain the 25/50/25 rule. Do you agree with it?

10-4. People are often resistant to change—it's just human nature. What are some of the reasons why people resist change? Which do you think is the number one reason people fear change? What can the consultant do to mitigate fear of change?

10-5. What are some tools and techniques used by consultants in the change management process?

10-6. How are change teams used in change management? Who makes up the change team? What kind of team do you think would make the most effective change team?

EXERCISES

10-7. Imagine that your university is contemplating new parking regulations. Under the new rules only seniors will be able to have cars on campus. All other students will be required to use public transportation to travel to campus.

  a. Identify what individuals or groups must be involved in the change process.

  b. Describe how the change will be implemented.

  c. What resistance do you expect to exist?

  d. Identify ways to mitigate expected resistance.

  e. Should a change agent be used? If so, who do you suggest as the change agent?

10-8. Some management approaches to change include business process reengineering, total quality management, just-in-time manufacturing, and time-based or cycle management. Using the Internet, locate companies that employed each of the above management approaches. Were each of the companies successful with these strategies? What resistance to change did the companies meet? How did the company mitigate the resistance?

10-9. The Denver airport was known for taking an inordinate amount of time to get up and running. The problems mainly appeared to be due to the new baggage system that apparently, despite its state-of-the-art technology, failed to work properly. Based on what you have learned in this chapter, how might consultants have been helpful in the change process?

10-10. You've been hired as a consultant to assist a small restaurant in automating its business. There are 25 employees, including a bookkeeper, Amber, who has done all of the bookkeeping by hand for the past 10 years and is not computer literate. Amber is very opposed to the new system and feels she can do her job just fine without a computer. The waiters and waitresses are also opposed to computerizing the process. The owner of the restaurant, Samantha, is very interested in the computerization and determined to go forward. How would you as a consultant approach this engagement?

REFERENCES, RECOMMENDED READINGS, AND WEB SITES

References and Recommended Readings

Blake, Robert, Jane Mouton, and Anne McCanse, *Change by Design* (Reading, MA: Addison-Wesley, 1989).

Block, Peter, *Flawless Consulting,* 2nd edition, (San Francisco: Jossey-Bass Pfeiffer, 2000).

Burnes, Bernard, *Managing Change: A Strategic Approach to Organisational Dynamics* (London: Pitman, 1996).

Cannon, Tom, "Managing Change," *The Guardian* (August 31, 1996), p. 17.

Carr, D. K., K. Hard, and W. Trahant, *Managing the Change Process: A Field Book for Change Agents, Consultants, Team Leaders, and Reengineering Managers* (New York: McGraw-Hill, 1996).

Carson, Kerry D., *The ABCs of Collaborative Change* (Chicago: American Library Association, 1997).

Cohen, Allan, *The Portable MBA in Management* (New York: John Wiley & Sons, 1993).

Galpin, Timothy J., *The Human Side of Change* (San Francisco: Jossey-Bass, 1996).

"Getting Started," *Journal of Accountancy,* vol. 29 (December 1, 1998).

Grollman, William, *The Accountant as Business Advisor* (New York: John Wiley & Sons, 1986).

"Managing Change through Leadership," *The Irish Times* (November 17, 1995), City Edition, Supplement), p. 4.

Moorehead, Gregory, and Ricky W. Griffin, *Organizational Behavior,* 3rd edition (Boston: Houghton Mifflin Company, 1992).

Morris, Daniel, and Joel Brandon, *Re-Engineering Your Business* (New York: McGraw Hill, 1993).

O'Neil, James M., *Organizational Consultation: A Casebook* (Newbury Park, CA: Sage Publications, 1992).

Pawlak, Jim, "Managing Change Takes People Skills," *Pittsburgh Post-Gazette* (November 26, 1995), p. E-1.

Pritchett, Price, and Ron Pound, *Handy Booklets on Managing Change, The New Straits Times* (January 28, 1997), p. 12.

Redwood, Stephen, Charles Goldwasser, and Simon Street, *Action Management: Practical Strategies for Making Your Corporate Transformation a Success* (New York: John Wiley & Sons, 1999).

Reeb, William, *Start Consulting—How to Walk the Talk* (New York: AICPA, 1998).

Tan, Victor S., "Seven Stages for Managing Change," *The New Straits Times* (November 13, 1996), p. 11.

Thomas, Joyce, "The Future—It is Us," *Journal of Accountancy* (December 1, 1998), p. 23.

Trapp, Roger, "Managing Change From Top to Bottom," *The Independent* (November 12, 1995), p. B3.

Web Sites

A web site that provides resources for training and change management is: www.trainingsupersite.com/publications

The following web site provides information for managing change with respect to corporate databases: www.bmc.com/technews/973/973tn6.html

The Expertise Center provides a complete list of speakers for various corporate topics, including change management: www.expertcenter.net/members.htm

J. D. Edwards provides a software tool that facilitates management of the change process using a set of change management tools, including: activators, process models, documentation, and other content. See: www.jdedwards.com/ideatoaction/E-Business/Foundation/Forchange.asp

Chapter 11

Legal and Ethical Issues

Nothing works better in preventing lawsuits than being professional and above reproach

> Elaine Biech and Linda Swindling, *The Consultant's Legal Guide* (San Francisco: Jossey-Bass Pfeiffer, 2000), p. 15

INTRODUCTION

Suppose you are hired as a consultant on an engagement to design a custom accounts receivable module. You don't possess the programming skills necessary to do the job; however, you believe you may be able to subcontract the programming work to a qualified party. You don't want to disclose this fact to the client because you have already represented to the client that you have the programming skills needed to do the job. Is this legal? Is it ethical? Where is the line drawn between what is legal and what is ethical?

The first section of this chapter looks at the difference between legal and ethical issues affecting consultants. The following two sections discuss legal versus ethical concerns in some detail.

Legal versus Ethical: What's the Difference?

The line between what is legal versus what is ethical can sometimes be difficult to distinguish. Generally speaking, legal issues are related to specific laws or statutes in effect at either the local, state, or federal (national) level. Breaking a law carries a civil or criminal penalty, depending on the circumstances, such as whether it is a state or federal law, how serious the infraction is, and whether the offender is a repeat offender. In addition to prohibiting certain acts, laws may also mandate behavior. For example, while the Child Labor Law prohibits children from working more than a limited number of hours a week, the Fair Labor and Standards Act requires the federal minimum wage as well as overtime to be paid to certain hourly employees covered by the act.

The distinction between criminal versus civil law is an important one. Criminal laws must state specifically what action constitutes breaking the law, as well as the penalties that can be applied in the event the law is broken. The element of "intent" must also be present to successfully prosecute one for breaking a criminal law. The penalty for breaking a criminal law ranges from monetary fines to incarceration.

In contrast, violations of civil laws do not result in incarceration; rather the penalty ranges from monetary damages to court orders to probation. Additionally, civil statues may provide for a positive action. For example, a person who sues for discrimination under the Equal Opportunity Employment Act may have his or her employer required to halt the discriminatory actions.

What about the example presented at the beginning of the chapter, subcontracting a portion of the consulting engagement? This is an instance of an ethical rather than legal concern. It doesn't break any law; however, without disclosure of the circumstances to the client, it crosses the line into dishonesty by omission. While the act of subcontracting work out is in itself not unethical, by hiding relevant facts about the engagement and the consultant's ability to perform the work for which he or she was hired, the consultant is engaging in unethical behavior. Thus, it is the act of misrepresentation of skills that makes this act unethical.

LEGAL CONCERNS

Let's look at some of the legal concerns that an accounting consultant will undoubtedly face. They include issues surrounding employment laws, confidentiality, copyrights, contracts, inappropriate behavior, misrepresentation, litigation services, and the statute of limitations.

Employment Laws

There are a number of employment laws[1] consultants should be aware of, both from the standpoints of competently advising clients and observing proper labor practices within their own consulting firm. These include: the Americans with Disabilities Act of 1990 (ADA), the Age Discrimination in Employment Act of 1967, Title VII of the Civil Rights Act of 1964, the Occupational Safety and Health Administration Act (OSHA) of 1970, the Fair Labor Standards Act of 1938, the Employee Polygraph Protection Act of 1988, the Immigration Reform and Control Act of 1986, the Equal Pay Act of 1963, the Pregnancy Discrimination Act of 1978, and the National Labor Relations Act of 1935 (NLRA).

- **The Americans with Disabilities Act of 1990 (ADA).** A relatively recent law, the ADA, has required sweeping changes in the workplace. As with most employment laws, the ADA applies to companies with a minimum number of employees. For the ADA, the law applies to firms with at least 15 employees. The ADA prohibits discrimination of employees with disabilities. Further, it requires companies to make reasonable accommodations for handicapped employees, unless doing so imposes an unreasonable hardship. The ADA also requires companies that serve the public to provide reasonable access for disabled persons. For example, restaurants that serve the general public are required to provide handicap ramps and restrooms to accommodate handicapped patrons.
- **The Age Discrimination in Employment Act of 1967.** This act, amended by the Older Workers Protection Act of 1990, prohibits discrimination against workers aged 40 or older in any employment decision, including hiring, firing, and personnel evaluation decisions. The act applies to companies with 20 or more employees.
- **Title VII of the Civil Rights Act of 1964.** Title VII of the Civil Rights Act of 1964 prohibits discrimination in employment practices on the basis of race, religion, sex, or national origin. The act applies to companies with at least 15 employees.

---

[1] This discussion of employment laws is adapted from E. Bieche and L. Swindling, *The Consultant's Legal Guide* (San Francisco: Jossey-Bass Pfeiffer, 2000), pp. 102–104.

- **The Occupational Safety and Health Administration (OSHA) Act of 1970.** The OSHA Act protects employees by requiring companies to establish and maintain safety standards in the work environment. OSHA requires strict adherence to the guidelines and conducts safety checks to ensure compliance with the act.
- **The Fair Labor Standards Act (FLSA) of 1938.** The FSLA protects employees by providing standards for employee pay. Minimum wage is required by the FLSA as a minimum to be paid to all employees. Further, the act requires that nonexempt (i.e., nonmanagers) employees be paid overtime when they have worked more than 40 hours in one week. FLSA also sets the minimum age for workers, depending on the type of employment.
- **The Employee Polygraph Protection Act of 1988.** The Employee Polygraph Protection Act, enacted in 1988, prohibits mandatory lie-detector testing of employees, unless certain security devices are provided or the company is involved in the manufacture, storing, or distribution of drugs.
- **The Immigration Reform and Control Act of 1986.** U.S. employers are prohibited by this act from hiring employees who are not U.S. citizens or alternatively do not have permission to legally work in the United States. The consultant should seek appropriate proof from non-U.S. citizens that they may work legally in the United States.
- **The Equal Pay Act of 1963.** The Equal Pay Act of 1963 requires that employers pay men and women equally for equal work.
- **The Family Medical Leave Act of 1993 (FMLA).** The FMLA, hailed as one of the strongest pieces of legislation to pass in recent history protecting families in medical crisis, provides up to 12 weeks of unpaid leave if the employee or a family member is ill, or in the event of birth or adoption of a child. The Act applies to companies with at least 50 employees.
- **The Pregnancy Discrimination Act of 1978.** This act requires companies with pregnant women employees to extend the same treatment regarding medical leave as they would to employees with any other type of temporary medical disability.
- **The National Labor Relations Act of 1935 (NLRA).** The NLRA provides employees with the legal right to engage in union activities, including forming a union, joining a union, and engaging in collective bargaining. The right-to-work provisions also give employees the right to not join a union if they so desire.

Confidentiality

Confidentiality is a crucial component to consulting. It is both a legal and ethical issue (covered under Rule 301 of the AICPA *Code of Professional Conduct*). Depending on the nature of the engagement, the consultant will often be privy to sensitive product and trade secrets, financial data, personnel information, and other proprietary company information.

For example, let's say you are hired to assist in reengineering a company's manufacturing plant, which involves completely redesigning the product lines to maximize operational efficiency. To carry out your job, you must gain intimate knowledge of the products the company produces. This will undoubtedly mean that you will gain access to information the company would like to protect from its competitors.

You are bound by confidentiality to keep all information you become privy to as a result of your consulting relationship.

It is equally important to protect confidentiality in electronic communications with the client. In today's global business environment, e-mail is an effective and efficient means of communicating. However, due to the informal nature of e-mail, often a lowered standard and a more relaxed attitude toward e-mail communication is assumed. Consultants should take care to guard against this relaxed attitude, and observe confidentiality in these communications.

Additional consideration should be given to protecting the client's data, including interviews with employee personnel, financial records, trade secrets, and proprietary client data. The consultant should have a plan for where data gathered will be kept and who will have access to the data gathered during the consulting engagement. The consulting contract should also specify that all data gathered during the engagement are the property of the consultant, with the stipulation that if the engagement is terminated, all data gathered would revert to the client.

It is a wise practice for a confidentiality agreement to be incorporated into the consulting contract, stating specifically what the consultant is bound to with respect to confidentiality. If desired, a separate confidentiality contract may be drawn up that the consultant and the client both sign to affirm the terms of the confidentiality agreement.

Copyright Infringement

Title 17 of the U.S. Code Section 101 governs copyright law. Copyright law is a federal law that covers original works such as books, music, cartoons, graphics, images, and so on. It prohibits using materials that have been copyrighted for commercial use without permission or compensation.

With the rise of the Internet, individuals often overlook the need for obtaining permission to use documents, graphics, images, custom backgrounds, animated GIF files, and other multimedia files copied from the Internet. The consultant should not forget that, even when it is not noted, many items on the Internet are, in fact, protected by copyright.

Music is an often overlooked area in which copyright laws apply. In designing web sites for clients, consultants will sometimes use a famous or popular tune on the web site. If done without permission, this constitutes violation of copyright law.

> *Case-in-Point 11.1*   The recent fight in court between Napster and the Recording Artists Association is a copyright dispute. The question is whether Napster violated copyright laws by allowing users to download music. This case was decided in a lower court against Napster but is currently under appeal. Although one media giant, BMG, is working with Napster to create a legal fee-based service in which copyright holders would receive compensation for downloaded music files, Napster's future is still unclear. Even if the BMG-Napster deal is successful, Napster may still be held liable for copyright infringement at a later trial, and if found guilty, could face stiff fines.[2]

So how does one go about obtaining permission to use a copyrighted item? If the author of the item is known, the first step would be to contact the author. For Internet-

---

[2] Lee Gomes, William Boston, and Anna Wilde, "Bertelsmann, Napster Agree on Service," *Wall Street Journal,* November 1, 2000, p. A3.

related questions, the site owner or maintainer is usually listed on the site and would be the first place to seek permission. Permission to use the item should be made in writing. The owner of the copyright may charge a fixed license fee for a set number of uses or may imposed a fee-per-use charge. Be sure to retain all documents with respect to copyright requests. Copyright permissions obtained for a particular consulting engagement should be placed in the documentation file for that engagement. If permission is obtained, be sure that the permission is so noted on each occurrence of the use of the copyrighted material. For example, if a PowerPoint presentation is made that incorporates the copyrighted material, each slide that uses the material should have a notice on the bottom such as: "©*Coca-Cola,* used with permission."

What about use of items for which there is no copyright? This now crosses over into the ethical realm. It is unethical to use another individual's ideas without proper attribution or citation. Even if the materials are not copyrighted, the responsibility to obtain permission to use the ideas, words, and so on still exists ethically. To fail to do so may damage both your and (inadvertently) your client's professional reputation.

Contract Disputes

Unpleasant as they may be, contract disputes between the client and the consultant do exist. What are the consultant's responsibilities, and how can such disputes be avoided? This section discusses those issues.

A contract may take any of a variety of forms, including an oral agreement, a letter of agreement, or a formal contract. Some consultants view the engagement letter as the contract, and require the client to sign a copy attesting to the agreement of terms. Contract law dictates that the elements of a contract must be present in order to enforce the contract under a breach-of-contract legal action. These include: an offer, an acceptance, and exchange of consideration. Consideration involves something bargained for in exchange for performance of services. Additionally, the parties must both demonstrate intent to enter a contract.

Although a written consulting contract is not mandatory, the best defense against a contract dispute is a well-written contract. Should legal action become necessary, the contract will serve to clarify what the parties specifically agreed to. As discussed in Chapter 4, the contract should specify the objectives of the project, what deliverables the consultant agrees to provide, a timeline for completing the project, and an estimate of the fee to be paid.

The consultant's and client's responsibilities should also be specifically stated in the contract. In broad terms, the consultant has the responsibility to perform the work to which he or she agreed in the contract, within the timeline specified and for the fee agreed on in the contract. The consultant should include a clause in the contract to provide for unforeseeable circumstances. For example, if a snowstorm keeps the consultant from traveling to the client's for a week, this would be an unforeseeable event that should not indicate a breach of contract on the consultant's part. Language related to unforeseen circumstances can protect the consultant. The client is responsible for providing access to all aspects of the client's business that are relevant and necessary for the consultant to complete the engagement, including financial records, product data, and employees. Additionally, the client is responsible for providing answers to relevant inquiry to facilitate completion of the consulting engagement.

Inappropriate Behavior

Although unintended, the consultant can sometimes be guilty of engaging in questionable behavior in the client's presence, including inappropriate humor, sexual harassment, and discrimination.

In presentations to "warm up" the audience, a speaker commonly uses humor. However, the consultant should never use off-color, demeaning, racist, religious, or ethnic references within jokes. However innocuous the speaker may view them, such references inevitably alienate large portions of the audience and indicate profound insensitivity on the speaker's part.

Sexual harassment is another pitfall that consultants should be aware of and strive to avoid at all costs. The consultant should treat the client's personnel with the utmost courtesy and respect. Sexual harassment can take many forms: pictures, jokes, e-mail—virtually any form of communication can be used that demeans an individual based on sex or gender. Off-color e-mail jokes are commonly circulated on the Internet. While employees may not realize the seriousness of the offense, companies often take a harsh view of passing offensive e-mail.

> *Case-in-Point 11.2* During the summer of 2000, Dow Chemical Corp. fired 50 employees for downloading and sharing pornographic e-mail. Although the employees didn't intend to engage in sexual harassment, the company viewed the act of saving and then sharing these e-mail messages as creating an environment of harassment, and the employees were fired. The Dow Chemical case is not an isolated case. In 1999, the *New York Times* fired 22 employees for similar reasons, while Xerox Corp. fired employees for downloading and sharing potentially offensive e-mails.[3]

Consultants need to be aware of these problems both from an advisory standpoint and also as owners and administrators of consulting firms. Some consultants, constantly alert to opportunities for a new consulting niche, have created a specialty service aimed at detecting computer-related misconduct such as downloading and sharing objectionable e-mail.

> *Case-in-Point 11.3* In 1998, Ernst & Young hired James Holley to help train and assemble a team of forensic consultants. Today Holley's team has grown to over 120 forensic consultants who investigate all types of computer fraud and misconduct.[4]

Consultants must also guard against actions that may be viewed as discrimination, including any form of treating employees differently based on racial, gender, age, or religious criteria. Each employee should be treated with professionalism and respect.

Statements such as "We don't hire people over 25" indicate an inherent bias against older workers. It is not only unprofessional, but also illegal. It is the job of the Equal Opportunity Employment Commission (EEOC) to oversee and enforce federal antidiscrimination laws.

---

[3] "Fifty Dow Chemical Workers Fired After E-Mail Investigation," *The Canadian Press,* July 28, 2000, p. A-1.
[4] Greg Miller, "High-Tech Snooping All in a Day's Work: Some Firms Are Now Using Computer Investigators to Uncover Employee Wrongdoing," *Los Angeles Times,* October 29, 2000, p. A-1.

Misrepresentation

Misrepresentation is an issue that falls within both the legal and ethical realms. The example at the beginning of the chapter is a case of an ethical breach. While no laws were broken, the consultant misrepresented that he had employees with the skills needed to successfully complete the job. However, misrepresentation can also be a legal issue. There are several areas in which a consultant can misrepresent credentials. For example, a consultant may represent to a potential client that she has worked on several previous engagements similar to the current job being proposed, when in fact she has never worked on this type of engagement. This type of misrepresentation can lead to legal action for malpractice if the client is unsatisfied with the consultant's work. A similar situation occurs when the consultant misrepresents education or professional certification of himself or his employees. In claiming to possess such education or certification, the consultant misrepresents his credentials. Such misrepresentation, again, can lead to legal malpractice action.

The consultant should carefully check the qualifications of potential employees reported on employment applications and resumes. It is not uncommon for individuals to overstate their qualifications in an effort to obtain a job. The consultant cannot afford not to check qualifications and references thoroughly to verify information reported by an applicant.

Litigation Services

Many accounting consultants have ventured into a specialized area of consulting called "litigation services," wherein accountants are hired to provide professional assistance to attorneys. These services include serving as expert witnesses, serving as arbitrators or mediators, and serving as receivers in bankruptcy matters. Accounting consultants who are members of the AICPA and engage in litigation services are subject to the same standards of ethics to which other CPAs are bound. The topic of ethics is discussed in the next section. They are also held to the general standards of professional competence, due professional care, planning and supervision, and sufficient relevant data.

An interesting issue for accounting consultants who provide professional assistance to attorneys involves attorney-client privilege. Attorneys maintain that such protection is important to facilitate open, honest communication between a client and the CPA consultant who is providing the litigation services. The courts concur, and have extended the attorney-client privilege to accountants' services that enhance legal advice and when the parties do not waive the privilege. Consultants should be careful to document the nature of these services to show that they enhanced the legal advice being provided by the attorney.

Statute of Limitations

Case-in-Point 11.4   CPAs who serve as consultants are exposed to a myriad of legal risks. One issue in consulting engagements is the statute of limitations. What is the window within which a client may legally bring charges of negligence against a consultant? There are several standards that may be applied to determine the statute of limitations in the absence of a provision in the consulting contract; however, in *IBM v. Catamore,* 548 F.2d 1065 (1st Cir. 1976), the court upheld a clause in the contract stipulating a one-year statute of limitations for claims arising from a consulting engagement. Thus, a contractually agreed on statute of limitations less than the state-defined statute of limitations is legally binding.[5]

Clients of consultants have a statute of limitations in effect during which time they may make a claim of negligence, incompetence, or malpractice against a consultant for his or her direct or indirect actions. The statute of limitations on professional negligence or malpractice is set, and thus varies, by state. However, two to three years is the normal period for most states. As in the case-in-point at the beginning of the chapter, some consultants opt to incorporate a shorter time frame for claims into the consulting contract. Courts have generally held that a time frame shorter than the state statute of limitations is legal and valid. Consultants would be well advised to consider such a strategy when writing the consulting contract.[6]

Now that we have covered some of the many legal issues a consultant may face, let's turn to a discussion of some ethical issues a consultant may face.

ETHICAL CONCERNS

Ethics, quite simply, is doing the right thing—being professional in all aspects of behavior and decision making. Following this simple rule will often ward off potential legal problems. Each professional organization that represents consultants maintains a formal code of ethics. A practicing member of the professional organization is bound to the code of ethics set forth by that organization (see Figure 11-1).

Professional Codes of Ethics

Two professional organizations that maintain codes of ethics are the American Institute of Accountants (AICPA) and the Institute of Management Consultants (IMC). Let's look at the provisions of each of these ethics codes.

AICPA Code of Professional Conduct

The AICPA maintains a *Code of Professional Conduct* that all CPAs who are members of the AICPA are bound to follow. CPA consultants are subject to the code of professional conduct with a few exceptions. The *Code of Professional Conduct* is composed of four components: principles, rules of conduct, interpretations, and ethical rulings.

The **principles,** which are unenforceable, represent six ideals of ethical conduct. They typify the highest level of conduct that CPAs should strive to meet. They are unenforceable because they represent ideals.

The **rules of conduct** are numbered and organized by topic. They consist of the *minimum* standard of ethical conduct and are binding on all practicing CPAs who are members of the AICPA. AICPA members who disregard any of the rules of conduct are subject to disciplinary action. Note that independence, while crucial for attestation services, is not relevant for consulting services. That is, consultants who perform services for clients are not barred from owning stock in client companies.

---

[5] "Legal Scene, Statute of Limitations: A Primer," *Journal of Accountancy,* July 1999, pp. 24–25.
[6] Ibid.

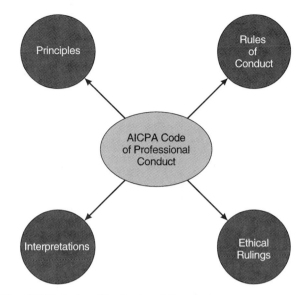

FIGURE 11-1 The AICPA Code of Professional Conduct.

Integrity means that consultants are honest and candid while honoring client confidentiality. The AICPA identifies objectivity as the distinguishing feature of the profession, which means the consultant is free from conflicts of interest. Conflict of interest is discussed below.

Each of the rules of conduct has **interpretations,** which arise from frequent questions to practitioners concerning a specific rule of conduct. The AICPA's Division of Professional Ethics, in consultation with a committee of practitioners, prepares these interpretations. A number of key people in the accounting profession are afforded the opportunity to comment on the interpretations before they are finalized. While not binding, interpretations are important in providing direction in the event of a disciplinary hearing.

When interpretations are not specific enough to cover a particular set of facts, an ethical ruling may be requested from the AICPA Division of Professional Ethics. In response, the executive committee of the Division of Professional Ethics takes the facts under consideration, determines the outcome, and fashions an **ethical ruling.** Ethical rulings have been set forth on a myriad of interpretations. Consult the expanded version of the AICPA *Code of Professional Conduct* for further examples of ethical rulings.

The AICPA has also promulgated seven standards for management consulting services (SSCS) aimed specifically at CPAs engaged in consulting. These consulting standards are binding on CPAs engaging in consulting services who are members of the AICPA.

The SSCS repeat four of the general standards stated in Rule 201 of the Code of Professional Conduct: professional competence, due professional care, planning, and supervision. The SSCS set forth three additional standards, including serving the client interest; understanding with the client regarding the nature, scope, and limitations of the work to be performed; and communication with the client regarding conflicts of interest, significant reservations concerning the scope or benefits of the engagement, and significant engagement findings or events. See the AICPA web site at www.aicpa.org/members/div/mcs/stds/sscs.htm for complete details on the seven consulting services standards.

The Institute of Management Consultants (IMC) Code of Ethics   The Institute of Management Consultants, known as the IMC, publishes its code of ethics on the Internet. The IMC organizes its code along four dimensions: clients, engagements, fees, and profession. Many of the AICPA Code of Ethics components are included in the IMC's Code of Ethics. The basic overriding ethical themes of competence, objectivity, independence, client confidentiality, and client communications are covered in both the AICPA and IMC Codes of Ethics. See the IMC web site at www.imcusa.org/ethics.acgi.

You will notice that legal and ethical issues are often intertwined. What starts out as an ethical issue (e.g., accepting a job for which you are not completely qualified) may turn into a malpractice suit for negligence or incompetence, should the client be dissatisfied with the final end product. This section will focus on five specific ethical issues, including conflicts of interest, inability to meet timelines, job offers, accepting personal responsibility, and fiscal responsibilities.

Conflicts of Interest

Conflicts of interest are covered in Interpretation 102-2 of the *Code of Professional Conduct.* A conflict of interest is a situation that interferes or appears to outsiders to interfere with the consultant's objectivity. For example, suppose the consultant's husband is employed by a client's competitor. This may or may not interfere with the consultant's ability to carry out her job to the best of her ability; however, the client will most likely be uncomfortable with the situation, given that the consultant will be privy to proprietary client information. Thus, a conflict of interest exists. The client's interests should always be the consultant's number one priority.

What does the consultant do in the event of a conflict of interest? SSCS #7, "Communication with Client," requires the consultant to inform the client about the conflict as soon as the consultant becomes aware of the situation. This is true even if a substantial portion of the engagement has been completed. The consultant has a duty to inform the client of the conflict. The client then has the right to terminate the engagement if he or she so wishes. Should the client choose to continue the engagement, it is a good idea to obtain a statement from the client that he or she is aware of the conflict and has agreed that the conflict does not detract substantially from the consultant's ability to carry out the engagement to the client's satisfaction. Both the consultant and client should sign the statement, and each party should retain a copy. The consultant's copy should be retained in the engagement documentation. If a legal situation arises related to the conflict of interest, the signed statement will attest to the client's knowledge and acquiescence of the situation.

Inability to Meet Timelines

Suppose you are a consultant on an engagement and find that you are unable to complete the engagement within the timeline specified in the contract. This situation was presented earlier and is another example of an ethical or legal dilemma. Any significant deviation from the contract should be brought to the attention of the client as soon as it is known. To delay informing the client would be an ethical breach. Minor deviations are usually not an issue; however, major deviations can be reason for concern, particularly if the client has expressed that time is of the essence on this engagement.

Experience is helpful in teaching how much time is needed to complete a particular type of engagement. The consultant should plan carefully to ensure that enough time is allowed. If the client insists on a schedule that the consultant knows is unrealistic, the consultant should be honest. It is better to decline an engagement when you know the client-imposed deadline is unrealistic. On the other hand, if the client is willing to pay overtime or for subcontracting of a portion of the job, this would be a perfectly ethical proposition for the client if time is a critical issue. The client then has the prerogative of declining or accepting the terms in order to complete the job within the desired time schedule.

Job Offers

When clients are happy with a consultant's work, it is not uncommon for job offers to result. The question is whether it is ethical for a consultant to consider a job offer from a client.

Normally, job offers come at the end of the consulting engagement. If so, it is ethical for a consultant employee to entertain and accept such offers. The key is that the consulting engagement should be over or at least substantially over.

Consider the following case. John Doe is employed by a consulting firm as a programmer. He is assigned to an engagement to design a web page using Visual Basic programming. John really hits it off with the client company. The owner of the company approaches John, and the following conversation ensues:

Client: "John, I think you are a very talented programmer. I think you could have a great future here at our company. We are prepared to make you an offer you can't refuse if you come to work with us. We can get out of the consulting engagement. You can design the web page for us as our employee. What do you say?"

If the offer were to come at the end of the engagement, John likely would not have an ethical dilemma, unless, of course, John has signed an employment contract that prohibits him from accepting client or competitor job offers for a certain period of time. The existence of an employment contract outlining specific criteria on job offers is not uncommon in the consulting world, and such a contract will prevail in any type of legal dispute about what job offers may be accepted and when. The most valuable asset a consulting firm has is the intellectual capital of its employees. Most firms will take care to protect their investments in their employees. In this example, however, the client is asking John to do something that is unethical because the client is soliciting the consulting firm's employees and bypassing the firm in awarding the engagement. John should politely decline the offer.

Accepting Personal Responsibility

The consultant should always strive to be ready to assume responsibility when the circumstances indicate an error or misjudgment on the consultant's part. It may be tempting to blame client personnel or subcontracted employees of the consultant. The fact remains, however, that the consultant is ultimately responsible for the quality of the end product. Personal integrity dictates that the consultant assume any loss to the client as a result of consultant personnel actions or recommendations. For example, suppose you have been hired as a consultant to oversee installation of a new accounting system. However, in the implementation stage, something goes terribly wrong and the new system does not work as intended. You trace the problem to an incorrect procedure by one of your employees. As the overseer of the project, you have a responsibility to remedy the problem as efficiently and effectively as you can. If you and your employees must work overtime, you should absorb that loss, since the situation was caused by your personnel.

Fiscal Responsibilities

Consultants may charge consulting fees using a variety of methods. A common practice is to estimate the number of hours the job will take and multiply by a standard rate structure for each consultant expected to participate in the job. Expenses may be separately reimbursed or the consultant's rate structure may factor expense reimbursement into its rates and not bill expenses separately. For a particularly long consulting engagement, the consultant may wish to designate an installment billing agreement in which the client is billed as the project progresses. For example, a project that is expected to last three months may contain a billing stipulation of one-third of the total expected cost to be rendered for payment at the end of months one, two, and three. Other fee arrangements may tie the installment payments to completion of the deliverables. Whatever the consultant's procedure for billing the client, it should be clearly stated in the signed consulting proposal or the consulting contract. Further, the consultant should take care to ensure that the client fully understands and agrees to the billing procedure.

When applicable, the consultant should pay particular attention to the handling of expense reimbursements. Only expenses directly attributable to the client should be billed to the client. Such expenses might include, for example, travel to the client's place of business, parking fees, road tolls, meals while traveling, overnight accommodations, and other similar expenses incurred in the course of carrying out the consulting engagement. The consultant should also keep all receipts to substantiate the expenses and provide documentation when requesting reimbursement.

Ethical situations can be quite difficult to deal with. The consultant should always err on the side of honesty. Even if an engagement is lost, it is far better to preserve one's reputation as an ethical, honest businessperson.

SUMMARY

The consultant faces many legal and ethical considerations. While the line between what is legal and what is ethical may appear blurred at times, generally speaking, legal issues relate to a law or statute. Ethical issues may not relate to breaking a law; however, an ethical issue may turn into a legal issue in some cases. For example, misrepresenting credentials may be an ethical breach when the information misrepresented is very minor. Misrepresenting that you have the basic skills necessary to complete a consulting engagement may well turn into a legal issue if the client is dissatisfied with the final work product or service provided. Breaking a criminal law carries a civil or criminal penalty, depending on whether it is a state or federal law, how serious the infraction is, and whether the offender is a repeat offender. Penalties for breaking a criminal law range from monetary fines to jail time, while penalties for breaking a civil law range from monetary damages to probation.

The consultant should be aware of a number of legal issues, including employment laws, client confidentiality, copyright infringement, contract disputes, discrimination, sexual harassment, misrepresentation, litigation services, and statute of limitations. Eleven employment laws are summarized in the chapter. Some employment laws are applicable to companies with a certain minimum number of employees, while other employment laws are applicable to all companies. For example, the Americans with Disabilities Act of 1990 (ADA) applies to companies with at least 15 employees, while the Equal Pay Act of 1963 applies to all companies.

Confidentiality is both a legal and ethical concern. Rule 301 of the AICPA *Code of Professional Conduct* requires consultants to keep client information confidential except under stated provisions. Confidentiality is important in oral, written, and electronic communications. Copyright law is governed by Title 17 of the U.S. Code. It prohibits using materials that have been copyrighted for commercial use without permission or compensation. This includes all original copyrighted works, including books, music, cartoons, graphics, and images. Legal problems may also arise from disputes about what the consultant agreed to do or what the client's responsibilities were. Contract disputes can be mitigated by having a written, formal contract that clearly states what is expected of both parties. Inappropriate behavior such as sexual harassment and discrimination are prohibited by employment laws. Consultants should take care that they are familiar with the appropriate laws and that they foster an environment free from harassment and discrimination.

Providing litigation services wherein accounting consultants offer support to an attorney thereby enhancing the attorney's legal advice is another area consultants have attempted to establish as a consulting niche. Accounting consultants who are hired by attorneys and enhance the quality of the attorney's services have been held by the courts to have the attorney-client privilege extended to their work in that capacity. Consultants should be knowledgeable about the statute of limitations and would be well advised to include language regarding the statute of limitations for their work product or services in the consulting contract. State law usually determines the statute of limitations unless the client and consultant agree to a shorter period of time in the consulting contract.

Accounting consultants who are members of the AICPA are bound to the AICPA's Code of Conduct with respect to ethical matters, as well as seven standards for management consulting services (SSCS) promulgated by the AICPA. These seven standards cover the following topics: professional competence, due professional care, planning and supervision, sufficient relevant data, client interest, understanding with client, and communication with client. Other ethical considerations include how to handle conflicts of interest, what to do when the consultant cannot meet promised timelines, what to do when the consultant receives a job offer, accepting personal responsibility when something goes wrong in the consulting engagement, and what the consultant's responsibilities are with respect to billing time and expenses to the client.

Anticipating and planning for legal and ethical concerns are important for consultants to safeguard their business. Employee training may also be beneficial in raising awareness of such concerns. The important thing is to be aware of these pitfalls and proactively address them.

DISCUSSION QUESTIONS

11-1. Describe the difference in penalties between breaking a criminal law versus breaking a civil law.

11-2. Describe the basic intent of each of the following employment laws: the Americans with Disabilities Act of 1990; the Age Discrimination in Employment Act of 1967; Title VII of the Civil Rights Act of 1964; the Occupational Safety and Health Administration Act of 1970; the Fair Labor Standards Act of 1938; the Employee Polygraph Protection

Act of 1988; the Immigration Reform and Control Act of 1986; the Equal Pay Act of 1963; the Family Medical Leave Act of 1993; the Pregnancy Discrimination Act of 1978; the National Labor Relations Act of 1935.

11-3. Identify the minimum number of employees a company must have for each of these employment laws to apply.

11-4. When is client confidentiality a legal issue and when is it an ethical issue?

11-5. What sections of the AICPA standards apply to confidentiality?

11-6. What is the responsibility of the consultant with respect to electronic communications with the client?

11-7. What types of issues should the consultant be especially sensitive to with respect to client confidentiality?

11-8. Identify the section of the U.S. Code that applies to copyright law.

11-9. What types of works are covered by U.S. copyright law?

11-10. How does copyright law apply to the Internet?

11-11. Suppose a client wants you to use the "Theme to *Mission Impossible*" on their website. Is this legal? What are the consultant's options?

11-12. How do you obtain permission to use a copyrighted work?

11-13. How do you acknowledge on your work that permission to use a copyrighted work has been granted by the author?

11-14. What is the consultant's responsibility when a copyright is not present?

11-15. What types of contracts are applicable for consultants?

11-16. What are the elements of a contract?

11-17. Is a consulting contract required to be written?

11-18. What should be included in the consulting contract?

11-19. What types of sexual harassment might a consultant need to be particularly mindful of?

11-20. How can a consultant engage in misrepresentation to the client?

11-21. What are litigation services? Give some examples of litigation services a consultant might engage in.

11-22. Describe the provisions of the statute of limitations regarding a consultant's actions or work product.

11-23. Identify and describe the four components of the AICPA *Professional Code of Conduct.*

11-24. Is a consultant required by the *Professional Code of Conduct* to be independent? Explain why or why not.

11-25. List and describe the components of the AICPA's seven standards for consulting services (SSCS) per the AICPA's Statement on Standards for Consulting Services No. 1.

11-26. List and describe the four components to the Institute of Management Consultant's Code of Ethics.

11-27. What is the consultant's responsibility regarding conflicts of interest?

11-28. What is a confidentiality agreement?

11-29. What should the consultant do if faced with a deadline for which he or she knows it will be impossible to meet?

11-30. Is it ever ethical for a consultant to accept a job offer from a client?

11-31. Suppose a consultant causes a financial loss to a client directly from the consultant's advice or work product. What is the consultant's responsibility to remedy the financial loss to the client?

11-32. What are the consultant's responsibilities regarding billing of time and expense to the client?

EXERCISES

11-33. Identify an issue you recently confronted that you were unsure about regarding its legal versus ethical nature. Describe why you were unsure. Do you have a better sense of which type of problem it is now?

11-34. Perform an Internet search to locate a recent court case on a consulting issue. Identify the following components of the case: the issue involved, the parties involved, which jurisdiction ruled on the case, the facts of the case, and the final outcome. Do you agree with the court's findings? How do you think the case will impact or influence consultants' actions in the future?

11-35. Locate through Internet search a web site that you believe violates copyright law. Give the URL. Why do you believe the web site violates copyright law? What suggestions would you make to the web site owner to remedy the problem?

11-36. CPAs often serve as expert witnesses on a variety of financial consulting engagements. Research this issue and write a short paper on the legal issues involved when CPAs serve as expert witnesses.

11-37. Locate a recent article in the popular press on one of the following topics as related to consultants: sexual harassment, the statute of limitations, or litigation services. Summarize the article and provide your comments on the impact of this article on accounting consultants.

REFERENCES, RECOMMENDED READINGS, AND WEB SITES

References and Recommended Readings

Arens, Alvin, and James Loebbecke, *Auditing: An Integrated Approach,* 6th edition (Englewood Cliffs, NJ: Prentice-Hall, 1994).

Biech, Elaine, and Linda Swindling, *The Consultant's Legal Guide* (San Francisco: Jossey-Bass Pfeiffer, 2000).

Block, Peter, *Flawless Consulting,* 2nd edition (San Francisco: Jossey-Bass Pfeiffer, 2000).

Eyres, Patricia, *The Legal Handbook for Trainers, Speakers, and Consultants* (New York: McGraw-Hill, 1998).

Reeb, William, *Start Consulting—How to Walk the Talk* (New York: AICPA, 1998).

Web Sites

The AICPA maintains a web page, "Consulting Service Links," that contains a wealth of consulting services links for legal issues at:

www.aicpa.org/members/div/mcs/links.htm

The AICPA maintains a web page, "Practice Aids," that provides consulting engagement practice aids in the form of publications on a number of legal issues:

www.aicpa.org/members/div/mcs/pubs/pa.htm

Chapter 12

Consulting Services

From thought to finish.™

Ernst and Young, 1999

INTRODUCTION

So what is it that consultants do? According to Ernst and Young, they take ideas and make them happen—"from thought to finish." This chapter looks at what a few of the services consultants, those with accounting backgrounds in particular, offer to their clients. Just a few—to name them all would take lots of books. Also note that not everyone would call all the services we talk about "consulting." However, in this book we have taken a *broad* view of consulting. Offering a client help in developing an Internet privacy policy might be part of a firm's assurance services, but it's also a type of advisory service.

In the first chapter we described three consulting firms—Harry Ballman, Kevin Martin and Associates, and the Andersens. Harry Ballman, a sole proprietor, offers small business clients one-stop shopping for audit, tax, software selection, and legal work. Alliances with law firms and other professionals allow him to provide a wide array of financial, legal, and IT-related services. Kevin Martin's firm primarily provides its client base with software selection and implementation services. Ninety percent of their revenue comes from this work, with the other 10 percent consisting of more traditional accounting assurance and financial services. Andersen Worldwide, of course, offers its clients about any consulting service imaginable. Andersen Consulting grew by specializing in IT consulting. Arthur Andersen, while mostly thought of today as an assurance and tax service provider, offers its own wide variety of consulting services. These include business process reengineering, e-business consulting, data analysis, and so on.

This chapter discusses only some of the services accountants can provide—just to give you an overview and get you to think about all the possibilities. Accountants have, arguably, the best understanding of a business in terms of its processes and information flows. For this reason, accountants can, with some additional training, competently offer many different kinds of consulting help.

Just as fashions change, so do the consulting services in vogue. A few years ago, many large consulting firms were deriving much of their revenues from implementation of enterprise resource planning (ERP) systems. Business was great because many companies were purchasing new systems to avoid the Y2K problem. Today, e-business is the service offering on which consulting firms are pinning their hopes for revenue growth. This chapter discusses software implementation and other IT-related services, e-business, data analysis (including data mining), costing, performance measurement, business process, and assurance services. We also briefly mention other services, including human resource, corporate finance, legal, and tax services.

ACCOUNTANTS AND CONSULTING SERVICES

Different types of professionals bring specialized skills to consulting. A company needing help in profiling its customers might look to a consultant trained in marketing. Businesses needing assistance in creating contracts that protect their interests would get help from a lawyer.

Accountants are the best choice to consult about financial, process, and strategic matters. They are trained to think analytically and solve problems. Accountants are also educated about the flows of information, particularly financial information, throughout an enterprise. In learning about transaction processing, accountants develop an understanding of business processes. Increasingly, today's accountants are also well educated in the area of information technology.

This chapter section discusses several consulting services that accountants might provide. The list isn't comprehensive, and not every accountant is qualified to offer the services described. But it's a start. If you're an accountant considering a career in consulting or seeking to expand your service lines into consulting specializations, you should look at the web sites of professional service firms or professional accounting organizations' web sites and journals to learn more about the consulting services other accountants are offering.

SERVICES LINES

Assurance Services

The traditional services of accountants are audit and tax work. As explained in Chapter 1, these professional services are at a mature stage in their "product life cycle." The accounting profession, recognizing in the early 1990s that audit revenues for accountants were stable and not likely to grow, began looking for related services to offer to both internal and external clients. They also expanded the definition of audit to encompass other types of assurance.

CPAs and Assurance Services The AICPA's Committee on Assurance Services has been charged with looking for assurance service line opportunities in the marketplace. (Professional service firms began in the 1990s to refer to audit services as assurance services.) Auditors, or assurance providers, have redefined the audit process. They've moved from a control-focused, reactive approach to a risk-based, proactive audit approach. The difference is a simple but important one. Rather than investigating a client's practices for evidence of controls, auditors now evaluate the business risks faced by their clients. For example, an internal auditor would not simply check to see if its businesses' payment process included a list of prescribed internal controls. Instead, the auditor would identify the risks in the process and the cost-effective controls that could mitigate that risk. This approach creates a more value-added and proactive approach to auditing.

The Committee on Assurance Services estimated the revenue potential of various service offerings and recommended those with the most promise. The first set of assurance services they recommended were six services with potential revenues in excess of $1 billion each. The committee identified seven others in a second tier and suggested hundreds of others that accountants might consider. As part of their analysis, they surveyed 21 large and mid-sized CPA firms about their current service lines. Figure 12-1 is a partial listing of these services. A complete list is available at the AICPA web site (www.aicpa.org). The first set of assurance services the AICPA chose

---

Six Assurance Services with Revenue Potential > $1 Billion:
Risk Assessment
Business Performance Measurement
Information Systems Reliability
Health Care Performance Measurement
ElderCare
E-Commerce

Seven Additional Potential Assurance Services:
Policy Compliance
Outsourced Internal Audit
Trading Partner Accountability
ISO 9000
Association for Investment Management and Research (AIMR) Compliance
WWW Assertions
Mergers and Acquisitions

Hundreds of Other Potential Assurance Services, including:
Productivity Improvement
Internal Audit Quality Assurance
Operations Scorecard
Fraud Assessment
Adequacy of Billing Systems
…

FIGURE 12-1 The Committee on Assurance Service's list of potential CPA assurance service offerings.

to endorse formally—offering training, practice standards, conferences, and tools— were *CPA WebTrust*^{SM}, ElderCare,^{SM} and *SysTrust*^{SM}.

World Wide Web Assurance *CPA WebTrust* is a third-party assurance seal for business's Internet web sites. The seal, on a client web site, promises that a CPA has verified the company's on-line privacy, security, and business policies. Although it makes sense for accountants to use their "brand identification" to provide this type of assurance, *CPA WebTrust* is only one of such services. Professional service firms, such as Ernst and Young, can provide their own form of assurance at a web site. Other organizations, including the Better Business Bureau, offer still more forms of web site third-party assurance.

Apart from security seals, other forms of assurance for web sites also exist. An example is assuring that a company selling advertisements on its web site has the number of hits on the site it promises. You would not be willing to pay much to advertise on a web site that has only a few hundred visits by customers each week. A company could inflate its "hit rate" through artificial means. Accountants with IT skills can verify that the rate is accurate and estimate the number of customers visiting the site, the number making purchases from the site, and so on.

Ensuring Care for the Elderly How do you consult about caring for elderly citizens? This consulting practice is based on the idea that elderly individuals and their families want assurance about their well-being in many aspects. Elderly individuals who lack the ability to live independently need some reassurance that their care dollars and financial investments are well spent. The services these individuals need are partly financial—tax preparation, estate advice, bill payment, and investment advice. They are also partly caretaking. For example, a middle-aged child may need to find an assisted living residence for an elderly parent. The person is likely to know nothing about such residences and may turn to his or her CPA for advice. The CPA practice will have researched these types of businesses and can make a recommendation tailored to the client's specific needs. The child can feel some relief knowing that a trusted professional assures the quality of care the parent will receive. At this point, the ElderCare practice is in early stages. The AICPA makes many resources available to practitioners, but we do not yet know how widespread this assurance service will ultimately be.

Systems Reliability Assurance   A very promising service line for accountants with IT skills is *SysTrust*. This service assures the availability of a client's information systems for operation and use, the physical and logical security of the system, integrity of information processing, and the system's maintainability. At the heart of this service line is the basic accounting capability to audit. The difference is that the focus of the audit is the information system, rather than the financial reporting system. Auditors, particularly those with IT training, should find this work lucrative and within their skill set. To date, this AICPA assurance service appears to be the most promising of the new assurance lines. Several large companies have adopted the principles and criteria internally and it has been used in a number of large audit engagements. As IT increasingly becomes the focus of audits, *SysTrust* promises revenue growth for those accounting consultants who offer it.

Other Assurance Services   As with *WebTrust* and *SysTrust,* many of the assurance services accounting consultants can offer their clients are IT-related. For example, apart from the AICPA services discussed, some consultants offer their clients *penetration testing* or *hacking* services. On-line companies are concerned about the vulnerability of their web sites to hackers. When a business decides to have an Internet presence for customers and suppliers, they increase the risk that outsiders can access data and other assets within their organization. To assess the likelihood or extent of vulnerability, the company's management can "hire a hacker." A consultant will try to penetrate the system to demonstrate the potential of others to do so. Sometimes professional service firms offer penetration testing services for a small fee—hoping to obtain more consulting business in eliminating the exposures they find. The Big Five professional service firms all offer some form of penetration testing services. The professionals they hire in this practice may be trained IT professionals or accountants with an IT interest or specialty.

There are two important advantages to providing assurance-type consulting services to accounting clients. First, accountants are trained in assurance. Auditor education develops skills in problem-solving and the appropriate skepticism necessary for assurance-type work. It's also a line of consulting work less likely to create independence issues for accountants. The perception of independence is more likely to be impaired when accountants *create* systems, not when they *assess* them. The next type of consulting service we discuss is more problematic in this regard.

Software Selection and Implementation

It's natural that over time business executives develop close, respectful relationships with their internal and external auditors. So it is logical that when management feels a need for a new information system, particularly an accounting or enterprise resource planning (ERP) system, they turn to their accountants for advice. Auditors and other accounting professionals have knowledge of a company's current system and its strengths and weaknesses. Sometimes, they also have knowledge of software markets. Software selection requires both a needs analysis and knowledge of technology and software features. Many accounting firms, like Kevin Martin and Associates (described in Chapter 1), have made this type of consulting service their niche. The largest professional service firms generated a hefty portion of their revenues from this consulting service during the last decade. Figure 12-2 lists various types of accounting and enterprise software categories.

There are several distinct stages in software selection and implementation. These are: (1) needs analysis, (2) system design, (3) system development or selection, (4) system implementation, and (5) follow-up and maintenance. Figure 12-3 charts these stages and briefly explains each one. The software selection and implementation process varies with the level of software under consideration. Of course, you'd expect the process to be different for a small company considering low-end accounting software versus a Fortune 500 company choosing an enterprise package that may cost tens or hundreds of millions of dollars. Consultants can help clients through each of these stages. In the latter example, the company may even determine that there is no existing software available to meet its particular needs. In this case, they'll hire a consultant who can develop custom software. Companies today have another choice to make about software. They can purchase it or "rent" it from an application service provider (ASP).

Often a company's top management believes that the Chief Financial Officer and Chief Information Officer can make a software selection decision without outside help. While these executives are likely to be most knowledgeable about the company's own needs, their normal job responsibilities don't lend themselves to being informed

Software Type	Adopter Characteristics	Examples
Low-End General Ledger (Entry Level) Software	Small transaction set and no special information needs; $100,000–$5,000,000 revenue	*Peachtree, QuickBooks, Profit, M.Y.O.B., Simply Accounting, NetLedger*
Middle to High-End Modular Systems	Moderate to large transaction set with some special information needs; $1,000,000–$20,000,000 revenue	*Accpac, AccountMate, ActPlus, Cyma IV, BusinessWorks, MAS90, Open Systems, Solomon, Great Plains, Macola*
Middle to High-End Enterprise Type Systems	Large transaction set, custom needs, desire to integrate systems; $20,000,000–$249,000,000 revenue	*Acuity, Dynamics C/S+, SAP* (light), *Navision*
Large Enterprise Resource Planning Systems	Large transaction set, custom needs, desire to integrate systems and reengineer processes; >$250,000,000 revenue	*SAP, BAAN, JD Edwards, PeopleSoft, Oracle*
Special Industry (Vertical Accounting Software)	Large transaction set, custom needs, specialized industry information needs; >$10,000,000 revenue	Construction, retail, healthcare, manufacturing, government, not-for-profit, banking, insurance, and other industry packages
Custom-Built Solutions	Moderate to large transaction set with very specific information needs; >$20,000,000 revenue	Available from software developers/consultants

FIGURE 12-2 Categories of accounting and enterprise software.

---

1. **Needs Analysis** – Perform an analysis of requirements for a new accounting or enterprise information system.
2. **System Design** – Develop the detailed specifications and features required for the new system.
3. **Software Selection or Development** – List options available and decide whether software exists to meet needs (at least 80%) or develop custom product.
4. **Software Implementation** – Go live with the new system.
5. **Follow-up and Maintenance** – Obtain feedback about how well the new system meets needs. Maintain the software.

FIGURE 12-3   Steps in software selection and implementation.

about the domain of software available. A consultant in this field has the opportunity to work with many clients and become knowledgeable about software choices.

There are many tools available to help consultants become well versed about accounting and ERP software and the selection process. The Internet, in particular, is a powerful tool for this purpose. Accounting software vendors all have web pages describing their software in some detail. Other consultants, such as K2 Enterprises (www.k2e.com), have sites that list software packages and their features, describe the software selection process, and provide links to selection tools and resources. (The web site references at the end of this chapter point to some of these sites.)

Consulting firms typically specialize in a few accounting or enterprise packages in one market or cost niche. The higher the cost of software and hardware, of course, the more clients are willing to spend on consulting help. Companies spend about $15 billion per year on ERP systems and the fees for consultants who advise about and implement these systems is about $10 billion per year.[1] Consultants were particularly busy with accounting and ERP software selections and implementations at the end of the last decade because many businesses chose to implement new software to avoid year 2000 software glitches. ERP systems were also popular because companies were excited about the possibility of integrating information across organizations through a common database. Today, this consulting business has slowed a bit, but consultants are still helping clients solve software problems. Consultants are implementing both enterprise systems and "bolt-on" products that solve specialized software issues, such as those related to e-commerce, activity based costing (ABC), supply chains, and customer relationship management (CRM).

Data Analysis

In Chapter 8 we discussed data analysis with respect to collecting data from consulting clients. Here, we talk about using data analysis tools to solve client problems, not as a part of the consulting process. Sophisticated data analysis tools can help clients with decision-making and can also assist them in using company databases more effectively.

Databases and Data Warehouses   Today's Knowledge Age is characterized by the vast quantities of data at our disposal. Having so much data is great if someone can organize it for productive analysis and interpretation. Consultants and IT professionals do this by building useful databases and data warehouses.

---

[1] Thomas H. Davenport, *Mission Critical* (Cambridge, MA: Harvard University Press, 2000), p. 4.

Legacy systems (old mainframe information systems) typically used data organized in files. Each different application, such as payroll or marketing, employed a separate set of data files. Advances in database technology, notably relational and object-oriented databases, allow IT professionals to merge a company's files into one large database. Each application can access certain parts of the database and extract relevant data.

Building a database is not a simple task, particularly for a company that doesn't have a large IT staff. Businesses often look to consultants for help in this effort. Many accounting students today learn how to model data for databases and use database software in their degree programs. With this training, they can help companies build small and large databases. For example, an accounting graduate could help a consulting client to build a customer database or other type of database to support its business processes.

Unlike a database, which collects data for a current specific business purpose, data warehouses consist of secondary or used data. The data in a data warehouse is a by-product of past data processing. For instance, a company processes customer sales orders and extracts from those orders the data needed to create shipping documents, invoices, and financial statements. Some of the data collected from the sales order is simply stored and not used. This is the data that consultants use to create data warehouses. These data can have strategic value to a company—for example, in tracking sales patterns. Data warehouses can be very large or smaller with a narrower focus (e.g., a data warehouse that supports just the sales process). A data mart is a small-scale data warehouse. You can create a data mart from scratch, but most often it is a subset of the data warehouse.

Since 90 percent of Fortune 2000 companies either have a data warehouse or plan to construct one, there's a lot of potential business here for consultants.[2] Consultants who help clients construct databases and data warehouses need training in data modeling. They also need some technical training in products for constructing and interrogating databases and data warehouses. Some of these products are *Microsoft Access, Oracle,* or *Microsoft Structured Query Language (SQL).* Accountants with database training are highly valued consultants in this area because of their knowledge of data and information flows in a business environment.

Leveraging Data   Building a data warehouse or data mart is a hefty investment. The return on the investment comes from using the data to support business decisions. There are various ways consultants can help clients extract and analyze data. The simplest of these is to construct queries or questions. Queries, a type of business intelligence, largely answer questions about the past. For example, you might construct a query to find out the gender, geographic location, and profession of customers who bought a specific product.

Queries are limited. For more sophisticated analysis, such as analysis about why certain customers bought a specific product, users need to not only extract data, but they need to manipulate it and then look at the data anew. On-line analytic processing (OLAP) systems transform data so that users may access it in ways they need to. With OLAP, a user can leverage data in a data warehouse to drill down through the data and answer questions that data query tools cannot address—for example, "What were the changes in purchase patterns for certain customers of a specific product over a particular time span?"

---

[2] Julie Smith David and Paul Steinbart, "Drowning in Data," *Strategic Finance,* December 1999, p. 32.

Queries and OLAP systems can provide business intelligence about the past. Data mining is a technique that is both capable of this type of discovery-oriented data analysis and can also help make predictions about the future. Marketing staffs and consultants are using data mining techniques to help clients leverage their data investments with large payoffs. One popular approach is customer relationship management (CRM). CRM systems maximize customer relations even in situations in which the customer has no face-to-face interaction with company personnel—for example, as with on-line retailers. Data mining is the business intelligence tool behind CRM. Figure 12-4 shows the various steps in the data mining process.

As we said, data mining can be either descriptive or prescriptive. Descriptive data mining searches for patterns in data that tell an interesting story. CRM is one application area for this service and there are others. Auditors and accounting consultants can use data mining to search for patterns of fraud. Predictive data mining is closely related. Using this, a consultant can help clients use data from the past to predict, for example, the likelihood of fraud in the future from specific sources, which customers are most likely to default on their accounts, or the employees who are likely to leave the company.

Data mining uses statistical analysis and artificial intelligence tools. Consultants trained in these techniques are well positioned to help clients get the most from their investments in data collection and storage.

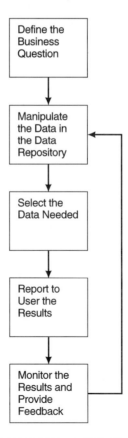

FIGURE 12-4   Steps in the data mining process. Note the iterative nature of the process.

Performance Measurement

Accountants have always been in the performance measurement business. The income statement and balance sheet are the traditional tools they use to see how well a company is doing. Many specific measures of performance evaluation, such as financial ratios, are based on these financial reports. Accounting consultants can help their clients to develop optimal performance evaluation systems.

Managers understand the behavioral impact of performance measurement. People perform according to the measure used to evaluate them. For example, if a department's return on investment is measured and used for evaluation, then there is no incentive for the department's managers to increase investment by acquiring assets—whether or not they need them for long-term profitability. The trick is to create a performance evaluation scheme that fosters the behaviors that lead to meeting established strategies and objectives.

Increasingly, business is realizing that financial performance is not the whole story. Measures of financial success were largely adequate for the Industrial Age, but since they tell the story of past performance, they are not sufficient for the forward-looking Knowledge Age. Accounting consultants today are helping companies to value both financial and nonfinancial performance. Operational factors, such as customer satisfaction, product development cycle time, employee retention, and product quality contribute to future performance on financial dimensions.

The Balanced Scorecard is a technique that businesses and other entities use to measure performance along all the dimensions that contribute to performance. Any individual, business segment, corporate or government entity can construct its own unique set of financial and nonfinancial performance measures. The specific measures are linked to goals and are characterized as financial, customer, internal business, and growth and learning perspectives. The Balanced Scorecard is so named because the approach seeks a *balance* between financial and nonfinancial performance measures. The assumption is that the nonfinancial dimensions drive the financial measures. Figure 12-5 shows a Balanced Scorecard for a sample manufacturing firm. In developing the scorecard, the company and consultants first identify objectives for each perspective. The Balanced Scorecard, used strategically, links objectives with a set of performance measures designed to report how well an organization is meeting its goals.

Consultants can play a value-added role in helping companies to implement a Balanced Scorecard or another performance measurement system. Familiarity with the process and experience with implementing it at a variety of organizations are assets that in-house management needs. The process by which performance measures are developed is important. Managers and staff should be involved in designing their own evaluation system, but they are likely to need help from outsiders who are both familiar with the process and also have an objective viewpoint. Consultants can also access Best Practices databases that describe the measures the consulting organization's premiere clients' use. Many large corporations, including AT&T, have implemented the Balanced Scorecard.

Strategic Cost Management

An important dimension of performance evaluation is strategic cost management. Profitability is a function of both revenue enhancement (largely a marketing role) and cost containment. Traditionally, management accountants have been responsible

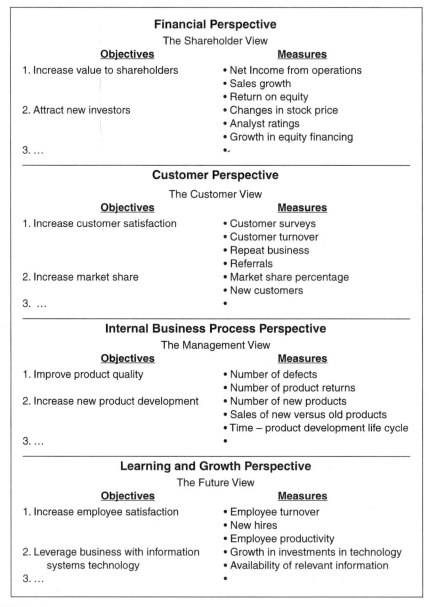

Financial Perspective
The Shareholder View

Objectives	Measures
1. Increase value to shareholders	• Net Income from operations
	• Sales growth
	• Return on equity
2. Attract new investors	• Changes in stock price
	• Analyst ratings
	• Growth in equity financing
3. ...	•

Customer Perspective
The Customer View

Objectives	Measures
1. Increase customer satisfaction	• Customer surveys
	• Customer turnover
	• Repeat business
	• Referrals
2. Increase market share	• Market share percentage
	• New customers
3. ...	•

Internal Business Process Perspective
The Management View

Objectives	Measures
1. Improve product quality	• Number of defects
	• Number of product returns
2. Increase new product development	• Number of new products
	• Sales of new versus old products
	• Time – product development life cycle
3. ...	•

Learning and Growth Perspective
The Future View

Objectives	Measures
1. Increase employee satisfaction	• Employee turnover
	• New hires
	• Employee productivity
2. Leverage business with information systems technology	• Growth in investments in technology
	• Availability of relevant information
3. ...	•

FIGURE 12-5   A sample Balanced Scorecard for a manufacturing company.

for measuring and tracking costs. In increasingly competitive business environments, managing costs and linking them to strategic initiatives have assumed greater importance. Fortunately, as competition has increased, new tools have become available for managing costs. Activity Based Costing (ABC) and Target Costing are two tools consultants can use to help businesses and other entities manage their costs.

Activity Based Costing (ABC)   Direct costs are those that can be easily linked to products and services. For instance, a consultant's time is a direct cost in a consulting project. Direct materials and direct labor are so-called because management can easily associate their use with units of finished goods in manufacturing systems. Indirect costs, or overhead, are more difficult to trace and in the past it was often inefficient to do so. Yet indirect costs, including many overhead costs such as supplies and managerial functions, may be related to specific activities. Activity Based Costing (ABC) links indirect costs to the activities that cause them to change. Computerized information systems allow for tracking these costs and their cost drivers efficiently.

An ABC system consists of the following steps. First, a company's managers, together with cost management consultants, identify cost pools. These are the groups of costs associated with certain activities. For a manufacturing firm, these activities could include finishing, inspecting, and packaging finished goods.

Next, you need to identify cost drivers. These drivers are the activities that create changes in cost. Cost drivers for direct materials and direct labor are, by definition, directly associated with changes in volume of goods or services produced. Drivers for indirect overhead costs are sometimes also linked to volume. For example, packing costs are likely to be a function of volume of goods shipped. The number of inspections drives inspection costs. Other indirect overhead cost drivers are less obvious. What factors cause changes in costs for employee training programs, for example? While one driver would be headcount, there are other contributing factors as well. Perhaps training costs are high because there is high employee turnover or new innovations in the company require extra training sessions.

The final steps are to determine the rate used to assign the cost to each unit of cost driver and make the assignment to units. For instance, if total packaging cost for a period is $20,000, and 5,000 units of finished goods were packaged, the cost per unit of cost driver (units packaged) is $4. Managers can then use the $4 to assign costs to various products or groups of products.

Target Costing A relatively new tool in cost management is target costing. As Figure 12-6 shows, the approach is an inversion of traditional cost-based pricing. Rather than calculate cost, set an acceptable profit margin, and then determine the price to be charged for a good or service, the price is set first, during the product design stage. The price is a competitive one that the market will bear. Subtract allowable profit margins from the preset price, and you have target costs. These are the ceiling on allowable costs for specific components of the product or service. For example, if you're manufacturing a clothing item, you would calculate target costs for fabric, buttons, detail, and so on. If a quality product or service cannot be produced at the target cost, then engineers may drop or redesign features cost-effectively. In some cases they may need to scrap an entire effort.

Target costing is used mostly for new or newly modified products and services. Kaizen costing is a cost-cutting tool for existing products. Target costing's appeal is that it tracks costs before they are spent—this way companies can avoid costly mistakes. As an example, Ford Motor Company incurred a large loss on its Thunderbird—perhaps

Target Costing
Target Sales Price – Target Profit Margins = Target Cost

Standard Costing
Standard Cost + Desired Profit Margins = Sales Price

FIGURE 12-6 Target costing versus standard costing systems.

because they did not know at the time that production costs were an extra $1,000 per car.[3] Consultants, working collaboratively with accountants and engineers, can help companies develop the products with high margins and optimal market potential.

Business Processes

Business processes are the value-added activities within a business. The nature, configuration, and functionality within these processes are key to an organizational entity's success. For this reason, consultants have long been advising companies about these processes. Increasingly, consultants are *doing* these processes for clients.

Because they understand business processes through familiarity with the information flows along them, accountants are well suited to offer advice about business processes. Consulting goals with respect to business processes are to help companies define or reengineer their processes, decide which of these to outsource, and, in some cases, handle the outsourced work.

Business Process Reengineering (BPR)   For many years, managers "tweaked" their business processes when things weren't going right. The business process reengineering (BPR) approach that became popular in the late 1980s and 1990s was to tear down existing business processes and create them anew, rather than adjust the status quo. Increasing competition and more discriminating customers were some of the impetus for process change. Technology was a driver too, as the business processes companies created to function in the Industrial Age became less effective. Advances in information technology created both problems and opportunities with respect to radical process changes.

As an example of BPR, consider a business experiencing an increase in missed customer delivery dates. This occurrence signals a problem in the distribution process. Tweaking the process might mean adding more employee resources or a new computer system to fix the problem. Reengineering the process would entail rethinking the distribution process in light of the best practices for that process used in the industry. The resulting process might use fewer rather than more resources. Perhaps there were too many employees involved in the old process, creating a communications mess regarding delivery schedules. BPR would address this. Figure 12-7 describes the seven principles of BPR.

Many companies realized significant improvements in performance through BPR. Stories about successful efforts at companies such as Taco Bell and Ford Motor Company spurred other businesses to engage consultants to examine their processes. However, the fact that BPR frequently streamlined processes so that fewer employees were required made the term synonymous with downsizing, not a welcome effort in many businesses. This is just one of the problems that BPR ran into. In fact, it appears that a majority of BPR projects fail to meet all their established goals. Why are there so many stories of high-cost BPR consulting investments with poor returns? One reason is that managers sometimes confuse processes with tasks. A process is a set of tasks that is of fundamental importance to success. Other reasons for BPR failures can be resistance to change, lack of support from top management, and cost. Nonetheless, the potential rewards are huge and businesses are increasingly

---

[3] German Boer and John Ettlie, "Target Costing Can Boost Your Bottom Line," *Strategic Finance,* July 1999, pp. 49–52.

- Combine multiple tasks and assign a single point of contact for each process. An important feature of BPR is integrating activities and assigning business process responsibility to one individual called a case worker.
- Allow workers to make decisions. Avoid decision hierarchies that require workers to go through layers of management for decisions about the work they are doing.
- Perform process steps in their natural order. Rather than following a linear sequential set of tasks, perform process activities as needed, sometimes in parallel.
- Create multiple versions of processes. There can be more than one version of the same process, dependent on situational variables, such as customer or product characteristics.
- Minimize checks and controls. Only use those checks and controls that are cost-effective.
- Use information technologies to centralize data management. This allows companies to capture and store data only once, yet disperse it as needed.

FIGURE 12-7 Some characteristics of business process reengineering (Adapted from Michael Hammer and James Champy, *Reengineering the Corporation* [New York: Harper-Collins Publishing, 1993].)

realizing that their success depends on the efficiency and effectiveness of their business processes, as well as making sure that they have the *right* processes. The move today is toward a process-focused enterprise in which managers become process owners. In fact, BPR is often realized through adopting enterprise information systems, rather than as an initiative of its own.

Business Process Outsourcing According to the Outsourcing Institute, "Outsourcing is the strategic use of outside resources to perform activities traditionally handled by internal staff and resources."[4] Increasing competition forces enterprises to examine what they do best. They need to decide which business processes relate to core business and which might be better offered by someone else. Increasing competition and advances in information technology are fueling a dramatic increase in the move toward outsourcing. This focus on directing resources to core competencies creates opportunities for consultants to help businesses decide which of their processes they can outsource effectively. In some cases it also provides opportunities for consultants to take over the outsourced business.

The most frequently outsourced functional area is information technology. There are several reasons why. Information technology is expensive and personnel are a scarce resource. Also, IT changes rapidly and it is difficult for an in-house operation to keep up without continuing investment. IT services outsourced typically include maintenance, training, application development, data center management, and, in some cases, the entire IT function. Staples, for example, recently outsourced its in-store computer configures and installation and support services to ICL, hoping for cost savings and the ability to focus on core competencies. And outsourcing e-commerce applications, where the outsourcer can integrate a client's traditional back-end systems with an e-commerce front, is a fast growth industry.

A new approach to outsourced IT and accounting functions is use of an application service provider (ASP), sometimes referred to as e-sourcing. The ASP is similar to the service bureaus of old. A business using an ASP need not make software investments, but rather leases the software and services such as training and maintenance

---

[4] www.outsourcing.com.

from the service provider. Typically, the ASP hosts software applications on its own servers and makes them network-accessible to clients who run them through their browser applications.

> ***Case-in-Point 12.1*** PricewaterhouseCoopers (PWC) is an example of a professional service firm offering ASP services. One of their ASP service areas is human resources. They will run remote applications for clients for human resource functions such as payroll and benefits administration. PWC can either operate systems at the client or move the client's processes, people, and applications to a PWC site.

There are many advantages to the ASP model. One is that companies can generally cut costs by forgoing software ownership. The other is that outsourcing business processes allows companies to focus on the processes in which they have expertise. A manufacturing firm, for example, may possess expertise in making and selling their products. They are not necessarily experts in information technology or human resource management.

Apart from ASPs, business entities are outsourcing their basic accounting functions in other arrangements. For instance, General Motors Corporation contracted with Arthur Andersen for administrative accounting functions, including payroll processing.[5]

Another trend in outsourcing involves the internal audit function. Some consulting firms, including Deloitte and Touche, co-source, rather than outsource this service. Co-sourcing leaves some of the functional employees intact in the company and works with them. Interestingly, the professional service firms who employ external auditors are among those offering internal audit services, despite auditor independence implications. Former internal auditors are getting into the action too, offering their internal audit services on an independent contract basis, rather than as company employees. Jefferson Wells International is a professional service firm that specializes in outsourced internal audit services. The organization avoids the independence problem because they do no external audit work.

Since many accounting-related services are not core competencies, they are a prime area for outsourcing. Accountants who are displaced by the outsourcing may win the business back by offering their accounting services as consultants outside the business.

E-Commerce

Perhaps no other service line offers as much potential for consulting opportunities than e-commerce or e-business. The scramble for businesses to develop on-line presence and learn how to take advantage of e-business opportunities has them hiring consultants for help at an unprecedented rate. The Big Five professional service firms were particularly quick in jumping on the bandwagon. Print and television advertisements extolling the e-business services of these companies abound.

E-commerce services range from implementing on-line interfaces to existing or new enterprise systems to assurance services for e-commerce transactions. Figure 12-8 describes five "waves of evolution" of the Internet. Each of these waves carries with it a particular array of consulting services. For example, at the first stage, consultants can simply help companies determine which of their existing materials or ser-

---

[5] Lee Copeland, "GM Strikes Deal to Outsource Accounting," *Computerworld,* November 29, 1999, p. 6.

vices to put on the web, and they can help them do it. When companies begin to use the Internet to connect with their customers, suppliers, and other stakeholders, they need even more consulting services. Assurance is a major one. Opening up a company's information system to external parties creates significant security and privacy issues.

The e-commerce services advertised by Ernst and Young on their web site provide an example of the range of e-commerce consulting services that a professional service organization might offer. The firm has a venture group that makes investments in Internet companies and assists the company in management, finding partners, and providing consulting advice on technology, operations, and so on. Ernst and Young also offers what it calls "eRisk solutions." These are its e-business assurance services and they include security, e-commerce enablement, information technology risk management and assurance, and enterprise systems management and cost control.

Accounting consultants have many skills that enable them to offer advice to companies engaged in or entering into e-business in several arenas. The assurance services associated with e-commerce are an obvious example. Cost control issues are another. Helping clients to manage their supply chain across the Internet is another area in which accounting expertise is useful. Many accountants and accounting consultants have experience with electronic data interchange (EDI). This experience transfers well to the Internet environment. Further, while most businesses today realize that they need to sign up with trading partners to exchange goods and services online, they need help doing it. Consultants can assist clients in deciding what b-to-b model is best for them, and which trading partners offer the best deal. Apart from

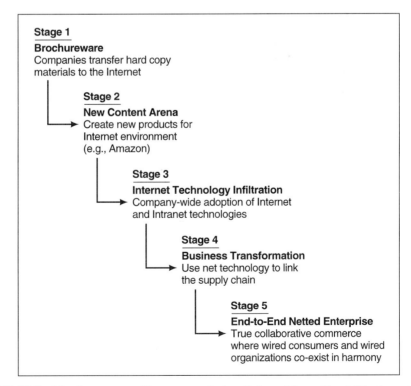

FIGURE 12-8 The five waves of Internet evolution (Adapted from Chuck Martin, *net future* [New York: Mc-Graw Hill, 1999].)

these examples, many of the other service lines mentioned previously in this chapter offer consulting opportunities with respect to e-commerce. For instance, many companies today need help in linking their ERP systems to the Internet. *WebTrust,* discussed earlier, is an example of an e-commerce assurance service.

More Service Lines for Accounting Consultants

A recruiting partner at Arthur Andersen commented recently that it was becoming almost impossible to keep track of all the service lines within the firm, and he needed to so that he could advise students about career opportunities. So far in this chapter we have focused on just a few of the services that consultants with accounting backgrounds offer to their clients. This section of the chapter more briefly describes a few others.

Services   Basically, you can consult about anything. In Chapter 1, we explained that a consultant is one who offers advice. Consultants with an accounting background may offer anything from personal financial planning to mergers and acquisition, personal tax advice to succession management, or accounting software selection help to ERP implementation. Some consulting firms organize their business around various service lines; other consultants may choose to focus on specializing in one or more industries, such as financial or manufacturing sectors. Some professional service organizations characterize "consulting" in a narrow sense. Their form of organization separates consulting practice from assurance services, for instance. However, we take the view that many of these assurance services are a form of consulting. If you help a client to develop an Internet privacy strategy, for example, this assurance is hard to distinguish from consulting advice.

We have mentioned many different kinds of consulting services in this chapter and throughout the book. Most fall under one of six general service categories for consulting. These are: assurance services (covered earlier), information technology (IT) consulting (which includes e-commerce and software selection and implementation), financial services, tax and legal services, human resources, and management services.

Assurance Services   As we noted earlier, the AICPA has developed a list of literally hundreds of possible assurance services accounting and consulting firms currently provide. Two that are popular today are worth further mention. One is forensic accounting. The public may not realize it, but usually accountants do not search for fraud in the course of an audit. Forensic accounting is fraud detection. Many professional service organizations employ forensic accountants, who are trained to recognize patterns of fraud, specifically financial fraud. One other "hot" assurance area is environmental auditing. Many businesses need to ensure compliance with environmental regulations. They may engage a consultant to help them assess their risk in this area and develop plans for minimizing their organization's impact on the physical environment.

IT Consulting   Andersen Consulting built a practice around IT consulting, beginning with helping General Electric to implement a payroll processing system, the first computerized business application. IT consulting can cover any advice relating to hardware, software, or perhaps just managing information.

Financial Services   Financial services are a natural for accounting consultants. Personal and business financial planning are one aspect of this service area. Costing and performance evaluation are other services in the financial category. Real estate management and mergers and acquisition are other examples of financial consulting services. One other popular financial consulting service is transfer pricing. Consultants can also help businesses to raise capital, whether through acquiring debt or managing an IPO.

Tax and Legal Services   Tax and legal services are closely related to financial services. Just as the financial audit creates an outgrowth of many types of assurance services, tax compliance and planning lead to other tax consulting services. Tax implications can be the "make or break" part of a business deal. International trade, for example, has many associated tax issues that require the help of experts. Many accountants are tax specialists; so are many lawyers. Because accountants and lawyers often team together in helping clients, professional service firms often employ large legal staffs. Apart from tax work, these consulting teams can help clients with a variety of litigation. For instance, a client who is facing fraud litigation can employ the services of a legal staff and forensic accountants.

Human Resources Consulting   The fifth area of consulting services we will mention is human resources consulting. The association between accounting and payroll makes this a rich potential service area for accounting consultants. Some of the human resource services that consultants can help clients with include: actuarial and insurance advice, health plan analysis, developing compliance plans relative to equal opportunity employment regulations, productivity measurement, and developing compensation policies.

Management Services   A final classification of consulting services are management services. These include management support services, such as strategic planning. Consultants bring many assets to the table in this area. They lack the biases of internal parties, have a broad understanding of a client's industry, and may be skilled in strategic planning processes. Other management support services overlap some of the previous categories. Helping clients to manage their IT and knowledge resources is an example.

Professional Alliances

Even large consulting firms cannot be experts at everything. Forming alliances with other consultants and professional organizations is important if you plan to offer your clients "one-stop shopping." The alliance may be a loose one—where you refer your clients to other experts or subcontract their services. Harry Ballman, for example, has formed professional alliances with law firms so that he can meet all his client's needs with respect to financial and tax planning. As another example, accounting consultants offering their clients financial planning services often form a third-party relationship with brokers or other investment professionals.

A more dramatic approach is for a professional service firm to sell one or more of the service lines it develops, but maintain some professional ties. Finally, you might actually invest in other companies, even clients, that are doing things your consulting organization does not. This may take the form of providing venture capital to start-up businesses. Ernst and Young, for example, has a Venture Group that will provide consulting services to start-up e-commerce businesses, and may even invest in them.

SUMMARY

A consultant with accounting knowledge combined with communication and technology skills can literally advise businesses about almost anything. In this chapter we looked at several of the consulting services that are a particularly good fit. By no means did we cover all the possibilities.

This chapter first discussed assurance services. Auditors have been trained in risk analysis and control. Although traditionally accounting auditors concerned themselves with financial auditing, today they are assuring businesses and individuals about information systems reliability, Internet security and privacy, and care for elders. Next we talked about software selection and implementation. When a CEO decides to acquire a new accounting or enterprise information system, he or she often looks to the company's accountant for help. Data analysis is another rich consulting area for people with accounting backgrounds. To analyze data, you must first accumulate it. Today that means building databases and data warehouses. Leveraging that investment requires extracting the data through data analysis tools, including queries, OLAP, and data mining. Consultants can use data mining in particular to help businesses detect patterns for marketing and control purposes. Next, the chapter discussed performance measurement. This is what accountants have traditionally done in preparing financial statements. Since the measurement system may drive the performance, developing appropriate metrics is critical to business success. The Balanced Scorecard has helped companies to focus on more than financial measures, and has become a lucrative niche consulting service area for many. Accountants, too, are well trained in costing. These skills translate well into helping companies to manage their costs. Two tools that can help here are activity-based costing systems and target costing. One more consulting service we elaborate on in this chapter concerns business processes. Accountants' familiarity with information flows around business processes prepares them for helping companies to improve these processes through reengineering. Helping clients determine what processes to keep and which to outsource, certainly from a cost perspective, is another service line accounting consultants can offer with expertise.

Consulting services, including those discussed in detail, that are potential opportunities for accounting consultants, generally fall into one of six categories. These are: assurance services, IT consulting, financial services, tax and legal services, human resources, and management services. The section of the chapter on other services provided examples of each of these.

No one person, and none but the largest professional service firms, can offer clients every type of consulting service they require. For that reason it often makes sense to form alliances with other professionals with specialized skill sets. The final section of this chapter briefly discussed these professional alliances.

DISCUSSION QUESTIONS

12-1. Discuss the skill sets an accountant can leverage in performing consulting services.

12-2. Make a list of five or more assurance services that a $250-million manufacturing firm might need to hire a consultant to provide.

12-3. If you were the CEO of a $250-million manufacturing firm, would you consider hiring a CPA offering the *SysTrust* service to evaluate the reliability of your information system? Why or why not?

12-4. Discuss the steps a small CPA firm might go through to begin offering *ElderCare* services.

12-5. What special training would an accountant need to obtain expertise in software selection consulting?

12-6. Discuss how a company might use its data warehouse to increase profitability.

12-7. Explain the differences among queries, OLAP, and data mining.

12-8. Activity based costing and target costing are two tools consultants can help clients use to manage their costs. What are some other cost management-related services accounting consultants can offer?

12-9. To some degree, business process reengineering is now incorporated in enterprise software implementation. Explain.

12-10. What are some criteria you would use in helping a client decide whether to outsource its internal audit function?

12-11. Suppose you are the managing partner of a small professional service firm. You offer accounting and consulting services to clients. Currently, consulting accounts for about 50 percent of revenues. The firm employs 18 staff members; most are quite skilled in information systems and technology. You recognize that e-commerce affords opportunities to expand your consulting practice but are not sure what specific services you might offer clients associated with it. Describe two or three possibilities for the firm.

12-12. This chapter described six categories of consulting services that accounting consultants offer. Can you think of any others?

EXERCISES

12-13. *CPA WebTrust* is one of several third-party assurance services. Use the Internet to answer the following questions about this type of assurance practice. What are the specific assurances it provides? How many companies have purchased the seal? What are the other third-party assurances available and how do they compare in terms of the assurances they offer?

12-14. A consulting firm can not only help others develop Balanced Scorecards for performance measurement, it can also adapt the approach in-house. Create a Balanced Scorecard for a consulting firm that specializes in information systems consulting to mid-size (less than $500-million revenue) clients. List the likely performance measures and objectives for each of the four categories in the scorecard.

12-15. ABC Company is experiencing problems with its accounts payable process. Payments to vendors are often late and the company frequently fails to take advantage of cash discounts. The current system has many controls designed to avoid duplicate payments. For instance, the information system matches purchase orders, receiving reports, and vendor invoices before creating checks. Each day the system produces a discrepancy report listing inconsistencies. Accounts payable clerks follow up on these. Unfortunately, there are many discrepancies, although usually they are due to minor issues, such as use of different specifications in the various documents. How might you reengineer this accounts payable process?

12-16. Each of the five largest public accounting firms offers tax and legal services to clients. Use the Internet to examine these practices in some detail and compare them. Do the firms organize their practices differently? For example, do some include mergers and acquisitions services in this category or under financial services?

12-17. Suppose you are managing partner of a small professional service firm, specializing in accounting, auditing, and tax work. Increasingly your clients come to you for advice that you cannot provide. What are some of the professional alliances you might make to give your clients a complete range of services?

REFERENCES, RECOMMENDED READINGS, AND WEB SITES

References and Recommended Readings

Bagranoff, N. A., "Select Your Next System with High-tech Tools," *Strategic Finance* (May 1999), pp. 75–79.

Banham, Russ, "The B-to-B Virtual Bazaar," *Journal of Accountancy* (July 2000), pp. 26–30.

Barcus, Sam W., III, and Joseph W. Wilkinson, Editors in Chief, *Handbook of Management Consulting Services,* 2nd edition (New York: McGraw-Hill, 1995).

Bellis-Johnes, Robin, Alf Oldman, and Roger Mils, "Trends in Cost Management Practice," *Management Accounting* (July/August 1999), pp. 28–30.

Boer, German, and John Ettlie, "Target Costing Can Boost Your Bottom Line," *Strategic Finance* (July 1999), pp. 49–52.

Castellani, D. J., "ASPs: Changing Information Technology Delivery," *Strategic Finance* (March 2000), pp. 34–37.

Collins, J. Carlton, "How to Select the Right Accounting Software, Part 3," *Journal of Accountancy* (October 1999), pp. 67–77.

Collins, J. Carlton, "How to Select the Right Accounting Software, Part 1," *Journal of Accountancy* (August 1999), pp. 61–69.

Davenport, T. H., *Mission Critical* (Cambridge, MA: Harvard Business School Press, 2000).

David, Julie Smith, and Paul John Steinbart, "Drowning in Data," *Strategic Finance* (December 1999), pp. 30–34.

Figg, Jonathan, "Outsourcing: A Runaway Train," *The Internal Auditor* (June 2000), pp. 48–55.

Frieswick, Kris, "Special Report: Outsourcing from Soup to Nuts," *CFO Magazine* (February 2000), www.c fanet.com.

Gordon, Lawrence, *Managerial Accounting Concepts and Empirical Evidence,* 5th edition (New York: McGraw-Hill, 2000).

Hammer, Michael, and James Champy, *Reengineering the Corporation* (New York: HarperCollins Publishers, 1993).

Hammer, Michael, *Beyond Reengineering* (New York: HarperCollins Publishers, 1996).

Hammer, M., and S. Stanton, "How Process Enterprises Really Work," *Harvard Business Review* (November/December 1999), pp. 108–118.

Hayes, D. C., and J. E. Hunton, "What You Better Know About Databases," *Journal of Accountancy* (January 1999), pp. 61–65.

Kaplan, Robert S., and David P. Norton, "The Balanced Scorecard—Measures that Drive Performance," *Harvard Business Review* (January/February 1992), pp. 71–79.

Kaplan, Robert S., and David P. Norton, "Using the Balanced Scorecard as a Strategic Management System," *Harvard Business Review* (January/February 1996), pp. 75–86.

Kaplan, Rober S., and David P. Norton, *The Balanced Scorecard* (Cambridge, MA: Harvard Business School Press, 1996).

Linoff, G., "Data Mining," *Inform* (November/December 1999), pp. 18–24.

Lozinsky, Sergio, *Enterprise-Wide Software Solutions* (Reading, MA: Addison-Wesley, 1998).

Martin, Chuck, *net future* (New York: McGraw-Hill, 1999).

Mottl, Judy N., "IT Outsourcing Gives Staples the Tools to Grow," *Informationweek* (May 15, 2000), pp. 112–116.

Ostrenga, Michael, *The Ernst and Young Guide to Total Cost Management* (New York: John Wiley and Sons, 1992).

Romney, M., "Business Process Reengineering," *Internal Auditor* (June 1995), pp. 24–29.

Sauls, W., "Leveraging the Data Warehouse," *Management Accounting* (October 1996), pp. 39–43.

Shank, John K., and Joseph Fisher, "Case Study: Target Costing as a Strategic Tool," *Sloan Management Review* (Fall 1999), pp. 73-82.

Simon, A. R., *Data Warehousing for Dummies* (Foster City, CA: IDG Books Worldwide, 1997).

Thomson, Jeff, and Steve Varley, "Developing a Balanced Scorecard at AT&T," *Journal of Strategic Performance Measurement,* vol. I, (August/September 1997), pp. 14-20.

Web Sites

www.k2e.com (accounting software site)

www.ctsguides.com (*The Requirements Analyst*—software selection tool)

www.excelco.com/tal.htm (*The Accounting Library*—software selection tool)

www.aspindustry.com (site for the ASP industry)

www.outsourcing.com (The Outsourcing Institute)

APPENDIX A

Using *Microsoft Project 2000*

INTRODUCTION

The purpose of this appendix is to familiarize you with *Microsoft Project 2000.* Given the limited amount of space allocated to this objective, you will receive a high-level tutorial on how to use the most basic features of *Microsoft Project 2000.* If you want more details about the many features built into *Microsoft Project 2000,* you should purchase a guidebook from a bookstore since there are many hands-on texts dedicated to *Microsoft Project 2000.*

Throughout this tutorial, you will be asked to perform functions commonly found in Microsoft business applications, such as open a file, change a view, and use some tools. Because it takes a great deal of space to provide point-and-click instructions at the lowest level of detail, the tutorial expects that you are already familiar with other Microsoft applications, such as Word and Excel. Therefore, such detailed instruction is not provided herein. With these caveats in mind, let's begin to use *Microsoft Project 2000.*

In the back of this text, you will find a CD that contains *Microsoft Project 2000* and some accompanying files. Please load the CD into your CD drive and install *Project 2000* on your computer. Once this is accomplished, open *Microsoft Project 2000,* and choose the Gantt Chart view (using the icon in the left-hand frame). If the Help screen appears in a frame on the right-side of your screen, close Help by clicking on the X button in the upper right-hand corner.

From the top toolbar, choose |Project|, |Information|, and set the project start date to Monday, January 6, 2003. Save the project with the name STAR in a folder of your choice on your computer. Using your left mouse button, hold and slide the vertical bar over so that you can view the following columns: Task Name, Duration, Start, and Finish. Your screen should look like the one provided in Figure A-1.

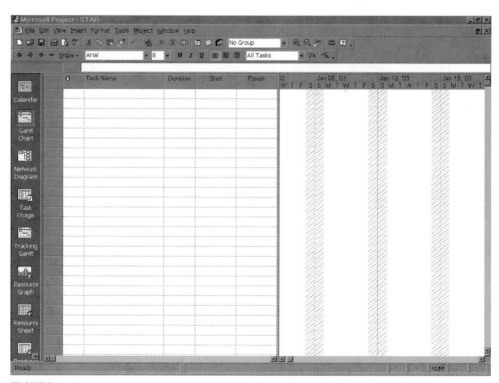

FIGURE A-1   Starting screen for using *Microsoft Project 2000.*

THE STAR PROJECT

Let's begin the tutorial by using the Sales Transaction Accounting Register (STAR) project developed in Chapter 6 of this text. Since the STAR project is quite simple in nature, it offers an easy-to-understand starting point for using *Microsoft Project 2000.*

Entering a Relatively Simple Work Breakdown Structure (WBS)

Please refer to the WBS shown in Figure 6-2 entitled "Abbreviated Work Breakdown Structure (WBS) for the Sales Transaction Accounting Register (STAR) Project." The first step in entering the WBS is to establish the WBS code or indexing system. In our example, we use a numeric indexing system (i.e., 1.0, 2.0, 3.0 and 4.0). Click on the |Project| menu item and choose |WBS|, then |Define Code|. Using the drop-down box shown under the heading Sequence, choose Numbers (ordered). Under Length, select Any and under Separator, choose the decimal point. Repeat this procedure for two more levels. At this point, your screen should look like the one shown in Figure A-2. Notice in the Code Preview portion of the window that the WBS code will take the form X.X.X (three levels deep). Although the STAR project uses only level one, the next tutorial example will use all three levels. Click the OK button.

The next step is to enter the tasks and their estimated duration times. To complete this operation, please refer to the duration times for the STAR project shown in Figure 6-4 entitled "Activity-on-Node Network Diagram with Durations." Enter the tasks and duration times shown for the STAR project. When finished, your screen should look like the one shown in Figure A-3. You have now successfully entered the WBS into *Microsoft Project 2000.*

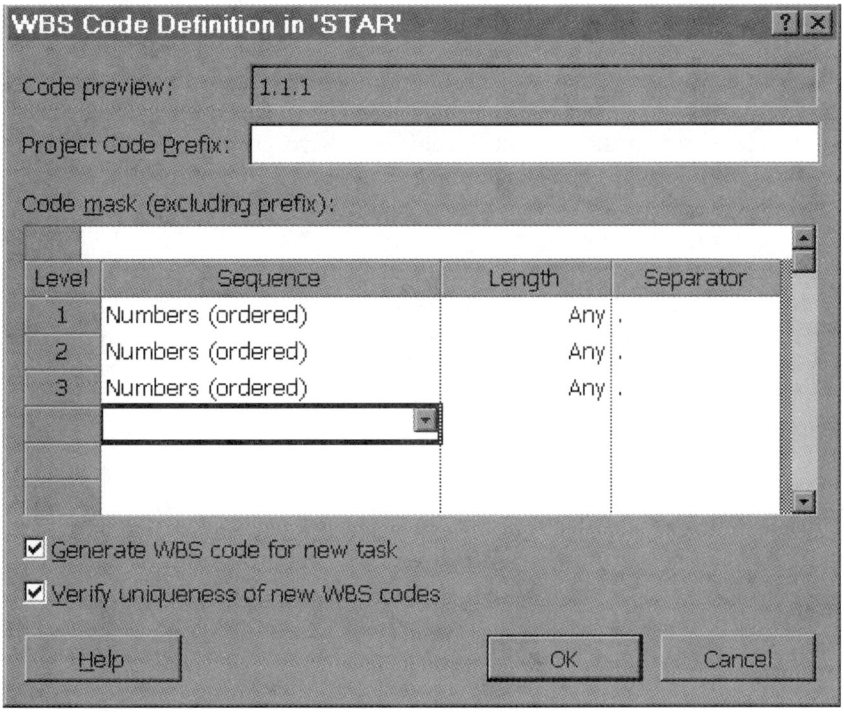

FIGURE A-2   Setting the WBS code for the STAR project.

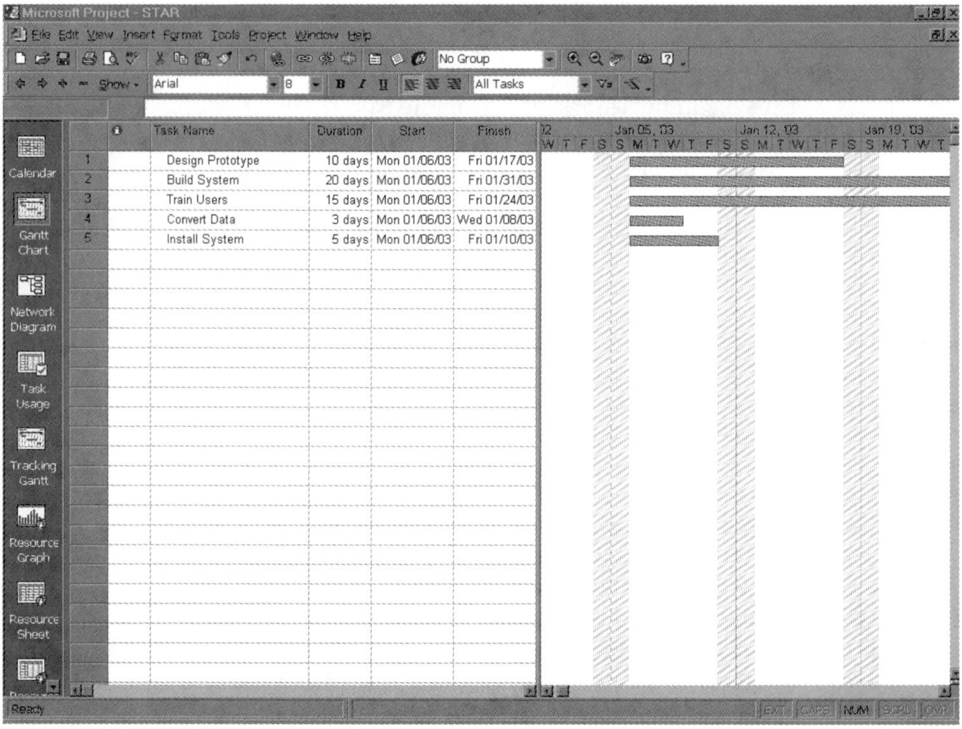

FIGURE A-3   Entering the WBS for the STAR project

Configuring a Relatively Simple Network Diagram

Notice that all tasks begin on Monday, January 6, 2003, and the project ends on Friday, January 31, 2003. The end date is 20 workdays from the beginning date because the longest duration is 20 workdays for the task labeled Build System (weekend days are not counted in the project estimate). Based on what we learned in Chapter 6, we know that the project should last 35 workdays, rather than 20. The difference comes about due to the sequencing of the tasks. Presently, all tasks are assumed to begin simultaneously. Thus, we next need to configure an activity-on-node network diagram for the STAR project.

Click on the Network Diagram icon in the left-hand frame of your project screen. You should see all the tasks stacked on top of each other. Using your mouse, place your cursor inside the first task box (Design Prototype), click and hold the left mouse button, and drag the cursor to the second task box (Build System). An arrow should appear from Design Prototype to Build System, indicating a sequential path. Perform the same procedure from Build System to Install System. Then, create paths from Design Prototype to Train Users, from Train Users to Convert Data, and from Convert Data to Install System. At this point, your network diagram should resemble Figure A-4. The red line on the network diagram indicates the critical path.

Click on the Gantt Chart icon in the left-hand frame of your project screen. Slide the vertical bar over so that you can see the Task Name, Duration, Start, Finish, and Predecessors columns. Notice that Design Prototype has no predecessors, whereas the other tasks have the predecessors as indicated in the network diagram. The start and finish times shown represent the early starts and early finish times, as determined using the critical path method (CPM) in Chapter 6. Next, we will have *Microsoft Project 2000* determine the late start, late finish, and total slack times.

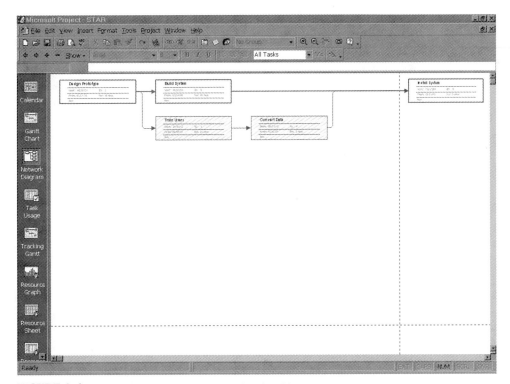

FIGURE A-4   Building a network diagram for the STAR project.

Place your cursor in the label box (on top of the column) of the Predecessors column. Left click the mouse once and the whole column should become shaded. Using the toolbar on top of the screen, select |Insert|, |Column|, and then select the field name Late Start (press OK). A new column should be inserted. If the column is too small, you might see a series of pound signs (#). If so, click and hold the rightmost portion of the column in the top label box and expand the column to the right until the dates appear. Perform this procedure again and insert two more columns: Late Finish and Total Slack. When finished, your screen should look like the one shown in Figure A-5.

The start and finish times are stated in calendar days and elapsed days (as shown in Chapter 6). Also, notice that the slack times match Chapter 6. As you can see, by changing estimated dates and/or resequencing tasks, we can easily create activity-on-node network diagrams with slack using *Microsoft Project 2000.*

Preparing the Resource Sheet

Now let's take the STAR project to another level of planning by assigning resources to tasks. To accomplish this objective, project resources must first be entered into a resource sheet. Begin by clicking on the icon in the left-hand frame called Resource Sheet. Under the column heading Resource Name enter John Smith. The next column, Type, designates whether the resource is Work or Material. Choose Work. Had we chosen Material in the third column, Material Label, we might enter a type of material that is being consumed or used during the task, such as Computers or Supplies. The fourth column, Initials, is used in future reporting when you might not want lengthy resource names appearing, such as the names of people; rather, an abbreviation would appear. For our tutorial, enter JS for John Smith. The next column, Group,

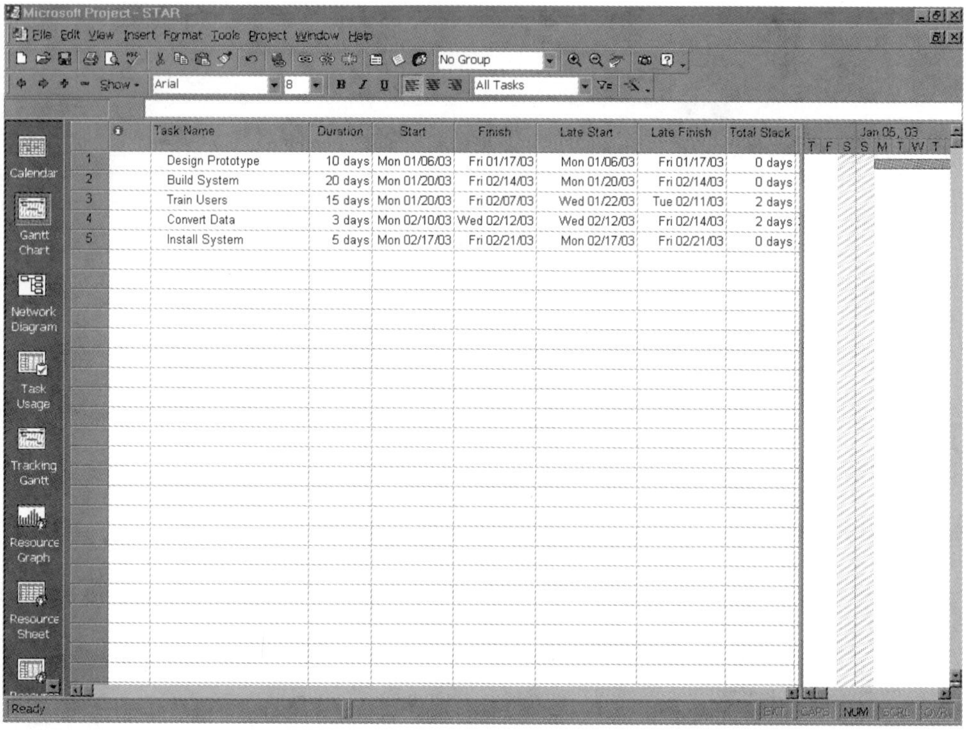

	Task Name	Duration	Start	Finish	Late Start	Late Finish	Total Slack
1	Design Prototype	10 days	Mon 01/06/03	Fri 01/17/03	Mon 01/06/03	Fri 01/17/03	0 days
2	Build System	20 days	Mon 01/20/03	Fri 02/14/03	Mon 01/20/03	Fri 02/14/03	0 days
3	Train Users	15 days	Mon 01/20/03	Fri 02/07/03	Wed 01/22/03	Tue 02/11/03	2 days
4	Convert Data	3 days	Mon 02/10/03	Wed 02/12/03	Wed 02/12/03	Fri 02/14/03	2 days
5	Install System	5 days	Mon 02/17/03	Fri 02/21/03	Mon 02/17/03	Fri 02/21/03	0 days

FIGURE A-5 Gantt chart with early and late times and total slack.

is used to categorize similar resource types, such as analysts, programmers, and so on. Please enter Analyst here. The Max. Units is used to indicate the maximum percentage of time the resource can be used on the project. For instance, some programmers might spend all their time on a project, while other programmers might spread their efforts across multiple projects. In our case, John Smith is allocated at 100% to the STAR project. In the Std. Rate column, we can enter the standard rate at which the resource will be billed to the project. Let's assume that John Smith's billing rate is $80.00/hr. Next, enter John Smith's overtime rate (Ovt. Rate) as $120.00/hr. At this time, enter the information shown on Figure A-6 (page 259) into your resource sheet.

Assigning Resources to Project Tasks

The next step is to assign resources to tasks. In Chapter 6, we assigned elapsed days to tasks. For instance, the task Design Prototype was assigned ten working days. *Microsoft Project 2000* assumes that 10 working days equates to 80 hours of work (although, this assumption can be changed in the software, if desired). Thus, a single analyst can build a prototype in two weeks, assuming 40-hour weeks. With this in mind, let's start out by assigning one human resource to each task in the STAR project.

Click on the Gantt Chart icon in the left-hand frame. Then, click on the first task Design Prototype. Then, on the top tool bar, click on the Assign Resources icon, which looks like two human faces. Click on the name John Smith and then click the Assign button. You have just assigned 100 percent of Smith's time to the first task. Now, click the Close button. To the remaining tasks (Build System, Train Users, Convert Data, and Install System) assign Philip Sickles, Jane Kelso, Joan Billings, and

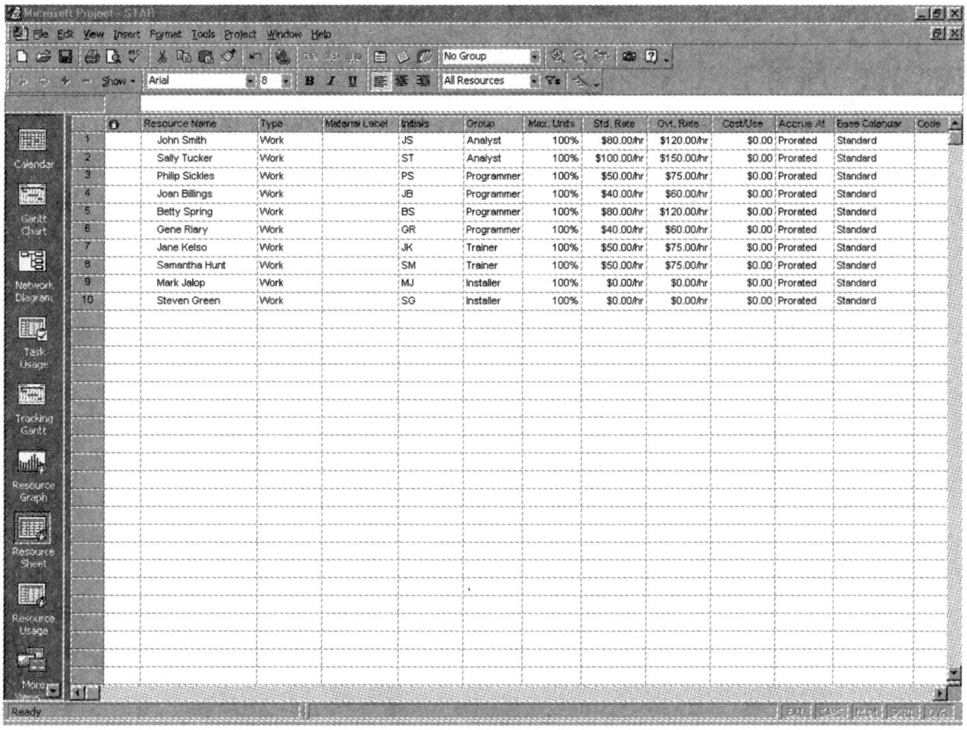

FIGURE A-6 Resource sheet information for the STAR project.

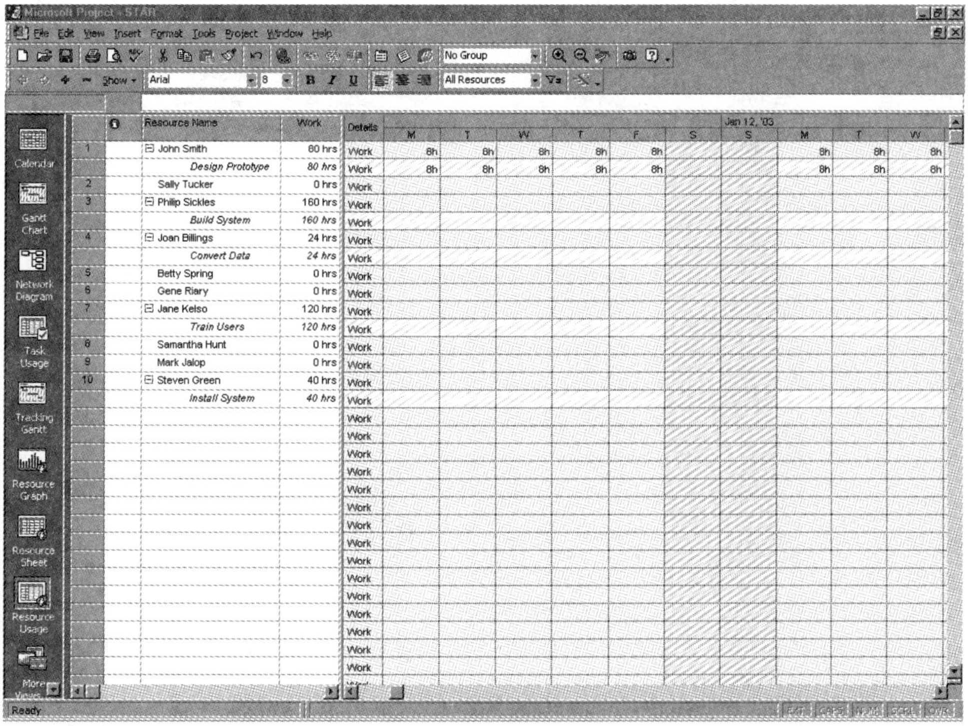

FIGURE A-7 Resource usage for the STAR project.

Steven Green, respectively. Click on the Resource Usage icon in the left-hand frame. Move the navigation bar on the bottom of the right-hand frame to the week of January 5, 2000, and then keep looking forward in time. You will notice that the assigned resources are allocated for eight hours per day throughout the duration of their assigned task (see Figure A-7).

Shortening the Project Schedule

One way to shorten the overall project timeline is to add more resources to tasks. The project manager would first consider adding resources to tasks along the critical path, since these tasks represent the bottleneck in the timeline. In the STAR project, the critical task is Build System, which is expected to take 20 workdays. Let's add another full-time programmer to this task and see what happens to the Gantt Chart. Click on the Gantt Chart icon in the left-hand frame. Place your cursor in the cell called Build System and then click on the Assign Resources icon located on the upper toolbar. Assign a second programmer, Joan Billings, to this critical task. Now, click on the Network Diagram icon in the left-hand frame. Notice that the critical path now runs through Train Users and Convert Data, since the Build System task has been reduced to 10 workdays (rather than one person working for 20 days, we have two programmers working for 10 days). Your new Gantt Chart should look like Figure A-8. At this point, if the project manager wanted to further shorten the schedule, he or she would have to add more resources to either or both of the tasks along the new critical path.

It's important to remember that merely throwing additional resources at a task might not work as planned. That is, due to overlap issues, communication problems

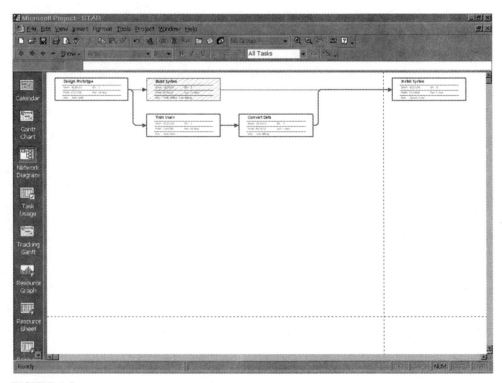

FIGURE A-8 Network diagram with new critical path.

and so on, a team of, say, three programmers might be much more efficient than a team of six. Hence, the project manager must be very careful to think through the ramifications of adding more human and material resources to tasks.

Setting the Baseline Project

Microsoft Project 2000 allows you to save a baseline project. That is, once you have entered the WBS, established the network diagram and assigned resources, you should save the original project plan as a baseline estimate against which actual project results can be compared. Thus, a baseline allows you to track project progress over time.

Once a baseline is established, *Microsoft Project 2000* saves the original plan data as part of the overall project file. At this time, create a baseline by selecting |Tools|, |Tracking|, and clicking on Save Baseline for Entire Project. This action does not create a separate baseline file. If you desire to keep the baseline project file in isolation, you should create a backup copy of the file before entering any actual tracking data. You may do so by selecting |File|, |Save As|, and entering another name for the original project file.

Let's take a look at some baseline statistics. Select |View|, |Reports|, and click on Overview and Project Summary. You should see a report similar to the one shown in Figure A-9. Notice that the baseline information appears, but there is no actual data at this point. If you want a further breakdown of the $20,560 estimated project costs, select |View|, |Reports|, and click on Costs and Budget (see Figure A-10). As you can see, the budget report shows the estimated cost of labor for each task, based on the assigned resources. Please feel free to examine other reports available to the project manager, which are listed under |View|, |Reports|.

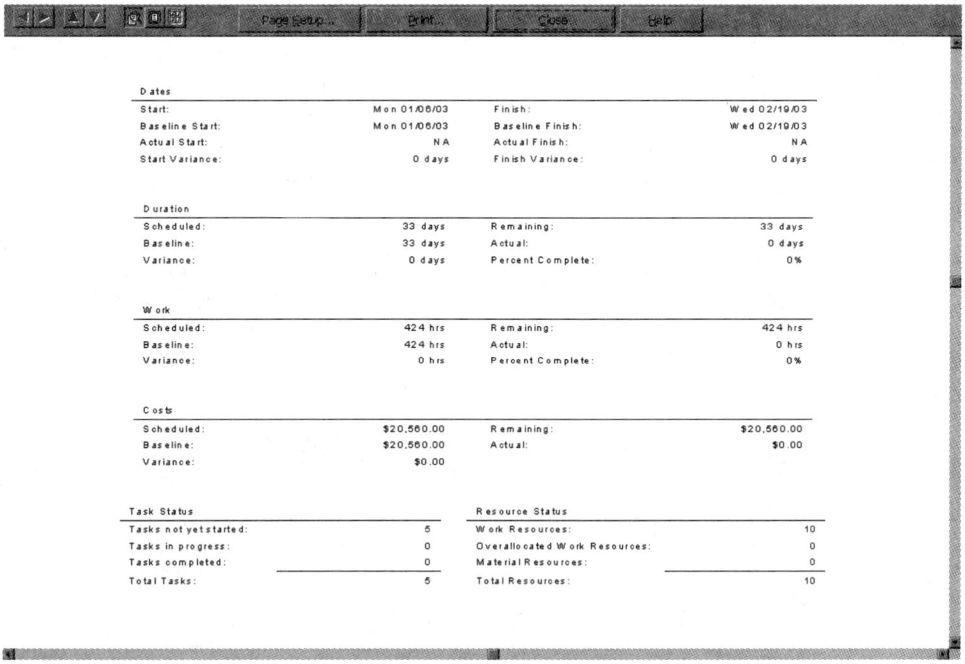

Dates			
Start:	Mon 01/06/03	Finish:	Wed 02/19/03
Baseline Start:	Mon 01/06/03	Baseline Finish:	Wed 02/19/03
Actual Start:	NA	Actual Finish:	NA
Start Variance:	0 days	Finish Variance:	0 days

Duration			
Scheduled:	33 days	Remaining:	33 days
Baseline:	33 days	Actual:	0 days
Variance:	0 days	Percent Complete:	0%

Work			
Scheduled:	424 hrs	Remaining:	424 hrs
Baseline:	424 hrs	Actual:	0 hrs
Variance:	0 hrs	Percent Complete:	0%

Costs			
Scheduled:	$20,560.00	Remaining:	$20,560.00
Baseline:	$20,560.00	Actual:	$0.00
Variance:	$0.00		

Task Status		Resource Status	
Tasks not yet started:	5	Work Resources:	10
Tasks in progress:	0	Overallocated Work Resources:	0
Tasks completed:	0	Material Resources:	0
Total Tasks:	5	Total Resources:	10

FIGURE A-9 Report on STAR project overview.

Budget Report as of Wed 10/04/00
STAR

Task Name	Fixed Cost	Fixed Cost Accrual	Total Cost	Baseline	Variance
Build System	$0.00	Prorated	$7,200.00	$7,200.00	$0.00
Design Prototype	$0.00	Prorated	$6,400.00	$6,400.00	$0.00
Train Users	$0.00	Prorated	$6,000.00	$6,000.00	$0.00
Convert Data	$0.00	Prorated	$960.00	$960.00	$0.00
Install System	$0.00	Prorated	$0.00	$0.00	$0.00
	$0.00		$20,560.00	$20,560.00	$0.00

FIGURE A-10   Budgeted labor costs for the STAR project.

Tracking the Project

The next step in managing a project is to track actual progress over time. Let's assume that the first task (Design Prototype) is 100 percent complete, the Build System task is 50 percent complete, and the Train Users task is 75 percent complete. Click on the Gantt Chart icon in the left-hand frame and place your cursor in the Design Prototype task. Next, select |Tools|, |Tracking|, and click on Update Tasks. Use your cursor to roll the % Complete box to 100 percent then click the OK button. Now, navigate back to the same Update Tasks box for the Design Prototype task. Notice that *Microsoft Project 2000* changed the actual duration to 10 days and remaining duration to zero days (see Figure A-11). Naturally, the start and end dates could be

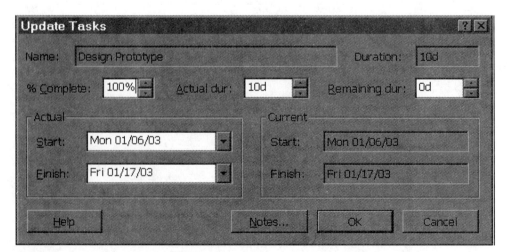

FIGURE A-11   Update the design prototype task.

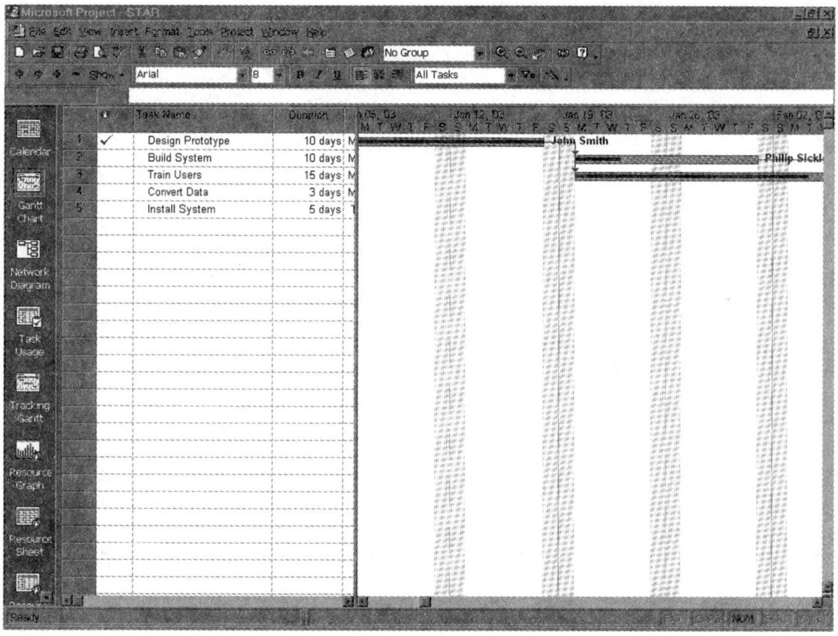

FIGURE A-12 Gantt chart after entering percentage completions for three tasks.

changed from the original plan, if necessary. Perform the same procedure for the Build System task (set the task at 30 percent complete) and the Train Users task (set the task at 75 percent complete). Your resulting Gantt Chart should look like Figure A-12. Notice that the Design Prototype task has a checkmark beside the task name, indicating that the task is complete. The bars in the right-hand frame representing the first three tasks have lines running though them, which visually reflect the percentage of completion for these tasks.

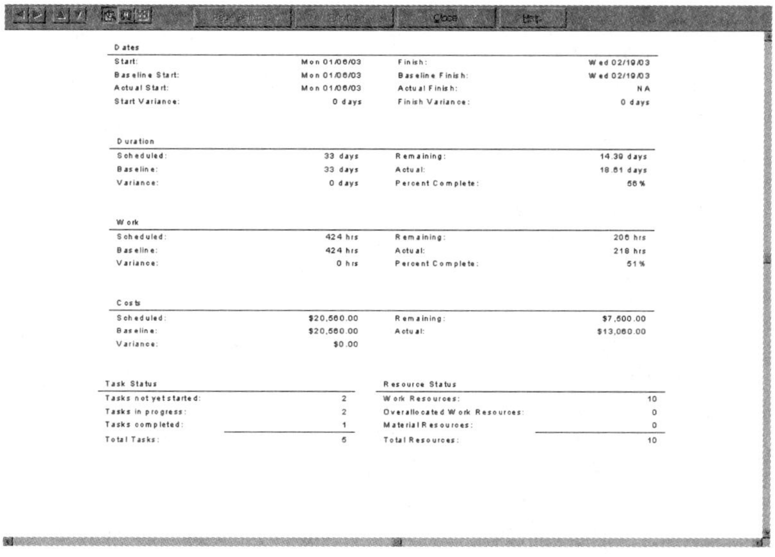

Dates

Start:	Mon 01/06/03	Finish:	Wed 02/19/03
Baseline Start:	Mon 01/06/03	Baseline Finish:	Wed 02/19/03
Actual Start:	Mon 01/06/03	Actual Finish:	NA
Start Variance:	0 days	Finish Variance:	0 days

Duration

Scheduled:	33 days	Remaining:	14.39 days
Baseline:	33 days	Actual:	18.61 days
Variance:	0 days	Percent Complete:	56 %

Work

Scheduled:	424 hrs	Remaining:	206 hrs
Baseline:	424 hrs	Actual:	218 hrs
Variance:	0 hrs	Percent Complete:	51 %

Costs

Scheduled:	$20,560.00	Remaining:	$7,500.00
Baseline:	$20,560.00	Actual:	$13,060.00
Variance:	$0.00		

Task Status

Tasks not yet started:	2
Tasks in progress:	2
Tasks completed:	1
Total Tasks:	5

Resource Status

Work Resources:	10
Overallocated Work Resources:	0
Material Resources:	0
Total Resources:	10

FIGURE A-13 Overview report including tracking information.

Let's look once again at a project report to see the impact of entering actual task information. Select |View|, |Reports|, and click on Overview and Project Summary. You should see a report similar to the one shown in Figure A-13. The remaining project costs total $7,500, whereas $13,060 has already been spend on the project.

If you haven't already done so, please save your project using the name STAR in the folder of your choice on your computer. Of course, we entered tracking information into the STAR project as if everything were running smoothly—the tasks were starting on the planned dates and the duration estimates were accurate. In the real world of project management, this rarely occurs. However, you can probably start to see by now how you can adjust beginning dates, durations, and ending dates on a task-by-task basis. Resources can also be reallocated within and among tasks at any time. We hope that it is clear just how valuable *Microsoft Project* can be to project managers, particularly as projects become very complex.

THE CIRCLES PROJECT

The next project example, Completely Integrated, Regulated, Coordinated, and Linked Enterprise Software (CIRCLES), can be found in Chapter 5. Whereas the STAR project has a simple WBS structure, the CIRCLES project is considerably more complex. Entering the WBS structure and configuring the network diagram will be discussed next since these two project events are a bit more difficult when the project is fairly complex. However, this section will not cover the remaining project events (preparing the resource sheet, assigning resources to tasks, shortening the project schedule, setting the baseline project, and tracking the project) because the way you handle these is not notably different in simple versus complex WBS structures.

Entering a More Complex Work Breakdown Schedule (WBS)

Let's begin by establishing a start date for the project and saving the project file. From the top toolbar, choose |Project|, |Information|, and set the project start date to Monday, January 6, 2003. Save the project with the name CIRCLES in a folder of your choice on your computer. Next, establish a three-level WBS code, as explained in Section 2.1 of this appendix. Although we did not utilize the WBS structure codes in the STAR project (since its WBS reflected a single level), we will look at the WBS structure for the CIRCLES project. We are now ready to enter the WBS into *Microsoft Project 2000*.

Click on the Gantt Chart icon in the left-hand frame. Place your cursor in the text box labeled Task Name and click the left mouse button. The entire column should darken. From the top toolbar, select |Insert|, then click on Column and select the WBS field name. Once completed, a new column labeled WBS should appear on the left side of the Task Name column. We will now enter the entire WBS structure for the CIRCLES project shown in Figure 5-2 entitled "Function-Based Work Breakdown Structure (WBS) for CIRCLES Project."

For the first task name, enter Analysis. Then, enter the next task name Document Existing Processes. Once this task is entered, press the Enter Key, stay in the task name field, and click on the indent button shown on the top toolbar (|). Enter three days duration for this task. Next, enter three more consecutive task names: Develop New Models, Create Process Maps and Specify Business Events. Move back to Create

Process Maps and click on the indent button and move to Specify Business Events and click on the indent button. Enter four duration days for Create Process Maps and five duration days for Specify Business Events. Notice that the WBS codes match the CIRCLES project codes we developed in Chapter 5. Also notice that the elapsed days for the Analysis phase of the CIRCLES project is five days at this point, reflecting the longest elapsed days of the two subtasks (1.1 and 1.2), which is Develop New Models. The five elapsed days for the Analysis phase presumes that all subtasks can be performed simultaneously. Hence, *Microsoft Project 2000* uses the longest elapsed days for the subtasks to determine the duration of entire phase. As we will see later, if these tasks are connected in a serial manner (i.e., one task must be completed before another is started), the total elapsed days for the Analysis phase will change accordingly.

On the next row, enter the task name Design, then click twice on the outdent button on the top toolbar ($\Leftarrow$). On the next row, enter the task name Create Database Schema, click on the indent button, and enter a duration of three days. Continue by entering the following five task names: Produce Application Systems, Design Input Screens (click the indent button and enter 8 days duration), Design User Reports (click the indent button and enter 7 days duration), Write Application Code (click the indent button and enter 11 days duration), and Test Application Code (click the indent button and enter 3 days duration). Sometimes the WBS code numbers get out of sequence. If they are, you can select |Project| and click on WBS and Renumber as often as needed. This action will correctly resequence the WBS numbers. At this point, you have entered the WBS structure up to task 2.2.4. Refer to Figure A-14 and finish entering the WBS structure for the CIRCLES project as shown.

Configuring a More Complex Network Diagram

Click on the Network Diagram icon in the left-hand frame. Let's presume that the first task Document Existing Processes must be accomplished before Develop New Models. To indicate this relationship, place your cursor in the Document Existing Processes box, hold the left mouse button down, and draw an arrow to the Develop

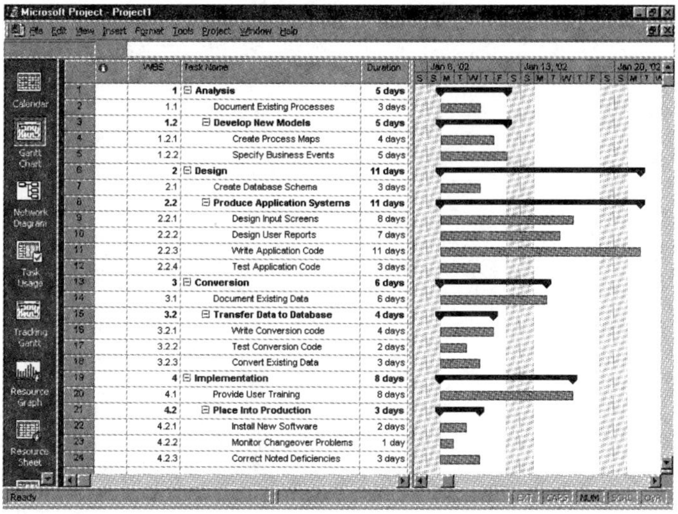

FIGURE A-14 Gantt chart view of CIRCLES project before establishing the network diagram.

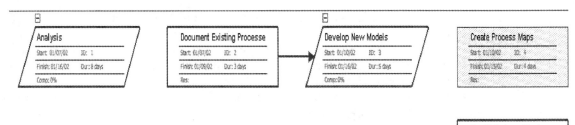

FIGURE A-15A   Network diagram of the CIRCLES project.

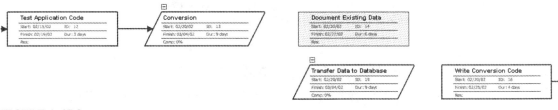

FIGURE A-15B   Network diagram of the CIRCLES project.

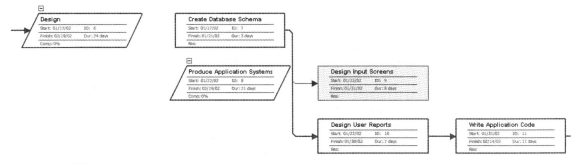

FIGURE A-15C   Network diagram of the CIRCLES project.

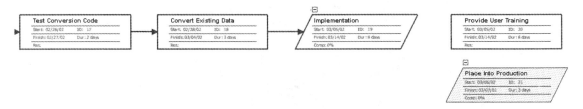

FIGURE A-15D   Network diagram of the CIRCLES project.

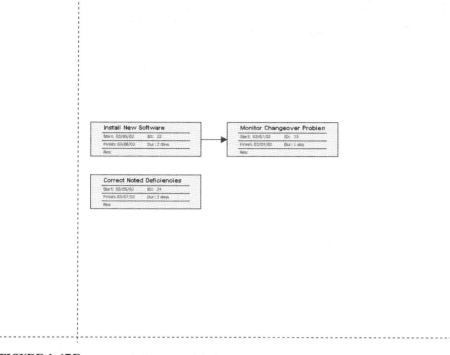

FIGURE A-15E   Network diagram of the CIRCLES project.

New Models task (release the left mouse button). Now, presume that Create Process Maps and Specify Business Events can be performed simultaneously. However, once Specify Business Events is finished, the Design phase can begin. To depict this relationship, draw an arrow from Specify Business Events to Design. At this point, your network diagram should look like Figure A-15A.

Draw an arrow from Create Database Schema to Design Input Screens. Then, draw another arrow from Create Database Schema to Design User Reports. Also, draw an arrow from Design User Reports to Write Application Code. Your network diagram should now be extended to look like Figure A-15B. The interpretation of these relationships is that Create Database Schema must be accomplished first, Design Input Screens and Design User Reports can be performed concurrently, and Write Application Code can only be performed after Design User Reports. Finish the network diagram by following the illustrations shown in Figures A-15C, A-15D. and A-15E.

The Gantt Chart view provides a concise way for visualizing the relationships just established. Click on the Gantt Chart icon on the left-hand frame. Slide the middle bar to the left such that you can see the whole network structure, as shown in Figure A-16. Notice the sequential and interdependent nature of the CIRCLE project tasks.

Next, slide the middle bar back to the right so that you can see the Task Name and Duration columns (see Figure A-17). Notice that the duration days are different now that the network diagram has been established. For example, before the network diagram, the Analysis phase was estimated to take five days to complete, based on the longest elapsed time for Specify Business Events. After the network diagram, the Analysis phase duration is eight days. This is determined by adding three days for the Document Existing Processes task (which must be performed first) to five days for

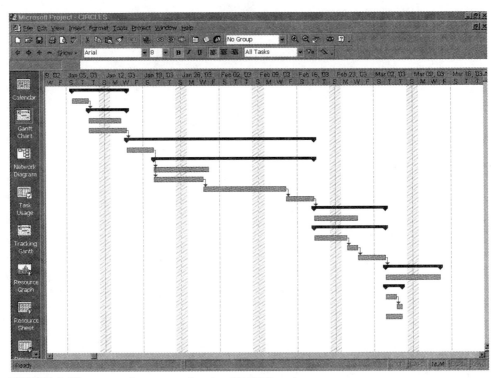

FIGURE A-16   Gantt chart view of entire CIRCLES project.

		WBS	Task Name	Duration	Start	Finish	Predecessors	Resource Names
1		1	⊟ **Analysis**	**8 days**	**Mon 01/06/03**	**Wed 01/15/03**		
2		1.1	Document Existing Processes	3 days	Mon 01/06/03	Wed 01/08/03		
3		1.2	⊟ **Develop New Models**	**5 days**	**Thu 01/09/03**	**Wed 01/15/03**	2	
4		1.2.1	Create Process Maps	4 days	Thu 01/09/03	Tue 01/14/03		
5		1.2.2	Specify Business Events	5 days	Thu 01/09/03	Wed 01/15/03		
6		2	⊟ **Design**	**24 days**	**Thu 01/16/03**	**Tue 02/18/03**	5	
7		2.1	Create Database Schema	3 days	Thu 01/16/03	Mon 01/20/03		
8		2.2	⊟ **Produce Application Systems**	**21 days**	**Tue 01/21/03**	**Tue 02/18/03**		
9		2.2.1	Design Input Screens	8 days	Tue 01/21/03	Thu 01/30/03	7	
10		2.2.2	Design User Reports	7 days	Tue 01/21/03	Wed 01/29/03	7	
11		2.2.3	Write Application Code	11 days	Thu 01/30/03	Thu 02/13/03	10	
12		2.2.4	Test Application Code	3 days	Fri 02/14/03	Tue 02/18/03	11	
13		3	⊟ **Conversion**	**9 days**	**Wed 02/19/03**	**Mon 03/03/03**	12	
14		3.1	Document Existing Data	6 days	Wed 02/19/03	Wed 02/26/03		
15		3.2	⊟ **Transfer Data to Database**	**9 days**	**Wed 02/19/03**	**Mon 03/03/03**		
16		3.2.1	Write Conversion Code	4 days	Wed 02/19/03	Mon 02/24/03		
17		3.2.2	Test Conversion Code	2 days	Tue 02/25/03	Wed 02/26/03	16	
18		3.2.3	Convert Existing Data	3 days	Thu 02/27/03	Mon 03/03/03	17	
19		4	⊟ **Implementation**	**8 days**	**Tue 03/04/03**	**Thu 03/13/03**	18	
20		4.1	Provide User Training	8 days	Tue 03/04/03	Thu 03/13/03		
21		4.2	⊟ **Place Into Production**	**3 days**	**Tue 03/04/03**	**Thu 03/06/03**		
22		4.2.1	Install New Software	2 days	Tue 03/04/03	Wed 03/05/03		
23		4.2.2	Monitor Changeover Problems	1 day	Thu 03/06/03	Thu 03/06/03	22	
24		4.2.3	Correct Noted Deficiencies	3 days	Tue 03/04/03	Thu 03/06/03		

FIGURE A-17   Duration days for CIRCLES project after creating the network diagram.

Specify Business Events (the longer of the two simultaneous tasks associated with Develop New Models). The remaining recalculations of duration days can be determined in a similar fashion. Finally, click on the minus buttons that appear beside WBS numbers 1, 2, 3, and 4. Notice that the subtasks associated with each phase are collapsed, which provides a very concise view of the project at the phase level.

SUMMARY

The purpose of this tutorial is to provide a high-level overview of how to use *Microsoft Project 2000*. Although *Microsoft Project 2000* is capable of much more than what has been covered in this tutorial, due to space limitations we can't delve into more detail. However, at this point you should have a firm grasp of how to begin using *Microsoft Project 2000* for project management purposes. We encourage you to take the time to navigate through the software and discover its many intricacies. You'll find the Help function very useful in learning more about *Microsoft Project 2000*.

Also, you can look at some interesting project templates that are packaged with the software by selecting |File| and clicking on New and Project Templates. By doing so, you will notice prebuilt templates for projects such as Commercial Construction, Engineering, and Software Development. The last template might be especially interesting since it is an expanded version of a project much like the CIRCLES project we have developed in this text.

APPENDIX B

Glossary of Terms

Activity-based costing (ABC)—a technique that links indirect costs to the activities that cause them to change. A similar tool is activity-based management, which extends to using information about cost-driving activities to improve management.

Assurance services—a broader offering than attestation services. Assurance services can include any service in which an auditor, consultant, or other professional offers some comfort regarding the validity of the underlying subject. For example, an auditor can assure a web advertiser about the number of hits to a web site.

Attestation services—services offered by auditors in which they evaluate the accuracy of financial statements and "attest to" or offer opinions about their reliability.

Balanced Scorecard—a performance measurement technique that evaluates goal achievement with respect to financial, customer, internal business, and growth and learning perspectives.

Business processes—the value-added activities of a business enterprise. They include, for example, the sales or order-fulfillment process, the production process, and procurement.

Business process reengineering (BPR)—a consulting service that requires a fundamental rethinking of a business's underlying processes. BPR became very popular in the 1980s as businesses began to focus on making major changes to their processes; many of these changes were made possible by advances in information technology.

Change management—the process of effecting organizational change. Change management is a component of organizational behavior. Managers, consultants, and psychologists may all offer change management services.

Change teams—personnel who assist a client with transition. They may be a separate team of individuals assembled specifically to facilitate a change or a continuation of the consulting project team that has worked on an engagement from the beginning.

Civil laws—legislation prohibiting or requiring certain behaviors. Punishments for breaking these laws do not include incarceration.

Client proposal—a document and/or presentation that a consultant makes to a client. It describes in detail the work to be done, how and when it will be done, deliverables, and pricing.

Computer-assisted systems engineering (CASE) tools—software programs that include a wide variety of documentation and application development features. Programmers and systems analysts use them to develop and maintain software solutions.

Confidentiality—a crucial component in consulting. It is both a legal and ethical issue (covered under Rule 301 of the AICPA *Code of Professional Conduct*). Depending on the nature of the engagement, a consultant may be privy to sensitive product and trade secrets, financial data, personnel information, and other proprietary company information. Clients may require consultants to sign confidentiality agreements designed to protect the confidentiality of information gathered during the course of an engagement.

Coopers and Lybrand Change Management Framework—an approach to change management consisting of a four-step methodology: (1) assessment, (2) planning, (3) implementation, and (4) renewal. The approach, developed by the firm of Coopers and Lybrand (now part of PricewaterhouseCoopers), stresses the uniqueness of each change effort.

Cost plus contracts—a pricing structure that builds a profit margin on top of costs.

CPA Vision Project—a project initiated by the AICPA to identify how the accounting profession will adapt to the changing needs of the future. The project identifies CPA core competencies, values, services, and significant issues facing CPAs.

CPA Web Trust—a third-party assurance seal for businesses' Internet web sites. The AICPA developed this service offering. The seal provides assurance about a company's transaction processing, privacy, security, and business policies.

Criminal laws—laws that state specifically what action constitutes violation, as well as the penalties that can be applied. Penalties for breaking criminal laws range from monetary fines to incarceration. The element of "intent" must be present to successfully prosecute one for breaking a criminal law.

Critical path analysis (CPA)—is based on a network portrayal of project activities whereby the sequence of activities and their time duration are used to determine a project's most critical path. This path consists of the interdependent activities that make up the longest timeline through the project. CPA includes two similar network techniques: critical path method (CPM) and program evaluation review technique (PERT). The primary difference between CPM and PERT is that PERT allows variability in time estimates, whereas the times in CPM are fixed.

Critical thinking—the ability to analyze a problem from many perspectives to arrive at an optimal solution. Critical thinking requires constructing and analyzing hypotheses with limited information. Professionals often refer to critical thinking as "thinking outside the box" because it should allow those who practice it to arrive at innovative solutions.

Cross-selling—Offering additional, perhaps complementary, services to current clients.

Data flow diagrams—a graphical documentation technique that shows the flow of data and information around business events and processes. Systems analysts use this tool in designing information systems.

Decision tables—a graphical documentation technique that shows conditions and actions within a decision context.

Deliverables—what a consultant is to provide a client at the end of an engagement. Deliverables may include oral presentations, graphical documentation, user manuals, reports, software, methodologies, and so on.

ElderCare practice—a consulting practice that provides assurance about the well-being and care of senior citizens. The AICPA developed this service offering.

Entity relationship diagrams—a graphical documentation technique used to model a database structure.

Ethics—professional standards or rules of conduct. Behaving unethically carries no legal ramifications, but there may be professional sanctions and harm to reputation.

CPAs must observe the code of ethics of the AICPA. The Institute of Management Consultants (IMC) also provides a code of ethics for consulting professionals.

Flowcharts—a graphical documentation technique that shows the flow of data, documents, and information events through business processes

Focus group—a data collection technique consisting of an organized discussion among invited participants on a specific topic.

Forensic accounting—a consulting service offering that provides clients fraud detection by analyzing accounting data.

Gantt charts—a documentation tool used in project planning. Gantt charts represent work activities or tasks as horizontal bars on a chart. The length of the bar indicates the time each activity should or actually does take. These charts typically make little allowance for the interdependencies among various tasks.

Go-live—the date on which a consultant implements a client solution. The go-live date for a software implementation is the time you switch over to the new software system. In the case of immediate cutover, you would implement a new solution all at once, without using the old system to back up processes or systems.

Independence—the real and perceived lack of a conflict of interest. Independence issues for accounting consultants are quite complex. The Securities and Exchange Commission recently developed new standards of independence for CPAs.

Interpersonal consultant role—the role a consultant assumes when the engagement requires effecting, but not actually participating in, a change or new solution. The consultant, in this instance, is primarily a facilitator.

Just-in-time (JIT) manufacturing—a manufacturing approach that requires companies to minimize their inventories. JIT manufacturing relies on strong relationships with suppliers such that only the inventory or parts needed to complete the current job are on hand, thus minimizing inventory storage costs and thereby maximizing profit.

Lewin's process of organizational change—a model of organizational change developed by Kurt Lewin. The model presents change as a three-step process: unfreezing, change, and refreezing.

Likert scales—a set of closed-end questions that provide the respondent with a scale of responses, such as "agree, disagree, neutral."

Litigation services—a specialized area of consulting in which consultants provide professional assistance to attorneys. These services include serving as expert witnesses, serving as arbitrators or mediators, and serving as receivers in bankruptcy matters.

Management letter—a tool that auditors and some consultants may use to communicate to client management any concerns or observations made during the engagement.

Outsourcing—strategically using outside resources to perform activities traditionally done by internal personnel. Examples of outsourced functions are information systems, internal audit, manufacturing, and accounting. A similar approach is cosourcing in which the external parties work with a small internal staff to manage and execute a function.

Process maps—a graphical documentation technique that focuses on the events within business processes. Increasing levels of detailed maps show detailed breakdowns of activities.

Project management—leading a project team and ensuring that a project is completed on schedule, within budget, and meets its goals.

Parallel implementation—implementing a new solution (e.g., an information system), while the old system or process is continued along with it.

Phased implementation—implementing a new solution on a piecemeal basis. For example, you might implement one module of a software package at a time. In a business process reengineering engagement, a phased implementation would entail rethinking one business process at a time.

Project life cycle—The four essential phases of project management: planning, scheduling, monitoring, and controlling.

Prototype—a scaled-down, "bare-bones" version of a full model. The purpose of a prototype is to permit a client a preview of what the final model will look like. Typically, prototypes are not fully functional. For example, a prototype of a software system may include screen designs minus the programming behind them.

Request for proposal (RFP)—a document created for vendors to reference when bidding on projects. An organization might issue an RFP for a variety of consulting services. The RFP includes details about the problem situation, a company history, requirements for proposals, and a time frame for responding.

Services marketing mix—The well-known four "Ps" of product marketing are price, product, promotion, and place. The service marketing mix includes these elements along with people, physical evidence, and process.

Service recovery—how you "make up" for a poor service offering. For example, if consultants find that a recommended solution is not working, they may "eat" the cost or offer other remedies to ensure client satisfaction.

Step-check solution implementation method—an approach to implementing a consultant's solution. The consultant seeks client confirmation and feedback following each major project step.

SysTrust—a consulting service that provides assurance regarding the reliability of a client's information systems. The AICPA developed this service offering.

Statistical tests and analysis tools—these include t-tests, chi square, regression, and other forms of data analysis. Rather than defining each of them here, we refer you to Chapter 8's sections on Summarizing and Coding Data and Statistical Analysis.

Storyboards—a graphical documentation technique used frequently by advertisers and film producers. Storyboards depict a "story" in a graphical set of frames. They are useful tools for reengineering and activity-based costing projects.

Strategic thinking—the ability to think proactively and anticipate the future.

Target costing—a technique that requires a price to be set based on market conditions. Costs are then determined that will allow that price. These are the "target" costs that production must meet.

Technical consulting role—the role of consultants when an engagement requires solution implementation.

Time and materials contracts—a pricing structure in which consultants are paid by the hour for direct expenses as the work progresses.

Time-based management (also called **cycle management**)—a process that relies on an analysis of a manufacturing process to reduce idle time, thereby increasing efficiency and profitability.

Total quality management (TQM)—a business methodology that seeks to involve all employees in the change process as an organization focuses on its customer and the quality of its services and products. Often focus groups of employees or "quality circles" consisting of lower level employees participate in advising middle and upper management on how to best implement change. TQM is also characterized by an emphasis on constant improvement in the work process, and a focus on assessing and meeting customer needs.

Value-based pricing—a pricing structure in which a client pays consultants the perceived value of the work performed. For example, the contract could call for profit-sharing based on increased revenues or decreased costs accruing from improvements.

Work breakdown structure (WBS)—a hierarchical representation of a project's scope. The WBS breaks the project down into task levels and increasingly less complex tasks. A project manager can create a time budget by estimating the length it will take to perform each task at the lowest level of complexity.

Index